The
Courage
of
Children

For the Students of

Wilma Hanson
School

Peter D-

December 3/01

The
Courage
of
Children

My Life with the World's Poorest Kids

PETER DALGLISH

HarperCollins*Publishers*Ltd

http://www.harpercollins.com/canada

HarperCollins books may be purchased for educational, business, or sales promotional use. For
information please write: Special Markets Department, HarperCollins Canada, 55 Avenue
Road, Suite 2900, Toronto, Ontario M5R 3L2.

First edition

Canadian Cataloguing in Publication Data

Dalglish, Peter
The courage of children : my life with the world's poorest kids

ISBN 0-00-255752-5 (bound)
ISBN 0-00-638567-2 (pbk.)

1. Dalglish, Peter. 2. Street Kids International. 3. Homeless children. 4. Poor children. 5.
Child welfare. 6. Social work with children. I. Title.

HV28.D34A3 1998   362.7'092   C98-930602-X

98 99 00 01 02 03 04 HC 10 9 8 7 6 5 4 3 2 1

Printed and bound in the United States

For the street children of Khartoum,
who showed me their world

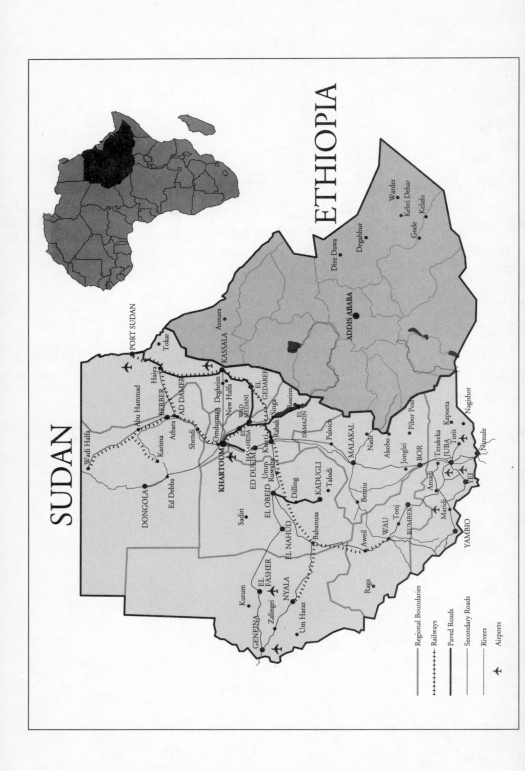

SUDAN

ETHIOPIA

PORT SUDAN

Tokar
Haiya
Abu Hammad
BERBER
AD DAMER
Atbara
Shendi
Karima
Wadi Halfa

KASSALA
Asmara

Degheim
New Halfa
Omdurman
EL GEDAREF
WAD MEDANI
Singa
Kosti Rabak
ELHASHEISA
Roseires
EL DAMAZIN
Paloich

DONGOLA
Ed Debba

KHARTOUM
ED DUEIM
Umm Ruwaba
EL OBEID
Sadiri
Dilling
KADUGLI
Talodi

MALAKAL
Nasir
Akobo
Jonglei
Pibor Post

ADDIS ABABA

Dire Dawa

Degahbur

Warder
Kebri Dehar
Gode
Kelafo

EL FASHER
Kurum
Zalingei
NYALA
GENEINA
Um Haraz

Babanusa
EL NAHUD

Raga

WAU
Aweil
Tonj
RUMBEK
Bentiu

Amadi
Maridi
YAMBIO

BOR
Terakeka
Torit
JUBA
YEI
Kapoeta
Nagishot
Nimule

Regional Boundaries
Railways
Paved Roads
Secondary Roads
Rivers
Airports

CONTENTS

ACKNOWLEDGEMENTS

I began writing *The Courage of Children* while working in refugee camps on the border between the Sudan and Chad in October, 1985. I finished the project in February, 1998 at my desk overlooking a frozen Canadian lake, with my infant daughter adding her coos and giggles to the clicking of the computer keyboard. Along the way many people have contributed their time, expertise and words of encouragement. Iris Tupholme and Tom Best at HarperCollins believed that the story of a wayward lawyer, and the gang of street children he fell in with, was worth telling. My editor Marie Campbell kept me focused and on schedule. I appreciate the contributions of Susan Thomas, who designed the book, and Jocelyn Laurence, who copy edited the text. Becky Vogan's keen eye picked out numerous inconsistencies and structural problems. For their assistance with research and fact checking I am indebted to Blanka el Khalifa, Peter Verney, Marc Abrioux, Dr. Deborah Cowman, Mark Connolly, Hawley MacDonald, Mary and David Melvill, Cole Dodge, Patta Scott-Villiers, and Jacques de Milliano. Nick Cater, Christopher Lowry and Aino Block read various drafts of my chapters and e-mailed specific and frank suggestions for improvement, most of which I have heeded. Sudanese politics are complex at the best of times, and Dr. Taisier Ali at the University of Toronto provided me with wise counsel. Penny Long invested hundreds of hours preparing the manuscript, researching, and fact checking. Thank you to Kuki Gallmann of Ol Ari Nyiro Ranch in Kenya, and Hemmie and Dirk Schaap of the island of Terschelling in the Netherlands, for providing me with inspirational settings in which to write, and to the bartenders at the Walvis Cafe on the island of Terschelling for the privilege of using their telephone to transmit my drafts of various chapters to Marie Campbell in Toronto. My wife, Nienke Schaap, demonstrated extraordinary patience and understanding during long periods when I was totally immersed in the project and had to be reminded to eat and drink. Finally, I am indebted to my daughter Annelie for learning to sleep through the night just when I most needed my rest. Despite the help of so many people the final manuscript will undoubtedly contain errors, for which I accept full responsibility.

INTRODUCTION:
WARRIOR CHILDREN

I cannot see what others see;
Wisdom alone is kind to me,
Wisdom that comes from Agony.
* * *
Wisdom that lives in the pure skies,
The untouched star, the spirit's eyes:
O Beauty, touch me, make me wise.

—John Masefield

This is a story about the courage of children. In particular, it is a story about those children who, desperate and poor, have been for the most part forgotten by the rest of society. It is also, unfortunately, an account of the arrogance and incompetence of many of the government agencies and international organizations that have been entrusted with their care.

Although I am a lawyer by training, for the past 12 years I have had the privilege of working with some of the world's poorest children. In your travels you may have met some of them. They are the girls and boys you find only a few metres from your hotel entrance in Rio de Janeiro, sifting through a steaming heap of trash for something to eat or to sell. They are the children who expertly juggle amidst Mexico City's traffic, who diligently shine the shoes of tourists in Manila, and who ingeniously fashion toys from bits of wire and tin in Nairobi's Blue Market. Invariably they are dressed in rags and are badly in need of a bath. They rarely have shoes on their feet. Although they do not appear to be threatening, you may be reluctant to approach them or speak to them. Local residents caution their own children to stay away from them and not to touch them. These girls and boys are clearly from another world, and we prefer not to think of the exploitation and misery that must surround them. It is safer for us to move on without acknowledging their presence, and so we quicken our pace.

But each of you who encounters these children has a choice to make. If you even for one moment look into their eyes, you will likely recognize the fear and loneliness of a child who lacks the love and support of a caring family. If you take the time to scratch beneath the grime that covers their skin, if you have the opportunity to break bread with them, you will find that, underneath, there resides the indomitable spirit of a child like any other.

When I started working with street children in 1986 in the desert city of Khartoum in the Sudan, courage was the last thing I expected to find. I had been warned that the children were dangerous and that they carried disease. Government officials claimed they were not Sudanese children at all but refugee children from Chad and Ethiopia, who were illegally in the country and who should either be imprisoned or trucked across the border and dumped into the sand. The Sudan's minister of social welfare, an educated woman from a prominent Muslim family, had called them trash, and suggested a wall be built around the city to keep them out. Few of the aid agencies were concerned about their plight; every day, representatives of Save the Children and UNICEF raced past the street children in their shiny, new four-wheel-drive vehicles, kicking up clouds of dust in their wake, either indifferent or oblivious to their wretched condition. Not even the churches wanted them; the children who turned up for Sunday mass at the cathedral on Khartoum's Nile Avenue were routinely sent away by the priests. They were told they did not have the proper clothes, they smelled, that there was no place for them in the house of God.

The first street child who entered my life was a modern-day Oliver Twist. I encountered him while he was breaking into my Land Rover in Khartoum armed only with a bent nail. In less than two minutes he had pried the door open. His name was Adam, he was 11 years old, and he was terrified I might hand him over to the police. Instead, I started a technical training school for Adam and his friends from the garbage dump, with the generous support of the Irish rock star Bob Geldof, the moving force behind Band Aid, which raised tens of millions of dollars for famine relief. Within a few months, 80 of the city's best house-breakers and pickpockets were being transformed into carpenters, welders, and car mechanics. The premise was simple: given the opportunity to learn in a supportive environment, children who were good thieves could also become fine artisans and tradespeople. The Sudanese teachers were impressed with the kids' innate ability with their hands and with their eagerness to learn. The children were like sponges that had not seen water in a long time, absorbing every lesson the teachers put in front of them. They easily outperformed their middle-class counterparts, for whom the expensive Belgian-funded school had been built. The graduates of the school were hired by the very businessmen whose offices they had once broken into. Today, Adam works with Iveco, the Fiat truck division in Khartoum.

Hired by UNICEF in February, 1986, I went on to establish Khartoum's first bicycle courier service run entirely by street children. Working out of my garage, we began the business with three borrowed bicycles and a contract to deliver the *Sudan Times*, Khartoum's only English-language newspaper. The paper's editor, Bona Malwal, sympathetic to the plight of the children and anxious to provide his readers with a reliable home-delivery service, unwittingly became the godfather of legions of children who had few allies. In a city where nothing works, the citizenry was dazzled by the couriers' efficiency. The kids made deliveries to the very offices and homes they had once plundered; along the way, they learned the importance of discipline and hard work. I quickly realized these children of adversity had special talents, and that small business projects that provided them with a modest income could dramatically transform their lives. The key was to build on the natural skills of the children rather than to smother them with charity. Traditional hand-outs made beggars out of them, reinforcing their subservience.

I returned to Canada in 1987 to found Street Kids International, with the aim of beginning similar self-help programs for street children in other countries. Street Kids International has grown to become one of the leading agencies supporting innovative programming for poor girls and boys living in cities around the world. With our local partners, we have developed projects for street children in India, Zambia, Tanzania, South Africa, and the Sudan. Our animated films on AIDS and substance abuse are distributed in 25 languages and over 100 countries, making them the single largest initiatives for street children anywhere in the world. In 1994, Street Kids International was the first Canadian organization to be honored with the prestigious Peter F. Drucker Award for Non-Profit Innovation.

I started Street Kids International with $200, a borrowed office, and an American Express card. But by far my most important assets were the lessons I had learned from my days with Issam, Pio, Sunday, and the many other Sudanese children who had become my good friends when I was a guest in their country. The desert children of Khartoum, intrepid explorers and adventurers, continue to inspire my work. But I will never see them again. In June, 1989, Brigadier Omar Hassan Ahmad al-Bashir seized power in Khartoum, terminated peace negotiations, and stepped up efforts to rid the country of any dissenters to brutal authoritarian rule. Street children were placed on the list of undesirables, alongside trade-union leaders, feminists, and human-rights activists. Conscripted into the military by the Sudan's racist and extremist regime, many of these same children have since died fighting a bloody and unwinnable war in the remote southern region of their country. This book is dedicated to their memory.

If I were a historian I would write a book challenging the myth that the 20th century has been kind to children and youth. It's true that ambitious vaccination campaigns and state-funded primary-schooling programs for girls and boys alike have made a significant impact. England's poorest kids no longer toil as chimney sweeps. But over the last 100 years, barbarism and nationalism have exacted a heavy toll, and children and youth have suffered disproportionately at the hands of adults. It was in the fetid trenches of the Great War that Europe lost over 10 million of her youngest and most promising citizens. In 1914, entire graduating classes of boys from British, French, and German schools went marching off to war and never returned. Between 1937 and 1945, the Nazis systematically exterminated more than one million Jewish and Gypsy girls and boys in history's largest mass murder of children. Even their memory has been obliterated. We know nothing of their dreams, their favorite teachers, or their best friends. Their naked bodies were thrown into muddy pits by slave children who waited their turn to be executed. We can only imagine the horror of their last days on earth, separated from their families, herded into cattle cars, transported and re-transported, then seeing the camps where they must have known their lives would end. What were their last thoughts as they moved in long and silent columns to the crematoria? Did older children take the hands of younger sisters and brothers to provide, in their final moments, a modicum of comfort? Did some children, in defiance of the Nazis, dare to raise a fist in the air or curse the darkness?

Throughout the 20th century, children from minority religious and ethnic groups were singled out for "special treatment" at the hands of authorities. In 1915, Turkish soldiers hunted down and massacred Armenian girls and boys. In the 1930s, Nazi doctors began the elimination of handicapped

4

and "imperfect" children by phenol injection. Doctors working in the Nazi concentration camps selected children for gruesome scientific experiments, subjecting them to extremes of heat and cold, ear-bursting sessions in pressure chambers, injections of dye into their corneas, and exposure to live typhoid and cholera bacillus. The results of their experiments were methodically recorded with scientific precision in prestigious medical journals. Visitors to Auschwitz and Dachau can see the same tables where the children, their bodies still warm, were dissected by some of the world's most eminent physicians. Today, medical ethicists believe entire areas of scientific research have been contaminated by results obtained only through the torture and murder of young girls and boys by Nazi doctors.

During the 1970s, Khmer Rouge soldiers surrounded and burned down schools in dissident areas, shooting any child who escaped. Children who could read, who wore eye glasses, or who had parents suspected of being intellectuals or professionals were warehoused, photographed, tortured, and murdered. During Iran's eight-year war with Iraq, over 25,000 Iranian children died clearing minefields. They walked out into no-man's land holding hands, jumping up and down in an attempt to detonate the mines buried beneath their feet. The youngest children were tied with wire to older youths to prevent them from running away in fear. They all wore red sashes, and were given special plastic keys to put around their necks to guarantee quick entry into the kingdom of heaven. In 1995, Catholic priests shepherded Tutsi children who were in their care into local churches, then rang the bell as a signal for Hutu soldiers to slaughter them with their machetes.

The indiscriminate killing of children has continued to the end of the century. Just 14 years after hosting the Olympics, Sarajevo's most distinctive feature is its new cemeteries, the resting places for over 1,800 girls and boys slaughtered by Serbian soldiers who skillfully aimed their mortars at schools and playgrounds. Betrayed by all of Western Europe and its gutless politicians, the children of Sarajevo endured more than three years of relentless Serb bombardment before American intervention finally ended the bloodshed. During the siege, the Serbians employed 700 pieces of artillery and 120 tanks. Their leader, the silver-tongued psychiatrist Radovan Karadzic, promised that once his soldiers had finished the job, "The people of Sarajevo will be counting the living rather than counting the dead." If today you wish to find the boys and young men lured to the UN "safe haven" of Srebrenica in search of peace, you need only dig a few feet below the surface of the football fields surrounding that town, where 7,000 of them lie silent.

Too often governments and international aid organizations portray destitute children merely as the hapless victims of misfortune or harsh circumstances; there is great reluctance to point fingers—to acknowledge that certain governments actively seek to disenfranchise girls and boys who live on the margins of society. Today, more than 100 million children around the world are systematically denied access to primary schooling. Governments devise ingenious techniques to keep them out of school, requiring that they purchase expensive school uniforms, possess government identity cards, pay school fees, or prove their "parentage." Instead of learning to read and write, the children toil in coal mines, glass factories, and textile mills to pay off their parents' loans and supplement their families' income. In Pakistan alone, over seven million children, the majority of them girls under the age of 13, work for pennies a day in brick kilns and carpet factories despite the existence of national legislation that makes child servitude illegal. To offer the lame excuse that these children have no choice but to work is to condone state-sanctioned slavery that benefits only the ruling class. It is no coincidence that virtually every member of Pakistan's parliament is linked to a family business that relies on child labor. Entire economic systems are predicated on the availability of laborers who are cheap, young, easily intimidated, and unlikely to ever be organized into trade unions. The facile notion that poor children "choose" hours of back-breaking labor over attending primary school alongside other children is a lie perpetrated by those interested only in maintaining the status quo. Do hungry children ever have a choice?

Even recreation is off-limits to poor children in many developing countries; as a matter of course, they are chased off public football fields and cricket pitches by angry adults wielding clubs. Most competitive sports are reserved for children of the elite who belong to posh clubs and have access to equipment and training. If you check the rosters of Olympic and Commonwealth Games athletes from countries such as India and Pakistan, you will find they are stacked with athletes from the country's ruling class; many of them speak the colonial English they learned in their exclusive British-style boarding schools. The national sport-governing bodies, which choose the athletes who will represent their countries in international competitions, are dominated by high-society types who have only contempt for the poor. In most cities in the developing world, there are virtually no recreation opportunities for poor girls and young women; local officials offer the time-honored explanation that "only boys are interested in sports." Swimming pools and tennis courts remain the exclusive domain of upper-class children. In July, 1986, I invited a group of street children to swim after-hours at the venerable Sudan club; I returned the next day to find the club members—predominantly UN employees—had drained the pool out of fear of contamination.

The world's poorest children rarely benefit from the greatest achievements of the 20th century. Street children are seldom vaccinated and are routinely refused admission to government-funded clinics and hospitals. Their ailments go untreated, and they die of curable diseases such as tuberculosis and typhoid. Poor girls and young women are denied family-planning services on moral and religious grounds. Most working children and street children have never used a standard typewriter, let alone a computer, which remains a resource reserved for children of the privileged. Local businessmen in India were shocked by Street Kids International's plans to begin a computer-education program for Bombay street children. "Our own children don't have such nice computers. Don't waste them on the street children," they told us.

When pushed to take action, politicians resort to legislation as a cure-all for social ills. The 20th century has seen the proclamation of dozens of elaborately worded conventions and protocols intended to help those children who are most in need. But the laws have no teeth: there are no penalties for noncompliance. The legislation makes politicians look good, but does little else. The International Labor Organization passed its first convention banning child labor in 1919; there have been more than eight similar conventions passed since, each one making as little impact as its predecessor. No one pays any attention to them—certainly not the police, the judges, or even the social workers. UNICEF's crowning achievement, the 1989 Convention on the Rights of the Child, has no effective enforcement provisions and relies solely on the goodwill of nations for its implementation. The consequences are predictable: countries such as the Sudan and Guatemala, two of the world's most egregious violators of the basic rights of children, ran to the table to sign and ratify the convention, knowing it would never be enforced.

Many countries use their ratification of the Convention on the Rights of the Child as an excuse for their own inaction on children's rights, adding it to their laundry list of all the good things they have done for their children. Conferences are held and endless numbers of papers are published by foreign consultants charging $300 a day for their services. But children hardened by the reality of day-to-day survival can see through the charade; they know that laws exist primarily to protect the rich, including rich children. The Convention on the Rights of the Child guarantees access by all children to health care and primary education—but to what end? Every morning, street children watch more privileged girls and boys walking to school in their fine uniforms while they must work for their gruel. They have gone to public medical clinics for treatment, patiently waited their turn, then been told by white-smocked doctors they cannot be treated unless they first can pay. How does the convention help them? These children, considered by many authorities unteachable and untrainable, are wise enough to know that a piece of paper will not protect them from the local policeman who wants to hit them, or rape them, or extract a bribe from them. "We are graduates of the university of life," they tell us.

That young people with no voice, no vote, and no economic clout should be victims of injustice is predictable. But what sobers even the most hardened child advocates is the widespread public support for actions by governments against poor children. A survey in Brazil by the newspaper *Folha de São Paulo* showed that 30 per cent of the population supported the murder of street children by state policemen. In Guatemala, workers for the organization Casa Alianza who bravely defend local street children are continually taunted by local citizens. "Why do you speak up for such trash?" people ask. Ehsan Ullah Khan, the founder of Pakistan's Bonded Labor Liberation Front and a tireless campaigner for children's rights, has been hounded out of his own country and must now live as a refugee in Sweden. Street children are told they are thieves and perverts, that there is no room for them on the bus, that their place is in the gutter. Not even their bodies are wanted. In Bogotá, Colombia, the American child advocate Mark Connolly adopted a dead 12-year-old street child—the only way to ensure the boy would receive a proper burial.

In the United States, right-wing politicians compete to introduce regressive legislation aimed at punishing poor children and their families. In 21 American states, children of 16 can be sentenced to death. In 1994, the Florida legislature debated a bill that would lower the minimum age for execution in that state to 14; what remained unsaid was that the vast majority of young offenders who would thereby become eligible for the death penalty were black and poor. A popular initiative in California would deny the right to primary education for children of illegal immigrants. Many states have enacted laws prohibiting publicly funded family-planning agencies from providing services for women under the age of 18 without parental consent; of course, affluent youth always have the option of turning to their private physicians. In 1996, Republican Senator Bob Dole opposed a bill banning the import of assault weapons into the U.S., despite the fact that more than a quarter of a million people, many of them under the age of 18, have been murdered in the U.S. in the past 10 years, more than all the U.S. fatalities in World War II. Often the contradiction between words and deeds is lost on the politicians themselves. On September 30, 1990, then president George Bush, amidst much fanfare at the UN World Summit for Children in New York, signed a declaration on the survival, protection, and development of children; the next day at the White House, he approved legislation cutting in half the largest social-assistance program for American single mothers.

But children follow courage, not politicians. If, on a summer day in Amsterdam, you walk the old neighborhood of the Westerkerk, you will find a large crowd of young people gathered outside the house at Prinsengracht No. 263. Every year, thousands of youth from around the world make a pilgrimage to the attic where Anne Frank hid from the Nazis for over two years with family and friends. On the morning of August 4, 1944, after the Allied invasion of Europe was already under way, the occupants of the attic were betrayed by a Dutch collaborator and arrested by an S.S. sergeant and Dutch security police. They were deported on the last train of Jews to leave Amsterdam and interned at Westerbork, the holding camp for Dutch Jews en route to the concentration camps of Germany and Poland. Anne and her sister survived Auschwitz, but died in Bergen Belsen of typhoid just two weeks before the camp was liberated by British soldiers on April 12, 1945. Of the eight people who in 1942 had hidden in the attic, only Anne's father Otto ever returned from the death camps.

The young visitors to the Anne Frank House emerge visibly shaken by the experience. While waiting in line, they have heard the sound of the Westertorren bells similar to the ones Anne listened to every hour, before they were removed by the Nazis and melted down for the war effort. Once inside the house, they have seen the actual newspaper photographs of royalty and movie stars that Otto Frank pasted onto the walls of Anne's bedroom in an attempt to brighten it up. They have noted the pencil marks by the third-floor door tracking the growth of the three children during their two years in hiding. From the top floor they can reach out and almost touch the leaves of the same great chestnut tree that shaded the courtyard of the house when the Frank family was resident. Anne's spirit is near, and visiting children can sense it. When I last made a trip to the attic, a French couple were picking up their 12-year-old daughter, who had decided to spend the afternoon at the house. "Maman, elle est encore ici!" the girl told her parents, who appeared embarrassed by the intensity of their daughter's reaction.

Anne Frank's life is testimony to the quiet heroism of millions of children of the 20th century who, despite acts of extraordinary cowardice and savagery by the adults who surrounded them, continued to believe in a world free of violence, hatred, and persecution.

I began writing this book on scraps of paper while working in a refugee camp on the border of Chad and Sudan during the great African famine of 1985. The young nomads who lived in the camp had walked immense distances across the desert in the open sun in search of food and water, carrying their younger sisters and brothers on their backs. They had survived against overwhelming odds. All their goats and cattle had long before perished. Their skin was enamelled with dirt and their hair was matted into one piece. The girls wore only rags, the boys nothing at all. Many of their adult friends and family members had died on the way to the camp. But these children had fire in their eyes. They were the toughest kids I had ever encountered, and they personified courage in the face of adversity. I believed their stories deserved to be told. Since those days, I have worked in cities such as Bombay, Bangkok, and Port Moresby, helping local community-based organizations establish projects for poor children, and I have witnessed many examples of heroism by young people. But one image in particular always stays with me.

In May, 1987, I travelled by train from the Mediterranean coast of France to the city of Lyons to attend the trial of Klaus Barbie, to witness the testimony of two elderly women and, in particular, to learn of the fate of 44 girls and boys. In 1941, a home for children located in the village of Izieu, 60 kilometres east of Lyons, became the secret refuge for a group of Jewish girls and boys, many of whom had already lost family members to the death camps. The home was run by Sabina and Miron Zlatin, and was a place of peace and happiness for all its residents. The Zlatins thought they had an understanding with the local authorities that despite the war, the children would be left alone. One of the women in the courtroom that day, Mme Fortunée Benguigui, had sent her three sons to the home because she believed it was the safest possible place for them.

On a fine spring day in the packed courtroom in Lyons, we learned what happened to the girls and boys of Izieu. Acting on the written and specific orders of Klaus Barbie, on the morning of April 6, 1944, Nazi storm troopers arrived at the home aboard three trucks and immediately began to round up the children. One witness reported the children were tossed into the trucks "like sacks of potatoes." Mme Lea Feldman, an adult guardian at the home, rode with the children to Auschwitz in a sealed railway car; they had no food or water for the entire journey. Upon arrival at Auschwitz, she was forcibly separated from the children, all of whom were immediately marched to the gas chambers. She later heard reports that two girls who resisted the soldiers had been thrown into the crematoria without first being gassed.

Fighting to maintain her composure, Mme Benguigui read out to the courtroom the last letter she had received from her 12-year-old son: "My dear Maman: I send you from far away my best wishes. When you send me food, I share it with all the children who have no parents. I send you hugs and kisses. Your adoring son, Jacques."

Mme Feldman, the only one of the seven adult guardians to survive, testified that the Nazi storm troopers arrived in the morning at the orphanage without warning. She had no idea who in the village had betrayed them. Her most powerful testimony came at the end of the day, when she described to the silenced courtroom how the children, as they were being driven away in the three trucks, in defiance of their captors began to sing a popular song entitled "Ils n'auront plus l'Alsace et la Lorraine." She said they sang with great strength and pride—that you could hear them long after the trucks had disappeared from view.

I am a 39-year-old Canadian who was born into an affluent Catholic family, and I have never suffered any form of violence or oppression. I travelled to Lyons because I believe the children of Izieu who dared to sing patriotic songs taunting the Nazis have something in common with many of the children who have become my life. I have known boys who have hidden for days at a time under bags of coal aboard old Nile steamers to escape the war in South Sudan. My friends include children as young as seven and eight years of age who have been interned for months in brutal adult prisons. I have interviewed young girls who labor in decrepit factories, earning a few coins each day so their male siblings can go to school. I travelled to Lyons because I wanted to learn how 11- and 12-year-old children, who know they are being taken to their deaths, can find the courage to sing.

The courage of children is often unfathomable, and I have no easy answers. Children do not behave or think like adults, and their motives are usually beyond our comprehension. My hope is that in witnessing their courage, we learn of the heroism some people in extreme circumstances are capable of. The priests who zealously guard the doors to their fine churches may never understand, but the dirty, lice-infested girls and boys who dutifully turn up for Sunday mass are closer to God than most of us will ever be. Perhaps they are here on earth for a reason—to remind us that evil must be confronted, that in a single child who stands up to tyranny we can find hope for the whole world.

The courage of children is rarely recognized, rewarded, or remembered. We know that during World War II girls and boys played important roles in the

French resistance, that children as young as 11 and 12 sabotaged strategic rail lines in Italy and Germany, and that hungry kids armed only with slingshots took up rocks against the Nazis in the Warsaw Ghetto uprising. But when caught, these warrior children were invariably executed. Their graves are unmarked and their names for the most part are forgotten. We know little about how they lived or how they died. No monuments were built in their memory. Those of us who could never emulate their bravery can pay tribute to them today by remembering that in a century of unparalleled barbarism, there lived a special breed of young people who, with little regard for their own well-being, confronted the evil they found in an adult world. When, in your travels, you next encounter a rag-tag gang of street kids, remember that they are descended from children of noble blood.

KINDERSEHEN: SCENES FROM CHILDHOOD

By any standards, I enjoyed a golden childhood. I was born and raised in London, Ontario, statistically one of Canada's most affluent cities, a university and insurance town with clean and quiet neighborhoods that have a storybook quality to them. To most visitors, London appears a world apart from the rest of the continent—a kind of northern Charleston. Even today, the city remains primarily white and Christian. When I was a child in London, police cars did not have sirens and corner newspaper boxes worked on the honor system. Lawns in London suburbs were always perfectly manicured; house owners who left them unattended for more than two weeks at a time received written warnings from city hall. The River Thames, green and lazy, winds its way through the city core; on hot summer days, kids still drift along its banks in oversized, truck inner tubes. The city was the birthplace of Guy Lombardo, the band conductor renowned for hosting America's nationally televised New Year's Eve party. If London had its own theme song, it would be "Auld Lang Syne"; the city mirrors a way of life that doesn't exist in many other places.

I was the third of four children born to my parents, who had settled in London in 1953, four years before I arrived on the scene. My father, a fifth-generation Canadian from Montreal who spent his childhood and youth in Toronto, correctly predicted that London would grow and prosper, and that it would be a sensible place to raise a young family. My mother, a native Berliner who emigrated to Canada in 1952 and who was accustomed to a more cosmopolitan lifestyle than London could possibly offer, had to be persuaded by my father that they were making the right choice. The city had little to help her make it through a long and bleak winter. She had no interest in ice hockey, bowling, or curling.

I grew up in a neighborhood called Sherwood Forest in a house with six bedrooms and six bathrooms, a large swimming pool, and a three-car garage. Our driveway was electrically heated to help keep it clear of snow in the winter. My father owned one of the first Volkswagen dealerships in Canada, and over the years under his able stewardship, it flourished. He maintained a menagerie of at least a dozen very beautiful automobiles at a time, and people driving by our house would slow down to have a close look at whatever was parked in the driveway. At one point my father's personal fleet included three Rolls-Royces, a yellow 1949 MG TC, a blue 1963 Cadillac convertible, and a silver Porsche Speedster. But the Volkswagen Beetle was my favorite of all, and I regularly fought with my siblings for the privilege of sitting in the little storage space behind the rear seat.

The community we lived in was very homogeneous; while in London, I never met a single Jewish, black, or Oriental child. We were the closest thing to an ethnic family on our street simply because we were Catholic. My father was an active member of the Knights of Columbus. Every Wednesday evening he disappeared after dinner for a Knights of Columbus council meeting. I had no idea what the organization was about, and, as a young child, I imagined my father decked out in a full suit of armor.

My mother found London to be both limiting and parochial. International news in the *London Free Press* usually amounted to less than one page. Café life was non-existent. The only vegetables available at corner stores were canned peas and carrots. Restaurants locked their doors at 8:00 p.m. Alcohol was (and still is) only available at government-run stores, a hold-over from Prohibition days. People had little knowledge of Europe or the rest of the world. They couldn't place my mother's accent, and thought it unusual and unpatriotic that she would return to Germany every year, usually without her husband. "You're a Canadian now," they would remind her.

But London was a safe and nurturing environment for a curious and energetic boy. Our house backed onto a large and wild ravine that became my childhood refuge. To this day it remains for the most part undeveloped, and the creek is still swimmable. We built rafts, carved deep caves out of the sand cliffs, and constructed elaborate forts. Our imaginations ran wild. If the Russians ever invaded, I had my hiding place prepared: an underground bunker made from scrap lumber I had collected at nearby construction sites, complete with a working periscope and ventilation pipe. But at the end of one season, I camouflaged the bunker and lost interest in it over the winter. Years later, when I tried to relocate it, the area had filled with thick undergrowth and I never found it again. I suspect it has remained undisturbed, still on stand-by for an enemy invasion.

I attended local Catholic schools with my two brothers and sister. The nuns who taught us were fine educators but strict disciplinarians, who expected both academic and moral perfection from their students. Under their tutelage, I became, for a brief period, a devout Catholic boy, observing First Fridays of each month, going to confession every week, and taking Holy Communion at mass. At school, we prayed three times every day and learned how to say the rosary. I developed a keen interest in the lives of the saints, and in particular how each of them eventually met their fate. By the age of 10, I was an expert on the most grisly methods of martyrdom, from being barbecued on a gridiron (St. Lawrence of Toledo) to being thrown off a ship with an anchor wrapped around the neck (St. Clement). Catechism classes at St. Thomas More Elementary School were serious business. In Grade 2, the nuns gave each of us a special catechism coloring book. One picture was especially disturbing; it depicted people burning in purgatory for their sins, including an old man and a group of small children. Sister Ann showed no mercy for the penitent, specifically instructing us to "color the flames white, because white is the hottest color."

My sister Fran and I were inseparable. We both had blond hair and often people mistook us for twins. When she was in Grade 4, friends taught Fran their own version of pig Latin. It was called Avenglavish, and while most kids could quickly learn the simple rules used to form the words and sentences, adults found it impossible to decipher. Fran and I would have lengthy conversations in fluent Avenglavish in front of our parents. It drove them crazy, and eventually they banned the language from our household. This only caused us to devote more time and energy to its propagation. I taught all the kids in my Grade 2 class how to speak it, and wrote my name in Avenglavish (Pavetaver) on all my writing, arithmetic, and art assignments. The nuns condemned Avenglavish as "the devil's language" because, despite their considerable linguistic expertise, they couldn't make out a word of it. To this day I remain fluent in my secret language from childhood.

I loved reading from an early age. Every Thursday evening the London Public Library's "bookmobile," a large trailer fitted out as a portable library, arrived in our neighborhood. I usually signed out the maximum number of books and traded them in for replacements the following Thursday. My favorite subjects were the standard fare of a Canadian school boy and included aviation, space exploration, and North American Indians. When my father would go to England he would bring me back the latest *Boys' Own Annual*, which would last me for months. Our house was always full of magazines and newspapers, and I subscribed to a mail-order publishing house that sent me special science and history books that automatically arrived every month by mail.

Every Sunday we went as a family to St. Peter's Cathedral, and at my father's suggestion, I became an altar boy at the age of 10. The priests' elaborate robes, the music, the candles, and, incense created an aura of mystery, and were in rich contrast to my rather humdrum home town. I was intrigued by the rituals associated with the mass. I vehemently opposed the reforms brought in by the Second Vatican Council, because I had learned all the Latin necessary to assist the priest and now my efforts were completely wasted, as English was being introduced in its place.

My music teacher discovered I had a clear treble voice, so at the age of 10, I was recruited to become a student at St. Peter's Cathedral Choir School in the centre of the city. It was an intensive musical program requiring us to study music theory and comprehension, play three instruments, and attend rigorous daily choir practices. Mathematics and science went by the wayside, as music took up most of our school hours. We were talented choristers and we knew it. We won virtually every competition we entered. I loved everything about the Cathedral Choir School, and the music we sang became a central part of my life. I spent most of my time in and around the cathedral, serving mass six days each week with two of my best friends, Bill McKeough and Frank Vita, and performing in the choir on Sundays.

Every summer from the age of eight, I attended a boys' camp in Algonquin Park, a wilderness preserve teeming with lakes in the heart of the Canadian Shield that is one of the country's prime canoe-tripping regions. Camp Ahmek caters to children from some of Canada's most prominent families, but its conditions are quite primitive. None of the cabins have electricity or running water, and status at the camp has more to do with one's ability to stern and portage a canoe with style than wealth or power. Most of the time we wore rags or nothing at all. Discipline was almost non-existent. Meals were complete chaos. I loved every minute of it. If it were not for Ahmek, I'd be a geek. At the camp I learned how to sail and ride horseback, and developed a love of wilderness and an appreciation of solitude. Canoe trips were the highlight of the summer; we travelled for as long as five weeks at a time, carrying all our supplies and cooking all our meals over an open fire. I eventually became a skilled canoeist and expedition leader, attributes I owe entirely to 15 summers at Ahmek.

Counsellors at Ahmek were known to flip cedar-strip canoes with one arm and run them over two-kilometre portages. Dave Conacher, one of the camp's most gifted athletes and canoeists, was fond of carrying two canoes at a time over the 200-metre Joe Lake dam portage; for dramatic effect, he would have two of his youngest campers perch on top of the canoes. Guy Mayer held the Ahmek (and likely the Canadian) record for portaging a canoe over the historic 14-kilometre grand portage from Pigeon River to Lake Superior, finishing in less than 90 minutes. Rich Cureton was an American who spoke with a distinctive mid-Western drawl, and like many of our American counsellors, he lived in fear of being drafted to fight in Vietnam. Cureton was one of the camp's most renowned expedition leaders. When we were on canoe trips, he insisted we get up before sunrise and break camp within 60 minutes—that meant lighting the fire, eating breakfast, washing the dishes, taking down the tents, packing our equipment, and loading our canoes within one hour from the word go.

At the conclusion of the summer, Camp Ahmek organizes an Indian Council Ring, at which time competitions are held in traditional skills. The feature event is the water-boiling contest, which requires participants equipped only with one piece of wood of their choosing, an axe, a small pot, and one match to boil one cup of water. The winner is the first person to have his pot of water boil over. Since its inception, the competition had been won by burly Canadian lumberjack types who, when the whistle blew, would chop the piece of wood with wild swings of their axe, then build their fire out of the tiny pieces. In August, 1969, Cureton revolutionized water-boiling: at the sound of the whistle, he got down on his hands and knees and, with the razor-sharp edge of his axe, began to make thin shavings from the bone-dry piece of pitch pine he had found on one of his canoe trips. Within seconds he had a flame burning under his pot, and he smashed the record by more than one minute. The camp director, astonished that a Yank had taken the crown, demanded the stop-watches be checked for accuracy.

As a young boy I had a pantheon of gods to whom I was completely devoted, including Israeli Defence Minister Moshe Dayan, the explorer and cartographer David Thompson, the Canadian surgeon and communist Dr. Norman Bethune, the German rocket pioneer Wernher von Braun, and the rogue naturalist Rachel Carson. Searching for information about them, I soon exhausted the resources of our little mobile library and was directed to the downtown branch of the London Public Library, where the staff attempted to condemn me to the children's room.

Astronautics and aeronautics enthralled me. I knew the names and home towns of all the American Mercury 7 astronauts and what colleges they had attended. I cheered on the Israeli air force as they obliterated three-quarters of the Egyptian planes on the first day of the Six Day War. The Israelis had attacked at dawn with lightning speed; most of the Egyptian planes were destroyed while still on the ground. I alarmed my pacifist mother by subscribing to military and aviation magazines. With the money I earned selling American greeting cards door-to-door, at the age of 11 I bought a telescope and an aircraft-band radio receiver. Armed with both pieces of equipment, I tracked the progress of commercial airliners streaking across blue London skies.

At times my boyhood pursuits became an obsession. When an Air Canada DC-8 crashed just outside Toronto, killing all on board in what remains Canada's worst aviation disaster, I wrote to the Department of Transport in Ottawa for a copy of the official transcript of the inquiry, looking for any clues to the cause of the crash that the investigators might have missed. The captain, Peter Hamilton, was one of the airline's most experienced pilots; a simple error by his co-pilot resulted in premature deployment of the ground spoilers when the plane was still 50 metres over the runway coming in to land from Montreal en route to Los Angeles. The aircraft pancaked onto the runway, ripping one of the four engines off the wing. I was struck by the irony that it took a super-human effort by Peter Hamilton, unaware that he had lost an engine, to then get the plane off the runway, but his actions proved fatal: while attempting to bring the aircraft around to land, a series of explosions ripped the wing apart and the DC-8 slammed into a farmer's field at over 800 kilometres per hour. Many of the bodies were never recovered from the molten wreckage. From the Department of Transport documents, I learned that Hamilton had used full throttle and all his ingenuity in a heroic attempt to pull the aircraft out of its fatal dive, and that the co-pilot, until the moment of impact, begged the captain for forgiveness, pathetically screaming out, "Sorry, Pete, sorry." As I pored over the transcripts, Captain Peter Hamilton became a figure of mythical proportions to me, easily eclipsing any television or movie stars of the day.

I was a total space junkie. I studied everything that was available about the Apollo Project, America's attempt to put a man on the moon. I built elaborate models of the lunar module. When the first Saturn V rocket was launched, I watched in amazement as the panel of glass in the CBS trailer was blown by the force of the ignition blast out of its frame. Technicians had to come to the assistance of Walter Cronkite, who never missed a beat in delivering his live commentary from Cape Kennedy. I was inconsolable when the three Apollo 1 astronauts died in a fire during a routine test session on the Cape Kennedy launch pad on January 27, 1967, including Mercury astronaut Gus Grissom. In 1968, while other kids collected baseball cards of the Detroit Tigers and the St. Louis Cardinals, I sent away to NASA for photographs of Frank Borman, the commander of Apollo 8, the first manned space craft to circle the moon. On the night of July 20, 1969, I stood with more than 100 Camp Ahmek children and staff in the warm rain outside the director's house to watch live television images from the moon, and to witness Neil Armstrong's historic "small step" onto its surface.

Based on plans I copied from library books, I constructed model rockets in our basement, fashioning them from scrap metal and cigar tubes, using gunpowder I salvaged from firecrackers for fuel. My old sandbox became my Cape Kennedy. My creations were potent, and potentially lethal. The best rockets were lost from sight, never to be recovered. One hot summer morning, I almost killed our neighbor, Dr. Frank Lindsdale, when my latest two-stage engine delayed igniting until the rocket was already arching back toward earth; it hurtled into the ground, just missing him in his pink lawn chair. When I jumped over our fence to reclaim my rocket, I found Dr. Lindsdale clutching the morning newspaper, staring with disbelief into the crater that contained the smoking remains of the true-to-scale Honest John missile.

Watching the CBS evening news with Walter Cronkite at 6:30 every night was the closest our family came to a bonding activity. I was deeply affected by the weekly estimates of the U.S. and Vietnamese dead that closed every Friday broadcast. The pictures of the American soldiers reminded me of my favorite summer counsellors from Camp Ahmek. Images of the Vietnam War, the 1968 Democratic convention in Chicago, the assassination of Robert Kennedy in the kitchen of the Ambassador Hotel, and Martin Luther King's March on Washington marked me for life, and I became a young activist. In my Grade 6 class at the cathedral school, I organized a petition denouncing the Vietnam War that we planned to mail to the U.S. embassy in Ottawa; it was intercepted by the principal and destroyed. I proposed doing my end-of-year school project on Martin Luther King; my home-room teacher informed me that he was an inappropriate choice. He didn't offer any explanation. I chose Rachel Carson instead, of whom nobody had heard. The same teacher suggested that a man might be a more suitable subject for a boy, such as a famous politician or explorer. I reminded him that Dr. King was very much a man. I stuck with Rachel Carson, and spent a week reading and writing about her seminal work, *Silent Spring*, the book first published in 1962 that many credit with launching the environmental movement in North America. Chief Justice William O. Douglas labelled *Silent Spring* "the most revolutionary book since *Uncle Tom's Cabin* ... the most important chronicle of this century for the human race." I received a D on the project, my worst grade ever.

Looking back, I see we lived a charmed life throughout the 1960s. My father's business boomed. We enjoyed frequent family vacations. On a number of occasions, I travelled with my mother to Hamburg and Berlin, and spent weekends on the island of Sylt on the North Sea. My paternal grandparents lived in Arizona, and I visited them at their desert home. I remember being traumatized by the sight of kids my age and younger picking through piles of refuse in the Mexican town of Nogales just south of the Arizona border. I asked questions to which none of the adults in my life could provide satisfactory answers: why weren't the kids going to school? Where were their parents? How did they survive? One child had no shoes and I wanted to give him my pair of Keds, but my parents held me back. After Mexico, London, Ontario, never looked the same.

I was a challenging child for adults to contend with and my activities began to test my parents' patience. Without warning I started to bring kids home from school who were from disadvantaged families. I began to resist any form of discipline, and to resent my parents' authority. I talked about becoming an actor and joining a travelling theatre company. My brothers and sister were better behaved and were more comfortable in London than I was. At the age of 11, I wanted out.

With my usual cockiness, I announced to my parents that I had outgrown London. My cousin David Callahan was attending Upper Canada College in Toronto, reputably the country's finest school for boys. I proposed to my parents that I write the Grade 7 entrance examinations. I think they were relieved by the suggestion. I spent the night before the examinations at my cousin David's house in Toronto, and he and his mother peppered me with questions that they expected might be asked. From the start I suspected they might have inside information. That night I memorized all of Canada's prime ministers, their respective parties, and home provinces. The entrance examinations were held in the Upper Canada College Preparatory School gymnasium, which reeked of sweat and floor wax, and were officiated by a plump and pink-faced master who told us precisely when we could pick up our pencils and when we had to put them down. Most of the kids wore jackets and ties. I had on the play clothes I normally wore on weekends. The second question on the first examination—worth 20 per cent of the total score—required us to list the names, parties, and home provinces of all of Canada's prime ministers. Less than one month after I wrote the exam, a letter arrived at our home in London informing my parents that I had been admitted into Grade 7 at Upper Canada College Preparatory School and was to report at the college before 3:00 p.m. on September 7, 1969.

From my first day at the college I understood it was an unusual place and the students unusual children. The boys beamed with self-confidence and were well versed in the language and traditions of the Canadian establishment. With their every word and gesture, they let you know the whole world lay at their feet. Many were being groomed to take over their families' businesses. They were accustomed to long, drawn-out lunches with their fathers at places such as the exclusive Vancouver Club and the Badminton and Racquet Club in Toronto. My classmates addressed each other by their last names. Some spoke perfect French and Spanish. One kid came complete with his own title. A number had parents who were ambassadors, and they traded stories about their favorite postings. Paris and Bangkok were high on their lists. London, Ontario, sounded like a joke to them.

This was a new world for me, and it took me time to adjust. I was still a child and had barely begun to outgrow my Lego set. I knew nothing about the Royal Canadian Yacht Club, Bermuda Race Week, Wimbledon, or the Church of England. The boys were all fit, tanned, and smartly dressed. For me, high fashion meant my favorite T-shirts featuring the Road Runner and Wile E. Coyote; Prep kids preferred monogrammed golf shirts. They knew how to tie a Windsor knot with their eyes closed and when to wear a dinner jacket as opposed to their school blazer. Some had arrived with matched luggage; I had the same battered steamer trunk I took to summer camp.

When the daily newspaper appeared in the common room before breakfast each morning, I was astonished to see kids fighting not for the sports section or comics but for the business pages to see how their fathers' companies were faring. One incident in my first term speaks volumes about the school and its students: at dinner, a 12-year-old friend whose father was a powerful banker pointed to a younger boy sitting at the end of the table and informed me that, although neither the boy nor his family had received the news, his father, a prominent Canadian businessman, was to be fired the following week. Sure enough, one morning the next week the younger boy dissolved in tears when my friend and other kids waved the front-page business news of his father's untimely demise in his face. The boy went home for the Christmas holidays and never returned.

The school may enjoy a fine reputation, but the boys of the Upper Canada College Preparatory School with whom I lived were not angels. We had over 40 acres of prime real estate in the centre of the city to ourselves, and enjoyed the finest academic and sports facilities in the country. We had as masters a number of the nation's most distinguished educators—including occasional visits from pianist Glenn Gould and author Robertson Davies—but we were rotten, spoiled brats. The kids were merciless to one another. Bullying was the rule rather than the exception. It wasn't merely a case of school-boy shenanigans. Boys who were in any way considered to be weak, effeminate, or different were singled out and relentlessly persecuted. Ruthless and sadistic punishments were meted out by self-appointed dorm captains. Although live-in masters were present at meals and at roll calls, at other times we had to fend for ourselves. It was *The Lord of the Flies* cast in the heart of the Canadian establishment's preferred incubator. Kids' worst characteristics surfaced. I remember few acts of kindness or generosity. Pettiness and one-upmanship ruled the day. Cheating, lying, and stealing were endemic. I feared that, if left to their own devices, these prepubescent school boys, all decked out in their regulation gray flannel pants, school blazer, and school tie, would slice each other's throats.

The kids I roomed with had a highly developed sense of social hierarchy and they knew exactly where their natural place was: right on top. The criteria used to establish the pecking order in the boarding house were predictable. Money—or the appearance of it—was more important than anything else. I did well in the car department, because every time my father came to get me, he arrived in a shiny European automobile. But I flunked out when it came to clothes, vacation homes, and sports equipment. Athletic prowess was a critical factor in determining a boy's status, and in this category I lost points. I was good at sailing and canoeing, but not at any of the sports in which UCC kids traditionally competed. If you were suspected of having a smidgen of ethnic blood in your system, you started out with two strikes against you. Kids with ethnic names were labelled kikes, dagos, spics—whatever seemed to fit. A mulatto kid from Sudbury was dubbed "the mongrel." When Andy and Benny Yap, the school's first boarders from Hong Kong, arrived in September, 1968, most of their fellow students assumed they were there to do our laundry.

We taunted and baited our masters. We treated the kitchen and cleaning staff, known as "workies," as our personal servants. Two of them were war veterans, old enough to be our grandfathers; we addressed them by their first names, Johnny and Bill. I remember their having to pick up the wet towels we nonchalantly dropped on the floor of the locker room. We attempted to blow up the school plumbing with M80 firecrackers that David Basta imported from Chicago. One 13-year-old boy, whose parents lived in Central America, employed his own grandmother as a drug mule, returning to Toronto from Christmas and Easter breaks with plastic sandwich bags of hashish and marijuana. He controlled the Upper Canada College Preparatory School drug cartel.

On holidays we had to choose between the theatre trip to England or a snowmobile expedition to James Bay. A delegation of kids went to Osaka, Japan, for the 1970 World's Fair. We returned from our vacations with the latest in 35-millimetre cameras and electronic equipment from Hong Kong and Tokyo. Our lockers were bursting with equipment for hockey, football, and cricket. Extra space in the boarding house was set aside for our downhill skis and 10-speed bicycles. We enjoyed our own indoor shooting range, darkroom, and filmmaking studio. The college owned a 400-acre nature preserve with an architectural award-winning chalet for our exclusive weekend use. When our parents picked us up for Christmas and Easter breaks, the school parking lot looked like a scene from the Frankfurt Auto Show.

But the apparent wealth masked extraordinary levels of dysfunction within these respected society families. Some of the kids who were boarding at the Prep had been abandoned there by parents who did not want to have them around, and the kids knew it. Sunday nights, traditionally a time associated with family dinners, were the worst for boarders who had nowhere to go. I remember groups of sullen kids gathered around the television in the common room as more fortunate boys returned from weekends with family members. Some kids rarely heard from their parents. Children concocted wild stories to explain their parents' total lack of interest in them. One boy's mother was an ivory trader in Africa who lived 100 miles from the nearest phone or post office. Another was a Concorde pilot for Air France.

As bad as we were, none of us deserved the sadistic beatings we received from our house masters for the most minor transgressions. Being "slippered," caned, or cuffed was part of the routine of the institution. I was independent and assertive, and was able to negotiate my way out of many difficult situations. Other boys fared much worse.

One master was a drunk, and we most feared Friday evenings, when he would stagger home from the liquor store at the corner of Yonge and St. Clair streets with his brown bag loaded with his "groceries," as he called his bottles. He would get totally hammered, line up all the boys in the dormitory, and beat every one of us, often for no reason. One young teacher enjoyed stripping us naked in his apartment, then pulverizing us with his cricket bat. Once another house master I respected belted me across the face while I was standing in line waiting to go into the dining room. It was the hardest I had ever been hit, and although I was not bruised, I felt disgraced and humiliated. After he slugged me, I lost all respect for the man.

Why didn't I leave Upper Canada College and go back to London? For me, quitting would have been an admission of failure and was not an option. Instead, I learned to cope. I tried to steer clear of our house master when he was intoxicated, and did my best not to irritate any of the Grade 8 kids who controlled the various factions within the boarding house. Being a New Boy with few ties to the Canadian establishment (kids made fun of me because my dad was a car dealer), I was automatically relegated to the B list among boarders. The consequence was that I could not hope to become close friends with any of the kids whose parents were diplomats, distinguished Old Boys, or captains of industry. I fell in with kids from prairie towns, military brats, and boys being raised by single moms. Toby Cullingworth, Tom Lansey, and Thayer Cummings existed on the periphery of the school's social circles. They were decent, unpretentious kids from middle-class families and were therefore particularly vulnerable to being harassed and exploited by other boys.

But among the new arrivals in Grade 7 at Upper Canada College in 1969 was a brash, loud-mouthed upstart from the American South who took up the cause of challenging the landed gentry of Upper Canada College. Philip Raleigh was an unlikely champion of the underdog—he had Republican roots and displayed a Confederate flag on the dormitory wall—but he became our own William Wallace, and had the guts to stand up to the Prep bullies. He could swear like a sailor, was already well into adolescence, smoked rum-tipped Colt cigars, and knew everything about girls.

Philip Raleigh and I were in the same form room, with a 23-year-old bearded German named Peter Weintrager as our teacher. Mr. Weintrager, fresh out of Bishop's University and with no teaching experience to his name, conducted his classes like university lectures. At age 12 I became familiar with the historians Denis Mack Smith and Arnold Toynbee. From his first term on campus, Mr. Weintrager was the *enfant terrible* among the faculty.

The day before our Christmas holidays, he presented us with our own copies of *The Communist Manifesto*, which he paid for out of his own pocket. When Prince Philip visited the school, Mr. Weintrager had our Grade 7 class line the procession route leading up the Avenue to the Upper School and instructed us to wave underwear at the Duke of Edinburgh and his entourage as they passed.

Philip Raleigh and Peter Weintrager egged each other on. Neither had much time for the school's arcane traditions or royal pedigree. Who the hell was this Duke of Edinburgh guy, Raleigh demanded to know, that the entire school had to bow and scrape in his presence? We were all ordered to muster into the Upper School quadrangle to receive the royal laying on of hands. Just after the playing of "God Save the Queen," Raleigh fired a volley of spit balls in the direction of His Royal Highness, just missing the wife of the chairman of the UCC board of governors. Weintrager saw the incident, but never said a word.

Philip Raleigh loved America, defended Richard Nixon to the hilt, and believed that the Vietnam War was a noble endeavor. With respect to politics, we had no common ground. But he was the most colorful character the school had seen in many years, our own Artful Dodger, quick-witted, quirky, with no time for hypocrisy.

Institutions have no ability to tolerate dissenters, and when the school year wrapped up in June, 1970, Philip Raleigh was not asked back. But in nine months he had made his mark among the faculty and the students. A gaggle of younger kids was by his side to see him off, and cheered as Raleigh, defiant to the end, drove away in an airport limousine with his Confederate flag billowing out the rear window. Philip Raleigh had shown me that much of the language and ritual used by kids from powerful families was nothing more than posturing. It was like the Wizard of Oz. Rich kids weren't necessarily stronger, brighter, or quicker than any other kids. Their most important weapons were their egos and self-esteem, which the school, their friends, and families constantly buttressed. Raleigh had dared to question their competence to lead, and most had come up short. Among a very few he may have actually pricked their social conscience and engendered some level of concern for others, but most UCC boys were happy to see him go.

I had been warned by my parents that academic competition at UCC would be fierce. To my surprise, I discovered most kids at the school were quite average intellectually and a contingent were positively mediocre. We presumed their parents had made generous contributions to the Upper Canada College

Foundation or were well-connected Old Boys. It was well known among the student body that the really clever kids went to the University of Toronto Schools, located on Bloor Street near Varsity Stadium. At any one time there may have been three or four brilliant boys out of 850 students enrolled at UCC; I certainly was not one of them.

A good number of kids didn't care how they performed in their classes. No matter how discouraging their grades, they stood to inherit their fathers' companies. At Upper Canada College there were things to be learned other than history and Latin; these were the subjects at which many of the richest kids excelled. UCC kids at an early age acquired a finely honed ability to intimidate. Boys learned how to wield power and how to abuse those who were vulnerable. Compassion was not part of their vocabulary. Psychological torture was their specialty. Kids who were targeted for particularly harsh treatment had no one they could turn to for help or protection. If we had personal problems, we were expected to take them up with the school nurse, a 70-year-old witch named Agnes McQuistan who, a generation before, had been disciplined for severely beating a child.

Andy Yap from Hong Kong became my closest friend. We were in the same dormitory room with 12 other boys and Andy had the bed directly across from mine. I loved his tales about life in steamy Hong Kong—roving gangs of martial-arts experts who did battle in the city streets, typhoons in the South China Sea, airplanes overshooting the runway at Kai Tak airport and ending up in the harbor. On most long weekends Andy came to London with me. With his refined manners and quiet nature, he was an easy guest and a favorite of my parents. We went to movies, our favorites being disaster films such as *The Towering Inferno*, which featured O. J. Simpson, and *Earthquake*, presented with the latest theatre gimmick called Sensurround, which consisted of vibrations that shook the entire theatre. We both were fascinated by airplanes; our idea of a fun Saturday afternoon was to take a bus to the airport in the middle of a snowstorm, park ourselves at the top level of the four-storey garage, and watch the departures and arrivals while listening to communications from the control tower on my aircraft-band receiver. Andy and I remained close friends after we graduated from Upper Canada College, and at the age of 22, we travelled overland together to the ancient cities of Samarkand and Buchara in Soviet Central Asia, to Lake Baikal in Siberia, then by steam locomotive to Shanghai and throughout China.

In Grade 8, I was appointed a prefect and took up the task of protecting a number of the younger kids from the relentless bullying that went on at the boarding house. I launched a "first name" campaign, suggesting kids and masters might try to use the first name that every child came with. It was a total failure. To this day I remember the face of every student who took pleasure in terrorizing younger and more vulnerable kids. The aggressors were invariably social misfits themselves whose status depended entirely on putting others down. As adults, many of the worst kids have done well taking over the reins of the family business, but they have not changed. They rule their companies with an iron fist and they lead predictable lives. Materialism and consumerism reign supreme. A popular bumper sticker in the Upper Canada College parking lot read "He who dies with the most toys wins." It was meant to be taken seriously. I sometimes wonder how many people have suffered at the hands of graduates of the school, young men brimming with self confidence, with big bank accounts to back them up, who are let loose on an unsuspecting world. I once dated someone who believed there should be a support group for women who have endured relationships with UCC Old Boys.

In 1979, Upper Canada College ended boarding in the Preparatory School, and plans were made to tear the boarding house down. A number of crusty Old Boys protested and some even embarked on a campaign to save the wretched building, which dated from the 19th century and was of absolutely no historic or architectural significance. However, few boarders of my generation raised a finger in support of saving the boarding house. There were too many ghosts associated with the place, too many dark and disturbing memories that we, as grown men, do our best to repress. Luckily, the preservation efforts failed, and the Prep boarding house was reduced to rubble. I still can't walk or drive by the site without feeling the same pangs of profound sadness and loneliness that at times engulfed me when that building was my only Toronto refuge.

I started working with children when I was still a child myself. It wasn't entirely by choice. Boarders at the Prep were regularly rounded up for various political and charitable causes. Jean Pigott, the mom of my dorm-mate John, had once come through the residence with her son searching for boys willing to work for the local Conservative candidate for the Canadian Parliament, Ron Atkey. In September, 1970, while in my second year at Upper Canada College, I was drafted by an educator named Shirley McNaughton to join her team of young people who would be teaching non-verbal kids to "speak." McNaughton, a teacher at the Ontario Crippled Children's Centre, had been looking for a system that would allow children with cerebral palsy to communicate by way of pointing to symbols. Our own language, relying on combinations of letters and words to form sentences, was too slow and cumbersome for her kids. McNaughton stumbled across a new language based on symbols, each of which, like Chinese or Japanese ideograms, stood for a word or concept. "Blis-symbolics" had originally been invented by an Australian linguist, Charles Bliss, as his contribution to the search for a universal language.

McNaughton and her colleagues arranged the Bliss symbols on boards in a logical manner that reflected normal sentence structure. The boards were fixed to the wheelchairs that the children used at the school at the Ontario Crippled Children's Centre. By pointing to the symbols in order, non-verbal kids could suddenly communicate with the outside world. They were liberated from their disability and it transformed their lives. McNaughton wanted young students to introduce the children to the symbols. She visited Upper Canada College and interviewed a number of the boarders. She told me that she selected me because I was talkative—something that usually got me into trouble at school.

A new world opened to me. Working with handicapped children my own age, none of whom had ever spoken with anyone in their lives, was a powerful antidote to the smugness and arrogance that plagued Upper Canada College in the 1970s. The Ontario Crippled Children's Centre was a 20-minute subway ride and a world apart from Forest Hill, the school's exclusive neighborhood. Working with handicapped children was a humbling experience and it quickly cut me down to size. The kids I worked with had never heard of, and didn't care about, the glories of Upper Canada College. They would never play cricket, perform in a Gilbert and Sullivan musical, or attend The Proms in London. They simply wanted me to be their friend.

I first found courage in the form of Scott Bond, a mute, wheelchair-bound, 11-year-old hellion who was crazy about girls. He mastered his full tray of 250 Blissymbols in less than 30 minutes, and arranged them in unusual combinations to form swear words that he had often heard but obviously not quite understood. His first words to me, his friend and tutor, were "Fuck you." In 1970, many people considered children with cerebral palsy to have the mental capacity of infants and treated them accordingly. The handicapped kids at the Ontario Crippled Children's Centre were all very sheltered. Our job was to make their world big. The fact that we had no training as social workers or as special-education teachers was considered an asset. We had no cumbersome theories of learning or development to inhibit our relationship with these girls and boys.

Scott Bond was very clever and extremely curious. He liked sports and movies, so that's what we talked about. Shirley McNaughton wanted age-mates to serve as tutors for her children for the very reason that we could deal with sub-jects that were off-limits to adults. In this and other aspects, she was years ahead of her time. Scott Bond and his friends showed us all that they were kids like any others and that they expected to be treated as such. In those days at the Ontario Crippled Children's Centre, many of the myths about cerebral-palsy kids were smashed; I am proud to have played a small part in a Canadian success story.

In September, 1971, I moved 200 metres north to the Upper Canada Col-lege Upper School, for boys between the ages of 13 and 18, and was fortunate to be assigned to an island of sanity called Seaton's House. The housemaster was a diminutive, chain-smoking Frenchman named Louis Paichoux, and he was serious about his responsibilities to the 55 students in his care. The boys of Seaton's House were consequently ferociously loyal to him. Paichoux had served in the French Army during World War II, been taken prisoner, and spent years in a prison camp. He arrived at UCC in 1962 after a distinguished career teaching in Syria, Egypt, Morocco, and Cambodia. He instituted a system of authentic student leadership whereby the older students ran all aspects of house life, from setting up sports clubs to enforcing discipline. The system was democ-ratic, fair, and effective. It worked because he trusted and respected the students, and valued their contributions to the house and to the school. Idleness and sloth were not tolerated; we had to participate in sports and clubs and keep up with our academics. No matter how bad our house team was, Louis turned up to watch every football match we played; as a matter of principle, he challenged the referees when a call went against us.

For boarders like myself who had moved up from the Preparatory School, the Upper School was nirvana. We were allowed off the campus on our own, could visit the girls' school down the road, and were mostly left alone. Louis Paichoux's unwritten rule for Saturday leave was that no matter how late, we had to sign the book in the portico with the exact time of our return, and whether drunk or sober, we had to go directly and quietly to our room. Kids could smoke, and we kept beer in the water tank above the urinals. Louis saw us as members of his extended family. Discretion and honesty were the key words. If we followed these guidelines, there would be no repercussions. Phys-ical punishment by masters or prefects was strictly prohibited.

Paichoux selected his prefects on the basis of their ability to lead, not by their family's status. The Heads of House and prefects were respected by the stu-dents, and we tried to avoid making their lives difficult. Among their ranks were a number of gifted leaders. Joe Gibbons from Bermuda was brilliant, irreverent

29

of the school and its traditions, and a natural orator; he chaired the evening boarding-house meetings with the finesse of a seasoned parliamentary whip. Among day students, Paichoux's allies included Richard Meech, who single-handedly made community service a leading after-school activity years before this became fashionable at private schools.

Patrick Johnson, our principal, was born and raised in colonial India. His older brother had died in combat in Burma, and he himself had served as an officer with the 9th Gurkha Rifles from 1944 to 1948. Johnson was a graduate of Oxford, and with his upper-class mannerisms and almost regal air, he could have arrived at the school straight from central casting. He had his detractors among faculty and students alike, but he led the school with an even hand during a very turbulent period, when authority was being challenged and offices of university presidents across North America were being occupied by student demonstrators. I liked him immensely, and admired his ability to deal with idiosyncratic faculty whom he had inherited from his predecessor, bombastic parents, and a board of governors that read like the *Who's Who* of the Canadian establishment.

Robertson Davies once said that the advantage of private schools over state-run institutions was that they could tolerate a number of cultured madmen on staff without having to account to the government authorities. Johnson had a stable of eccentrics to contend with. My Grade 9 math teacher, Walter Bailey, came to most classes with a flask of gin in his pocket; he allowed us to play hearts at the back of the classroom while at the front, he instructed any students who happened to be interested in geometry. There were very few takers. Over the 1971 Christmas break, Wally lost all of our examinations and "divined" our marks. In January, 1972, after a particularly heavy bout of drinking, he failed to emerge from his on-campus apartment for more than four days. Patrick Johnson slipped a little note under the door with two words: "You're fired."

Our German teacher enjoyed riffling his fingers through our hair while we conjugated our verbs. Our classes often had little to do with learning German; he once volunteered that if his daughter ever asked his permission to go on the pill, he would poison her. Our chemistry teacher was a brilliant but high-strung young scientist who was terrified of his students. Using the hoses at our desk sinks, we flooded the classroom on a regular basis, and on one occasion, Louis Paichoux, who taught French in the classroom immediately underneath, had to cancel his classes because of the downpour. Our music teacher and organist exercised no control over his classroom; he almost suffered a heart attack when we once dangled him outside the window by his ankles three floors above the school entrance.

These characters, all part of the "Upper Canada College Family," were easily outnumbered by teachers who were dedicated and selfless educators. Men such as Ted Stephenson, Bernie Lecerf, and Roger Allen inspired and challenged their students. I never found finer teachers or role models. They provided me with a solid intellectual foundation that has served me well to this day. I learned to chase ideas, how to read a Shakespeare sonnet, that curiosity is a good thing. In Grade 9, Jay D. MacDonald was my English teacher, but he was best known as the director of the Upper Canada College Little Theatre. He devoted himself to running a theatre company that was in every way professional. It was Mr. MacDonald who convinced the UCC board of governors to allow girls from neighboring schools into the company. Previously boys from the Prep had played all the female roles. Productions ranged from Thornton Wilder's *Our Town* to Gilbert and Sullivan's *Pinafore*; they were all done with great style and attracted full houses. The Little Theatre enjoyed an independence from the rest of the school, which its members jealously guarded. It certainly was not a democratic institution. Admission was by audition only, with Jay D. making all the decisions.

MacDonald's talent pool was limited, but he squeezed the best performances possible out of every actor. In the 1974 and 1975 seasons, because of an almost unprecedented talent drought, I was cast in lead roles in *The Fantasticks* and *Anything Goes*. The cast included Geraint Wyn Davies and Louise Valence, both of whom went on to successful professional acting careers. Jay D. berated us during rehearsals for our flubbed lines, for upstaging other performers, and for our inconsistent and haphazard delivery. Once he angrily threw his copy of *The Fantasticks* script into the air and stormed out of the hall, telling us he would return when our level of seriousness as performers warranted his attention. We worked on scenes until we got them right, and both productions were well received by the public. I was conscious of the fact that I was operating at the outer limits of my ability as a performer, and had the sense never again to appear on stage.

As an adult, I am an avid swimmer, sailor, and canoeist, but as an adolescent, I was awkward and unco-ordinated. I had no innate ability for any of the sports that Upper Canada awarded prestigious First Team ties for. This could have made my life at the school very difficult, but what I lacked in athletic prowess I more than compensated for with my mouth. I excelled at debating. I enjoyed verbally sparring with my masters and fellow students. At the time, the Upper Canada College Debating Society was controlled by a junta who suffered from the delusion that they were running a junior version of the Oxford

Debating Union. I wasn't part of their clique, but in the debates between the school's eight houses, I was chosen to represent Seaton's House. The head of Seaton's House, Joe Gibbons, was my debating coach. He had a theatrical bent, and was intimately familiar with the parliamentary rules associated with the art of debate. Over the next four years I never lost a single contest.

In 1974, much to the chagrin of the Upper Canada Debating Society, I was selected as a member of the UCC team that would compete at the prestigious McGill International Debating Tournament in Montreal. The best schools from Eastern Canada and from New England would be present. Some members of the Debating Society openly voiced their grievance that I had not earned the right to compete at McGill, but the names of the UCC team members had already been submitted to the authorities at McGill and nothing could be changed. I won the competition for the school and was awarded the Best Speaker prize—the first Upper Canada student to be so honored by McGill. I went on to participate in other tournaments for the school and always came home with the big prize.

I wanted to make debating at Upper Canada College more fun and more accessible to the general student population. Nobody paid attention to debating. It was associated with people wearing Coke-bottle-lens glasses who needed to be reminded to take a weekly bath. At the House competitions, five or six students might turn up for each debate, all of which were held at lunch hour. In the spring of 1974, Seaton's House was so far ahead in the house debating competitions that we could not lose the championship, no matter how badly we did in our last contest, which was against our arch rival, Wedd's House. John Pigott and Glen Tugman were representing Wedd's House, and I met with them to negotiate both the topic and who the debaters would be for our house. They were concerned about the resolution I proposed: "Be it resolved that too much time and money are spent on hockey at Upper Canada College." I suggested that Wedd's House support the resolution, and that we would represent the opposition. Pigott and Tugman thought it would be an easy resolution to oppose, until I informed them that speaking for Seaton's House were two students who had never debated before, both of whom were first-team hockey stars: Al Walsh and Reuben Donnelly. Walsh was a strong student, but Donnelly was best known as an aggressive right wing who would drop his gloves and fight other players at the slightest provocation. He was no intellectual, but he was extremely popular among his fellow students. Pigott and Tugman immediately accepted the terms of the debate; they anticipated an easy victory.

The hockey debate, as it became known, transformed me into a kind of Don

King of verbal pugilism at Upper Canada College. We had to move it to a small assembly hall instead of a regular classroom on account of the throng that turned up. The school's faculty lined the back of the room. For dramatic effect, I had Walsh and Donnelly arrive a few minutes late for the contest decked out in their hockey sweaters. The room burst into applause as they entered.

Walsh did superbly in opposing the resolution, producing statistics that showed Upper Canada College spent more money maintaining the cricket pitches than it did running the school's hockey program. The Upper Canada College indoor arena had the best ice surface in the city. Teams from all over Toronto, from school and sport clubs alike, paid $200 an hour to use the arena, and it was a cash cow for the school's sports program. But Pigott and Tugman were skillful opponents, and in the end, we lost the debate. It didn't really matter; we won the overall house championship, and the hockey debate, the most raucous event of its kind for many years at the college, shook up the uptight UCC debating establishment.

Minutes after the debate concluded, a row broke out in the masters' common room over the release of the statistics that our team had used, showing that the UCC cricket program was much more expensive than hockey. Terrence Bredin, Latin master and cricket aficionado, was livid that these supposedly confidential statistics had entered the public domain. He suspected that his colleague, Brian Proctor, geography teacher and coach of the school's top-ranked hockey team, had fed Donnelly and Walsh the information. It couldn't be proven, though, and both students refused to reveal their source. More than 20 years later, hockey and cricket remain very popular at the school.

As much as I enjoyed life at Seaton's House, I searched for ways to expand my horizons. Volunteering was my ticket to escape the school grounds. From Grade 9, I expanded on the work with children that I had begun in the Preparatory School. I signed up as a tutor at an inner-city school in St. Jamestown, which was then, and remains today, one of Toronto's poorest neighborhoods. This nondescript block of apartment buildings was only a few streets south of Rosedale, Toronto's toniest address. The kids were mostly from immigrant Caribbean families with both parents working.

One 12-year-old Jamaican-born girl named Leticia was their leader; she worked part-time in two different convenience stores to supplement her family's income. Leticia was a superb athlete, easily beating all the boys in any competition that we organized, but she could not afford a single pair of decent running shoes. Another girl, Cordelia, age 11, worked in a laundromat and saved her earnings for piano lessons. Many of the children I tutored had never been far from their apartment buildings, so I started inviting them to Upper Canada College for sports activities, which raised eyebrows on campus. I thought Philip Raleigh would have approved. An American boarder, who lived in what was effectively a segregated community in Coral Gables, Florida, informed me the school was better off remaining "nigger-free." Most of the students were indifferent to the visitors, but my behavior puzzled them. The kids from St. Jamestown were dazzled by the green space, our indoor arena, and the size of the houses in Forest Hill that surround the school. "You're telling me that one family has that entire house to themselves?" one kid asked.

I found these inner-city children more engaging than many of my fellow students at UCC. They lived much less protected lives than we did, and they grew up quickly. They knew where drugs were for sale, about racism and corruption within local government. Although they had few possessions, they were generous with what they had. Upper Canada College kids were notoriously tight. I remember bratty Prep kids ordering pizzas on Saturday nights with the hefty allowances their parents had provided; one corpulent boy from Ottawa auctioned off the pizza crusts that he didn't want to eat himself. When I was in Grade 7, we were asked to take donation boxes around for UNICEF at Hallowe'en. When the woman from UNICEF came the next day to retrieve the boxes, she commented that we had not been very successful. What she didn't know was that the majority of the students pocketed the money they had collected. In Canada, WASPs are not known for their philanthropy. We don't have anything like the American tradition of the Dupont, Heinz, or Annenberg families giving hundreds of millions of dollars to charity. Boys who attend Upper Canada College are raised in the tradition that money is something to be hoarded and not given away. They learn their lessons well. Most graduates of UCC end up in professions where they act as the defenders of capital; their job is to guard against hostile incursions, whether by Revenue Canada, banks, competitors, or charities.

UCC was the express lane to the easy life—a cushy job with a bank on Bay Street in Toronto's financial district, a cottage in Muskoka north of the city, and March vacations in the Bahamas. What we didn't know in 1973 was that Canadian society was being turned upside down. Immigration from Asia, the emancipation of women, new technology, and the globalization of the economy were transforming the nation. For many years, virtually all of Canada's senior diplomats were graduates of Upper Canada College, but by the late 1970s, having played on the UCC first cricket team didn't carry the same weight as it had a generation earlier. In 1829, Upper Canada College adopted Admiral Nelson's motto: *Palmam Qui Meruit Ferat*, or "Let he who deserves the palm bear it." I always thought the school motto should be, "Let he who bears the palm deserve it."

In three years of boarding, I had only once been invited overnight at the house of a day student, so I was both honored and surprised when, after a few weeks of tutoring Leticia at Rose Park School, she asked me home for dinner. I had never been inside the nondescript apartment buildings that make up the St. Jamestown complex, and I was not sure what to expect. Leticia lived with her parents, one sister, and two brothers in a two-bedroom flat on the 23rd floor of a building at the corner of Wellesley and Parliament streets in Toronto. Her parents had emigrated from Jamaica five years earlier. Although their apartment was crowded, it was spotless. Everything had its place. Winter jackets were hung up in the corridor according to size, and boots and shoes were neatly arranged side by side in a long plastic tray.

Leticia brought me in to meet her family. No one was alarmed that she was accompanied by a white boy four years her senior. A place was set for me at the table. Dinner was being prepared, and Leticia's mother asked if I liked Caribbean cooking. It was only 4:30 in the afternoon, and I was surprised they would be eating so early. I learned that Leticia's mother and father both worked nights; eating dinner at 5 p.m. meant they would have time to help their children with their homework before heading off to their jobs.

When dinner was served I recognized few items on the table. At Upper Canada College, roast beef, potatoes, and gravy were standard fare. At Leticia's house, the staples included cornmeal bread, yams, plantains, and okra. They baked the bread themselves, and it was served warm with Blueband margarine smeared all over it. We were not allowed to touch anything before grace was said. Leticia came from a family of hard-working, God-fearing people. Conversation at the table was animated, but all four children were soft-spoken and well-mannered. Leticia helped her younger brother cut his food into bite-sized pieces. Without being asked, Leticia and her older brother collected the dishes off the table and washed and dried them. When the dishes were done, it was homework time. The dining table had already been washed down, and places were cleared for all four kids to complete their assignments, if they had any, or to practise their reading and spelling.

Leticia's parents had never met a boy from Upper Canada College before. Her father knew the school as the site of the city's finest cricket pitches, where uniformed maids served cucumber sandwiches to spectators and players at tea time. I returned to Leticia's apartment several times after that initial visit and on each occasion, I was made to feel at home. I encouraged other UCC kids to join me in volunteering at Rose Park School, but I was unsuccessful. In a way, I was happy I was on my own. I liked the fact that St. Jamestown had so little in common with the rest of my life. For the most part, I kept my experiences and stories about St. Jamestown to myself. I didn't want to be cross-examined by my fellow students about my new-found interest in the lives of inner-city children.

I combined community service with political activism, petitioning voters to stop the construction of a new airport on prime agricultural land east of Toronto and doing my best to persuade shoppers not to buy California grapes, picked by non-unionized migrant workers who were regularly exposed to harmful chemicals. I approached fur-clad housewives in the produce section of the local supermarket, dressed in my UCC blazer and Seaton's House tie. "Excuse me, ma'am," I earnestly pleaded. "Did you know that by purchasing the California grapes I see in your shopping cart, you are contributing to the exploitation of Mexican farm workers by powerful corporate interests? May I suggest these Ontario-grown apples as an alternative?" They looked at me bewildered and amused. Some actually backed away from the grapes as if they were radioactive.

By the age of 17 and after six years at an all-boys boarding school, I had had enough and wanted to move on. My choices were to apply to an American university or to stay for the final year of high school at Upper Canada College. Without telling my parents, I threw myself into the university-application process, researching schools, writing SATs, and lining up teachers willing to write letters of recommendation on my behalf, but I only really had one school in mind. Ever since the days when I had raced on my bicycle to the bookmobile in London to collect my weekly reading selections, my dream had been to attend Stanford University in California, the home of biologist Paul Ehrlich, anthropologist Jane Goodall, and author Ken Kesey. Robert Kennedy had attended law school at Stanford. It had its own marine-biology research station just outside Monterey where John Steinbeck had studied. Stanford was among the most competitive of American colleges, accepting fewer than 10 per cent of all undergraduate applicants, so I knew my chances of being admitted were slim. But I had been near the top of my class every year at UCC, and thought that if I were turned down, I could reapply after one more year of high school.

I filled out all the forms, and for the required essay about "a person or persons who were important to me," quickly typed 700 words about the girls and boys I worked with in St. Jamestown. I entitled the essay "The Courage of Children," and mailed the application materials off to Palo Alto, California, just before the Christmas break.

Four months later, on an unusually warm morning in April, 1975, I was handed an envelope at morning mail call embossed with the words "Stanford University Office of Admissions" in bright red letters. I knew it contained bad news. The conventional wisdom then was that letters of acceptance from Stanford, Yale, and Harvard came in thick envelopes, packed with information about classes and enrollment procedures, while rejection letters were only one page long. The envelope I had been handed was thin; I did not have the nerve to read it in front of any other students. I took the letter outside and opened it in the inner quadrangle in the shadow of the statue of the school's founder, Lord Seaton. I read the first five words with stunned disbelief: "It is with great pleasure..." I was overcome with emotion, and could read no further. I later learned that my essay about my young friends Leticia's and Cordelia's efforts to surmount the poverty and prejudice of inner-city Toronto was a compelling factor in the admission committee's decision in my favor. For several years I stayed in contact with both girls, but their families were being pursued by creditors, and they eventually moved to other parts of the city. I never saw them again.

From my first year of boarding at the Upper School, Louis Paichoux had hinted he looked forward to the day when I would become his head of house, a privilege reserved for one of his Grade 13 boys. I had earned the respect of the students. In particular, the Grade 9 and 10 boys looked up to me and were keen to have me as head of house. Inspired by the memory of Philip Raleigh, I was eager to run the house the way Paichoux wanted, in an atmosphere that fostered trust and co-operation between teachers and students. My admission to Stanford changed everything. I was 17 years old and I had done enough time at a single-sex boarding school. When I knocked on Louis's door that evening with the letter from Stanford in my hand, he guessed what news I was bringing. Choking back tears and with his wife at his side, he told me, "Don't say anything. I know I am losing you." That moment, my elation at having been accepted at Stanford was tempered by the sudden realization that as I had seen a father in Louis, he had found a son in me. I was profoundly moved and honored, and vowed that never again would I knowingly disappoint someone who had placed such faith in me.

My last few weeks at the school were the most difficult of all. Emotionally, I was being pulled in two directions. For day students, the buildings and grounds were just a school, another part of their busy lives. They had their homes and families to return to every evening. For boarders, with all its short-comings, Upper Canada College was still the place where we grew up, and the place that we closely associated with the happiest and most despairing moments of our childhood. No wonder the school provokes such strong reactions among former boarders. I knew every tree on the campus, the names of the grounds keepers and the caretakers who kept the place beautiful, and which meals in the cafeteria were best left uneaten. Now that I had decided to leave, I finally realized how much the school meant to me.

In those last days of June, 1975, all the memories came back to me. I remembered our finest Little Theatre productions. I remembered trooping off on bitingly cold February mornings to the Ontario Science Centre with my friends Mark Johnston and Peter Boeckh to work in the holography laboratories along-side one of their resident scientists. I remembered playing hockey on the artificial rinks under the stars in Grade 7 and 8, and walking back across the frozen fields to the boarding house, where steaming hot chocolate would be prepared for us. I remembered cricket games on long spring afternoons when the college fields were at their greenest. I thought of those very few teachers over my six years who had actually taken an interest in me, and mentored me, and spoken to me almost as a friend. I remembered the kindness of adults who played only minor roles at the college, but who had an obvious fondness for children—Mr. Gregory, who, although in his mid-70s, ably managed the residence at the college's property on the Credit River, and an elderly and diminutive caretaker in the Preparatory School we knew only as Bill, who spoke with a thick Glaswegian accent. The school would have been a much happier place if there had been more people on staff who actually enjoyed working with children.

I remembered my new friend in Grade 11, the scion of an establishment Connecticut family named John Eldridge, who never missed an opportunity to buck the system and who constantly fought with his house master, whom he detested. When I returned from summer vacation at the start of Grade 12, I searched throughout the entire boarding house for John. I had plans for us to go out for a pizza and exchange stories about our summer vacations. John always had a new girlfriend, and inevitably had tales of his latest exploits. But I couldn't find him anywhere, so I went to see his house master, who, with cool detach-ment, informed me that John had drowned while waterskiing just days after school had ended in June. "And how was your summer, Dalglish?" he asked me.

I remembered those precocious kids with the fancy cameras and sports equipment whom I had so envied in the Preparatory School. Some had shown such great promise, but then fallen by the wayside. In the end, Upper Canada College had broken them, and they never recovered their self-confidence. Some had taken up hard drugs; at least two were already in the criminal justice system. David Basta, the sassy kid who imported M80s from Chicago with which to demolish the school's plumbing, shot himself before he completed college. Most of the emotionally damaged kids simply disappeared. You never read about them in the school alumni magazines and nobody mentions their names. Years after I left Upper Canada College, I was picked up by a middle-aged cab driver who claimed he had attended the Preparatory School; he described it as the most painful experience of his life, and one that had shattered his self-confidence forever. I didn't believe him at first, so I quizzed him on names and places associated with the school that only someone who had attended the Prep would be able to answer. He easily passed my little test. He remembered being pummelled and humiliated in the annual Prep boxing competition, the teacher who photographed him skinny and naked at the edge of the school swimming pool, and being taunted by classmates for his ethnic-sounding name. So the abuse spilled over from one generation to another, casting a wider and wider net. I felt sick. I wished the subject of the school had never come up, and was happy to escape the cab when we reached our destination.

It all came to an end very quickly, which for me was just as well. I couldn't face saying good-bye to Louis Paichoux. In those days, there was no graduation ceremony at Upper Canada College; you simply packed your bags and left. Adolescent boys are rarely demonstrative with each other, so after six years of residential schooling, I peeled the posters off my bedroom walls, loaded my steamer trunk into my father's car, and exchanged cursory farewells with kids I had been through hell with, and with kids I had loved like brothers. Most of them I never saw again. Summer had arrived early that year, and my father had brought a 1952 Ford convertible Suncruiser from London for the occasion. It was gleaming white with red upholstery, and I remember he had the top down. We made our way down the Avenue with the big elm trees towering overhead and out the college gate into the city. I closed my eyes and felt the warm wind in my hair. As we left the school grounds, I thought I heard one of the Grade 9 kids calling my name from a distance, but I never looked back.

THOSE BRIGHT
COLLEGE YEARS

I arrived in California in the fall of 1975 as a refugee from Upper Canada College. I knew no one at Stanford and no one knew me, which suited me perfectly. I wanted a fresh start. Stanford is not as well known in Canada as Harvard or Yale; the only reason my parents let me go was because they thought it was located somewhere in Connecticut. One teacher at Upper Canada College had gone out of his way to discourage me from attending Stanford, telling me that I could not withstand rigorous competition from some of America's best students. UCC boys made disparaging remarks about the United States. The Vietnam War was just winding down, and anti-American sentiment in Canada was at an all-time high. Only four of the 110 members of the Upper Canada College Class of 1975 chose to study at American schools.

On Thursday, September 25, I took a bus packed with bubbly Stanford freshmen from the San Francisco airport to Palo Alto. I made sure I had a window seat. From my first view of the palm-fringed campus, I knew I had made the right choice. This was no Oxford, Cambridge, or Princeton. Stanford had an easy-going, West Coast ambience. I spied groups of students in shorts and T-shirts playing volleyball and tossing Frisbees. By the fountain of the Old Union building, five games of chess were under way. A bearded professor dressed in jeans was leading a seminar of some kind on the grass outside the main quadrangle. Nothing about the school appeared threatening; it looked more like a Club Med than one of America's top-ranked universities. I felt right at home.

The Stanford campus, located just west of San Francisco Bay and a 30-minute drive from the Pacific Ocean, is both spectacular and unique. Mrs. Stanford was a deeply religious woman and chose to have all the university buildings modelled after the famous missions built in California and Mexico in the 17th and 18th centuries by Spanish priests.

Leland Stanford, former governor of California and a U.S. senator, had made a sizable fortune building America's transcontinental railway, so there was no shortage of money for his wife's pet project. Frederick Law Olmstead, the most distinguished landscape architect of his day and the designer of New York City's Central Park, was commissioned to plan the campus. Stanford has nothing in common with America's historic and tradition-bound East Coast universities. In fact, ivy is banned from all buildings. Stanford's most distinctive feature is the red-tiled roofs which top everything from the 34 university libraries to the business school and the medical centre. Stanford undergraduates derisively refer to their school as the world's largest Taco Bell. The charter drafted by the Stanfords setting out the terms of their bequest includes a clause requiring all new buildings to have identical red-tiled roofs "so that Mrs. Stanford can see the campus from heaven." No cars are allowed within the main campus; students make their way from the residences to their classes on bicycles or on foot. If they choose, they can detour through the expansive eucalyptus groves that surround the school, visit the Rodin sculpture garden, or stop for a swim at the old boat house on Lake Lagunita. The hills and open fields located on the most western portion of the campus are a runner's paradise. The university facilities today include a stadium that seats 88,500 spectators, a sunken baseball diamond, 40 tennis courts, an Olympic swimming complex, and an 18-hole golf course rated among the top 50 in America. Visitors who are accustomed to more modest state-funded colleges are overwhelmed by the scale and opulence of the institution; nothing about it is understated. Stanford has more in common with Versailles than it does with the Sorbonne.

By the mid-1970s, Stanford had come into its own and was brashly self-confident. Its departments were studded with numerous Nobel laureates and Pulitzer Prize–winners. The chemist Linus Pauling and the geneticist Joshua Lederberg were on faculty. Stanford's schools of engineering, education, and business were rated the best in the nation. Its resources appeared to be limitless. Undergraduates in most North American universities share cavernous lecture halls with as many as 200 other students. Some never go to classes at all but monitor their lectures by way of videotapes. As Stanford freshmen, we enjoyed intimate seminars led by some of the nation's most acclaimed professors. The distinguished civil-war historian Donald Fehrenbacher hosted a freshman seminar on the role of Leland Stanford's Central Pacific Railroad in shaping California culture in the 1870s. The poet Diane Middlebrook taught a pioneering class on American feminist thought. Jane Goodall lectured on her work with primates in Tanzania. One of the most popular activities for aspiring biologists was to chase and tag butterflies alongside Paul Ehrlich, author of *The Population Bomb*, at Jasper Ridge, Stanford's own biological reserve. Students studying oceanography attended their classes sitting on the beach at Half Moon Bay with the breaking surf as their backdrop.

As good as Upper Canada College was, nothing could have adequately prepared me for the zeal of ambitious and hard-working American students. They arrived at Stanford equipped to do battle. For the first time in my life I had to fight to stay with the top half of the class. In chemistry and biology, the Americans were at least one year ahead of me; in mathematics, I had no chance of competing. Stanford freshmen were among America's finest high-school graduates and they were very good indeed. In their first year of college, they were already looking beyond Stanford at prestigious medical and law schools. Many formed study groups that met on Sunday nights to prepare for the following week. My friend Alex Armour would lock himself in his room the night before an organic-chemistry examination and, with his photographic memory, "copy" 200 pages of text into his brain. Students shared notes with each other and warmed up to graduate students who could help them with their assignments. Equal amounts of charm and natural talent had served me well at Upper Canada College, but at Stanford, these attributes had little currency. The only things that really counted were raw intellect and individual effort.

The one area in which I had a distinct advantage was the humanities. I was as puzzled by the American students' cultural illiteracy as I was impressed by their prowess in mathematics and science. At Upper Canada College I had been immersed in literature, reading at least two Shakespeare plays each year from the age of 12. We studied them the right way, performing many on stage and going to Canada's acclaimed Stratford Festival every fall. Before I graduated from high school, I knew many of Orwell's essays and was familiar with the *Iliad* and the *Odyssey*. We had read Eliot and Yeats, and studied the great modern American playwrights Tennessee Williams and Eugene O'Neill. European history had been drilled into us. We had studied the roots of parliamentary democracy in England, the Napoleonic campaigns, and the rise of fascism in Spain and Germany. For most Americans, including Stanford students, ancient history meant last year's Super Bowl game. Their entire culture was based on television. My fellow students knew little poetry and even less about classical music and Renaissance art. Some had completed high school without writing one essay. The majority could speak and write only one language—and not very well at that. They had been taught little grammar. Geography was clearly not their forte; most Stanford students thought the West Bank was a place to open an account.

I decided my only hope was to build on my natural strengths and focus on the humanities. The Stanford English department became my refuge. The faculty was strong, including leading authorities on Chaucer, Joyce, Yeats, and Eliot, and African-American literature. For freshman English, I was assigned to a seminar entitled *The Literature of the American West* led by Professor N. Scott Momaday, a Kiowa Indian who had won the Pulitzer Prize for his collection of poems, *The Way to Rainy Mountain*. He had taken the ancient Kiowa legends that he had heard as a child and written them in a modern and evocative form. Momaday had a commanding presence in the classroom, with a white beard and a resonant radio voice. He also drove a Porsche 911 and played a strong game of tennis. Momaday made a huge impact on me. His class was really only about one thing—the art of storytelling. He had us read out loud everything we wrote to hear the sound the words made on our ears. Momaday was as interested in the rhythm and balance of our sentences as in the actual content of the stories. He took my clumsy sentences, ripped them apart, and had me rebuild them over and over again. He once made me write the word "cadence" 50 times on the blackboard.

Stanford students must choose to live in co-ed or single-sex residences. After six years at a boys' boarding school, I was keen on getting to know the other half of the human race and I selected a co-ed residence. For most boarders at Upper Canada, relations with girls had been ritualized and sex had been furtive. Dances were organized with local girls' schools, but were formal occasions and heavily chaperoned. Girls had boys picked out well in advance, probably with the assistance of their mothers who ran the Cotillion Society and who practised a genteel form of eugenics. Hockey and football stars were in heavy demand, as were boys with cars.

In Toronto I had the same girl friend, Shelley Roberts, from Grade 10 through 12, which was rare, but we were perfect together. We had met at a debating competition. I was drawn to her unruly red hair and her quick wit. She skied, wrote poetry, and loved Shakespeare. Shelley was brilliant, and she shared the name of my favorite poet. She was one year behind me at school, and ended up joining me at Stanford, where she majored in human biology. Over the next three years we shared residences and classes; Shelley single-handedly got me through six months of organic chemistry.

In my freshman year, Julie Macey and Linda Nowlan, who were room-mates, became my confidantes and advisors. Both had Californian roots and knew their way around. Julie owned a red Fiat, which she drove with gusto. We travelled to Los Angeles for the USC football game and to San Francisco when-ever we needed a break from our studying. After school on Fridays, we drove over the hills to walk the empty beaches at Santa Cruz or Half Moon Bay. On the way home we always stopped in the village of Pescadero and ate fresh arti-choke soup at Duarte's, which became my favorite California diner.

Linda, Julie, and I studied together, played tennis, and shared as many classes as we could. Linda was only 16 when she arrived at Stanford but she more than held her own. Her mother was a Stanford graduate and her father a member of the Canadian Parliament from the Annapolis Valley in Nova Scotia. They had been married at Stanford's Memorial Church. As with many Stanford women, Linda was an overachiever: she was intelligent, ferociously independent, and very competitive. She was madly in love with my best friend, John Montgomery.

Stanford students were consummate overachievers and I was humbled by their accomplishments. Sally Ride, America's first woman in space, was finishing her second Stanford degree at the time. Robin Lee-Graham had sailed around the world alone at the age of 16 in his eight-metre boat named *Dove*; I recognized him from the *National Geographic* stories about his voyage. On weekends one guy in my residence would throw his pitons and chalk bag into his car and head off to Yosemite, where he would free-climb El Capitan, one of America's most demanding climbs. Athletes juggled academics with rigorous training schedules. I knew James Lofton and Tony Hill, two of Stanford's most versatile football players who became superstars with the Green Bay Packers and the Dallas Cowboys respectively. Both were good students. They went to classes in the morning, played football four hours every afternoon, and studied until late into the night. That was their life.

The school's tennis, swimming, and water polo teams are perennial national champions. Stanford alumni include John Elway, Tom Watson, and Tiger Woods. At the 1976 Montreal Olympics, Stanford undergraduates won five gold medals, more than most countries and five more than Canada. Unlike many U.S. universities, Stanford expected its athletes to meet all its academic standards and to complete their degrees. Most did. One notable exception was the tennis star John McEnroe, notoriously unpopular among his fellow students, who dropped out after winning the NCAA singles championship for Stanford in his freshman year. With typical McEnroe bravado, he told everyone he would soon be rich and famous and wouldn't need an education. And he was right.

Stanford students studied hard but covertly. Nobody wanted to be known as a nerd. The highest level of achievement at Stanford was to earn top grades without appearing to crack a single book. It was a bit of a game. Undergraduates stuffed their chemistry and biology text books into tennis bags and made a big spectacle of heading to the courts for the afternoon; in fact, they never got farther than the Meyer Undergraduate Library, known among students by the acronym UGLY, which indeed it was.

While at Stanford I needed to work part-time to help defray the costs of my education. The easiest job I have ever had was serving as a research subject at the Stanford Sleep Clinic, run by one of the nation's leading sleep researchers, Dr. William Dement. The Sleep Clinic was located in a trailer complex on the fringes of the university. I would bicycle to the clinic after finishing my evening studies at the undergraduate library. I would get undressed, and they would wire me up from head to toe. I would sleep my regular eight hours with the researchers, located behind a screen, monitoring my heartbeat, breathing, eye movement, and brain activity with a battery of computers and video cameras. In the morning I would have a shower at the clinic, eat a hot breakfast, and then would proceed to my first class of the day. For my services I was paid $6.50 an hour. The university research guidelines limited the number of days each week that we could work as lab rats, but it was still the easiest money I ever earned.

On weekends I abandoned my books and explored the California that was my new home. I was 18, and my only possessions were my blue Bottechia 10-speed bicycle, a small nylon tent, and a down sleeping bag, but they were everything I needed. Never had I felt such a sensation of complete freedom. All memories of boarding-school days had been vanquished. With my map and compass I could go anywhere I wanted. I bicycled hundreds of kilometres of coastline, from Point Reyes National Seashore to the Monterey Peninsula. At the end of each day, I would be sunburned and covered with a layer of sand, salt, and sweat. I slept in small state parks, or in eucalyptus groves alongside the road. I ate fresh melons, mangos, and strawberries that I bought from farmers' stalls.

The hills and horse farms between Stanford and the sea were my favorite biking destinations, but also the most dangerous. The switchback roads were steep, and for long periods I would be completely hidden in thick coastal fog. It was a punishing climb from Stanford up through the Redwood forests to the village of La Honda (the home of Neil Young and other celebrities), and then a wild ride down the edge of the hills to the Pacific Ocean. I would bicycle directly onto the beach and throw myself into the sea. Years later, I learned that

the director of the Stanford Earth Sciences Department and one of the origina-
tors of modern plate-tectonics theory committed suicide, after being charged
with the sexual assault of a child, by pointing his bike down the steepest section
of that same road and letting himself go.

Northern California was also the home of John Muir, one of America's first
conservationists and the founder of the Sierra Club. Since childhood, I had been a
keen environmentalist; the first demonstration I ever participated in was as a 12-
year-old Upper Canada College student marching on Toronto City Hall alongside
my chemistry teacher, Allan Whitely, to protest the city's lack of action on pollution
issues. I joined the Stanford Sierra Club, and hiked extensively in the back country
of Yosemite and King's Canyon national parks. Every January, we strapped on cross-
country skis and camped in the Sierra Nevada. I learned at least as much outside
the classroom as I did inside, and although my grades might have suffered, my
Stanford years were much richer than if I had locked myself into the Meyer Undergraduate Library for four years. While in my freshman year, I researched a canoe
trip in northern Saskatchewan and Manitoba, retracing the route of the American
wilderness writer Sigurd Olson, Blair Fraser, the Ottawa editor of *Maclean's* magazine who later drowned in a white-water section of the Petawawa River, and Eric
Morse, perhaps Canada's best-known writer about historic canoe routes. Olson's
accounts of the expedition, *The Lonely Land*, set the standard for canoe-trip journals. Unfortunately, my research efforts were in vain, as Manitoba Hydro constructed a massive diversion dam on the Churchill River, flooding thousands of
acres of land and displacing entire First Nations communities.

The San Francisco I came to know in 1975 was a world apart from uptight
and Orange Toronto, a city that the actor Peter Ustinov once described as
"New York run by the Swiss." The radical poet Lawrence Ferlinghetti gave free
readings at City Lights Bookstore in the North Beach—not really a beach at all,
but instead the heart of the city's Italian neighborhood. Daniel Ellsberg, the
author of *The Pentagon Papers*, spoke at sold-out lectures across San Francisco
Bay at Berkeley. Ralph Nader and Cesar Chavez were cult heroes. California's
governor of the day, Jerry Brown, the chosen representative of America's most
prosperous and populous state, had been trained as a Jesuit priest and refused
to reside in the official gubernatorial mansion; instead, he slept on a bare mattress in a spartan Sacramento apartment. A devotee of yoga, Governor Brown
once conducted an entire interview in an inverted semi-lotus position. On
weekends he was known to disappear into the rough-and-tumble Tenderloin
District of San Francisco to live anonymously with the homeless.

When I arrived at San Francisco airport in September, 1975, the country was just emerging from the turmoil of the Vietnam War. The sentiment in much of northern California was that those who had protested against the war had been proven right—the war was unjust, unwinnable, and had been bleeding America to death. Among mainstream Americans, however, there was still much bitterness associated with the anti-war movement. People had been outraged at the spectacle of Jane Fonda taking emergency supplies to the North Vietnamese. In their eyes, she was a traitor.

While Berkeley, only 50 kilometres away, had been a focus of anti-war activities, Stanford students had for the most part remained on the sidelines. Cynics would say they and their parents were too interested in making money to get involved one way or the other. As long as they maintained their academic status, the chances of Stanford students being drafted were almost nil. At Stanford for the length of the Vietnam War, it was impossible to receive a grade worse than C because faculty had no interest in failing a student who could thereby become eligible for the draft. More than any previous war, Vietnam was fought by Americans who were out of school, poor, or black.

Stanford students were largely a conservative lot. They went to their classes wearing pastel-colored Polo shirts, the unofficial uniform of America's country-club set. The most popular drug on campus was No-Doze, which allowed students to study around the clock—with their doors closed, so nobody could catch them. In keeping with Mrs. Stanford's instructions, no alcohol was available for sale on campus. The social life of most North American universities is centred around the campus pub; Stanford students would rendezvous at the post office and book store. Stanford student parking lots were littered with BMWs; VW buses and rusting Volvos were few and far between.

In 1976, Americans went to the polls, and although political activity was prohibited by the terms of my visa, I campaigned for the Democratic congressional candidate David Harris, a former Stanford student president from Fresno, California, who had been voted by his high-school classmates as most likely to succeed. As a Stanford undergraduate, David had challenged the draft system as unfair, burning his draft-deferment card and going to jail for his beliefs. The campaign team was young, highly motivated, and multi-talented. Ken Kesey was the speech writer. He was stoned most of the time. We knew when we went into the election that our chances of winning were slim. Stanford was in a congressional district that was represented by a Republican, Pete McCloskey. McCloskey was popular, had graduated from Stanford, and had earned the reputation in

Congress of being something of a maverick. At the 1972 Republican Convention, he was one of the few high-profile Republicans who had openly challenged Nixon's leadership of the Republican Party and had spoken out against the Vietnam War.

On behalf of David Harris, I knocked on hundreds of doors in local housing projects and learned first-hand about poverty in inner-city America. In Canada and in Europe, handguns are almost non-existent. Thanks to the political influence of powerful right-wing lobby groups such as the National Rifle Association, in the U.S. guns are everywhere—especially in inner-city neighborhoods. People flaunt their constitutional right to bear arms and to use them on their neighbors. Violence is endemic and people in housing projects live in fear. The homes I visited in 1976 had become virtual prisons for their occupants. When I knocked on their doors, people would open them a few centimetres with great caution while still keeping the chain fastened. I would see suspicious eyes peering at me and nothing else. I gave them David's campaign literature and before they had a chance to slam the door shut, I would recite the few lines I had rehearsed about the need for a national health-care program, and jobs, and better schools.

On one occasion, a woman who answered my knock at her door started screaming at me, calling David a coward and a traitor. Then she dissolved in tears. I quickly moved on to the next house, but her husband came after me. He apologized for her, saying they were lifelong Democrats, but that their only son had been killed in Vietnam during the last weeks of the war. His wife was inconsolable; the Vietnam War had destroyed their lives.

As a student in California, I was shocked by the disparity between communities that existed side-by-side. People with money in America usually opt out of publicly funded services, instead going to private hospitals and sending their kids to private schools. They pay into private insurance schemes. When I had appendicitis at Stanford, I wasn't admitted to the Stanford Medical Center until it was determined I had adequate insurance coverage. I lay squirming on the stretcher in the hospital emergency waiting room while administrators checked my documentation. The Stanford Medical Center was more like a four-star hotel than a hospital. We had a choice of white or red California wines with our meals, and a small sign above the sink reminded patients that check-out time was 10:00 a.m. Affluent Americans have little interest in preserving a social safety net, because they don't believe they ever benefit from it. When it comes time to vote, they oppose taxes that go towards public health-care or education. In California, even public swimming pools are rare because rich people living in suburbs have their own pools or belong to private clubs. Why fund recreation facilities they would never use themselves?

Just across the freeway in East Palo Alto was a neighborhood that was black and desperate. Some people lacked electricity and running water, and kids ran around in rags. Only a few miles away, Stanford had its own elementary school for faculty brats; it was as luxurious as everything else associated with the university, with a beautiful playground and a big library. Hewlett-Packard had equipped it with the latest computers. The elementary school the kids in East Palo Alto went to looked like something from Beirut. One day, while handing out leaflets for David Harris in East Palo Alto, I got lost on my bike, and three African-American children showed me the way back to Stanford. I was surprised when they told me they had actually never set foot on the campus but had only seen it from a distance. Kids pick up on signals. Although there are no fences around the university and nobody had ever barred their entrance, they already knew Stanford was a place for rich kids and not for them. I ended up launching a weekend basketball program on campus for them, supported in part by the Stanford Athletics Department.

We lost the election by a factor of more than 2:1. Our "victory" party was held in the old dirigible hangar at the U.S. Navy's Moffett Field anti-submarine base, the only facility we could afford. The irony wasn't lost on anyone. McCloskey's celebration was up the road at Rickey's Hyatt House, the unofficial Stanford Republican party headquarters. The hangar had the atmosphere of an abandoned opera house, with enough room for at least 3,000 people. We were no more than 500, including children. David was married to the singer Joan Baez, who had kept vigil for him during his days in prison. That night, when Joan, bathed in a solitary spotlight, belted out "We Shall Overcome" with David and their young son Gabriel at her side, her voice sounded clearer than it did in any concert hall, and we were all reminded why we had volunteered for the campaign. I thought of the kids I had met in East Palo Alto, and the old people who, out of fear for their own safety, never left their apartments. Long after the last votes had been counted, David gave his best speech of the campaign, and then we packed up our signs and went home. I have been to numerous political events since November 4, 1976, but none of them compares with the night that Joan Baez closed the campaign at Moffett Field.

As much as I loved Stanford, its affluence could be stifling and one could easily become complacent. Stanford was too close to perfect—more like a theme park than a real community. Volunteer work kept my enthusiasm for America in check. It was at least as demanding as many of my classes. Through Project SHARE, Shelley Roberts and I tutored inner-city girls and boys. After a few days, you became one of the most important adults in their world. The kids counted on us to turn up on time, to engage them and amuse them as much as to teach them. Poverty marked every aspect of their lives. Although many were illiterate, they knew how to test the purity of cocaine. They had grown accustomed to shoot-outs in their housing projects. When I brought them to Stanford, the first thing they wanted to do was take off their shoes so that they could run barefoot on the grass—something they had never done before. Was this America as conceived by the framers of the Constitution? It was difficult to be anything other than pessimistic about the chances of these children to receive a decent education, earn a respectable income, and raise a family of their own in happy circumstances.

My many hours shooting hoops and reading with poor East Palo Alto children affected my choice of classes. I became interested in the social sciences, at which Stanford excelled. Why did some of the kids I knew cope so well with adversity while others were devastated? What were the psychological roots of violence and racism?

Stanford psychology professor Philip Zimbardo is best known in professional circles as a leading expert on shyness and for his controversial 1973 prison experiment. Over a weekend, Zimbardo and his team converted the basement of the Stanford psychology department into a makeshift prison. Zimbardo advertised for student volunteers and arbitrarily appointed half as prisoners and half as guards. The guards and prisoners were issued appropriate uniforms, and the experiment began. The results were sobering: after only 24 hours, guards were becoming abusive and aggressive, and prisoners were increasingly passive and dependent. After only 36 hours, the first prisoner had to be released due to uncontrolled crying, fits of rage, and deep depression. The experiment, which had been scheduled to run for two weeks, was shut down after six days. Anyone who has worked with the military or the police knows the phenomenon: people with uniforms, weapons, and titles can easily lose their sense of judgement; they quickly depersonalize and brutalize the people over whom they have authority. Stanford students were no different than anyone else in their ability to be transformed into automatons. Zimbardo showed that, given the right stimuli, we could all become good Nazis.

Zimbardo was a legend on campus, and his Psychology 1 class was among the university's most popular courses. He implemented a system that allowed all students to set their own pace and to administer their own tests. Students who were not satisfied with their grades could retake tests as many times as they wanted. Zimbardo's theory was that competitiveness was a quality that did not need to be enhanced among most Stanford students. As part of the course, students had the option of doing their own research projects. At the time, the Unification Church, better known as the Moonies, was recruiting on California campuses, offering a free weekend at its ranch in Mendocino County north of San Francisco. A number of Stanford students had signed up for the junket and never returned. For my Psychology 1 research project, I proposed to visit the ranch, study the Moonies' methods, and search for lost Stanford students.

Zimbardo was intrigued by the idea, but concerned. What if I never came back? He and his small army of teaching assistants made me sign a waiver authorizing them to rescue me, even against my will, if I had not returned by Sunday evening. I met up with the Moonies at their mansion in Berkeley on the following Friday afternoon; that evening, we went by bus to the ranch.

I had no interest in joining a cult, and after years of indoctrination by Catholic nuns believed I was immune to evangelism of any kind. But Zimbardo had reason to be worried. I began my research the moment we departed Berkeley, interviewing all the students and asking them how long they intended to stay at the ranch. Only three of the 35 expressed any interest in anything other than the free weekend. By the conclusion of the weekend, only two of us were on the bus returning from Mendocino County to the mansion.

The techniques the Moonies employed were conventional, but effective. We slept less than five hours each night. The diet was very limited, consisting mostly of nuts, raisins, yogurt, rice, and juice. All activities were done in groups of 12, made up of three initiates and nine Moonies. We were never alone. A "brother" or "sister" accompanied us at all times—even when we went to the bathroom. It was a sexless and child-like environment, with regular hugging and holding hands—things I loathe. Group discussions were endless. There was much singing and each group had its own special chant, which it belted out at every opportunity. There was immense pressure to conform and to contribute to the group, and not to let "the family" down. Evenings were set aside for long and emotional testimonials by Moonies that followed a predictable pattern: they had grown up in abusive families with plenty of material possessions but no love, they were not wanted by their parents, now they had a new family and were the luckiest people on earth. There was never any mention of Reverend Moon or of his church.

I eventually located the two Stanford students but they were already lost to the world of Reverend Moon. One had hoped to attend medical school; now she was content selling teddy bears and flowers on behalf of the Moonies to tourists at Ghiradelli Square in San Francisco. The other had been studying to be a civil engineer and was in charge of all the plumbing, sewage, and solar power systems at the ranch. Both had turned their bank accounts over to the Unification Church. The engineer's family had sent batteries of lawyers, private investigators, and deprogrammers to the ranch, but they never got past the main gate. The Moonies were experts at security matters.

Sunday dinner was the climax of the weekend. The testimonials were more intense, with much singing and crying. Some people swayed back and forth in a trance-like state. After dinner, the big announcement was made: we were lucky. We had passed. We had all been good children and now were being welcomed into our new family. We would take new names and renounce our past. We could live on the ranch forever! People were ecstatic—in one fell swoop all their problems had been solved.

I had to fight to return to Berkeley. As soon as I expressed interest in leaving, I was portrayed in my group as a traitor. I had shamed them. They did everything they could to change my mind. When it was clear their efforts were of no use, I was abandoned by the group and taken to a room I had never seen before. I was interrogated by a man I had never met, who was all business— very un-Moonie-like. There was no more talk of love and kindness between brothers and sisters. Who had sent me? Was I a spy for deprogrammers? The interrogator insisted I stay another day. Besides, there was no bus after all. I had no choice but to stay. I imagined Zimbardo and his team of commandos storming the ranch the next morning; it was going to be very messy. I hoped they would remember to bring wire-cutters.

In the end, after it became clear I was a lost cause, they let me go. I left for Berkeley on the Moonies' Elephant Bus well past midnight, with only one other fugitive from the ranch. We were emotionally and physically exhausted, and when we arrived in Berkeley, we went directly to a 24-hour diner and ate junk food until we almost got sick. I took the 6:00 a.m. BART train to San Francisco, and the 7:00 a.m. bus to Palo Alto. I arrived at Professor Zimbardo's office at 9:00 a.m. just as he was preparing to set off for Mendocino with his rescue team to spring me from the ranch.

The episode showed me that we all have our limits and that we are all vulnerable to psychological abuse. Cultists search for people's weaknesses and ruthlessly exploit them. The Moonies prey on young college students because they have access to money, but also because many of them are looking for alternatives. My report to Zimbardo stated that among the most vulnerable people were those students who, as children, had received no formal religious training. Their parents had steered clear of churches; the kids now seemed to be making up for lost time. I had been exposed to everything the Moonies preached—the notion of redemption and rebirth is the cornerstone of the Christian faith. I vowed then that no matter what state my soul happened to be in, I would introduce my own children to some form of religious education.

Stanford has an extensive overseas study program, with campuses in England, France, Spain, Russia, Germany, Japan, and Italy. Students can spend up to two years abroad. Shelley Roberts and I chose to study in Florence, where Stanford had a program focusing on art, history, and political science. For one academic year, we lived and studied in Stanford's magnificent 18th-century villa named Il Salviatino, located in the hills of Fiesole overlooking the red rooftops of Florence. Our professors included the assistant curator of the Uffizi and the director of antiquities for the Rome region. There were only 45 students at the villa, of whom 30 were women. We had our own bar and swimming pool. From my room I could see our own vineyards; the sound of church bells echoing in the valley below woke me each morning in time for breakfast.

Renaissance Florence became my classroom and I embraced it. During the summer months, Florence is stiflingly hot and given over to busloads of foreign tourists. Only in the damp and chill of mid-winter, when the city is reclaimed by its own citizens, is it possible to have a sense of what Florence must have been like in the time of Dante and Brunelleschi. Much of the city's art is not displayed in the Uffizi Museum or the Pitti Palace, but is hidden away in tiny churches and walled monasteries that are rarely open to the public. When in the neighborhood of Via Tornabuoni, I always visited the tiny side chapel of the Church of Santa Trinità to see the scenes from the life of Saint Francis by Ghirlandaio. If the custodian at the Convent of Sant'Appolonia was in a particularly good mood, and if he fancied the Marlboro cigarettes that I offered him, he might unlock the doors to the room containing the giant fresco of the Last Supper by Andrea del Castagno. In January and February I could park my bicycle outside the cloister of San Lorenzo and walk up the only staircase ever designed by Michelangelo to the

Laurentian Library, perhaps the most beautiful room in all of Florence, and have its stunning collection of illuminated manuscripts all to myself.

I was fascinated by the politics of Italy and debated issues of the day with Italian students over the city's cheapest lunch served at the University of Florence *mensa* in San Marco. The phenomenon of political extremism has always concerned and intrigued me. While in Florence I studied the writings of Savonarola, the Jesse Helms of his age, who, for a period of time in the 15th century, was immensely influential in Florence, condemning all secular art as sinful and organizing regular book-burnings in Piazza della Signoria, the political crossroads of the Republic. Even Botticelli fell under his spell, abandoning pagan themes such as *The Birth of Venus* and painting instead traditional scenes of Mary and child. But over the centuries, Florentines have demonstrated little tolerance for austerity and self-restraint, and in 1498 they turned on Savonarola, burning him at the stake in the same square where he had led his populist rallies.

In May, 1978, the revolutionary Red Brigades assassinated former Italian premier Aldo Moro. These were dark days for Italy. The country was crippled by a series of strikes involving every sector of the economy, from truck drivers to university professors. Students suspected of having ties to the terrorists were arrested by the dozen and held without trial. Nobody in Italy trusted the police, who have historical links to the fascists of the 1930s and '40s. I was stopped twice on roads outside Florence by the carabinieri, the Italian state police, and thoroughly searched by one officer while the other kept me in the sight of his Uzi.

The director of the Stanford program in Florence, Dr. Giuseppe Mamarella, was a socialist and a respected political scientist. I studied modern Italian history with Mamarella and began to decipher the complex story of how Italy in the 19th century became a republic, and how it has always been threatened by the forces of nationalism. In the 1930s, Mussolini exploited an undercurrent of inferiority and a longing for glory that ran deep in many Italians, despite their extraordinary accomplishments. He promised to make Italy great again, to make people proud, to recapture and rebuild Italy's former colonies in Africa. People were vulnerable to manipulation: the economy was in ruins, and millions of Italians lived in abject poverty.

An important lesson of the 20th century is that citizens of all countries should be wary of leaders who invoke the destiny of their nation as their rallying cry. I will call myself a patriot, but never a nationalist. Millions have died at the hands of demagogues such as Hitler, Stalin, Amin, and Karadzic, who used the flag to consolidate their power and eliminate opposition. Their tactics were crude but effective, demonizing minorities and exaggerating historic and cultural differences between neighbors who for centuries had managed to tolerate each other. We continue to live in their shadow and must deal with their legacy of mass graves, millions of refugees on the move, and historic cities in ruins.

I returned to Stanford in the fall of 1978 for my final year of study. I reclaimed my bicycle from storage and travelled again and again to the places around Stanford that I loved. I spent hours at the Bender Rare Book Room on top of Stanford's Green Library, examining Steinbeck's original manuscripts and galleys for *Cannery Row*. I was finally old enough to legally consume alcohol in the state of California and hung out with my friends at an old road house in the Stanford foothills called the Alpine Beer Garden, but known universally as Rosotti's, after the proprietor who resembled a rodent. The historic bar is on the original stagecoach route from Los Angeles to San Francisco, and features a railing for patrons to tie up their horses.

Ambassador Andrew Young spoke at the Stanford commencement, which was held under the trees at Frost Amphitheater. Young was a preacher's son, and he delivered his message in the measured cadence of a Baptist minister. I thought that Professor Momaday would be pleased. After the brief ceremony, I lined up to shake the hand of the man who had apprenticed with Dr. Martin Luther King, and then I went off to take pictures and drink champagne with friends and parents.

At their commencement, Yale students sing an anthem entitled "Those Bright College Years." My four years at Stanford were a time of light and life, of intense friendships and the best possible kinds of learning. At Upper Canada College, good grades had come easily to me; at Stanford, after much effort, I finished with only a B average. The school had shocked me into the realization that I had to work hard to succeed, that there were others hungry for the best jobs who were blessed with far more natural talent than I.

People often comment that I act and think like an American, which is meant as a criticism, but I accept it as a compliment. Stanford students were doers, not complainers, and in this aspect were different from many Canadians I knew. My American friends thrived on chaos, were flexible and creative. They had little faith in government and believed in the capacity of individuals to make a difference in the world. I expect that America's global predominance in science, technology, and business will continue well into the 21st century, and that schools like Stanford will play a big part in ensuring that success.

After all my days at Upper Canada College, there are only two names of students from that period in my personal address book. My Stanford friends, on the other hand, remain close to me, and although they are busy, they go out of their way to track me down whenever they are within 500 kilometres of the Canadian border. I fly to California for our reunions every five years, and I note that these remarkable Americans continue to excel at whatever they choose to do.

MICHAEL

When I was 12 years old, I finally abandoned the idea of becoming an astronaut or an Israeli fighter pilot. Instead, I wanted to be a lawyer just like my hero Atticus Finch from Harper Lee's novel, *To Kill a Mockingbird*. On Hallowe'en in 1969, my fellow boarders and I watched the Academy Award-winning film, starring Gregory Peck, in the Gibson Room at Upper Canada College. I had eaten too much candy, and just before the crucial trial scene, I had to leave the room to vomit. I rinsed out my mouth at the nearby water tap and hurried back so as not to miss anything important. I was enthralled by this soft-spoken Southern lawyer who defended an innocent black man, who was a crack shot with a rifle, and who allowed his children to address him by his first name. Most of my friends' fathers who were lawyers wore stiff suits and spent most of their time shuffling papers in gray office buildings. Atticus Finch was different. I admired his quiet confidence, his obvious affection for his kids, and most of all, his ability in the courtroom. Finch worked from the rocking chair of his front porch, and he drove a dented Ford pick-up truck. He was poor but powerful, which confused me.

When I was 16, I was invited by my girlfriend, Shelley Roberts, to see Henry Fonda starring in the one-man show *Clarence Darrow for the Defence* at the Royal Alexandra Theatre in Toronto. It was a fine production and convinced me to pursue a career in law. From my debating experience, I knew I had a natural ability to move people, a useful skill for any lawyer. While at Stanford, I had done some research on a volunteer basis for the Sierra Club Legal Defense Fund. As a canoeist and environmentalist, I was outraged by the massive hydro-power projects in the provinces of Manitoba and Saskatchewan of the mid-1970s that had displaced thousands of aboriginal people and wiped out fragile wildlife habitats. At the same time, a law professor from British Columbia, Thomas Berger, had been appointed by the government of Canada to advise on which route through Canada's fragile Mackenzie Valley would be the best for a proposed natural-gas pipeline. He shocked everyone by taking his duties to heart, and by visiting aboriginal fishing and hunting camps in the remotest parts of the Arctic. Berger held hearings in tents and school gymnasia, and he listened to the stories of the old ways told by the community elders. He learned about the Porcupine Caribou migration, one of the world's great wildlife spectacles but rarely witnessed by people living south of the 60th parallel.

I had closely followed the proceedings of Berger's committee and typed up an excerpt from a presentation to the committee made by Chief Frank T'Seleie of Fort Good Hope. I kept the passage pinned above my desk at Stanford:

> There is a life and death struggle going on between us, between you and me. Somehow in your carpeted boardrooms you are plotting to take away from me the very centre of my existence. You are stealing my soul. By scheming to torture my land, you are torturing me. By plotting to invade my land, you are invading me. If you ever dig this trench through my land, you are cutting through me.
>
> You are the 20th-century General Custers. You are coming with your troops to slaughter us and to steal land that is rightfully ours. You are coming to destroy a people who have a history of 30,000 years. Why? For 20 years of gas? Are you really that insane?
>
> Our Dene nation is like this great river. It has been flowing before any of us can remember. We take our strength and our wisdom and our ways from the flow and direction that have been established by ancestors we never knew. We will live out our lives as we must and we will know that our people and this river will flow on after us.
>
> We know that our grandchildren will look after this land and protect it and that 500 years from now, someone with skin my color and moccasins on his feet will climb up these ramparts and rest and look out at the river and feel that he too has a place in this wilderness, and he will thank the same spirits that I thank, that his

ancestors have looked after his land well and he will be proud to be
a Dene.

It is for this unborn child, Mr. Berger, that my nation will stop
this pipeline. It is so that this unborn child can know the freedom
of this land that I am willing to lay down my life.

Berger's lucid two-volume 1977 report on the proposed Mackenzie Valley
pipeline was the first Canadian government publication to become a national
bestseller. It chronicled a vanishing way of life for the people of the Arctic that
would be extinguished by the construction of any pipeline. Berger recommended
that no pipeline ever be built in the Northern Yukon, and that there be a morato-
rium on the building of a pipeline in the Mackenzie Valley for 10 years, allowing
time for native land claims to be settled. The oil and gas industry executives were
furious, and accused him of overstepping his mandate, but a groundswell of
public support for Berger meant the government of the day had no choice but to
accept his report. No pipeline has ever been built in the region.

I learned from the lawyers at the Sierra Club and from the example of Professor Thomas Berger that, in the right hands, law could be more than merely a
means of making a living. It was potentially a powerful tool for promoting social
justice and for taking on the establishment from within the system. Lawyers
could do more than make money—they could actually make a difference. More
and more of my heroes, including Bob Woodward and Ralph Nader, were graduates of law schools who were using their legal education in non-traditional professions, such as journalism, consumer advocacy, and human rights.

In my last term at Stanford, I applied to three Canadian law schools: the
University of Toronto, McGill and Dalhousie. I needed to attend law school in
Canada so I could practise in my own country, perhaps in the burgeoning environmental field. I chose Dalhousie on the Atlantic coast because of its expertise in
the law of the sea and environmental law. I also relished the idea of living on the
edge of the Atlantic Ocean in one of Canada's oldest and most distinctive cities. I
had been warned that law school required hours of tedious memorization of cases
and rote learning of statutes, something for which I had no affinity. I therefore
decided to spend the interval between Stanford and Dalhousie at Ahmek, my old
summer camp in Algonquin Park. One last summer on staff at Ahmek would
provide me with an opportunity to charge my batteries before locking myself in a
law library for three years. It would be an easy summer. As the director of one of
the camp's five sections, the most serious situation I would likely encounter

would be a child suffering a prolonged bout of homesickness. I looked forward to having time for reading summer novels.

I had already spent four summers as a staff person at Ahmek and I knew the routine well. The camp had two one-month sessions; especially keen campers would stay on for the full eight-week period. As section director of the Mountaineers, I was in charge of nine counsellors and 63 boys, all of whom were 12 or 13 years of age. Each cabin group would spend three weeks in camp and one week on a canoe trip. The atmosphere in camp was so laid-back that at times, the place almost ground to a halt. While in camp, the kids more or less entertained themselves. They were encouraged to attend the daily canoeing and swimming classes, but otherwise the boys set their own schedules. Some kids didn't go near the horses or sailboats for the entire session but instead, like Huck Finn and Tom Sawyer, fished off Wigwam Bay bridge, dangling their legs in the lake. A boy might catch one good-sized bass during his four weeks at camp. At over $1,000 per session, it would represent the single most expensive fish in the world.

The Ahmek staff were far more problematic than the children. Most were former campers. The counsellors were expected to turn up for meals and swim classes, but not much more. Ahmek staff were notoriously uninspired except after sunset, when many made a beeline to the seedy bars of Dwight and Huntsville. Many would lie for hours on the main dock improving their suntans. The summer months provided them with ample opportunities to visit their counterparts at our sister camp for girls, located within sight on an island called Wapomeo. My biggest challenge would be convincing a number of the more lethargic types to get off their butts and devote a fraction of their valuable sunbathing time to the kids whose parents were paying their salaries.

From the moment that I met Michael Kane-Parry on the first day of camp, I knew he was a gifted child. He came from Old Greenwich, Connecticut, just one hour by commuter train from New York City, and my first conversation with him was about American politics. He announced he was a Democrat; I responded that we would get along just fine. Michael was the same age and size as the other boys in my section, but in other aspects he was light years beyond them. Emotionally he was on par with kids at least two or three years older. He was comfortable in the company of adults and familiar with ideas of the day, but he was no egghead. He arrived at camp with his own bongo board to practise gymnastics, at which he excelled. He was a strong runner and swimmer. In a group of children, people would pick him out because of his shock of blond hair. He was a handsome boy, and a favorite among the Wapomeo girls at the inter-camp dance we organized during the first week of camp.

After a few days, it was obvious Michael was not happy at Ahmek and although not homesick, he was lonely. His uncle had gone to Ahmek many years before and had encouraged Michael's parents, who had never seen the camp, to send him. But Ahmek wasn't as much fun as his uncle had made it out to be. More significantly, Michael's cabin mates were not coming together as a group and his counsellor was weak. Michael didn't feel he belonged anywhere at Ahmek and was already counting the days until he could return home.

Michael started spending more and more time with me, and I became his de facto counsellor. Without asking my permission he moved many of his belongings into my cabin by the lake, including his bongo board and his Coleco computerized football game. Eventually I put in a second bed for him. At night, by the light of my Coleman lantern, I heard all his stories about Camp Colgate, where he had spent several summers with his family and which he much preferred to Ahmek. He was very close to his sister Tanya, who was a student at Andover, and he missed her. Michael's mother was a lawyer, so he offered me free advice on what I could expect in my chosen career. His father worked in advertising in New York City. We traded stories about New York and our favorite things to do there, including visiting the World Trade Center and FAO Schwartz. Michael's disposition improved dramatically and he started participating in regular camp activities with his cabin mates, especially archery and crafts. I let him call home but it made him feel even more homesick.

I like to climb trees—the taller, the better. Camp Ahmek has a huge white pine located on a hill above the senior council ring, away from the main camp. One afternoon I invited Michael to climb it with me. The first branch is three metres above the ground, so it requires some deftness to scale, but Michael scampered up the tree with the agility of an acrobat. I followed cautiously a few branches below him. We were able to reach the highest branch and the view was spectacular. We could see the entire camp, from the horse stables at the beginning of the Ghost Walk Creek to Chubby's Island and the swimming pool. We stayed for more than an hour, until the dinner bell sounded. I told Michael he could climb the tree on his own if he wanted, that it was a good place for him to read a book, which is what I, as a kid, had always enjoyed doing in trees, but he didn't seem to read much. Instead, Michael went to the tree every day after lunch, taking along his Coleco electronic football game. It became his personal retreat. He found the perfect spot where he could brace himself against the tree trunk; he needed both hands free so he could manipulate the game's controls.

It didn't rain a drop during the first two weeks of July. Summers in eastern Canada are among the best anywhere in North America, and when a ridge of high pressure settles in, it can last for weeks. By breakfast on Thursday July 14, it was already hot and there was no hint of wind. Eight of my nine cabin groups were leaving that morning on their canoe trips; Michael's cabin was staying on for another five days before departing for Ahmek's wilderness base camp in the Temagami region of northern Ontario. I was planning to take two days off to visit my parents at their summer cottage on Lake Simcoe to the south of Algonquin Park. After all the other campers had departed, Michael and his cabin mates helped me clean up the section and then we had a long swim off our own section dock, Ahmek's best swimming spot. We played in the water with my Frisbee and then sprawled on the dock to dry off. I was happy that for the first time, the kids were doing something as a group and for once they were not fighting.

After lunch, Michael accompanied me back to my cabin and helped me pack up my things for my days off. I explained that I wanted him to devote more time to his cabin mates, that it was important he feel comfortable with them before their long canoe trip. Two of the boys, one from Mexico and one from France, were less rambunctious than the others and were good company for Michael. I suggested to Michael that he spend the afternoon with them and that they go to general swim together just before dinner. It was the hottest day of the summer and there was still no wind on the lake. Michael and I went for one more swim off the diving rocks near our section dock. Then we paddled to the main dock and walked to the blue 1969 VW Beetle I had borrowed from my father for the summer. I told Michael that I would see him in two days.

I had just finished dinner with my parents at their cottage on Lake Simcoe when the phone call came from Ahmek. The staff person on the end of the line explained there had been an accident, that Michael was hurt and was being taken to the Hospital for Sick Children in Toronto by helicopter. I was assured that he would be okay. There was no alarm in the caller's voice or even a hint of urgency, but the other kids in the cabin were upset and the counsellor was feeling a bit overwhelmed by it all. Could I come back to camp as quickly as possible?

As I drove back to Ahmek that night, I felt more inconvenienced than alarmed. I had not even had a chance to unpack my weekend bags. My guess was that, at worst, Michael had fallen and broken his leg or had hurt himself on his bongo board. It crossed my mind that the tree above the council ring might somehow be involved. In any case, he would not be able to go on his canoe trip. I left my car in the staff parking lot and made my way with a flashlight through the thick forest to the director's cabin.

When I walked into Dr. Tay's cabin that night, I immediately sensed I had misunderstood the nature of Michael's accident, as well as the gravity of the situation. The camp's senior staff were all there and they shifted about uneasily when I entered. I was the youngest person in the cabin by 10 years. For a moment, nobody said anything. Somebody sighed deeply. I felt like an intruder and considered excusing myself. Finally Dr. Tay spoke.

Michael Kane-Parry had gone to general swim at 5:00 p.m. with two cabin mates, Eric and Paul from France and Mexico respectively. The Ahmek pool consists of a series of floating docks on the lake, fastened together and adjoining the beach in front of the dining hall. Because of the intense mid-summer heat, it was filled to capacity. The boys swam together but then Michael said he wanted to jump off the seven-metre diving tower, which was too high for the other boys. Apparently he went up the tower by himself while Eric and Paul swam in the main pool. More than 10 minutes later, another camper dove off the same tower and came to the surface of the water screaming that there was a boy floating near the bottom of the lake. A Mexican counsellor named Fernando from the oldest section of boys dove into the lake, reached the bottom, and in one motion grabbed the boy by his Speedo bathing suit and brought him to the surface of the lake. It was Michael. When the counsellor threw him onto the dock, he was lifeless and his skin was already gray in color.

Complete panic ensued. All the other boys were evacuated from the pool. By coincidence, two parents who were visiting their sons were in the pool at the time; both were physicians and one was an expert in resuscitation. Michael was laid out on the canvas deck under the diving tower; the doctors immediately began cardiac massage and mouth-to-mouth breathing. Within minutes, a large syringe loaded with adrenaline was inserted between his ribs directly into his heart. An ambulance was summoned from the nearest hospital in Huntsville, about one hour away. The doctors loaded Michael into a camp vehicle and met the ambulance halfway to town. By the time he arrived at the Huntsville hospital, Michael's heart was beating and he was breathing on his own. He was then transported by helicopter to the children's hospital in Toronto. Months later at a public inquest I attended, the doctors who treated Michael at the Huntsville hospital maintained that his resuscitation in the primitive circumstances of the camp was a medical miracle, that they had never seen anything like it in all their years of medicine.

But Michael had been under the water too long and he was brain dead. He was on a life-support system in the intensive-care unit at the Hospital for Sick Children in Toronto, the same place I had gone as a young boy at Upper Canada College when I had been smashed in the head with a cricket ball that I had bungled. His parents had already given permission for the machines that kept Michael alive to be turned off and for his organs to be donated for transplant purposes. The camp staff didn't want to tell me Michael's condition on the phone; it was too long and perilous a drive back to Ahmek after dark for a section director who had just been told his camper was near death. They knew that I was close to Michael, and the doctors had found the key to my cabin on a bracelet around his wrist. What they didn't know was that only three days earlier Michael had proudly presented me with an identical bracelet. He had made it as a gift for me at the Ahmek craft shop out of red and white gimp, the colours of Stanford University.

Dr. Tay spoke the words without pausing but I heard him clearly enough. I wanted to say something appropriate in response and the other men in the cabin appeared to be waiting for me to speak. I started, but I faltered mid-sentence and could go no further. Only a few hours earlier, Michael and I had eaten lunch together at the long staff table in the middle of the dining hall, the physical and spiritual centre of the camp. He had been in very good spirits. That morning after our swim, he had used the calendar on my cabin wall to calculate that he would be going home in 15 days. Unless he had returned that afternoon to clean them up, his clothes and wet towel still lay on the floor of my cabin. I imagined the grief of his mother and father, and his sister Tanya whom he missed so much, but it was too painful to consider, so I moved on.

Years later in the refugee camps of the Sudan, I became familiar with the sights and smells associated with the death of children. I helped lower the bodies of dozens of girls and boys, their jet-black skin warmed by the equatorial sun, into the desert sand. I could tell at a glance which were marasmic, and which simply had wasted away due to dehydration. When they died of cholera they required extra care to prevent the spread of infection, so, wearing surgical gloves, we gingerly wrapped their dripping bodies in clear plastic and buried them alone. Otherwise, they were neatly laid in the sand side by side, girls on one side and boys on the other, like obedient school children standing in line. But in July, 1979, I had just celebrated my 22nd birthday, and the glow associated with my graduation from Stanford only four weeks earlier had not yet worn off. My last days in California had been among the happiest of my life. I was not yet intimate with death, nor its attendant rituals. With his few words that night, Dr. Tay had pronounced Michael gone, and that my prolonged childhood and adolescence were finally over.

In over 50 years of camping at Ahmek and Wapomeo, no staff member had ever lost a child in their care. I was the first. Although I was not responsible for the swimming program or the waterfront, I was his section director. I had helped Michael plan his days. He had moved into my cabin. I was the one he had turned to for advice and comfort. I was the one who had suggested he spend the afternoon with Eric and Paul and go to general swim together. I had explained to him that the time at camp would pass faster if he were busy. Michael was a good kid; he trusted me, and to the end he had followed every word of my advice.

In the moments after Dr. Tay spoke, I replayed in my mind my last conversation with Michael and how we had planned his schedule for the time when I would be away. I wanted to absolve myself of any lapse of duty that might in some way have contributed to his death. In the circumstances, my advice to Michael had been reasonable, and looking back, I could not think of anything I should have done differently. At Ahmek, we never sent kids home from camp unless they were injured and could not participate in camp activities. And we rarely moved kids from one cabin group to another. At the same time, I knew that if I had not taken my day off, Michael would have been with me for the afternoon and he would probably still be alive. He would have gone on his canoe trip with his cabin group and returned to Ahmek for the last few days of camp. Then he would have packed his bags and left for his home and family in Old Greenwich.

My first concern was the welfare of the kids in Michael's cabin, particularly of the two boys with whom he had been swimming. I walked directly from Dr. Tay's house to the Mountaineer section. It was past 11:00 p.m., but the boys were all awake, and they were relieved to see me. Apparently their counsellor was a wreck and had disappeared earlier in the evening. In true Ahmek fashion, someone had taken him to the Empire Hotel in Huntsville to get him drunk. No one was with the children. One of the boys, Stuart Eccles, explained to me that Michael had hurt himself but that everything would be fine. They had been told Michael would return in time for their canoe trip. I was not about to set them straight; the kids were tired and needed to sleep. They would know soon enough that Michael would not be coming back to camp or ever going home.

I was worried about Paul and Eric. From what Dr. Tay had told me, the two kids had been with Michael at the time of the accident. They had been buddied up together by the lifeguards and were expected to stay together in the pool. During general swim, the lifeguards routinely had buddy calls every ten minutes, requiring all the swimmers to stand on the docks and hold their partners' hands in the air. After Michael had disappeared, there had been a buddy call. Paul and Eric anxiously scanned the surface of the pool for Michael. For unknown reasons, neither boy had said anything about their missing friend and the lifeguard in charge had blown the whistle, allowing the swimmers to go back into the water. Precious minutes passed before Michael was spotted by the diver, floating near the bottom of the lake. Paul and Eric would have seen Michael, pale and lifeless, being pulled out of the pool. That night in the cabin they both were very sombre. I knew they were going through hell and would get little sleep.

The next morning after breakfast, I held a team meeting with the cabin group at the staff council ring just outside the dining hall. I told them Michael's situation was serious and he would not be coming back to camp. I did not want to divulge information that Dr. Tay had not provided the camp as a whole. I tried to recall the units on shock and mental anguish that Philip Zimbardo had taught us during our introductory psychology classes at Stanford. I proposed we do everything as a group until they left on their canoe trip. We would go to all the activities, and since we were the only cabin in our section, we would join in another section's evening program. They all agreed to the plan; we would have the best possible time at camp under the circumstances.

But rumors about Michael's condition were beginning to circulate and I couldn't keep the kids in the dark much longer. That night as they got ready for bed, Stuart took me aside and told me he knew that Michael was already dead; he could feel it, he said. During the previous winter, Stuart's 14-year-old sister, a particularly beautiful and outgoing girl whom I knew from Wapomeo, had been killed by a drunk driver while walking home from school. He had seen it all before and recognized the signs of adults using the routines of daily life in an attempt to cope with tragedy. Michael's accident was bringing back memories of his sister's death, and he was very subdued.

In fact, Michael was still being kept alive at Sick Children's Hospital. The laws in Canada required that 48 hours pass with no sign of core brain activity before the life-support system could be turned off. Then Michael would be allowed to die.

I needed help dealing with the cabin group and knowing when and what to say to them. I was a 22-year-old student on the way to law school, not a psychologist. No one in my family had even been seriously ill. By far the most supportive persons were Henri Audet, Ahmek's program director who was Stuart Eccles's favorite adult in the world, and Janet Creaser of the camp's music staff. They provided me with wise counsel and took over responsibility for the cabin group whenever I needed a break. Liz Calvin, the camp nurse, had looked after Michael at the infirmary when he was sick with an earache. She came by our table at meals, and with her easy manner made friends with Paul and Eric. The kids weren't eating, a problem that was aggravated by the fact that meals were taking a long time to arrive at our table. We were among the last tables to be served. I had a talk with André Bourbeau, the Ahmek chef, and from then on we were the first cabin in the dining hall to be served. Bourbeau was easily the most talented person at Ahmek, and is something of a legend in Quebec for the outdoor-survival classes he teaches at the University of Quebec. If I were the owner of the Taylor Statten Camps, Bourbeau would be running the whole show. Without making a big deal of it, he arranged for the kids to have whatever they wanted at mealtimes.

The following morning after breakfast, we canoed to the Portage Store at the end of the lake for hamburgers and milkshakes. The cabin group was feeling better: Stephen Dalgarno successfully stole seven chocolate bars—one for each of us—and Stuart Eccles got into a fight with a boy from another camp. I was relieved. In the afternoon we returned to Ahmek and went sailing, my favorite camp activity. There was no wind, so against all camp rules we hurled bailing buckets of water at each other. We submerged two of our three boats, and had to paddle back to shore, swimming alongside the boats whenever we wanted to cool off. I realized that while I had been focusing on how I was going to get these kids through the summer, they would likely be the ones who would salvage the summer for me.

It had been two days since the accident. On the evening of July 16, I met Dr. Tay while crossing the Trading Post bridge near the Ahmek dining hall; he had just spoken to the doctors at the Hospital for Sick Children in Toronto and his face had lost all its color. As soon as I saw his eyes, I knew what he was going to tell me. The life-support system had been turned off and Michael was dead. The body would go by plane to New York City and then on to Old Greenwich. He would tell the entire camp at breakfast the following morning. I searched for something to say in response. I came up with the awkward statement that when they founded the camps, Dr. Tay's parents must have known that this day would eventually come, but my words sounded empty and they did little to console him. Dr. Tay deeply felt the tragedy and the responsibility for Michael's death.

I chose to sit on Stuart's bed that night when I visited the boys to tell them that Michael was dead. I knew at the time that I should have waited with the news until the morning and let them sleep, but they had already sensed Michael was gone and they needed to know for sure. Stuart had taken on the role of advising the group about what it means to be on a life-support system, what hospitals call the death watch. He described for them in very matter-of-fact terms his visit to the hospital for the last time to say good-bye to his sister, and what she had looked like.

I told the boys without any kind of embellishment that Michael was dead, and then I listened. The kids wanted to talk, and their questions were very personal. Had Michael felt any pain? Had his parents come to the hospital to see him? What would they do with his body? Would he be buried or cremated? They were most concerned about Michael's parents and sister: how were they going to cope without Michael? We talked by the light of my kerosene lantern for at least an hour. I stayed with them until the last of the children had fallen asleep, and I made sure I was there when they woke up in the morning.

An Ahmek tradition is the morning meditation, commonly referred to as the medication, delivered by Dr. Tay in the dining hall immediately following breakfast. His stories have been tested over the years on thousands of campers and staff and they seldom vary. We heard about the five common dangers of canoe-tripping (burns, axe wounds, diving into shallow water, campfires, and being separated from the group), and about the historic figures associated with the camps and with the history of Algonquin Park. Once each summer Dr. Tay gives what we called his sex talk, warning about inappropriate activity among campers. Everyone snickers, except the eight- and nine-year-olds, too young to understand. Ahmek is completely secular, and in 15 years I never heard anything uttered that even came close to a prayer. The messages at morning meditation were simple and inoffensive. Most staff slept through them.

On July 17, 1979, Dr. Tay Statten II stood at the microphone and gave a meditation that had never been heard before in the history of the camp: he told us that another beautiful day had dawned but that unfortunately, he was the bearer of bad news. The doctors had done everything possible for Michael but he had never emerged from his coma. For the first time that I could remember in all my years at Ahmek, the cavernous dining hall was completely silent. André Bourbeau and his kitchen staff had emerged from the back of the hall to hear the news. Somebody dropped a coffee cup on the wooden floor and it sounded like thunder. Although I had told the cabin group the night before, hearing the news of Michael's death from the camp director confirmed it was finally over. Paul and Eric had been holding out for a miracle. Stuart began to sob and the other kids followed seconds later. We put our heads on the table through the playing of a short piece of classical music, and stayed at the table while the other campers filed onto the beach for the ritual flag-raising and singing of the national anthem.

Although I tried not to show it, I was devastated. Worrying about the cabin group had kept me going since the day of the drowning. Now I felt completely defeated. Later that afternoon, Dr. Tay stopped me as I was walking to main camp from the infirmary. He had just spoken with Michael's parents and repeated for me word-for-word what Michael's father had said over the phone: "We sent you a healthy, normal, 12-year-old boy. Look what you sent us back." I imagined Michael's body being transported by plane to New York City. I walked to my cabin, grabbed my paddle, and went directly to the Mountaineer dock. I slid a canoe into the water and paddled off toward Whiskey Jack Creek. I needed to get away from camp and to be alone for a few hours. I didn't return until well after dark. I checked in on the kids; in my absence, Henri Audet had looked after them. They had all changed their clothes for bed. Nobody asked where I had been. They had their flashlights out and had buried themselves in comic books and magazines. Stuart hid under his covers. Nobody, including me, wanted to talk.

Ahmek is a place that people associated with happiness and carefree summer fun, and there were those on staff who stated that any form of mourning would be macabre and inappropriate. The argument was made that few campers or staff actually knew Michael, and that we should get on with the summer. I disagreed vehemently; children express grief differently from adults, but they needed to mourn in their own way, particularly for the loss of another child. I thought the camp should hold a short memorial service in Michael's memory. To ignore the drowning, to pretend as if it had never happened, would only further distress the campers. But I had no fight left in me and I was facing considerable opposition from Ahmek stalwarts. The camp's culture is closely associated with demonstrations of male prowess, from running canoes over five-kilometre portages to holding mock Indian games. Grief was not part of their vocabulary and would be seen as a sign of weakness. The message to the campers was clear: boys don't cry or talk about their feelings. In true Ahmek form, the camp would be as laid-back in its darkest moment as it was every other day of the summer.

In the end, all that was done to mark the death of a 12-year-old child was the lowering of the flag to half-mast for one day; then it was expected to be business as usual. The loss of an expensive canoe in a rapid on the Petawawa River would have resulted in more consternation. Nobody again talked about "the accident," as it was referred to, in public. Apart from Michael's cabin group, I never saw anyone shed a tear. Few people ever asked me how the cabin group was coping. The drowning may have been an unavoidable tragedy, but the camp's unwillingness to drop its guard for even one moment and let flow the collective emotions of hundreds of distraught and confused children was profoundly unsettling to me then, and remains so to this day.

For parents, educators, and youth leaders, a critical issue is how we can nurture compassion among the young people for whom we are responsible. For complex reasons—including societal conditioning—it's much more difficult for boys than for girls to connect emotionally to another human being. Similarly, high-school environmental and human-rights clubs are made up primarily of young women. It's not unusual for Amnesty International clubs in high schools to be lacking a single male participant. How can we expect young males to become caring parents and husbands when we don't provide them with anything other than macho, testosterone-driven role models? Ahmek bills itself as "the maker of men." Teaching kids how to sail and canoe is easy; my old summer camp has much learning to do about meeting the emotional needs of boys and young men if it is to be relevant in the next century.

On their own, the cabin group decided they wanted to organize a private memorial service for Michael. Under Stuart's able leadership, they went to the craft shop for the morning, and as a group they made seven little colored candles, including one for Michael. They invited their favorite adults to join them for the service—Henri Audet, Janet Creaser and her music staff, and the camp nurses. That night around the Mountaineer council ring fire, the six boys each said something they remembered about Michael. Eric spoke in French and Paul in Spanish. Stuart wrote a poem, but was overcome by emotion and could not finish it. Without hesitation, his friend Stephen Dalgarno stepped forward and took over reading where Stuart had left off. I made some closing comments about friendship and then, Michael being an American, I read two poems by Robert Frost, including *Stopping by Woods on a Snowy Evening*. The service was simple but appropriate. At its conclusion, we walked to the Mountaineer dock and the boys set their candles adrift on little paper plates. We watched the wind carry them off across the lake and out of sight, and then the kids walked back to their cabin in silence.

All six boys had a summer in which they gained confidence and learned new skills, and they went home feeling good about themselves. They all received their swimming and canoeing awards. Eric and Paul stayed on for the month of August, so I was able to spend more time with them. If they wanted to talk about Michael, they knew I was willing to listen and I would try to answer their questions. Otherwise, I did not raise the subject of the drowning. Paul, a devout Catholic, wanted to know if Michael had believed in God. Eric wanted to write a letter to Michael's family. We never talked about what had happened among the three of them that last afternoon in the swimming pool, how they came to be separated or why they had remained silent during the buddy call when they must have been aware Michael was missing. I suspect they knew more about what happened to Michael than they let on, but I was not willing to pry. Children are entitled to make mistakes and to keep secrets. Nothing they told me would bring Michael back.

As a group, we packed up all of Michael's clothes and equipment and sent them home to Old Greenwich in his trunk. When I cleaned out my cabin at the end of August, I found two of Michael's green-striped Izod shirts under my bed; in the fall, I delivered them to a charity in Toronto working with poor immigrant children. Since July 14, I had not seen Michael's cherished Coleco electronic football game, which had been his constant companion. It turned up on the last day of camp when I took the sheets off the spare bed in my cabin, which had not been slept in since the day of the accident. Michael had hidden the toy under his mattress, probably just before he set off for general swim with Paul and Eric that last afternoon.

Months later, a government inquest revealed only that Michael had suffered an injury to his neck, but it may in fact have been a pre-existing condition. How a dexterous and athletic 12-year-old boy drowned in a pool with six lifeguards on duty remains a mystery. My guess is that he did in fact jump or dive off the seven-metre board but, when swimming around the diving tower to the dock, was hit by someone jumping off the three-metre board. He could have been winded and unable to swim. But this is only a theory and there is no proof. The diving tower instantly became a symbol of the camp's first fatality, and it was dismantled days after the drowning. For years after the accident, you could still see the stains on the canvas dock where Michael had bled from his mouth after being pulled from the lake. When I visited Ahmek to check in with my friend Judy Biggar, the camp's business manager, I avoided even glancing at the swimming pool.

During the autumn following Michael's death, I met with his parents at their house in Old Greenwich, Connecticut. It was a perfect home for kids, with huge hardwood trees providing shade. I had brought along photographs for them of Michael at Ahmek, swimming, playing football, and sailing. Over dinner, we traded stories about Michael and laughed, then after dessert was served, Michael's father put down his wine glass and looked me in the eyes. "Please tell us how our boy died," he whispered. I was dumbstruck. More than eight weeks after the drowning, they still had not been informed about the details of the accident. I did the best I could to answer all their questions, and it was almost midnight by the time we finished. Originally I had planned to return to New York for the night, but I had missed the last train back to Grand Central Station. The Kane-Parrys had no guest room, so I slept in Michael's bedroom, unchanged from the July morning he left for Canada.

Michael had described his bedroom to me in intimate detail one day while we sat on the edge of the Mountaineer dock, just a few metres from my cabin. Now his words came back to me. The walls were indeed painted electric blue, his favorite color. I recognized the posters above his bed. Michael said he could see the ocean from his window, and the next morning there it was—so calm that it reminded me of a huge Ontario lake. I knew that if I were the parent of a child who had drowned I couldn't live within a thousand kilometres of a body of water. I would move to Arizona or Kansas to be consoled.

Michael's mom had told me that no one had slept in the room since their son had gone off to camp. During the night I had awoken and stumbled along the corridor leading to the bathroom. I wondered if I had disturbed her sleep. Hearing noise from the second-floor bedroom, she might, in her state of half-wakefulness, for an instant have thought her boy was home, safe and secure, his death a nightmare that would soon be forgotten. But Michael was now only a dream and a memory. I, a 22-year-old law student from Canada with an incomplete explanation for his death, was the reality. She told me over breakfast that when Michael was lying in a coma at the Hospital for Sick Children, she had attempted to make a deal with the Creator: He could take her now, but please deliver Michael back to the land of the living. Her boy had committed no sin, was responsible for no error or omission that could justify his passing. But God doesn't make deals.

Michael's mother continues to write to me every year, but otherwise, over the last 18 years I haven't spoken with anyone about Michael or how his death affected me. My wife, Nienke, once came across a photograph of Michael hidden among the pages of a novel by Leon Uris I started reading that summer but never finished. The child in the photo has an impish smile and he cradles a basketball under his arm. She asked me about the boy, but I could not provide an honest answer. "Just an Ahmek kid," I replied, not meeting her eyes. They say that time heals all wounds. I'm not so sure.

Intrepid Ahmek children still climb the massive pine tree above the senior council ring. If they look carefully along the top branch they will find the initials MKP and the year 1979 inscribed in the bark, but few people at Ahmek today could attach a name or a story to the letters. I have kept Michael's Coleco football game safe over the years. I will present it as a primitive computer game to my own children some day, and will tell them about the American boy who was its original owner, who climbed the tallest tree in camp with such speed and grace, and who liked to score touchdowns while hanging from its highest branches.

THE ROOTS OF
COMPASSION

I come from a long line of successful business people whose goal was to make money, not to give it away to charity. I didn't spend seven years in college and one year slugging it out in the catacombs of a large law firm with the intention of devoting my life to street children. I hate the term "do-gooder" and I am no Mother Teresa. I have always enjoyed my fair share of creature comforts, including fine wine, good books, Prospector canoes, and expeditions in remote parts of Umbria, my favorite region of Italy. If it wasn't for the Ethiopian famine of 1984, I suspect that today I would be practising law, wearing red suspenders, and attending Upper Canada College reunions to check up on the progress of my age mates.

The defining moment of my life came in the last week of 1984 in a refugee camp located on the border between Somalia and Ethiopia that had become the temporary home for almost 25,000 women and children. The region was gripped by the worst drought and famine of the 20th century, and millions of Africans were on the brink of starvation. For the third successive year, the seasonal rains had failed. The land was dying. "You've come too late," the farmers told us. "Where were you last year when we were on our knees begging for help?"

When I first saw the camp, I had no idea of its size. We arrived at night; there were dozens of fires burning and the sky was filled with smoke. I was led by the hand through the camp by a young Ethiopian named Ahmed, who never spoke a word. People were huddled around the fires, wrapped in blankets and pieces of plastic in an attempt to stay warm. As I walked through the camp, they looked at me but did not move. Even in their desperate condition, I knew these were noble people from a noble tribe. They had lost everything on their great trek to the camp. They were pastoralists, but all their animals had perished weeks before. Their possessions were a few plastic bottles to carry water in and their simple clothes, really only rags. They had traded their knives and jewellery en route to the camp for grain, salt, and tea. The smell, a combination of dirt, faeces, disinfectant, urine, and punk from the fires, was almost overwhelming. I felt like an intruder. I tried to communicate to Ahmed that I had seen enough and wanted to go back to the safety of the Land Rover, but he did not understand. We kept moving deeper into the camp, negotiating our way around makeshift tukuls—huts constructed from sticks, mud, and plastic bags. There were sick and hungry children everywhere.

Only 10 weeks earlier, I had been an earnest articling student with a leading Canadian law firm in Halifax, Nova Scotia, dreaming of becoming a successful litigation lawyer and perhaps some day owning a ketch that I could sail the world in. My hours at the law firm, like those of all North American lawyers, were divided into discrete six-minute segments that I would methodically record during the course of the day and hand in to the accountants for billing purposes. Billable hours are the standard by which lawyers and articling students are ultimately judged, and I was already far behind my colleagues for the month. Two fellow articling students had been snapped up by the firm's star criminal lawyer for a long and complex case involving a notorious Halifax night-club owner. They were billing as many as 15 hours a day and wearing it like a badge on their chests.

I couldn't hope to compete with them, and I knew my chances of being kept on by the firm at the end of my 12 months of articling were rapidly fading. Two of the senior partners at the firm had already gone out of their way to inform me that perhaps law was not my calling. I was determined to prove them wrong and was hankering to be handed a thick file that required my attention— that contained, buried within the reams of paper, a problem that needed to be solved. I was 26 years old and still believed that lawyers, like the best scientists, had "Eureka!" moments, when everything became clear and a solution leapt off the page. Somewhere amidst the thousands of dusty books and legal documents that made up the library at Stewart, MacKeen and Covert lay my salvation.

My world fell apart on October 23, 1984, at 10:00 p.m. Atlantic Standard Time. I had bicycled home from the law firm via my favorite Lebanese pizzeria on Quinpool Road and parked myself in front of the television at JoAnne Hurst's house, the woman from whom I was renting a basement apartment for $250 a month. I knew JoAnne and her kids well, and I had the run of the house. They were accustomed to my coming home from the office at all hours of the night and helping myself to whatever was in the refrigerator. I poured myself a Keith's beer and made myself comfortable in the living room.

The lead item on the CBC News that night was a seven-minute piece from a place called Korem in northern Ethiopia, filmed by a 41-year-old Kenyan named Mohammed Amin. He had travelled to the capital, Addis Ababa, with the intention of doing a story on the regime's 10th anniversary celebrations. After two days of mind-numbing speeches from party apparatchik and almost endless military parades, Amin grew bored and decided to follow up on reports he had read of famine in the remote mountain region 400 kilometres north of the capital. He convinced an Ethiopian air-force pilot to fly him and a sound man in a banged-up DC-3 to the dirt air strip at Korem. He promised the pilot that he would stay only a few hours, just long enough to interview local officials and, with luck, film some hungry people.

Nothing in his 20 years as a cameraman had prepared Amin for what he found at Korem. In a newspaper interview in 1995, he described the scene: "There were about 60,000 starving people ... camped in an open field outside the town. There was almost no food and no real shelter, and the nights up there are cold, with temperatures falling to around zero. The early morning scenes were the worst, by far the worst thing I have ever seen. There was this tremendous mass of people, groaning and weeping, scattered across the ground in the dawn mist. I don't really know how to describe it, but the thing that came to my mind at the time was that it was as if 100 jumbo jets had crashed and spilled out the bodies of their passengers amongst the wreckage, the dead and living mixed together so you couldn't tell one from the other."

The news item depicted people who were in the last stages of life, completely destitute and completely desperate. The children were skeletal. They resembled little old men and women, with their bald heads and gnarled faces. I was reminded of newsreel footage I had seen taken by the U.S. Army when they liberated Dachau and Auschwitz. In my days working as a student volunteer with inner-city children in the United States, I had seen urban squalor, but I had never glimpsed starvation. These people in Korem were from another world.

I had a troubled sleep that night, and the next day, Amin's images were never far from my mind. The print media were beginning to pick up on the story; there were pieces that week in the *New York Times* and the *Washington Post* datelined Korem. On November 2, 1984, the *Halifax Chronicle-Herald* published a CP wire photograph of a young child being carried on his father's shoulders in an unnamed refugee camp in northern Ethiopia. The child had his arms around his father's head, and you could see he had total trust in his father's ability to provide. But if you looked in the father's eyes, you recognized the look of a desperate man. He had no idea where their next meal would be coming from.

I cut out the photograph and put it above my desk in the office I shared at the law firm with another articling student, Don Murray. Throughout the day, I kept returning to it. That afternoon I telephoned two Stanford friends working with UNICEF in New York. I put an idea to them: did it make sense to launch an airlift from Canada of food and medical supplies that would be delivered to experienced relief organizations that were already on the ground? We would appeal to the Canadian public for support; the people of the Atlantic provinces were famous for their generosity. For the most part, they lived in small towns, and many of them had experienced adversity in their own lives.

I went knocking on the door of John Godfrey who, at the age of 41, was the youngest university president in Canada. While professor of history at King's College, affiliated with Dalhousie University, John had attracted large numbers of students to his lectures through a format that was as theatrical and inspiring as it was didactic. King's College was a staid, tradition-bound institution, but John refused to play by the rules. He drove around Halifax in a lime-green Volkswagen Beetle convertible. His classes sometimes involved full-scale re-enactments of historical events. He loved Wagner, and every year organized marathon performances of the *Ring Cycle* with no breaks. Students brought along sleeping bags, air mattresses, and large thermoses of coffee.

The night I knocked on John's door, he was in the middle of his first political campaign, running for a seat in the Nova Scotia legislature. From the latest polls, he knew his chances of winning were slim, but he was determined to knock on every door in the constituency. I told him what I had seen on television and that I needed his help. "Do we have to do something before the election? Can it wait until after I lose?" he pleaded.

John knew the answer to his own question. Famine waits for no one. He had seen, along with millions of people around the world, those same images from Korem filmed by Mohammed Amin, and he knew we had to act quickly. John invited me into the President's Lodge and pulled out a Michelin map he had used during his travels in Africa. Much like players in a game of Stratego, we scrambled across the map, measured distances, searched for air strips, and plotted a strategy. If we were to launch a relief effort, how would it work? Where could we land a plane? Was the port at Assab still operating? We needed more information from the field.

The next morning, I telephoned the Canadian embassy in Addis Ababa and was referred to Terry Mooney, who was second in command at the embassy. He, too, was supportive of the idea of an airlift. Mooney was Canada's point man on the issue of the Ethiopian famine and hadn't slept in over 24 hours. He stated that I was "the only good news he had heard that day." Mooney said we were the first Canadian group to propose an airlift, and he expressed surprise that we were civilians with no African emergency experience to build on. But he shared all the information that he had on the current situation in Ethiopia with us. He related to me how grim conditions really were in the refugee camps and how the aid organizations were fighting to keep kids alive. Mooney suggested I look to the Ogaden region, which had been largely ignored by the media and by the development organizations. He told me the World University Service of Canada and the Lutheran World Federation were operating in the area and were very short of supplies. WUSC had just entered into a contract with the United Nations High Commission for Refugees and the Relief and Rehabilitation Commission of Ethiopia to provide food for 50,000 refugees of Ethiopian origin from Somalia and Djibouti. The LWF had been in the Ogaden for a number of years and were running an excellent medical project, headed by a German volunteer doctor named Klaus Hornetz.

John, in turn, recruited Dr. Arthur Andrew, a former Canadian ambassador to Israel, Sweden, and Greece, who was a visiting professor at the faculty of journalism at King's College. Arthur Andrew was 69 years old, wise, thoughtful, and patient—a good foil to both John and myself. He was also methodical, precise, and disciplined. He knew everyone at the Department of External Affairs and he was very experienced in dealing with bureaucrats. Arthur was also something of a rebel in tweed; while serving as professor of foreign affairs at the University of Toronto, he had published a book entitled *Defense by Other Means: Diplomacy for the Underdog*, in which he challenged mainstream thinking about the effectiveness of nuclear deterrents and the widely accepted theory of mutually assured destruction. He proposed that, when confronted by a vastly superior opponent, the only sane option for a country was capitulation. In his last book, *The Rise and Fall of a Middle Power*, Arthur Andrew argued that in cuddling up to the Americans, former prime minister Brian Mulroney had "diminished our detachment as a peace-keeper and our acceptability among Third World peoples." While stopping short of suggesting Canada should join the non-aligned movement, Professor Andrew believed that as a non-nuclear power, the most effective role for Canada was as a peace broker, zealously guarding our independence from the United States.

Arthur was initially skeptical of our plan for the airlift, but the more he became drawn in, the more he was convinced its simplicity and its reliance on organizations already well established on the ground made a good deal of sense. The ports were already clogged. An airlift could deliver food where it was most needed. For an academic, Arthur had an astute political nose: he reminded me that Canada's foreign policy is largely demand-driven, and that Ottawa would soon be facing pressure from the Canadian public to do something about those hungry kids in Africa whom everyone had seen on television.

I moved into high gear. I tracked down John Watson, the assistant director for the World University Service of Canada in Ottawa. I was surprised he took my call. A siege mentality had already settled in at the WUSC office; Watson was being inundated with phone calls from people all across Canada who wanted to do something for Ethiopia. Some of their ideas made no sense at all, such as sending Massey Ferguson combines to harvest the non-existent Ethiopian crops, or using oil tankers to transport water to irrigate the desert. The owner of a salvage company in New Brunswick had proposed towing icebergs across the Atlantic ocean. Some Canadians didn't understand that people in Ethiopia did not have the luxury of time; thousands were perishing every day waiting for assistance.

From my initial call, Watson offered generous amounts of his time to work on our fledgling scheme. On the ground in the Ogaden desert, WUSC had in place a team of dedicated Canadian relief workers, but they lacked even the most basic supplies to become operational. On our behalf, Watson telexed the field to obtain a wish list of their priority items. The next day, Walter Msimang, the WUSC co-ordinator in Ethiopia, telexed back to Ottawa that he needed three food items in large quantities: milk powder, sugar, and a high-protein food supplement. These materials would be used for emergency supplementary feeding of the hungriest and sickest children. Msimang said that without these supplies, his team had no program to administer. Our airlift would put WUSC in business in the Ogaden. His telex underlined the gravity of the situation: "The whole area is in the grip of a famine.... More than 40 per cent of the children are said to be severely malnourished.... Over 800,000 people here require food and medical relief.... Stores are empty.... Unless something is done quickly the horrors of Korem will be upon us.... We are in the midst of a disaster."

Arthur Andrew had been right; already the government of Canada was feeling pressure from concerned citizens who wanted to help out in Ethiopia.

TV changed everything. For many people, simply sending a cheque to their favorite charity would not be sufficient. They wanted to help with their own hands. Relief agencies were being besieged with phone calls from Canadians who were willing to volunteer as truck drivers, nurses, mechanics, and pilots. The Canadian prime minister appointed a former cabinet minister, David MacDonald, as the Canadian emergency co-ordinator for the African famine. His mandate was to assess the famine situation in Ethiopia and propose concrete steps to alleviate the suffering. MacDonald would work closely with the Canadian International Development Agency, the United Nations, and the aid agencies in determining Canada's response to the famine, which was now estimated to affect more than 30 million people.

MacDonald, a former United Church minister and one of Canada's most decent politicians, stated he wanted to hear from Canadians who had ideas for their own projects to help Ethiopians. John Godfrey, Arthur Andrew, and I took MacDonald's invitation literally. On November 7, 1984, the three of us drafted a proposal, sketching out the elements of our plan, including launching an airlift from Canada, linking up at the other end with WUSC and the Lutheran World Federation, and involving Canadian farmers and businesses who were keen on becoming partners in the famine-relief effort. We included as much detail as we could, and we got some things wrong. We had proposed the impractical idea that the Canadian military fly relief supplies on board C-130 Hercules aircraft from Canada to Africa, a trip that would take at least three days in each direction, allowing for refuelling stops. But otherwise, the document was quite comprehensive.

Through John Watson, Walter Msimang telexed us with even more precise information about the Ogaden and listed the priorities of the relief agencies already on the ground. At the same time Msimang was feeding identical information to representatives of the government of Canada and the Canadian International Development Agency, which had been deployed by Ottawa to carry out field reconnaissance and map out Canada's emergency-aid strategy for Ethiopia. But large bureaucracies take time to collect and process information, and our little group was able to beat them to the punch. Consequently, we often knew about things before Ottawa did. Working with the latest WUSC reports from the field, John, Arthur, and I drafted a new document that we called "Detailed Logistics: Airlift to the Ogaden Region." In it, we proposed that food and medical supplies be flown from Diredawa in eastern Ethiopia to five communities in the Ogaden desert: Callafo, Gode, Wardair, Kebri Dehar, and Degabur. All the villages had serviceable dirt air strips and were the logical staging points for relief operations in their regions. We knew Msimang had recommended exactly the same course of action to the CIDA officials who were at that very moment carrying out reconnaissance in Ethiopia, and who would soon be reporting back to their masters in Ottawa. We called ourselves Ethiopia Airlift, and sent an appropriately formatted and official-looking proposal to David MacDonald in Ottawa by courier, then waited.

Already our imaginary airlift was beginning to take over my life. Law went by the wayside, and the secretary I shared with the other articling students at Stewart, MacKeen and Covert was becoming familiar with the intricacies of the international-aid business. Cynthia Woodward had a typed list of common acronyms used by the aid agencies posted next to her computer, including ICRC, CRS, FAO, MSF, AICF, and CCODP. I was now receiving as many phone calls as many of the firm's senior lawyers, and I was beginning to monopolize her time, but she told me that working on the Ethiopia file, as she called it, was far more interesting than typing up lawyers' time sheets. Cynthia began to work after-hours on the project, donating all her spare time to the cause. Thanks to the support of Bill Mingo, Gerald Godsoe, and Don McDougall—three of the firm's (and the city's) most influential lawyers—nobody complained.

At King's College, we recruited students to run a makeshift office that we set up in the basement of one of the residences. An 18-year-old student named David Wilson, who had the self-confidence and presence of someone twice his age, became the Ethiopia Airlift project co-ordinator. We covered the walls of the office with maps from northeast Africa and photocopies of pages from *Jane's Fighting Aircraft* listing the specifications of various kinds of military transport planes, including the C-130 Hercules (21 MT capacity, requiring a runway of 1,500 metres), de Havilland Buffalos (7 MT capacity, requiring a runway of 300 metres), and DC-3s (3 MT capacity, requiring a runway of 1,200 metres). CNCP Telecommunications donated a telex machine for the office, the only reliable means of reaching Ethiopia. It started chattering away almost the moment we plugged it in and didn't stop for six months. By the end of November, 1984, I had spent my entire month's paycheque, about $800, on long-distance calls to Ottawa, New York, Geneva, and Addis Ababa. When the president of the local phone company learned of my plight, he couriered me a long-distance calling card for all our international telephone calls.

I did my first interview with a reporter from the *Halifax Chronicle-Herald* about my idea for an airlift to Ethiopia late on a Friday afternoon before heading off to the Midtown Tavern, which served a decent steak with fries for $3.25. I was fatigued, and I rambled through the interview, listing the supplies that were needed in Africa and how people in the Maritime provinces could help. I assumed the story would be buried somewhere in the Metro or Lifestyle sections between advertisements for tractor pulls and announcements of upcoming nuptials. On Saturday morning, JoAnne Hurst's eight-year-old son Jay ran down the stairs of my basement apartment waving the Saturday newspaper; the story had run front page with a big picture of me alongside it. "Peter, you're famous!" he screamed.

The following week, I did three more newspaper interviews about our air-lift, which still existed only in our imaginations. Lawyers I bumped into in the firm's library kidded me about my new-found celebrity. Although they seldom admit it, most lawyers love to see their names in print, and law firms, which were prohibited from advertising, nurture relations with sympathetic reporters to create high drama out of material that is mostly quite mundane. Publicity for lawyers means more clients and fatter fees. The most successful trial lawyers invariably have the gift of the gab and are tireless self-promoters. Alan Derschowitz, who represented both Klaus von Bulow and O. J. Simpson, and F. Lee Bailey, America's most famous trial lawyer, are frequent guests on CNN's *Larry King Live*. Spending hours researching arcane elements of Canadian law had done nothing for my status within the law firm; a few easy interviews with the Halifax media and suddenly I was earning my keep.

The Maritime provinces of Canada are primarily rural, and people eat their evening meal shortly after the sun goes down. The most popular supper-hour news program in the Maritimes was *Live at Five*, hosted by Dave Wright, a journalist who every year had been judged by viewers as among the most trusted people in the country. The show enjoyed stellar ratings, and Wright had been courted by all three major political parties to run in various provincial and federal elections. He always turned them down, saying he had no time for politics or politicians. Wright was an Ontario native, but his folksy manner gave him a down-home quality that endeared him to his audience. Over the years, he had emerged as Atlantic Canada's Walter Cronkite. People sent him presents on his birthday, get-well cards when he was sick, and advice on a whole range of issues, from the clothes he should wear on the set to the best places for ice fishing in the province of New Brunswick.

Dave Wright was eager to have me on his Friday show. I was reluctant. Ethiopia Airlift had no bank account, no charitable status, and no donors. We had not yet crossed the Rubicon and committed ourselves to collecting donations from the public. What if nothing materialized from all our efforts? I didn't want people to start dropping off cans of food and bundles of blankets at the steps of my house. I agreed to the interview on the condition he explain to his audience that the airlift was only a concept and we had neither the supplies nor the funds required to make it operational.

Live at Five has no script and was designed to accommodate Wright's freewheeling, roll-with-the-punches style. When I arrived at the studio, Wright sent me off for make-up, then sat me down at his desk in front of the cameras just minutes before going to air. We had no time to prepare for the interview, and Wright had nothing in front of him other than the *Halifax Chronicle-Herald* article, but he wasn't concerned. "Just let me run with the story," he said to me.

Running with the story for Wright meant getting the aircraft off the ground. Nothing less would suffice. Wright's intro for the piece was dramatic and to the point: "Kids in Africa are starving, and a young Halifax articling student has got an answer. It's an airlift." According to Wright, the airlift was a sure thing. All we needed was for the Ottawa bureaucrats to get on side. That we had no bank account, no charitable status, and no agreement with anyone in the federal government were all details that could be worked out later. Our scheduled three-minute piece ran to eight minutes; I had not even walked off the set when an assistant ran into the studio and shouted out that the switchboard was lighting up with calls from people across the Maritime provinces wanting to help with the airlift.

The following Monday morning, we learned about the power of media when the mail arrived at King's College. A stack of envelopes addressed to Ethiopia Airlift was awaiting us. Without even soliciting funds, we had already received over $1,500 in donations, most of the cheques made out personally to me. I was stunned. Arthur Andrew was speechless. Godfrey was strategic: we needed a real lawyer who could incorporate the charity and carefully deal with the contributions.

The next few weeks were a wild roller-coaster ride that took me twice to Ottawa to lobby pale-faced bureaucrats who had little interest in listening to amateurs like myself who had cobbled together mad-cap schemes for rescuing Africa from the century's worst famine. Compassion didn't fit neatly into any box on their government-issue forms. In his startling inside account of international charities, *Lords of Poverty*, Graham Hancock writes about "the rich and powerful bureaucracies that have hijacked our kindness." The book is subtitled "The freewheeling lifestyles, power, prestige and corruption of the multi-billion-dollar aid business." Despite efforts by UN agencies to debunk the book and its author, *Lords of Poverty* has become required reading for all students of international development and for anyone interested in knowing how governments and charities throw money around in the name of fighting poverty. Readers learn that Edouard Saouma, director general of the UN Food and Agriculture Organization, earned $813,276, excluding fringe benefits, for his third six-year term in office, which ended in 1993. He was criticized for running the agency as his personal fiefdom. Among his detractors was former Canadian minister of agriculture Eugene Whelan who remarked that any resemblance the FAO bore to a democratic institution was completely coincidental.

According to Hancock, the international-development business is run by well-placed people who assume the manner of the landed gentry when dealing with outsiders. More than 80 per cent of all the money passing through the UN system is spent on its 50,000 staff worldwide. Representatives of UN agencies in cities from Bangkok to Lagos are drawn disproportionately from the aristocracy of their country of origin, and soon grow accustomed to a life of luxury, with private schools for their children, personal servants, swimming pools, and air-conditioned vehicles all paid for by the UN and its donors. Their jobs are hardly taxing; while the public may have an image of UN employees feeding hungry children and parachuting into war zones, the vast majority of international civil servants sit behind desks and move paper. For this they are paid handsome salaries in tax-free U.S. dollars. The international-aid community is rife with people who went overseas to do good but who ended up doing very well. They are famous for their complacency and their arrogance. It was former secretary general Boutros Boutros-Ghali, himself a former deputy prime minister of Egypt, who once proclaimed that UN bureaucrats had to be approached "with stealth and sudden violence."

Responding to one of the great environmental catastrophes of this century was routine business for the people at the Canadian International Development Agency in Ottawa. They had seen it all before. My meeting with them was a mismatch from the word go. I came to their office armed with maps, statistics, and the loading specifications of various kinds of aircraft. I was passionate, and I wouldn't quit. I had the distinct impression the CIDA staff viewed volunteers like myself, who had been moved by what we had seen on television, as meddling in affairs beyond our expertise. They would be happier if we simply paid our tax dollars and left the business of feeding African children in the hands of professionals. Before the African famine of 1984, large government and private-aid agencies were not big on accountability to the public and were not set up to deal with ordinary citizens' legitimate concern for others. They preferred to work with institutional donors such as the World Bank, which spoke their language and was run by people like themselves. They had no idea what to do with the dairy farmer in southern Ontario who wanted to send milk powder to the hungry kids of Korem.

At my first session at CIDA in Ottawa, I was stymied by officials who poked holes in almost every aspect of our proposal, from the expense of using aircraft to fly basic relief commodities to the likelihood that our aircraft and vehicles would be bogged down in mud, as the heavy rains were imminent. I had to remind them that, in most areas in the Ogaden, it had not rained in over two years, and mud was probably the least of our problems. My intensity unsettled them; one man nonchalantly chewed gum through my entire presentation. The meeting came to an end with no words of support or encouragement from any of the participants. I returned to Halifax that night frustrated and angry. If these were the women and men who held the fate of the starving Ethiopian kids in their hands, then only a mass mobilization of resources by ordinary Canadians working in their own communities offered any semblance of hope.

John Godfrey once described me as having "a kind of restless energy that is very impatient of obstacles." It's true I don't suffer fools gladly and I enjoy breaking rules and challenging systems. I have no time for hypocrisy and I refuse to be intimidated by institutions. From the moment we conceived the airlift until the day the planes arrived in Ethiopia, we must have heard the word "impossible" at least 20 times from representatives of aid organizations and governments. Some people were merely unco-operative, while others were deliberately obstructionist. I was beginning to learn that many people who work on behalf of charities have little real interest in humanitarianism; preserving their jobs and increasing their charitable donations tend to be their paramount considerations. As a representative of one aid agency said to me in Ottawa, "The Ethiopian famine will be great for business."

We may have had very little expertise on the subject of the loading requirements for C-130 Hercules aircraft but we had a growing constituency of people behind us. More than anything else, what got Ethiopia Airlift off the ground was the determination and generosity of the people of the Maritime provinces who shared our suspicion of government and large institutions. The school children, business people, and farmers who made their way to our office at King's College all believed that people acting in concert were the only real hope for the hungry kids they had seen on television. In their minds, the best thing the government of Canada could do was to provide us with an aircraft and pilot and then get out of the way.

The local media were becoming our biggest allies. On November 14, I was interviewed by CBC Radio for their Halifax drive program, *Information Morning*. Bill MacLellan, president of Farmers' Co-operative Dairy Ltd., heard me while he was en route to his office that morning and called me minutes after I had arrived at the law firm. The employees of the dairy had only days earlier approached the management of the co-operative with the idea of becoming involved in a direct way in a project providing assistance to the people of Ethiopia. No specific plan had yet been hatched by the company or its employees. MacLellan suggested that if milk powder was one of the commodities we would be needing, his co-operative could be a major partner in the airlift. Over the phone, MacLellan and I did a quick calculation and estimated we would need approximately 13,500 kilograms of skim-milk powder for WUSC's emergency supplementary-feeding program.

Apart from milk powder, Walter Msimang and his colleagues in the Ogaden desert required sugar and a high-protein food supplement. On November 20, 1984, I telephoned Murray McEwen, the president of Redpath Sugar of Canada in Toronto, and explained our proposal for the airlift. The advantage of a CEO over a mid-level CIDA official is that the CEO can make a decision without consulting an assistant deputy minister. McEwen was enthusiastic about our plans, and with no hesitation agreed to become a partner in Ethiopia Airlift, but he wanted more information. I sent him documentation the same day and within 24 hours, he telephoned me at Stewart, MacKeen and Covert to say Redpath was on board. How much sugar did I need? We estimated 8,500 kilograms, an amount that did not throw him off.

Finding a Canadian supplier of the high-protein food supplement proved much more difficult. Walter Msimang had requested we locate a source of CSM, a combination of corn, soya, and milk developed 30 years earlier by the U.S. Department of Agriculture. After an extensive computer search, we found no Canadian supplier of CSM. However, John Godfrey stumbled across a Toronto-based company called Griffiths Laboratories that, in the 1970s, had received $700,000 in federal government assistance to develop a successor to CSM that was more nutritious and more consistent with the African diet. Mixed with water, the compound, which combined skim-milk powder with wheat and soy protein, could be served as porridge or in the form of pancakes. As the Griffiths product is precooked, no fuel or fire is required for its preparation. Even the hungriest kids could stomach the mixture, as it is easily digestible. Griffiths had gone to great lengths to produce a quality product; their tests showed that a four-year-old child could live on a diet of 100 grams per day of the substance, which would supply 365 calories of food energy, 60 grams of carbohydrates, 20 grams of protein, and six grams of fat. Unfortunately, the project was shelved in 1980; no customers for the wonderfood had ever been found.

John Godfrey ordered a sample from Griffiths and had it couriered to his house in Halifax. We followed the directions printed on the side of the tin and produced something with a cream-of-wheat consistency. Godfrey tested the product on his King's College students, none of whom balked at the taste. Some of our guinea pigs even liked it and asked for extra portions for breakfast. Within days of learning about the product, we placed a conditional order for 34,000 kilograms—the first order that Griffiths had ever received. We decided it had a better chance of being marketable if it was known by something other than its official name, Nutritional Cooked Food Supplement, and dubbed it Canadian Food Supplement, or CFS.

We were putting ourselves in a precarious situation. Arthur Andrew, who served as our voice of reason and moderation, reminded us that we still had no means of transporting any donated commodities to Africa. Our only airplanes were made of paper. David Wilson and fellow 18-year-olds from King's College had already completed an extensive search of container-shipping companies operating from Halifax harbor. Sending our supplies in 40-foot containers would be relatively inexpensive, but we had to allow for at least four weeks at sea. More importantly, telexed reports were arriving at our office on a daily basis from WUSC, the Lutheran World Federation, and the United Nations in Ethiopia on the status of Ethiopia's two major ports, Assab and Massawa. Both were severely congested and strained far beyond their operating capacity. There was no guarantee any food commodities arriving by ship would ever get to their intended destination.

We knew it made little economic sense to transport relief commodities by air. The bureaucrats in Ottawa had laughed at the suggestion. David Wilson had obtained quotations from various air-charter companies. By his calculations, the cost of airlifting supplies from Halifax to Addis Ababa came to $42 per kilo—about the same cost as Willy Krauch's finest Nova Scotia smoked salmon. The irony was that the commodities we were assembling were for emergency supplementary feeding, and relatively small amounts—as little as

150 grams per child per day—were needed to sustain human life. Essentially, what we and other aid agencies had to do was use emergency supplementary feeding to buy time until the freighters with grain and other food stocks arrived at Massawa and Assab and could be unloaded.

Our orders for Canadian Food Supplement, milk powder, and sugar were conditional on Ethiopia Airlift finding the means to transport them to Africa. Now we faced a dilemma with our suppliers: they needed adequate lead time to produce and package their supplies but we were not in a position to proceed until we had some indication that we would be able to locate an appropriate aircraft. David Wilson had been on the phone with Robert Engle, the founder of Northwest Territorial Airways, based in Yellowknife. Engle is a pioneer of aviation in northern Canada and one of Canada's most daring entrepreneurs. He founded his airline in the 1961 with two bush aircraft, and over the years acquired a small fleet of planes that serviced some of Canada's most isolated northern communities. His pilots were legendary for their skill at finding and landing their planes on icy and snow-covered strips that other pilots would consider unserviceable. Bob had a C-130 Hercules that was configured for long-range cargo transport and was perfect for our needs, but it would be expensive to operate over long distances. He suggested jet aircraft, such as Boeing 707s that had been retired from passenger service and were now being used for freight. He told us to give him the word and he would find any aircraft we needed anywhere in the world.

I had gone down in flames at CIDA. Networking with government officials was not my strong suit. We needed a heavy-hitter in Ottawa to lobby on our behalf for funding for the aircraft to carry our CFS, sugar, and milk powder. George Cooper, former MP for Halifax, close friend of Prime Minister Brian Mulroney, and a Rhodes scholar, travelled to Ottawa on our behalf during the first week of December, 1984. He met with David MacDonald and with senior CIDA officials. His formidable diplomatic skills were put to good use in restoring their faith in Ethiopia Airlift after my stormy session. Cooper reported back to us that, while our plans for an airlift had initially been received by the bureaucrats and politicians with skepticism, dispatches from aid agencies and the Canadian embassy in Addis Ababa confirmed our initial assessment that transporting goods by sea was not an option. Ships were already being diverted from Assab and Massawa to Port Sudan and Mogadishu, thousands of kilometres from the population most in need. Transport trucks in Ethiopia were at a premium and could not be relied upon. Our networking with Walter Msimang and the WUSC field personnel was paying off, and eventually the same data we were working with were getting into the hands of CIDA decision-makers. Two weeks after my disastrous meeting with seemingly callous bureaucrats at CIDA, the federal government was warming to the idea of a private airlift from Canada of emergency relief commodities.

Over the next few days, we scrambled to put our house in order. We registered Ethiopia Airlift as a charitable organization, and as money was already pouring in, made application for charitable status with Revenue Canada. We had a logo designed, organized our first meeting with prospective volunteers, and purchased a second-hand coffee machine.

Dave Wright now had me on his *Live at Five* program every Friday afternoon to report to his audience on the progress of the airlift. The story was gathering momentum. I was becoming as familiar with the ATV staff as with my colleagues at the law firm. For all intents and purposes, I had ceased being an articling student with Stewart, MacKeen and Covert and had embraced the airlift as my full-time employment. I had no idea how I was going to eat or how the Law Society of Nova Scotia would view my informal leave of absence from my legal apprenticeship. I was now regularly being stopped in the streets of Halifax by total strangers forcing bills of various denominations into my hands; I had to institute a policy of keeping my own personal money in one pocket and donations to Ethiopia Airlift in the other.

Ethiopia Airlift was being fuelled by a kind of Battle of Britain mentality. Thanks to the extensive coverage by Dave Wright's program, the entire region of Atlantic Canada was signing on to volunteer for the cause. We certainly required their help. Even taking into account substantial contributions by the companies themselves, we needed to raise at least $50,000 for the relief commodities that were to be transported on our aircraft. Arthur Andrew, only half joking, informed me that if things did not go exactly according to plan, I would not become a lawyer. Instead, I would need a lawyer.

While I knew the people of the Atlantic provinces were known for their generosity, none of us were prepared for the avalanche of goodwill that headed our way. I also learned what kind of people traditionally give to charity. Cheques poured in from the most remote outports of Atlantic Canada, towns and villages where unemployment levels were among the highest in Canada and where many people lived below the poverty line. People who had encountered adversity in their own lives were deeply disturbed by the television images of hungry children. It didn't matter that they were African kids and that they lived thousands of kilometres away. David Wilson and his fellow student volunteers in our basement office opened many envelopes containing pension and disability cheques from people who we guessed were in need of assistance themselves. I travelled to the hamlet of Boutiliers Point and spoke at the town's only elementary school. Many of the kids were dressed in ill-fitting, out-of-fashion clothes handed down from older siblings. The library was sparsely furnished and there was not a computer in sight. The Grade 6 class had worked for more than two weeks to raise money for Ethiopia Airlift; I was shaken up when a blond sprite representing all the students handed me a cheque for $1,200 with the admonition, "You had better make sure every cent of this money gets to those poor kids in Africa."

The Boutiliers Point Elementary School kids, and the thousands of school children across the Atlantic provinces who held bake sales, raffles, and car washes on our behalf, placed their faith in our little charity and our team of volunteers. They believed that somehow, some way, we would find the means to connect with the hungry kids they had seen on television. By accepting their cheques, we were entering into a special kind of trust with every one of them. Simply doing our best was not going to be good enough—at least not for these kids. For the first time in my life, my level of achievement would not be measured by the grades I received on a test or the money I was paid for a particular job. Success or failure in the eyes of these Nova Scotian children would be judged according to the misery that would be spared and the mouths that would be fed, in a country I had never set foot in.

In Glace Bay, Nova Scotia, the roots of compassion run deep. The town, located on the eastern tip of Cape Breton Island, usually tops the list of the poorest communities in Canada. Glace Bay lives off mining, but its economic fortunes over the last 20 years have slipped in concert with the steady decline of the Nova Scotia coal industry. At any one point in time, 40 per cent of the adult population in Glace Bay is out of work. Unemployment insurance, providing only the most marginal existence, is all that stands between the town's population and absolute poverty. Commercial Street is dotted with "For Sale" and "Out of Business" signs. The busiest shop in town is the thrift store run by the Salvation Army. In 1983, the coal mine was closed down after a flash fire, and in January, 1984, the town's largest fish plant burned to the ground, putting another 800 people out of work.

Although the administrative office of Ethiopia Airlift may have been in the prosperous government town of Halifax, the heart of our organization was centred in Glace Bay and other down-and-out Maritime communities. Over the next few weeks, we received over $10,000 in individual donations from the citizens of Glace Bay, which has only 23,500 inhabitants. In a one-day relief drive organized by the Nova Scotia Teachers' Union, Glace Bay students contributed more than $35,000—almost four times the average annual income of a worker in Glace Bay. Other charities raising funds for African famine reported similar stories. The Glace Bay Central Credit Union raised $6,600 for the Canadian Catholic Organization for Development and Peace (CCODP).

With a borrowed Volvo, I began a road trip to dozens of towns and villages across the province, from Barrington Passage to Margaree Forks. Kids were mailing us their allowances, some of them being delivered in piggy banks that we had to smash open. At Amherst Centre Mall, customers assembled a 60-square-metre gingerbread village, all of which was auctioned off to shoppers with the proceeds of $1,600 going to Ethiopia Airlift. At Farmers' Co-operative Dairy in Halifax, employees held yard sales and donated their working time to assist the airlift, while the company scrounged old juice barrels to sell as scrap as a donation for the airlift. At Fairview Junior High School near Halifax, Grade 7 student Cairi May came up with the idea of holding a penny parade for Ethiopia at her school's winter carnival. Students, teachers, and parents collected pennies for one month until they had enough to cover a gigantic map of Africa made by the school's art department. The project, organized by librarian Maureen Leiper, raised $1,200 and produced a line of pennies that extended for 195 metres. Geary Elementary School in Oromocto, New Brunswick, with a student body of only 220 girls and boys, netted $1,500 hosting a spell-a-thon that featured questions on New Brunswick's history.

You know what they say: be careful what you pray for. On December 6, David MacDonald telephoned our King's College office from Ottawa. Thanks to the unflagging support of George Cooper, our MP Stewart McInnes, and various business people, our airlift had been approved. The federal government was allocating not one aircraft for Ethiopia Airlift, but two. They had agreed to charter two Air Canada stretch DC-8s from Montreal and Halifax with a total capacity of 88 MT. The planes would be departing on December 24. Could we be ready by then?

Our office erupted with hoots and cheers. Even Arthur Andrew got into the act. But after the noise died down, he reminded us of the enormity of the task we had taken on. David Wilson had held off placing firm orders for milk powder, sugar, and the Canadian Food Supplement until we had been able to confirm transport to Africa. We had less than three weeks to collect, package, and transport all the items. We didn't want to spend our Christmas in jail, so we had erred on the side of caution. Now we had planes, but could we fill them?

David Wilson and his team of volunteers placed frantic calls to our friends at Farmers' Co-operative Dairy and Redpath Sugar. David was appointed the loadmaster for the operation, and after consulting by telex with Walter Msimang in the Ogaden, came up with a shopping list of the commodities we needed, based on a total capacity of the two stretch DC-8 aircraft. We placed an order for approximately 40 MT of Canadian Food Supplement, 16 MT of milk powder, and 10 MT of sugar. Luckily, no one asked for a down payment for the commodities that were not donated. Our suppliers immediately began production, even developing special packaging that would withstand anticipated rough handling by forklift operators on the other side of the world. Griffiths Laboratories in Toronto put on extra shifts to make our Christmas Eve departure date.

If any doubt remained about the necessity of an emergency airlift to the Ogaden desert, an article in the *Globe and Mail* by its Africa-based correspondent, Michael Valpy, erased it. Dr. Klaus Hornetz was a young physician working with the Lutheran World Federation in Ethiopia, seconded by the German medical-aid agency Dienst in Übersee. Valpy described walking through a refugee camp alongside Dr. Hornetz, who had the responsibility of co-ordinating medical operations in the Ogaden, Ethiopia's largest and most populated region, located more than 600 kilometres southwest of the capital city. With a flick of his hand, Hornetz identified children who had a slim chance of surviving and those whom no one could save. "This one will die in maybe seven days. This one will die in two weeks." Hornetz was staggered by the task he faced, and resigned to the fact that one medical doctor could do little to keep the thousands of children in his care alive. The responsibility was weighing heavily on his shoulders; Valpy began the piece with the words, "Only God should know what Klaus Hornetz knows."

Valpy described what he called "famine in the penultimate stage." While the international media had flocked to Wollo Region, north of Addis Ababa, where, by some estimates, approximately 10,000 people each week were perishing in front of their camera lenses, little attention was being paid to those areas where famine was merely imminent and where it could be averted. A catastrophe was unfolding in the Ogaden and no one seemed to care. Hornetz was working in virtual isolation out of a canvas military tent. He had no medical supplies for the children who stumbled around the refugee camps, disoriented, cut off from their families, their animals long dead, their stomachs so empty they could not tolerate solid food. Some children were already going blind from chronic and prolonged vitamin deficiency. There were 50,000 kids in Hornetz's waiting room who needed immediate medical attention and emergency supplementary feeding or they would perish within days. Only an airlift would save these children, but as Valpy wrote, "There is no emergency airlift to the Ogaden."

We were beginning to feel overwhelmed. The design, procurement, and shipping of emergency medical supplies is a complex business, requiring technical skills we did not pretend to have. As in the case of identifying a high-protein food supplement, we followed Arthur Andrew's words of advice distilled from the old *Canadian Field Manual*: "Time spent in reconnaissance is seldom wasted." We needed to quickly identify what medical supplies were most useful in the Ogaden, which of the supplies required refrigeration, where they could be obtained in bulk, and how they should be packaged to survive the harsh desert conditions.

The United Nations has its own specialized packing facility called UNIPAC, located in Copenhagen. Its official mandate includes the preparation of emergency medical kits for exactly the kind of crisis we were facing in Ethiopia. We assumed it would be a perfect partner for Ethiopia Airlift, and were willing to pay in full for the medical kits we required, no matter what the cost. Over a 10-day period, Halifax lawyer David Copp attempted to get a commitment from UNIPAC that it would be able to procure 10 World Health Organization medical kits by our December 24 deadline. Copp asked for the details of its bank account, so we could transfer the necessary funds when required.

But UNIPAC turned out to be a spectacular failure. Despite its billing, it had little ability to assemble any medical supplies on anything other than a business-as-usual time frame. If there was an emergency in Africa, the people at UNIPAC in Copenhagen were the last to find out about it. As with many UN agencies, UNIPAC appeared to be infected with the kind of institutional lethargy that paralyzes large organizations. The people had no sense of mission. The UNIPAC officials gave Copp an earful about their policies and procedures, the forms they had to fill out, and the need to put the orders to tender—a process that would take at least three months. We knew that by that time, all of Dr. Hornetz's kids would be lying cold in their graves. David Copp, normally cool and level-headed, emerged on December 12, 1984, from his UNIPAC negotiations totally exasperated. We had less than 12 days to locate, order, package, and load the medical supplies we had promised to Dr. Hornetz.

What we were able to obtain from UNIPAC was an itemized list of exactly what made up a WHO emergency kit for a population of 50,000 people. We discovered there was nothing magical about the kits, and with a little legwork, we could assemble a reasonable facsimile ourselves. With some modifications, the list could be amended to accommodate the specific needs of a semi-nomadic population as found in the Ogaden desert. We also had to deal with the fact that there was little in the way of refrigeration; kerosene refrigerators had been ordered by the Lutheran World Federation but they had not yet arrived in the Ogaden.

We were getting in over our heads and badly needed someone with medical expertise on our Ethiopia Airlift team. We didn't have much time. John Godfrey tracked down Dr. Robert Tonks, the dean of health professions at Dalhousie University in Halifax, who was in the midst of supervising Christmas examinations for medical students, and asked him to spearhead the medical component of the airlift. Tonks's first reaction was that the airlift "seemed slightly crazy." In his opinion, the interval between the idea and take-off was too short and the resources in the Maritimes were too meagre, but he agreed to give it his best.

Using the long-distance credit card provided by Struan Robertson at Maritime Telephone, Dr. Tonks had several late-night conversations with Dr. Klaus Hornetz, who could be reached at his tented camp via satellite phone. He needed very specific drugs, including deworming pills, intravenous fluid, rehydration salt sachets, multi-vitamin tablets, and antibiotics. And he needed them desperately. Hornetz scratched out a five-page wish list, radioed it to the LWF country representative, Niels Nikolaisen, who in turn telexed it directly to the Ethiopia Airlift office at King's College. Within two days, Tonks and his associates at the Faculty of Health Professions had compiled a chart with over 300 items, including drugs to combat tuberculosis, dysentery, typhoid, and bilharzia. Some of the items could only be scrounged by way of a cross-country search of computerized inventories of provincial hospitals and departments of health. Amoebic dysentery was not a major health problem in Nova Scotia, but Bob Tonks was convinced we could find the antidote, Flagyl, in quantity somewhere in Canada. Working in close co-operation with Gerry Moulton, director of pharmacy services at the Nova Scotia Hospital, Dr. Tonks in seven days gathered $400,000 worth of drugs and medical equipment—enough to supply 12 clinics reaching a total of 50,000 children for three months. He and Moulton then conscripted pharmacy students, who were just emerging shell-shocked from their examinations, to package and label the supplies. All drugs came from new stock and none required refrigeration or sophisticated handling.

Walter Msimang and his co-workers at WUSC in the Ogaden were ecstatic when they heard that two DC-8 aircraft with their names on them would be arriving at Addis Ababa on Christmas Day. They had two last-minute requests. Ideally, the Canadian Food Supplement, milk powder, and sugar should be combined with vegetable oil for emergency feeding purposes. Vegetable oil is high in kilocalories and would dramatically increase the nutritional value of the CFS porridge. David Wilson, in co-operation with Bernie Miller, the director of freight operations for Air Canada in Atlantic Canada, did a recalculation of the space allocation on the aircraft. Somehow they were able to find room for 13,620 kilograms of vegetable oil, half of which would be donated by Canada Packers and half paid for through contributions to Ethiopia Airlift. Canada Packers did not have the oil in stock and had to initiate a separate production run. Their employees, just a few days before Christmas, worked around the clock to produce and package the oil in 44-gallon drums, which were then shipped to Mirabel Airport, where both DC-8s would be loaded.

A second problem related to the mechanics of eating. We had food for hungry kids but we had nothing for them to eat it with. Kids, whether they be from the Ogaden or from Oklahoma, need bowls and eating utensils. Because of weight restrictions, the items had to be plastic, but they also had to be durable. Could we find bowls and spoons for approximately 12,500 children?

Since it was housed within the confines of Canada's oldest university, Ethiopia Airlift addressed the challenge of feeding hungry children much like a student preparing for an examination: our first stop was the library. Our volunteer managers at the Ethiopia Airlift office, Barbara Daniels and Alan Riches, had already accumulated a small collection of erudite texts on the subject of disaster management. Their titles included *The Emergency Supply Logistics Handbook*, published by the League of Red Cross and Red Crescent Societies in Geneva, *Model Rules for Disaster Relief Operations*, and the *World Food Program Handbook on Food Storage Practice*, 1979 edition. From the *United Nations High Commissioner for Refugees Handbook for Emergencies*, we gleaned the essential components for a lightweight and useful feeding kit. A "family cooking set" for emergency purposes comprised 11 items: one six-litre and one four-litre cooking pot with bail handles and covers, four aluminum dinner plates, four plastic mugs, and a two-litre aluminum coffee pot. According to the *UNHCR Handbook for Emergencies*, "The set is packed in a cardboard carton 25 x 25 x 20 cm, weight 2 kg. The set does not contain cutlery: five stainless-steel soup spoons and one stainless-steel cook's knife, blade 15-17 cm, could be supplied separately if not available locally.... The advantages of the emergency set are lower weight, packed volume, and price. It is therefore particularly suitable when supply by air is necessary."

It made sense. We were getting progressively better at scrounging, and as the month progressed, John Godfrey began to assume the guise of a battlefield commander. Now that he had officially lost the first election of his life, he could devote all his energy to the cause of the airlift. Someone else could run King's College. John was becoming more strategic and developed a nose for potential donors who we could hit up. No one would be spared. For feeding kits, he turned to the president of Mount Saint Vincent University, Dr. Margaret Fulton, who in turn circulated photocopies of the relevant pages from the *UNHCR Handbook for Emergencies* among local Halifax businesses. With dogged determination, Dr. Fulton scavenged the city for suitable materials to include in the feeding kits. Thousands of plastic bowls, featuring a cartoon image of a leprechaun, were obtained from an ice-cream company that had recently gone bankrupt. When I visited the Ogaden desert more than two years later, I discovered to my amusement that many of the bowls were still in use.

As CFS led to feeding kits, so the provision of pots and bowls necessitated cooking and storage tents. Not any tent would do. The *UNHCR Handbook for Emergencies* came complete with a warning for civilians stumbling around in the dark searching for temporary accommodation for refugees:

> Tent specifications are to be understood as minimum in material weight and floor space. Only quality, heavy-duty, finished tents must be offered. Canvas to be equally strong in warp and weft. Chemicals used for treatment of the canvas must not smell offensive; salamander flame-retardant, rot and waterproofing process, or equivalent. Sufficient iron or steel pegs and pins to be supplied to anchor tent and fly every 50 cm (pegs 40 cm, pins 15 cm long). Stitching—machine stitched with extra strong, weatherproof thread. Ridges to be canvas or cotton-tape reinforced. Cabs and taps strongly stitched at outer and inner ridge for upright poles. Eyelets must be non-ferrous. Hems to be wide enough to accept eyelets. Entrance fasteners, zippers, clips, ties to be of heavy duty, where applicable non-ferrous quality, flaps well overlapping, unless zipped. All openings for ventilation or windows to be protected with mosquito netting. Zippered door flaps to have spare ties sewn

on, in case zipper breaks. Guy ropes to be equivalent in strength to 12-mm sisal rope, ultra-violet stabilized. Wooden or bamboo poles are not acceptable. Lengths of pole sections not to exceed 1.5 m. Mallet with 40-cm handle (10-cm diameter wooden or hard-rubber head) advised.

The instructions were daunting, but Godfrey merely appended them to the orders he was sending to his next victim—Canada's Department of National Defence. It turned out the specifications were in line with the military's own requirements, and within 48 hours, 850 kilograms of tents and related materials—including six wooden mallets—had been delivered to the Air Canada Maintenance Hangar at Halifax International Airport.

It didn't end there. The Annapolis Valley Women's Association knitted blankets by the dozen for the airlift. Other last-minute requests from the field, which, with a single phone call to Dave Wright, were fulfilled with relative ease, included 10 pressure-cookers to be used as sterilizers, 50 oil stoves, mattresses, teaching charts, weigh scales to check the progress of the kids we were feeding, and 100 rolls of plastic sheeting. ("Black seamless polyethylene sheeting, 250 microns [1000 gauge], width 5–8 m, supplied double-folded in lengths usually of 100–800 m, approx. Weight 1 kg/4m2. For multi-purpose use: roofing, walls, ground sheets, linings, etc. Widely available.")

Somehow we forgot to inform Air Canada in Montreal that one of the DC-8 aircraft would have to land in Halifax to take on supplies. They had quite reasonably assumed that all of the equipment and food items would be trucked to their cargo facility at Mirabel Airport, just outside Montreal, but we didn't have time. Now the loadmaster at Mirabel would have to calculate how much of the volume of one aircraft had to be set aside for goods we were accumulating in Halifax, including 14,528 kilograms of milk powder from Farmers' Co-operative Dairy. Just days before the planes were scheduled to leave, we still had not finalized the waybill for Air Canada and Canada Customs purposes. What complicated the matter was that large aircraft cannot land on full fuel tanks; the plane being routed through Halifax would therefore only load enough fuel for the Halifax portion of the flight at Mirabel, and would be topped off in Halifax. David Wilson, who was majoring in history, was becoming extremely well versed in the language of the international air-cargo business. At the conclusion of the airlift, Bernie Miller of Air Canada Cargo offered him a full-time job with the airline.

I was being haunted by the words of the blond-haired kid from Boutiliers Point Elementary School. Already the press had written lurid stories datelined Assab and Massawa about 40-foot containers of relief supplies being ripped open and pillaged by thieves at the country's two main ports. According to several reports, shiploads of grain were rotting on the docks, exposed to the sun and the rats. How could I keep the promise I had made that "every cent" of the money we raised would get to the kids in Africa?

It was becoming clear to John, Arthur, and me that someone would have to travel with the aircraft to Ethiopia to ensure the supplies actually got into the hands of the people for whom they were intended. From the telexes we were receiving from Niels Nikolaisen, director of the Lutheran World Federation in Ethiopia, and Walter Msimang, this would be no easy feat. Getting the aircraft to Addis Ababa was in fact the easy part of our little logistics operation. We would need trucks, preferably rugged, four-wheel-drive vehicles, to transport our 88 MT over 700 kilometres to our destinations in the Ogaden desert. However, almost all the trucks in the country were being employed in Wollo Region for the massive relief operation taking place there, in the wake of the flood of international media attention the famine had received.

In Addis Ababa, we might be able to hire market lorries, usually 20-year-old Bedford trucks, but even they were only to be had at a premium. For Ethiopian businessmen with access to transport equipment, the famine was a gold rush. It was a truck-driver's market and they demanded to be paid up front with U.S. dollars. Even then, there was no guarantee our supplies would ever arrive. Pilfering from trucks was rampant. Much of the Ogaden was not secure, and all truck convoys required military escort. But military escorts take time to arrange and need to be provided in advance with diesel fuel and food for the journey. Little fuel was available in the Ogaden and had to be flown in from the capital, but no aircraft were available. Nikolaisen warned us that we faced the possibility of all our supplies being unceremoniously dumped onto the tarmac at the Addis Ababa airport, where they would remain until we were able to secure transport. If they weren't moved within 24 hours, we could even face stiff fines from the airport authorities. I suggested to Godfrey that if things didn't go according to plan, all we would require was a one-way ticket to Ethiopia.

At the same time, no one in Ethiopia ever discouraged us from going ahead with the airlift. Walter Msimang and Niels Nikolaisen were consistently upbeat about it all. "Don't worry," Walter said. "In Africa, we always find a way." One thing was clear: at this point, turning back was not an option for us. Dr. Hornetz was already dreaming of shiny new sterilizers for his clinics and of his empty shelves suddenly overflowing with $400,000 worth of fresh pharmaceuticals from Canada. The WUSC field personnel were planning how the supplementary-feeding supplies would be allocated among the Ogaden communities they were responsible for.

It was the Toronto publisher Larry Heisey who suggested John and I travel with the aircraft to Ethiopia. Godfrey had been to Africa before and was an experienced traveller. He is a natural troubleshooter and diplomat, skills that could come in handy when dealing with stubborn local officials requiring that before our trucks move, we produce documentation, translated into Amharic, in triplicate. I needed to go to Ethiopia so I could report back to Dave Wright's audience and to all the schools I was visiting on what we had done with the funds they had contributed.

The Ethiopia Airlift office was now operating 18 hours a day. We had to install two new phone lines and buy a second coffee-maker. The walls were covered with relief maps from the Ogaden, long telex printouts from Hornetz, Msimang, and the Canadian embassy in Addis Ababa, and discount coupons from my Lebanese pizzeria. Arthur Andrew assumed the role of comptroller, drafting a budget for the airlift and supervising the deposit of cheques and cash that came in. He also intervened when we faced ethical issues, most commonly when substantial cheques arrived from pensioners or other people who were in financial need themselves.

Dave Wright at ATV created an Ethiopia Airlift thermometer for the studio, tracking the amount of money we had raised to date. Every night on *Live at Five*, Dave Wright featured an item about a school or a bingo hall that had sponsored an event for the airlift. He urged all of Atlantic Canada to "get on board for Ethiopia." On my regular Friday appearances, Dave peppered me with questions about airlift logistics, conditions in Ethiopia, and stories of generosity on the part of his viewing audience. He announced with glee that I had decided to travel with the two DC-8 aircraft to Ethiopia, promising his entire viewing audience that "under Peter's watchful eye, not one gram of our relief supplies will go to waste." I didn't dare mention the scarcity of trucks, the lack of fuel, highway bandits, or the idea that our supplies might be baking in the sun at Addis Ababa airport for a considerable length of time.

Atlantic Canada did in fact get on board for Ethiopia. The employees of Bathurst Mining in New Brunswick initiated a payroll deduction program, with all proceeds going to Ethiopia Airlift. The City of Halifax set up a program in all the city's banks and raised $50,000 to fund the Canadian Food Supplement, which was now rising like Lazarus off the shelves of Griffiths Laboratories in Toronto. The inhabitants of the island of Campobello, New Brunswick, in the Bay of Fundy launched "Campobello on the Move for Ethiopia," which included a series of fundraising events for the airlift. Schools by the dozen held raffles, dances, and trivia contests. The Académie Notre Dame in Dalhousie, New Brunswick, sold popcorn and hot-dogs, raising $1,275.84. The girls and boys of Sackville Heights Elementary School in Nova Scotia held a concert in their gymnasium and raised $279.17. The Liverpool Town Schools on the South Shore of Nova Scotia contributed over $900. The showing of a noon-hour film at Nashwaaksis Junior High School in Fredericton, New Brunswick, resulted in a donation of $64.47. The students from Room 316 at Westisle Composite High School in Elmsdale, Prince Edward Island, contributed $102. Sister Blanche Dupuis of École Élémentaire Champlain in Moncton, New Brunswick, mailed us a cheque for $300, the proceeds from a school concert.

The donations kept pouring in from all across Atlantic Canada. Within six months from its launch in mid-November, 1984, we had raised a total of $465,000. No donations came from government, other than the charter of the two aircraft. Our typical donor was a rural family with young children with an income of less than $30,000 a year. Many of our donors were elderly people, and numerous cheques came with heartfelt letters testifying to the poverty and hardship in their own lives that they had overcome. Our donors crossed all political and cultural boundaries; we had contributions from large companies and from union halls, from synagogues and Sikh temples. A number of donors were in prison and wanted to know if they could help us with research or any other tasks, as they had plenty of spare time on their hands. I was particularly moved when a homeless person, standing outside the Midtown Tavern in Halifax, handed me half the proceeds from his day of panhandling. "I may be poor," he said, "but those kids in Africa are dirt poor."

The outpouring of support from people of all walks of life, their letters, the meals people brought to volunteers working in our office, had a humbling effect on everyone involved with the airlift. I had never before witnessed such generosity. I learned that in most people there lies untapped a reservoir of goodwill. Despite the cynicism of the media, people still feel a strong need to demonstrate compassion for fellow human beings. People need to be needed. Bernard Kouchner, the founder of the humanitarian relief organization Médecins Sans Frontières, has travelled the world on behalf of hungry and sick people, and knows the restorative power that flows from coming to the assistance of people in need: "I have known the exaltation of solidarity; the pride, for example, of French children collecting rice for their friends in Somalia," he once wrote for *EnRoute* magazine. "Can there be any greater happiness than seeing hope reborn in the eyes of someone whom we have helped save from death?"

Ethiopia Airlift was essentially one big barn-raising and everyone wanted to be part of it. We were witnessing the birth of an authentic community-to-community aid program, designed and run by volunteers. Television, the telephone, and the telex machine had made it possible to link two very disparate worlds. We were defying the experts, the executives who run the charities that have brought about the institutionalization of compassion. We were proving that the farmer from the Annapolis Valley and the fisherman from Mahone Bay, Nova Scotia, had something besides their wallets to offer the people of Africa.

Over the years, my work designing community-service projects for children and youth has shown me that even hardened adolescent young offenders have the capacity to care for other human beings, and that we gain strength when we are asked to give something of ourselves. I have seen young people who have been living in the streets of Canada's largest cities acquire extraordinary self-confidence when given a chance to volunteer. I have visited recycling projects run by former street youth who, when trusted with the responsibility of managing a business, became productive members of the community. A door had been opened for them to mainstream society. Helping others is life-affirming. The street youth employed by the recycling centres tell those who will listen to them that, for the first time in their lives, someone actually needed them. Volunteering is an effective antidote to cynicism and apathy; we are reminded over and over again that there is a place for us here on earth. While Ethiopia Airlift and all the other organizations that responded to the great African famine did extraordinary things for the people of Africa, the challenge of responding to the famine made better citizens out of everyone who decided to get involved. We learned, once again, that it is better to serve than to be served.

We christened the airplanes Donner and Blitzen, and hastily organized a departure ceremony at the Air Canada maintenance hangar for Christmas Eve. In a spare moment, Arthur Andrew took me aside and, in the manner of a concerned parent, warned me of the human suffering I was likely to encounter in Ethiopia. I had spent little time in developing countries, and Arthur knew from his experience overseas how debilitating it can be to experience human catastrophe first-hand. He had lived through war in Europe. Arthur told me I had to steel myself, to insulate myself from the worst of it, or I would not be able to function. I appreciated his concern, but I doubted I would be able to follow his advice. I throw myself completely into whatever project I take on, and I am not good at constructing a protective bubble for myself. I would make a poor journalist and probably a worse judge. Whatever lay in store for me in Ethiopia, I simply hoped I would be able to cope. I worried instead about very practical things, such as how I was going to be able to eat and where I would sleep at night, although I was not concerned about my physical security. I allowed myself one luxury: I brought along a diminutive Sony short-wave radio so I could pick up the CBC's broadcasts to Africa. I wanted to receive hockey scores from back home.

When I arrived at the Halifax cargo terminal, Blitzen had not yet arrived from Montreal. Air Canada cargo employees, sacrificing their Christmas Eve, were buzzing about on forklifts moving pallets of powdered milk from the Farmers' Co-operative Dairy. Blitzen's other cargo were the tents and blankets, Dr. Hornetz's treasured pressure-cookers, oil stoves, the UNHCR-approved plastic sheeting, mattresses, disinfectant, teaching charts, weigh scales, and 550 kilos of drugs and medical supplies. We had designed a simple red-and-white Ethiopia Airlift sticker that was affixed to every package. Kids and parents were having their photographs taken standing next to the pallets. Bill MacLellan, the president of the Farmers' Co-operative Dairy, looked like a proud father.

Earlier that day in Montreal, Paul-Émile Cardinal Leger, the former Roman Catholic archbishop of Montreal, had presided over a brief inter-faith prayer ceremony at Mirabel Airport to commemorate the airlift. Given the lateness of the hour, I did not expect anyone to be at the Air Canada maintenance hangar to see off Blitzen, but more than 100 people had braved an early snowstorm, and instead of gathering around the Christmas tree in their homes with their families, had decided to spend Christmas Eve in a dark and cold hangar large enough to house eight games of basketball played simultaneously.

At one end of the terminal, a makeshift stage had been constructed with pallets of milk powder and medical supplies as a backdrop. When I arrived, a school choir was singing Christmas carols, ending with "Silent Night." Dr. Russ Hatton of the Atlantic School of Theology led this unusual congregation in a short but memorable Christmas Eve service, reminding us that as the Christmas star in the far east attracted the wise men bearing gifts to Bethlehem, so the cause of fighting famine in Africa was drawing these shiny aircraft across the Atlantic Ocean, the Mediterranean, and the Sahara Desert. John Godfrey took the microphone and thanked all the volunteers who had made the airlift possible. When it came my turn to speak, I held up the clipping from the *Halifax Chronicle-Herald* of the child who had been clinging so desperately to his father in northern Ethiopia that had inspired me to launch the airlift in the first place. I had no idea if the boy was dead or alive, but for thousands of other children, our efforts meant they would at least have a fighting chance.

The Air Canada pilots who flew Donner and Blitzen that night volunteered their time, which was in keeping with the spirit of the airlift. We had even managed to scrounge pilots! Both Donner and Blitzen had just returned from trips to France, where they had delivered 88 MT of live Nova Scotian lobsters, which many French evidently prefer for their Christmas dinner. Now they would be loading a very different cargo. After the speeches had ended and the choir had finished singing, Arthur hustled John and me along. We had to get moving or we were going to miss our flight. I needed to eat and I hadn't slept in two days. I was leaving Canada with a sense of exhilaration about what we had accomplished, but also with apprehension about what lay ahead. Just as I exited the hangar I thought I saw the blond-haired kid from the Grade 6 class at Boutiliers Point Elementary School among the crowd, but then I lost him. If we had had a moment to speak, I would have said to him that I hadn't forgotten my promise.

Shortly after midnight, the Air Canada cargo stretch DC-8 lumbered down the runway, using up almost all of its length, then slowly climbed into the winter sky. Bernie Miller was standing at the end of the runway, motioning with his hands as if to encourage the plane to fly. He later said it was the happiest moment of his life. While the people of the Maritime provinces slept, Donner and Blitzen made their way out over the Atlantic, where the light of Christmas Day would greet them.

THE WORLD I
NEVER KNEW

The Ethiopian farmers who employed pick axes, hoes, and shovels to break the earth and plant their crops knew years before the foreign experts that a devastating famine was imminent. They didn't need infrared photographs taken from satellites to understand that urgent action was required if their land was to be saved. Seasonal rains were declining and ground water was disappearing. Wells that for 20 years had produced good water had run dry. Certain species of birds vanished. In scenes reminiscent of the dust bowls of the Great Depression, the rich, red earth of Wollo and Tigre turned from brown to white dust that was swept up in windstorms and carried away to the sea. Almost overnight, entire farms disappeared. Villages were transformed into ghost towns as people began the long walk to the cities, their children in tow.

Most accounts of the Ethiopian famine begin on October 23, 1984, the night the BBC devoted a few minutes on the evening news to the story of hunger in a place called Korem. The international community, including donor nations such as Canada and the United States, takes great pride in the manner in which it responded to Mohammed Amin's horrific images of destitute women and children. But why did it take a television newsreel for the developed world to react to a famine that, for more than two years, had been predicted by the UN World Food Program in Rome and by the Ethiopian government's own advanced Early Warning System, which had been established several years earlier with the specific purpose of providing sufficient lead time for donors and aid agencies to respond to drought and famine? In the final report issued in 1986 by the umbrella group of Canadian non-governmental organizations that responded to the African famine, there is only one short reference to this issue. "Why donor countries did not respond to earlier and frequent calls for help from authoritative agencies that had been closely monitoring the famine's gruesome march is perhaps best left to historians."

Historians rarely conduct post-mortems, however, and most donor countries are loath to examine the shortcomings of their own largesse. No government can be proud of the way it responded to the plight of hungry people in Ethiopia prior to the night of October 23, 1984. The 1984 Ethiopian famine was not the first episode of mass starvation that went ignored by the international community. In 1968, the developed world stood by while Nigeria starved hundreds of thousands of Biafran children caught up in that country's civil war. Even mass murder fails to move the policy-makers of Washington, Paris, and London. In the 1970s, the West closed its eyes and ears to repeated and consistent reports of genocide being practised in Cambodia by the Khmer Rouge. At secret prisons such as Tuol Sleng, code-named S-21, Cambodian men, women, and children were tortured and killed by the followers of Pol Pot. I have the photographs of some of the victims, painstakingly compiled by the U.S.-based Photo Archive Group, in front of me now as I write. Many of them are young girls and boys. The condemned have numbers pinned to their chests—some fastened directly onto their skin. From the terror in their eyes, they must have known they were only minutes away from their own execution.

At the international level, there are few good Samaritans. Countries rarely provide protection or assistance to people in need out of the goodness of their hearts; furthering their own national interests is a much more common motive. In 1984, Menghistu's Marxist Ethiopia was no one's priority. An entire country fell through the cracks of the international aid system.

Similarly, it has always been in the interests of non-government organizations, whose business it is to address the needs of populations in danger, to avoid asking questions that might explore the limits of their arrogance, indifference, and incompetence. Throughout 1983 and 1984, the tight-knit fraternity of non-government organizations working in Africa—despite their large staffs with representatives posted throughout the Sahel, and despite the enormous resources at their disposal—paid scant attention to the regular reports from the field that a human catastrophe was imminent in Ethiopia, the dimensions of which were both immense and incalculable.

A few charities, such as Catholic Relief Services and some of the smaller church groups, played the role of Cassandra, predicting the famine but never being believed. For most international development agencies, however, the 1984 Ethiopian famine was not their finest hour. Some of the agencies didn't care one way or another about Ethiopia; the regime in power at the time was brutal and repressive, and out of favor with the West. Yet it should not be the business of humanitarian organizations to play favorites, or to punish farmers and pastoralists for the errors of their leaders. For the larger agencies, their failure to respond to the Ethiopian crisis reflected the bias of their institutional and government donors. Many humanitarian organizations depend for a vast proportion of their budgets on the donor nations' international development agencies, such as the U.S. Agency for International Development (USAID) in Washington, DFID in London, and ECHO in Brussels. Too often their programming is based not on the needs of a given region or population but rather on the funding priorities of the day. For whatever reasons, in 1984, famine in Ethiopia was not on the agenda for the world's international community.

Amin's footage changed everything. When the full horror of the famine was revealed, representatives of governments and the media scrambled for cover. Under the guise of investigative journalism, the West searched for excuses for its inaction in order to salve its wounds and to alleviate its collective guilt. There was much finger-pointing. In the months that followed, American and European journalists went out of their way to portray the Ethiopian authorities who were managing relief operations in their own country as poorly trained, undisciplined, and lacking dedication. There were repeated reports in the Western press of corruption at the highest levels of government in Addis Ababa, and accusations that Ethiopian authorities had ignored warnings of famine in the Wollo and Tigre regions. Inevitably, investigative journalists used the civil war under way in the north to condone the West's indifference to famine in Ethiopia. Ethiopia was an international outlaw among nations, and its citizens were not considered to be worthy of food aid.

The stories made newspaper editors happy, but were largely without merit. For over two years, the Relief and Rehabilitation Commission in Addis Ababa had issued specific warnings of the extent of the famine engulfing the northern half of Ethiopia. The Relief and Rehabilitation Commission, which had the overall responsibility for planning and carrying out relief operations throughout Ethiopia, was unmatched in Africa for its professionalism and technical expertise, and was held up by many donor nations as a model for the entire continent. The RRC's Early Warning System functioned exactly as it was designed. Rain levels and market prices for various commodities had been plotted, recorded, and telexed off to development agencies and press offices around the world. The RRC and Ethiopian officials fully expected the West would respond, and that the trucks, irrigation equipment, seeds, tools, and food would be forthcoming in the quantities that were needed to maintain the rural population until there was a good harvest. But repeated appeals issued by the RRC, and backed up by independent reports from the United Nations Food and Agriculture Organization, were met with silence.

As each month passed, as huge tracts of arable land turned to dust, as local storage systems set up by farmers were emptied, and as entire herds of livestock perished, the authorities in Addis Ababa grew desperate. By May, 1984, when the short rains failed in virtually all regions of the country, they knew with absolute certainty that unless the international community intervened on an unprecedented scale, thousands of people would perish. Urgent appeals were issued to Western donors, as they had been during the previous 18 months, but again, they were met with silence.

Throughout 1984, the Relief and Rehabilitation Commission produced five reports on the drought and famine situation in the country, listing the relief requirements needed by the drought-affected population, region by region. The reports are remarkably passionate, written with an intensity that one rarely finds in government publications. In early August, 1984, the RRC estimated that approximately 6.4 million people needed immediate relief assistance for a period of 12 months. The emergency requirements included food, medical supplies, water systems, and transport. The international donor community was urged to provide 521,428 MT of emergency food assistance. At its October, 1984, donors' meeting, after its appeals had been for the most part ignored and in the face of catastrophic famine, the RRC raised its estimated emergency food requirements to one million MT. At the same meeting, the United States pledged 40,000 MT of grain, but by the end of December, 1984, not one sack had arrived. The United Kingdom, under the leadership of Margaret Thatcher, had delivered a total of 3,005 MT, a paltry amount by anyone's standards. The Iron Lady was determined to punish the people of Ethiopia for falling into step with their left-wing dictator. Her intention was to starve the Menghistu regime out of power.

In its 1984 year-end report issued in Addis Ababa, the Relief and Rehabilitation Commission wrote, "With its well-established framework of prediction and response to drought situations, and with its certain knowledge of what would happen unless massive support was forthcoming from early in the year onward, the RRC viewed with grave and mounting concern the lack of support from the international community on the one hand, and the increasing dislocation and migration from their homes and villages in search of food of those affected by the serious drought on the other hand. There was little recognition of the problem on the part of the donor community and therefore little serious response, in spite of the RRC's strong and urgent appeals for assistance, both at individual meetings with donor agencies and after its March and August, 1984, appeals."

In its December, 1984, report, the Relief and Rehabilitation Commission acknowledged with appreciation that, at last, the international community was beginning to respond to the nation's plight. Well aware of the fickleness and short attention span of many donor nations, however, the RRC appended a warning: "...the visits and words of the hundreds of visitors the RRC has hosted over the last two months must be translated into the arrival of grain at the ports, the filling of regional and sub-regional stores with the grain, and the immediate distribution of this grain into the hands of those who need it now and who will need it over the coming months. It is only if this happens on a much-increased scale that the present tragedy will be overcome; if it does not happen, the situation will deteriorate to a horrifying and almost unimaginable extent, and the world will have on its conscience the responsibility for a catastrophe which it could so easily have prevented."

The writers of the RRC's December, 1984, report pleaded with foreign governments that this time, its words of warning be heeded. The sense of despair and impending doom is unmistakable:

> The situation is now clear. Death and starvation are all that millions of drought-affected people can look forward to, unless the requirements noted in this review are met. In spite of repeated attempts by the RRC throughout the year to gain the wholehearted support and commitment of the international donor community, this has not been forthcoming to the degree warranted by the present catastrophic situation. The world now has a chance to show that, from its feelings of common humanity, it has the will to face up to the challenge that now confronts it: this would entail changes in its present position, a revision of its present attitudes, a revision of its institutional response mechanisms so that bureaucracies can be broken through, and the taking of a major decision that it is not willing, at this late stage, to countenance a growing number of deaths amongst the drought-affected population for the lack of the simplest and most basic commodities of which the world has a surplus. Grain is what is needed in Ethiopia immediately, and the

means to grow grain in the future. Pledges have been made, and methods must be found, on the most urgent and priority basis, of bringing the grain pledged to the country without any delay. Large additional amounts of grain need to be pledged, with all the logistic support that is needed, to bring relief to those who are now dying for the lack of it.

This is the challenge, which could be met by the donor community without difficulty, providing the will to meet it was there. Let it not be said in future that the world forgot Ethiopia at the time of one of its gravest crises.

Drought is nothing new to Ethiopia or to Africa. Rwanda was devastated by famine in 1653 and Guinea in 1716. The first historical record of drought in Ethiopia dates back to the 9th century. We know that 23 famines took place in Ethiopia between 1540 and 1800. When Ethiopians speak today about the Great Famine, they are referring to the years between 1888 and 1892 when, in many villages, there were children who had reached their fourth birthday without having seen one drop of rain; two-thirds of the country's population perished.

In recent years, drought in Africa has worried scientists because of signs of a long-term trend that has been developing over the last 25 years. Rainfall levels have been declining to 50-year lows, and the Sahara Desert relentlessly advances south along a front stretching thousands of kilometres from Dakar on the Atlantic Ocean to Djibouti on the Red Sea. The 1984 Ethiopian famine represented a widening ecological catastrophe, the causes of which were varied and complex.

Apart from humans, the animal that has caused the most damage to the ecology of the region is the same cow that provides life to hundreds of thousands of pastoralists. The hooves of cattle are hard and sharp, and often dig up the ground cover. When cattle graze, they usually uproot and destroy the plants. In comparison, a camel's feet are large and soft, and do not damage the earth. Camels are known as "high browsers": they forage at the tree-top level, and mostly leave plants, bushes, and trees intact. Camels also graze over a much larger area than cattle. In recent years, development agencies such as Oxfam working in east Africa have initiated camel-breeding projects in an attempt to encourage pastoralists to switch from cattle to camels. Camel milk is high in protein and the animals are prized for the quality of their meat. It has been proven that as long as pastoralists can keep their camels alive, their children are essentially immune to the effects of a famine. Nutritionists are often surprised to find nomadic children who are healthy and well nourished in the midst of a horrific famine. Inevitably, their animals are still with them.

Much of the African rangelands are entirely unsuitable for year-round cattle-grazing. Since time immemorial, pastoralists have moved their cattle to coincide with wet and dry seasons and the resulting availability of water and areas for grazing their livestock. Over the course of a year, cattle may be moved along a circuit hundreds of kilometres in length. When cattle are not present, the land has the opportunity to recover and new plants soon take root.

Unfortunately, in many parts of the Sahel the indiscriminate drilling of boreholes by well-intentioned aid agencies has caused irreparable damage to what were previously only seasonal pastures. The site of a borehole gushing clear, clean water in the middle of a desolate plain makes a great photo opportunity for charities that are largely dependent on donations from the public for their day-to-day operations. Unfortunately, the increased availability of water due to borehole construction has resulted in much larger herds of cattle remaining for longer periods of time in marginal areas, leading to reduced vegetation cover, increased water and wind erosion, and sand drifting. Inevitably the demands for clean water for animals proves insatiable. Over-grazing by larger and larger herds of cattle has transformed millions of acres of arable African land into desert. New boreholes also create intense population pressures on the land as people tend to settle around reliable water sources. Boreholes are often drilled in areas totally inappropriate for human settlement, with no protection from the wind or sun and poor-quality soil that does not lend itself to cultivation.

When the desert moves, people move too. The process of desertification leads to the displacement of entire populations. Pastoralists in search of range-lands for their animals are forced to move south, where they come in conflict with sedentary farmers. At the same time, governments, in an attempt to fend off starvation, relocate entire populations considered to be in danger. During the 1970s and early 1980s, the government of Ethiopia declared large parts of Wollo and Tigre uninhabitable; between 1971 and 1978, as many as 110,000 families were reported to have been evacuated from Wollo to the more southern regions of Sidamo and Bale. Although the evacuation was billed as being only a temporary measure, the families never returned to their homelands.

Over the last century, much of Africa's virgin forests have been cut and burned as a source of cooking fuel for ever-growing populations. In 1900, 44 per cent of Ethiopia was tree-covered. By 1984, only 4 per cent was covered by trees. As trees are cut down, the temperature of the surrounding land increases and the moisture content drops, resulting in reduced evaporation and less chance for rain in the surrounding area. The destruction of Africa's forests has facilitated soil erosion as root networks and natural windbreaks are destroyed. Millions of tonnes of valuable soil are swept away. In addition, trees are natural reservoirs, retaining within their cell structure vast quantities of rain water. In regions where clear-cutting has taken place, seasonal flooding is now a perennial problem, resulting in loss of millions of tonnes of topsoil every year.

*   *   *

It was the middle of the night and I was the only passenger awake on the plane. Under the dim, unfocused light of my overhead reading lamp, I scanned the reports of the Relief and Rehabilitation Commission and the UN Food and Agriculture Organization as we approached the coast of Scotland. The statistics flowing from the famine underlined the scope of the emergency. Millions of cattle had already died as a result of the continuing drought. The famine had been so intense in many parts of the country that farmers and their families had resorted to eating the seed they had dried and stored for the upcoming planting season; the RRC was therefore requesting 32,220 MT of maize and sorghum seeds for distribution at the village level. Fertilizers were needed to rejuvenate the soil.

The existing RRC truck fleet consisted of 278 vehicles, most of which had been in operation for over 20 years. The trucks, primarily Mercedes and Volvo diesel transports, were badly in need of maintenance and spare parts, as well as fuel and lubricants. Some of the trucks hadn't been used in more than 10 years and were sitting derelict on blocks. The RRC required tires, fan belts, air filters, brake pads, and springs. In order to facilitate the transport of relief commodities, the RRC requested that donors provide 496 new trucks of 10-tonne capacity and 834 22-tonne trucks with trailers. In addition, many roads were impassable and numerous bridges had collapsed. Appended to the RRC report was a long list of equipment required for road construction and maintenance, including 20 dozers, 25 dump trucks, and 10 D8K crawler-tractors. Water for drinking, washing, and crop irrigation was a priority. Wells needed to be drilled and capped; for this purpose, the RRC urgently required four percussion well-drilling machines and 50 generators, as well as hand pumps, polyurethane piping, and casings.

From the documents it was apparent that the emergency relief operation under way in Ethiopia was already a huge undertaking and was getting bigger every day. As of the middle of December, 1,350 foreign pilots, technicians, and truck drivers were employed in the delivery of relief commodities. The Soviet

Union had seconded 12 Antanov cargo aircraft and 24 helicopters to the RRC. Already 131 foreign medical staff were on site in hospitals and clinics across the country. But the critical issue was speeding up the delivery of grain and supplementary feeding materials to food-distribution centres in the worst-affected areas.

Although 181,486 MT of grain had been pledged by donor nations since October, 1984, by December only 83,608 MT had arrived in the country. Between October and December, 1984, Canada had delivered more grain than any other nation, approximately 20,105 MT. Politics had much to do with who was and who was not helping to feed Ethiopia. The People's Democratic Republic of Yemen had managed to deliver 2,614 MT of grain, North Korea 1,012 MT, and 10,000 MT of grain had already arrived from the USSR. The U.S. and France had delivered nothing.

I was exhausted, and the numbers on the charts spread out on the fold-down table began to blur. Feeding hungry kids in Ethiopia had become my obsession, and I had paid a personal price. Relationships with friends had suffered. I had forgotten my sister's and father's November birthdays, and I hadn't even begun my Christmas shopping. My banker was on my back; for weeks I hadn't returned his phone calls. My law books had gone untouched for over a month, and I was now more familiar with traditional irrigation practices in northern Ethiopia than the intricacies of the Nova Scotia Civil Procedures Rules. In less than five months, I would have to sit for bar-admission examinations. If I didn't pass them, my years at law school would be wasted and no one would hire me. In any case, my chances of being kept on as a lawyer at Stewart, MacKeen and Covert were not improving. Publicity for the firm only counted for so much. The number of billable hours I had recorded for the firm since mid-October had dropped off the charts, setting a new record for inefficiency by an articling student. One lawyer had gone so far as to warn that the Law Society would have serious reservations about my application for admission as a barrister and solicitor. He suggested I consider taking up farming.

On board the aircraft I drifted between sleep and wakefulness, and my mind wandered back to my hometown and to memories of Christmases past. My mother being German, we began our Christmas celebrations on December 24. My mother would treat herself to smoked turkey breast, eel, herring, and other northern European specialties. My father, sister, brothers, and their families preferred ham and home-baked beans. For dessert, we would have the famous Nuremberg lebkuchen—gingerbread flavoured with honey, cinnamon, cloves, and cardamon. There would be fine wines to drink, and cognac after the meal by the fire. Eleven thousand metres over the Atlantic, my traditional Christmas dinner consisted of a few peanuts and pretzels washed down with a can of warm soda water.

I first crossed the Atlantic at the age of four with my mother en route to England aboard one of the most graceful airliners ever designed, the Lockheed Super Constellation. We stopped for fuel at Gander, Newfoundland, and were high over the water when my mother told me it was time to go to sleep, then disappeared toward the back of the plane. The only suitable place to retire for the night was the overhead luggage rack, which reminded me of my own bunk bed back home. Using my seat as a ladder, I slipped in among the coats and luggage items and made myself comfortable. By the time my mother returned from the lavatory, I was lost in my dreams, so with the assistance of the stewardess, she covered me with a blanket, and I slept soundly until we touched down in Reykjavik, Iceland.

Our landfall on the African coast was near Tobruk, the site of one of the most ferocious tank battles of World War II. Canadian kids were not expected to hold out German soldiers as heroes, but for me, General Rommel was the most intriguing character of World War II. It was at Tobruk on June 21, 1942, that Rommel's Afrika Corps with his mighty Panzer III and Panzer IV tanks routed the British 8th Army commanded by General Ritchie. For the British, the fall of Tobruk marked the nadir of the North African campaign. Rommel had proved to be a formidable adversary, and his Panzer tanks—especially the Panzer IV—were vastly superior to anything in the British arsenal. Things for the Allies looked bleak. Not even the military censors could disguise the magnitude of the defeat. British papers portrayed the fall of Tobruk as a national disgrace rivalled only by the fall of Singapore, which Churchill later described in his memoirs as "the worst loss and the greatest capitulation in history."

At Tobruk, the English under Ritchie turned tail but they couldn't run fast enough. Approximately 80 per cent of the transport used by the Germans to chase the retreating British forces that day was made up of captured British vehicles. Entire British tank brigades were handed over to Rommel in perfect running order, as well as warehouses filled with foodstuffs, fuel, and beer. Over 25,000 Allied prisoners were taken by the Germans, including a contingent of white South African officers who demanded to be held in separate detention quarters from black South African conscripts. Rommel refused their request, noting in his diary that the black African troops "wear the same uniform and they fought side by side with the whites. They are to be housed in the same POW cage." Today, if you walk the desert where the battle took place, you can still find empty shell casings and see shattered tank bodies protruding from the sand. There is a little memorial at Tobruk, and a cemetery maintained by the Commonwealth War Graves Commission, but from the air I could see only sand.

As a child I was captivated by Africa, and for my 10th birthday I received a *Boys' Own* collection of biographies of the continent's most famous explorers, including Burton and Speke. I had a marionette collection, and at the age of 11 I created a short play about the discovery of the source of the White Nile, performed by marionettes I had made myself. The story of the 1881 Mahdi Rebellion in Sudan, in which religious fundamentalists overwhelmed the Egyptian armies that administered the territory, enthralled me. I read over and over again the accounts of the emergency expedition sent by the British to relieve General Gordon, whose palace in Khartoum on the bank of the Blue Nile was under siege by the Mahdists. I was proud that Canadians had played a part in the attempted rescue of Gordon: young Iroquois from Ontario and Quebec were recruited by the British for the expedition because of their ability to navigate rapids in canoes. But the relief expedition did not arrive in time, and Gordon was killed as he stood on the steps of his palace.

I was 11 when I ordered my first map from the National Geographic Society in Washington. It was of North Africa, and around its edges were drawings of major events in African colonial history. To make room for the map on my bedroom wall, I had to take down my posters of Rocket Richard and Bobby Orr, two of Canada's hockey legends. I inserted red pins in locations where strategic battles had taken place, from ancient times through World War II. With the proceeds from my lucrative part-time job shovelling the snow off neighbors' driveways, I purchased a dog-eared copy of Winston Churchill's *The River War*. As a young reporter, Churchill tells the story of the British relief expedition sent to rescue Gordon, and of the Battle of Omdurman. Churchill wrote eloquently about the desert, and about the Nile.

> The area multiplies the desolation. There is life only by the Nile. If a man were to leave the river, he might journey westward and find no human habitation, nor the smoke of a cooking fire, except the lonely tent of a Kabbabish Arab or the encampment of a trader's caravan, till he reached the coast-line of America. Or he might go east and find nothing but sand and sea and sun until Bombay rose above the horizon. The thread of fresh water is itself solitary in regions where all living things lack company.

In the account of the River War the Nile is naturally supreme. It is the great melody that recurs throughout the whole opera. The general purposing military operations, the statesman who would decide upon grave policies, and the reader desirous of studying the course and results of either must think of the Nile. It is the life of the lands through which it flows. It is the cause of the war: the means by which we fight; the end at which we aim. Imagination should paint the river through every page in the story. It glitters between the palm-trees during the actions. It is the explanation of nearly every military movement. By its banks the armies camp at night. Backed or flanked on its unfordable stream they offer or accept battle by day. To the brink, morning and evening, long lines of camels, horses, mules, and slaughter cattle hurry eagerly. Emir and Dervish, officer and soldier, friend and foe, kneel alike to this god of ancient Egypt and draw each day their daily water in goatskin or canteen. Without the river none would have started. Without it none might have continued. Without it none could ever have returned.

In my estimation, for sheer storytelling ability, F. W. Dixon, the author of the Hardy Boys mystery books for kids, couldn't hold a candle to Winston Churchill. In an unprecedented act of generosity, I donated my 24-volume Hardy Boys set to my nine-year-old brother Michael. Generations of British youth had been raised on stories about the Nile, the men who explored its length, and the battles fought on its shores. I reckoned the same stories were good enough for me.

*   *   *

Somewhere between Lake Tana and Bole Airport in Addis Ababa, I fell asleep. I was jolted awake as the plane slammed into the runway. I still had my RRC reports and maps spread around my seat and they went flying about the cabin. It was almost midday and within minutes of the four jet engines being shut down, the cabin was stifling hot. I was hungry and tired and I badly needed a shower. I looked a wreck. John Godfrey had fared much better during the night, sleeping most of the flight. Somehow he had managed to shave and had changed into a clean, white, ironed shirt. I assumed he was gearing up for his role as diplomat and negotiator for Ethiopia Airlift.

We were prepared for the worst. We had been forewarned by officials of Canada's Department of External Affairs of Ethiopia's byzantine bureaucracy, that we could expect all our relief supplies to be held up for hours—even days—while papers were being processed. We did not relish this prospect. Although John and I had secured entry visas for ourselves, we still needed special permission to travel to the Ogaden desert, which was a high-security region with frequent and continuing skirmishes between Ethiopian and Somali soldiers. With the prospect of chronic ground-transport problems, we knew we could be in for a prolonged and frustrating stay in Addis Ababa.

But within hours of our arrival in Ethiopia's capital, all our relief supplies had been processed, our passports had been stamped, and we had been issued with all the necessary documentation for travel throughout the Ogaden desert. I could only imagine the red tape that would ensnarl any aircraft with foreign markings arriving at a Canadian airport stuffed full of African commodities.

We were not merely the beneficiaries of good fortune or Christmas cheer. In fact, Walter Msimang and his colleagues at the World University Service of Canada office in Addis Ababa had worked through the night to smooth the way for the arrival of Donner and Blitzen. Walter is a two-metre-high South African Zulu who had settled with his wife, Faith, and three daughters as a refugee in Canada, then been recruited by WUSC to head up their emergency-relief team in Ethiopia. I knew him only by way of his many telexes to our office. Walter exploited all his contacts within the Ethiopian government, the RRC, and the airport authorities to ensure the speedy processing of the Ethiopia Airlift supplies. His friend Niels Nikolaisen of the Lutheran World Federation had been in Addis Ababa for several years, and had an extensive network of associates within the aid agencies and the government itself. Niels had been very effectively lobbied by Dr. Klaus Hornetz to do everything in his power to clear the medical supplies through customs and transport them to his clinics without delay.

John Godfrey and I hit the ground running. There was no time to check into the Ghion Hotel. The penetrating African sun was our enemy. After clearing customs, we supervised the unloading of the supplies of the aircraft onto the tarmac and began a frantic search for tarpaulins that might offer some level of protection. It was the crew from the Royal Air Force C-130 Hercules who recognized our distress and came to our assistance, offering to stockpile and patrol all our supplies in their temporary compound erected at the southwest corner of the air field. They had transformed their allocated bit of asphalt into a home away from home, complete with folding chairs, a dart board, and the ubiquitous Union Jack fluttering in the breeze.

Addis Ababa was much more orderly than I had expected it to be. I had incorrectly assumed the capital city of a nation slowly wasting away would be a chaotic, even dangerous place, but Addis Ababa did not appear to be suffering any ill effects from the famine, and reminded me of a sunburnt Geneva—efficient but sterile. I noticed many cars had bumper stickers featuring the Ethiopian Airlines logo that proclaimed: "The 767 is coming!" Along the main road leading into the city from the airport I spotted a huge billboard erected by the Ethiopian Tourism Corporation with a pathetically ironic slogan: "Ethiopia—thirteen months of sunshine."

We needed trucks. According to the *UNHCR Handbook for Emergencies*, a "medium lorry" had a capacity of between six and eight MT. We therefore would require at least 11 trucks to carry our supplies to Diredawa, the staging point for relief operations in the Ogaden. From Diredawa, the supplies would be broken down into smaller units for transport by Land Rover and any other available means. A return trip from Addis Ababa to Diredawa could take as long as four days, depending on the condition of the roads.

Msimang and Nikolaisen had a better idea. From foreign pilots flying relief flights between the port of Assab and Addis Ababa whom they had met in local hotel bars, they learned there was an unexpected break in the off-loading of ships; suddenly there was a surplus of military-transport aircraft and crew members with nothing to do. Using all their persuasive powers, Msimang and Nikolaisen convinced representatives of three air forces to fly our supplies at no cost to Diredawa. After all my worrying, we had no need of medium lorries. The Luftwaffe, the East German, and the Libyan air forces came to the rescue of Ethiopia Airlift, the farmers who produced the milk powder, the students who packed the pharmaceutical supplies, and the good women of the Annapolis Valley who knitted the blankets. It was an unlikely alliance. The Ethiopian military donated the fuel, and the Canadian Embassy provided cases of Heineken beer as an incentive for the air crew who flew the missions. Within 48 hours of our arrival in Ethiopia, every commodity aboard Donner and Blitzen was flown to Diredawa aboard Antanov 12, C-130 Hercules, and Transal aircraft. After arrival in Diredawa, all the supplies were carefully packed in five warehouses and placed under 24-hour armed guard. Walter Msimang was right. In Africa, they always find a way.

*   *   *

Seasoned pilots in Africa prefer to fly as early in the day as possible, before the big cumulonimbus clouds begin to build and the sky becomes turbulent. On our second full day in Ethiopia, we made the mistake of leaving Addis Ababa on an Ethiopian Airlines DC-3 late in the afternoon, and within minutes I was turning green. Walter Msimang was sympathetic: "The Vomit Comet has claimed another victim." I was happy when we touched down in Diredawa, a beautiful town whose architecture and tree-lined streets betray its Italian colonial heritage.

With Walter behind the wheel of the Land Rover, we bumped up and down the road that took us out of Diredawa alongside the railway line in the direction of Djibouti. Behind us were trucks loaded with our supplies. We were the advance party, and our job was to ensure that in the towns of the Ogaden where the food and medical supplies would be distributed, there was adequate storage. Meanwhile, the real work was being undertaken by the Canadians of the World University Service of Canada, who were based in Diredawa but who spent most of their time in the desert. They included two former teachers and a drill operator from Alberta by the name of Jim Stevens, who knew everything there was to know about water and how to find it.

Like John and me, Jim had been moved to action by hungry kids he had seen on television and read about in the newspapers. He wore a baseball cap, and in the tradition of Canadian prairie towns, carried his cigarettes rolled up in the sleeve of his T-shirt. He was neither an academic nor a lawyer, but in the Ogaden, divining water is a particularly useful trick. Jim was at the top of the pecking order among relief workers, just above the niche reserved for mechanics and forklift operators. WUSC had purchased a $200,000 drilling rig specially outfitted for desert conditions; sitting behind the wheel, Jim looked like the captain of a ship. In a milieu that puts a premium on getting things done, and when the task at hand often involves feeding kids by the thousands at a single sitting, lawyers and university presidents are of limited value. Amidst the chaos of famine in the Ogaden Desert, a meritocracy emerged in which people were ordered not according to the degrees they had earned at fancy universities but rather according to their social utility. Pilots, nurses, doctors, engineers, excavators, agronomists, and veterinarians had all earned the right to be there. John and I were consigned to the role of spectators to human tragedy.

Drought and famine hit the Ogaden just as the region was emerging from more than 10 years of civil war with its neighbor, Somalia. The war was prolonged by the involvement of the USSR and the United States, which used the

With my big sister Fran.
People thought we were twins.

Michael Kane-Parry.

PAT KANE

PETER DALGLISH

Displaced women and children in the Ogaden,
December, 1984.

Korem, Northern Ethiopia, in February, 1985. These were the scenes of human devastation that moved millions of people around the world to take action.

Rations being distributed at a feeding center near Khartoum in February, 1985.

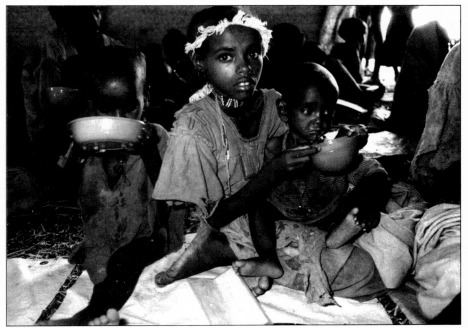

Refugees at a feeding center in Ethiopia in February, 1985. No matter how hungry or desperate, the children always sat quietly waiting for their rations to be distributed.

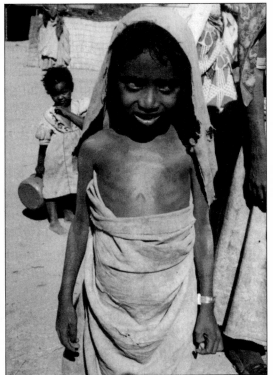

The child in Errer who inspired John Godfrey to launch Adopt-a-Village, September, 1984.

Dragging my
Toyota Landcruiser
across the wadi at
Bir Abu Zaima,
September, 1985.

Child in Northern Kordofan
amidst ruined crops,
September, 1985.
In some areas it hadn't
rained for three years.

Nomadic child
in Kordofan
near Bara,
August, 1985.

The lake at El Fasher,
September, 1985.
El Fasher was the
beginning of the
Forty Day Road,
the legendary
camel route across
the desert to Egypt.

PETER DALGLISH

Arriving at the refugee
camp at Assirni,
September, 1985.
In my journal I wrote,
"I arrived at Assirni
and remember why I
came to the Sudan in
the first place. Green
tents stretch as far as
the eye can see. I am
mobbed by hungry
stick children—
hundreds of them."

PETER DALGLISH

With my drivers, in
October, 1985, in
a village south of
El Geneina, having
delivered the first
relief commodities
to arrive in several
months. Garret
Adam is on my right
with the cigarette.

Christine Brown, the Joan of Arc of El Geneina, alongside Juicy Lucy, in October, 1985.

PETER DALGLISH

Peter Verney's camels loading up with American sorghum at the El Geneina market, October, 1985.

PETER DALGLISH

Child with truck constructed of reeds near El Geneina, October, 1985. There is no such thing as Toys Я Us in the Sudan. Refugee children working only with their hands constructed elaborate toys from whatever materials they had on hand. Some cars and trucks had working suspensions and steering wheels that turned.

PETER DALGLISH

Street children
searching for food in a
Khartoum dumpster,
January, 1986.

In the streets of
Khartoum with
my friends,
February, 1986.
Yassir is the child
in the foreground
sitting next to the
cardboard box.

Marie de la Soudière, the star of the
UNICEF office in Khartoum,
February, 1986.

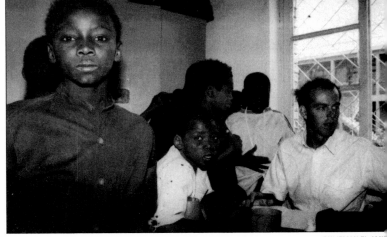

First day of classes at the Technical Training School for Khartoum Street Children, May 13, 1986.

Sunday, SKI Courier, January, 1987.

SKI Courier boys making a delivery in Khartoum, March, 1987. The children stood out from the pack in their distinctive yellow and blue uniforms.

Ogaden as another opportunity to showcase and sell their latest weapons. At one point, the two superpowers actually switched allegiances but continued to supply armaments.

For the Somali government, the Ogaden was a source of national pride, and its occupation by Ethiopia constituted a national disgrace. The Somali flag features a five-pointed star; one of the five points symbolizes the Ogaden, which is now the possession of a foreign power. Another point represents Djibouti, now a sovereign state.

The Ogaden conflict left both Ethiopia and Somalia impoverished, and displaced tens of thousands of people. When we arrived in the Ogaden, the UNHCR was embarking on an ambitious feeding program for 50,000 of the estimated 321,000 "returnees"—residents of the Ogaden who during the war had fled to Somalia, but who with the promise of peace had now returned home. But by the time the UNHCR program became fully operational, conditions for the entire Ogaden population had deteriorated to the point that returnees were no worse off than anybody else. By December, 1984, an estimated 881,000 people in the Ogaden faced famine. Indeed, with their official UNHCR registration papers, the returnees from Somalia enjoyed a privileged status and were the only population receiving regular food rations. In any case it was absurd to differentiate on the basis of official documentation. For centuries these people have identified themselves as Afar, Issa, Oromo, and Gugura tribespeople, not by any particular national flag.

Our first stop was the village of Errer, just 57 kilometres east of Diredawa. The adjacent camp had a population of 2,500 people who had staggered into the area over a period of only a few weeks. The British Save the Children Fund had established a feeding station for some of the worst-affected children. We arrived the week it opened. It was a relatively small project; only 500 kids under the age of five and their mothers were involved. A British nurse named Jenny was in charge, and she gave John and me a tour of the facilities.

The mothers and children were sitting in the shade of a temporary shelter that had been erected by Save the Children. The women who accompanied the children were not old but they looked ancient. Everything in the feeding station was orderly and efficient. One part had been transformed into a kitchen, with a heavy gruel bubbling away in pots suspended over an open fire. A well-organized storage room had been set up. Children were brought in from the camp, weighed and measured, and if they fell below the critical measure of 80 per cent of weight-for-height, a red band was fastened to their wrist. They would be fed four times a day, and with luck, they would live.

To this point, my involvement with the Ethiopian famine had been at a safe distance, through the buffer of telex and telephone lines, reports, and statistics. I had been so busy over the previous seven weeks that I had not fully comprehended what it would be like to encounter famine first-hand, to look into the eyes of an emaciated child. It was in the village of Errer that the famine became real for me.

I never imagined children could be so thin and still be alive. There was really nothing to them; some kids could barely stand. Their skin was gritty and had lost its natural elasticity. When you grasped a child with your hand, you would leave an imprint on her skin, a shallow depression. I noticed a girl whose hair had turned a rusty-red color, a sign of chronic vitamin deficiency. Having the mothers at their side was critical, because some children could not eat without their assistance. It was bad. In the heat and direct sun, I felt faint. There were flies everywhere. The mothers would do everything they could to keep the insects away from their children's eyes, mouths, or open wounds. The kids wore rags wrapped around their waists. Some had a leather locket fastened around their necks that contained a passage from the Koran, placed there by their parents to offer protection. I had expected that hungry kids would jostle to be the first in line to be fed, but these children were far past that stage. They sat passively and waited their turn. I wondered where their brothers and sisters were, and how many of them had survived.

The camp at Errer was the place where only a few weeks before, Dr. Klaus Hornetz had led the *Globe and Mail*'s Michael Valpy and identified the children who had a chance of making it and those who would soon be dead. On the way to the SCF feeding station, John and I had passed a newly dug cemetery with rows of small, unmarked graves. I didn't inquire, but I guessed the graveyard was the final resting place for many of the children whom Valpy had seen. We had arrived with our supplies only eight weeks after his story appeared in Canada, but many of the kids who had inspired us to act in the first place were already long gone.

Jenny was an awesome relief worker. "Welcome to our little restaurant," she announced upon our arrival, pouring us tea from her military-issue vacuum bottle. Jenny moved with grace and authority through the rows of children and mothers, pointing out to her assistants the kids who required immediate attention, comforting a girl who had no parent at her side, making a silly face for a handicapped boy who clung to a primitive wooden crutch. She had made up records for all of the children in her care, neatly listing their height and weight.

Jenny had been in the Ogaden for several weeks and had seen more than her fair share of human suffering, but she had not lost her sense of perspective. More than anything else, she said, she craved an English beer.

This hastily improvised feeding station was probably the happiest outpost for many kilometres around. A borehole had been drilled so there was plenty of drinkable water. Kids were scrubbed clean with warm water and soap before they were fed. Fluorescent orange plastic feeding bowls were stacked up on the serving tables. There was already a routine to the place. Within days, the Canadian Food Supplement would take the place of a tasteless gruel that was being served and Dr. Hornetz would have all the drugs he needed for his clinic. Even if we went no farther than Errer, we knew our mission had been accomplished.

But I felt no sense of elation. I wanted to be left alone. Although many said the famine was of biblical proportions and could not have been averted, there was no doubt that timely intervention on the part of the West would have prevented much of the misery we were witnessing. It was hard to avoid the conclusion that for the people of Errer, this was the end of the road. Over thousands of years, the pastoralists of the Ogaden had developed strategies that would allow them to cope with one of the world's harshest environments. Nomadic and semi-nomadic people have the reputation for being proudly independent, and are suspicious of people who choose to live in towns and cities. They are rarely involved in any kind of government programs. They are usually left out of government surveys, and are wary of researchers and academics. The famine had cost them everything, including their dignity. They had lost their fighting spirit. In other camps, members of the media wandered about the tukuls with their betacams and sound booms, interviewing fatigued relief workers, recording for their global audience the last act of this human tragedy. But the Ogaden was only a side show and had attracted little international attention. At least the people of Errer would be spared this final humiliation.

Over the next seven days, John Godfrey and I travelled with Walter Msimang and Dr. Hornetz by DC-3 and Land Rover to Kelafo, Warder, and Kebri Dehar. On the perimeter of each town, we found masses of people who had walked in from the edge of the desert. They had little in the way of protection from the sun and wind. People had collected sticks, cardboard, and bits of plastic with which they ingeniously engineered huts that approximated as closely as possible their traditional tukuls. Water was brought in by cart or truck from great distances. We met one man who had walked for three days to the Ogaden with his two young sons after their only donkey had died. Making his way to the town of

Warder was his last resort, and he hoped that there, he would find food and water for his surviving children. We went with him to the warehouse where he was given a ration of Canadian wheat, as well as milk powder and sugar. He carefully washed his sons and gave them cool water to drink, and then they headed back in the direction they had come from.

We heard the same story all across the Ogaden: people had not seen rain for over two years, and the drought had forced them to abandon their traditional way of life. For generations, their ancestors had moved with the rains, always searching for food and water, using their camels to transport their possessions from place to place. Theirs was a cashless economy; they traded for the few objects they couldn't make for themselves. Now their livestock were dead, and for the first time in their lives they were forced to depend on outside assistance for their sustenance. They made the most miserable of beggars.

The arrival of mountains of relief supplies could not compensate for the years of war and neglect that had crippled the infrastructure of the Ogaden. The region's only rail line linked Diredawa with Djibouti on the Red Sea; there was no southern branch serving the Ogaden. Most wells had run dry and pumps for irrigation purposes were inoperative. Diesel fuel was almost impossible to come by. We saw war wreckage everywhere, and had to be careful where we walked for fear of land mines. The retreating Somali troops had destroyed most bridges and many roads were in ruin. Schools had been shot up and their corrugated steel roofs pilfered. School supplies consisted of perhaps one or two books and a few pieces of chalk. In Kelafo, we visited a medical clinic the size of an average North American living room that was the only facility for the local population of over 100,000 people. There was no doctor at the clinic, and the supplies on the shelves were limited to a few bottles of aspirin, some containers of unmarked and discolored liquids, and three packages of bandages. Immunization programs for children had ground to a halt, and there were no veterinary services for livestock.

It was Dr. Hornetz's idea that John and I visit Gode. The people in the camp near the town had arrived over a period of a few days. Some were returnees from Somalia, but most were simply people who could no longer feed themselves or their children. Hornetz said that, at last count, there were over 25,000 people in the camp, but no one really knew for sure. "After a while you stop counting," he remarked with resignation. The shelves of the local warehouses were bare, and the RRC officials, already overburdened with the crisis, had experienced great difficulty finding any food for the new arrivals. Everything in Diredawa had already been committed to other towns. The UNHCR had nothing. UNICEF had offered to carry out a weight-for-height survey, but had no emergency supplies to offer.

When we arrived in town, it was already dark. We stopped just short of the camp so we could sip some tea and eat some biscuits. We were downwind from the camp, and you could smell the smoke from the many fires that were burning. I heard a sound that at first I thought was singing and then realized was the wail of women crying out, which rose and fell, stopped completely, and then started up again. Hornetz just closed his eyes and leaned against the side of the Land Rover. We had been on the road for over a week and we were all dirty and fatigued. Gode would be our last stop.

Arthur Andrew had warned me about moments like this when he had suggested I steel myself against the worst of what I was going to see in Ethiopia. But there is no way to prepare one's senses for the wholesale suffering of thousands of people, all clinging to life by the thinnest of threads. We had a few cartons of high-protein biscuits donated by the West German government in the back of Hornetz's truck, but it was pointless to even think of beginning a distribution. We would need dozens of trucks and thousands of boxes of biscuits to offer even faint hope to the people sitting clustered around the fires that burned that night.

To the uninitiated, there are no patterns that emerge from the chaos of refugee camps and no apparent forms of social organization. But even among people in the most extreme circumstances, from the holds of slave ships to the Nazi death camps, there are women and men who, without any formal endorsement, emerge as leaders and who assume responsibility for the tasks that must be performed for life to continue. Babies have to be bathed, and bodies wrapped and buried. Here in Gode, someone had allocated jobs to people who were still strong enough to walk and who had not lost their sight or sanity. For reasons unknown to me, young Ahmed had been assigned the role of tour guide. With no words being spoken, he led me away from the Land Rover into the heart of the camp.

I needed a guide for this inferno, as Dante needed Virgil for his. Ahmed knew where to take me and what places should be avoided. Hornetz had whispered a few words into his ear just before we had departed, probably cautioning him that Hornetz needed me to be strong for at least another day. Then I could retreat to Canada. In most camps, those people who are only hours away from death are carried away to a place that is dark and quiet, where final prayers are said. In Gode, people were dying everywhere, out in the open, even by the main gate where we had entered. We had to step around little mounds where people had stumbled and fallen. The stench was excruciating, and I almost gagged. My eyes stung from the smoke that filled the air. I wanted to turn back. A woman with one arm wrapped around her husband motioned with her free hand for us to approach, but Ahmed led me in the opposite direction.

It was at the back of the camp, where only one small fire was burning, that they had laid out the bodies of the children, some still warm. An ancient woman tended them, keeping vigil for the night. In the morning, they would be collected on a donkey cart, covered with lime, and rolled into a common grave just a few kilometres from the town. Ahmed took me to the side of one child and held my hand as I stroked the forehead, then the hair. The eyes were open. You could still see beauty in the child's face. I wondered how many hours had passed since he had last breathed, and if our few stale biscuits could have saved him.

There were six children lying on a single sheet of plastic spread out on the ground. Someone had arranged the bodies neatly according to height. The youngest was only an infant, and the oldest perhaps 11 years of age. One girl had a shiny copper bracelet around her wrist that caught the light from the fire. A boy grasped a length of wire that someone had skillfully fashioned into a little truck for him to play with. It had wheels that turned and doors that could be opened. For me, the toy was proof that someone here in the camp had loved the boy, and cared for him, and now grieved for him.

In David Mathews's English class at Upper Canada College, I had learned about the moments called epiphanies—episodes of heightened perception when, for an instant, things became startlingly clear. Here in Gode on the last day of the year, in the presence of children who had just lost the great gift of life, I found my calling. I realized my place on earth was with desperately poor kids who had few friends or allies. I had no idea what I had to offer, or exactly what my contribution would be, or indeed how I would support myself. But I knew at that moment that these girls and boys of the desert, with whom I had virtually nothing in common, were now my life.

Of all the children we saw, there was one kid who moved John more than any other. It was a tiny boy he met in Errer, who had covered himself in a dusty brown shawl to keep warm. He was standing all by himself and he was excruciatingly thin. He was patiently waiting his turn in the food line, holding one of our leprechaun ice-cream bowls in his hand. He looked at the green cartoon character with bewilderment. John sat down next to him and held out his hand. The boy smiled back. They couldn't speak, of course, but a kind of connection was made. John later wrote, "At that moment I made a pact with the child, and with myself, and with God that all we had done would not be in vain, would not be squandered, would not be forgotten, that we had to continue."

In late-night discussions under the brilliant stars of an African sky, John put an idea to Walter Msimang and his colleagues. We could not in good conscience simply take our pictures and leave; there had to be some kind of follow-up. Ethiopia Airlift had demonstrated the power of linking one community to another. What if we matched up the communities we had visited in the Ogaden with communities in Canada? Even among the semi-nomadic tribes, towns such as Gode and Kelafo were the critical link in reaching people. Schemes implemented by Western charities to support individual children through sponsorship programs often ignored the fact that healthy children are raised by healthy communities. It made no sense to single out a particular girl or boy for special attention while overlooking the fact that the local school had no books or that the local well had bad water.

John called his idea "Adopt a Village," and to everyone sitting around the fire that night, it made a good deal of sense. Donors could address the challenges in manageable bits instead of being overwhelmed by the scale of the disaster in Africa. Priorities could be identified, such as building a new medical clinic or launching a vaccination program. Ideally, there would be an exchange of information between the communities that would help people in the West to learn more about the developing world. The West had first come to know about famine in Ethiopia through the medium of television, but television audiences are notoriously fickle, channel-surfing from one story to another, while the crisis in Africa would continue for many years. Matching up communities would help to sustain interest long after the television crews had left.

The last village John and I visited was called Degahbur, and more than any other, it seemed like a good candidate for adoption. It needed almost everything, and in meetings with local officials we came up with an appropriate shopping list. The first priority was a mobile medical clinic that would begin to meet the health requirements of the local population, while at the same time have the capacity to reach people in outlying areas. Too often, tribespeople had been forced to travel for many days to town for treatment for their children. The second item was a 10-tonne Mercedes truck that the community could use to pick up equipment in Diredawa, including heavy equipment for well-drilling purposes and bags of grain for food distribution. It should be equipped with a collapsible rubber tank for transporting water. The truck would be useful long after the drought came to an end. The Degahbur public school had been badly damaged during the war; it needed to be rebuilt from the ground up and to be fully equipped with supplies. Finally, vaccination was a priority. The local authorities requested that Ethiopia Airlift work with WUSC to set up a cold chain—a system of kerosene-powered coolers—so that vaccines for children and livestock alike could be transported and stored in outlying areas that had no electricity.

We returned to Canada after 14 days in Ethiopia inspired and invigorated. In Canada, we had heard much about feuding between aid agencies, but in the field, we witnessed only co-operation between Save the Children, Oxfam, the Red Cross, and others. People shared aircraft, trucks, and graders. WUSC was regularly asked to dig boreholes for other charities at strategic locations, which they willingly agreed to do. Most of the relief workers we had met were volunteers who had given up employment in their native country for the opportunity of assisting in the famine-relief effort. They represented the best of their generation. I admired their can-do attitude, their idealism, and their ability to cope with everyday hardships. They were Hawkeye Pierces of the 1980s, combining professionalism with a healthy irreverence for the institutions that employed them. I had watched one Save the Children team in the course of 24 hours feed more than 600 children, tend to their immediate medical needs, counsel their mothers, prepare six bodies for burial, file a report on the day's activities with their head office in London, deal with a cantankerous British film crew, and end the day with cribbage and cold beer around the same table that only hours before had been used to weigh and measure malnourished kids.

John and I had been inspired by the humility and the dedication of the Ethiopians who were involved in the emergency-relief operations. Many of them had family members who themselves were affected by the famine, but they put their personal needs on hold in order to perform their professional responsibilities to the full extent their limited resources would allow. Their country had taken in hundreds of foreign experts who in one day earned the equivalent of their monthly income. The Ethiopians received little credit for their contribution to the relief efforts. Many, solely on account of being employees of government agencies, were suspected of corruption. While the BBC and other media selected foreign-aid workers who had been in the country only a few weeks for starring roles in their documentaries, Ethiopian experts, many of whom spoke excellent English, were rarely interviewed.

For hundreds of thousands of Ethiopians, the planes and trucks carrying emergency supplies arrived too late. It cannot be said that the response by the

West to the plight of a country on its knees was any kind of success story. The fact is that Amin's images of emaciated children shamed the charities and the donor governments into action. Nor should the people who organized relief efforts, including those of us behind Ethiopia Airlift, be portrayed as heroes. Our efforts pale in comparison to the herculean efforts of ordinary tribespeople in Wollo, Gondar, Sidamo, and the Ogaden who, through the conservation of traditional famine foods and ground water, were somehow able to keep their families alive. That anyone at all survived the great famine of 1984 is testimony not just to the generosity of the West but also to the resilience and ingenuity of the Ethiopian people.

On the return flight to Canada I attempted to sort out what my next steps would be. Somehow I would have to inform my parents, and the law firm, that my career path was about to take a 180-degree turn. My parents had invested thousands of dollars in my education. I had attended some of North America's finest schools. How would they react to my decision to give up law and work instead alongside the poor? I sought a way to present my interest in helping kids as honorable, at the same time recognizing that my father would inevitably confront me with two questions: who would hire me and what salary would they pay me? I had no answers for him.

After our return to Canada, John and I, working closely with the Ethiopia Airlift board and volunteers, began to raise funds for our adopted village of Degahbur. I resumed my duties as an articling student at the law firm during the day, and volunteered for Ethiopia Airlift at night and on weekends. Arthur priced out the items on our shopping list at a whopping $194,063. This sum included $100,000 for the renovation of the Degahbur elementary school and $22,835 for the kerosene-powered cold-chain refrigeration units and Oxfam water bladder. Dave Wright created a new thermometer for *Live at Five* and I went back on the air. In February, 1985, we dispatched a container from the port of Halifax packed with Canadian Food Supplement. Our fundraising efforts for Adopt a Village continued unabated; if anything, we gained momentum. We raised more money than anyone had ever imagined possible. By December 31, 1985, Ethiopia Airlift had collected approximately $465,000 from more than 10,000 donors. Our total expenses as a charity had been $24,694, representing 5.3 per cent of all cash donations. If the value of the goods from our airlift were included ($773,376), our overhead was less than 2 per cent of the total donations. Our biggest expenses by far were printing and postage.

With the additional contributions, Ethiopia Airlift was able to provide extra items for Degahbur. The collection and storage of rain water for long-term use would be insurance against drought and famine in future years; we therefore invested $139,000 for 10 drilled wells and two sub-surface dams to trap riverbed water during rainy seasons. In addition, we set aside $27,000 for an expanded immunization program based out of our mobile medical clinic for 10,000 children living throughout the Degahbur region. All the projects would be undertaken by WUSC.

The involvement of the people of the Maritime provinces did not end with the airlift. Two Nova Scotian teachers, Wayne Hamilton and Brian Alloway, launched Project SHARE (Students Helping African Relief Efforts), an ambitious campaign involving 17,000 students from across the province. On March 17, 1985, students collected funds in specially marked SHARE lunch bags and raised $130,000. Of this sum, one-third went to the Red Cross, one-third to Oxfam, and one-third to Adopt a Village. John Godfrey worked closely with Dr. Kenneth Hare, a leading expert on desertification at the University of Toronto, investigating practical, community-based interventions involving the planting of trees that could protect our village, and thousands of other communities in the Sahel, from encroachment by desert sands.

In January, 1986, I returned with Dave Wright to Degahbur to check on the progress of the Ethiopia Airlift projects and to account to the *Live at Five* audience how the funds they had contributed had been spent. The famine had lingered far longer than anyone had expected, and the town's feeding centre for malnourished children was still in operation. The best news was that the number of children below 80 per cent weight-for-height had dropped from 108 in May, 1985, to 38 in January, 1986. All children in the centre were being fed twice a day. Canadian Food Supplement was their food of choice. The Degahbur area vaccination program was under way, implemented by WUSC in co-operation with the Ministry of Health. UNICEF and WHO provided technical assistance and support. Children were being inoculated for six diseases, including tuberculosis, polio, whooping cough, and tetanus. Through our Adopt a Village program, we had provided the cold-chain equipment, vehicles, syringes, kerosene, and salaries for local health workers.

The WUSC water program, funded in part by Adopt a Village, was ambitious in scope, and Dave and I were impressed with everything that had been accomplished. A detailed survey of water needs throughout the region was carried out. Based on the survey, borehole locations were established. A $500,000 boring-bucket rig nicknamed Super George, capable of drilling to a depth of 85 metres, had been brought in especially for the project. All wells were lined with pre-cast concrete sections and included side troughs for thirsty livestock. Rugged hand pumps were installed that could be maintained by the local population. The entire project was carried out in close consultation with the Water Resources Commission of Ethiopia.

On the other hand, the progress of the elementary-school reconstruction was disappointing. Three months after the contract for reconstruction had been signed, only a simple fence had been built. Dave Wright shook his head in disgust. "What are we going to say to our audience?" he asked me. The Ministry of Education had proved to be very slow and bureaucratic. Dave and I met with the local party secretary and administrator, who were sympathetic but who had no answers for us.

In the end, Adopt a Village needed to make a direct connection with the school and its principal, Mr. Getachew Sheferau. Once again, governments and institutions were getting in the way of communities that wanted to help each other. The teachers understood exactly what they needed, and provided us with a list of important supplies, including mathematical instruments, English books, charts, maps, and basic scientific equipment. We sent this list off to teachers in Canada and pledged to follow up with the principal. Dave Wright's one-hour feature report on our visit to Degahbur entitled *The Maritime Miracle—One Year Later* attained a record-high audience share for ATV news broadcasts and helped to sustain interest in the Adopt a Village project.

After witnessing the horrors of drought and famine, I found it almost painful to lock myself into the Stewart, MacKeen and Covert library to learn—and then forget—everything about Canadian income tax law. Images of desert children were never far from my mind. Among the many people I had met in the refugee camps of the Ogaden Desert were unaccompanied nomadic children who, through their raw courage, had somehow managed to survive. Their talents were unique. By the age of 12 or 13, they were assuming many of the responsibilities of adults, looking after their younger siblings and the family's livestock. They knew the land for hundreds of miles around. They were familiar with the seasons of the Jerer River, which ran the length of the desert, and their calendar was based on the phases of the moon. They knew how to build simple structures in which to live and how to look after their own medical needs. They had no money to their name; what they didn't have, they could trade for. They could sing and dance and were proficient storytellers. These children had relationships with their parents, grandparents, and great-grandparents. They told me that as long as they had their land, they had their freedom. They dreamed of having healthy animals to care for once again. I admired their guts, and I vowed that someday, I would have a chance to work alongside these remarkable girls and boys.

By March, 1985, the epicentre of the famine in Africa had shifted westward from Ethiopia to Sudan, where in some areas up to 77 per cent of all children between the ages of one and five were suffering from malnutrition. The Nile flood waters were at their lowest level in 350 years. Ships carrying grain had arrived at Port Sudan on the Red Sea, but the country's antiquated railway system had collapsed and little grain was getting through. Millions of lives were at risk. WUSC had been awarded a contract by the UN World Food Program to set up a transport-management system between the capital city of Khartoum and those areas in the west of the country that were most affected by the drought and famine. Instead of taking a job with a Halifax law firm, I decided to sign on with WUSC as a field worker in a remote part of northern Darfur, an area of vast and open desert that had changed little since time immemorial. I knew almost nothing about trucks, but I was willing to learn.

Thanks to the efforts of my law school colleague Elizabeth May, who served as my personal tutor, I did manage to pass the bar-admission examinations and was admitted to the Bar of Nova Scotia in June, 1985. I gathered up all my law textbooks and sold them to the university's second-hand bookstore for $160. With the proceeds, I bought a new pair of hiking boots and a Silva compass. On August 7, my parents hosted a farewell party for me on the schooner *Mar II* in Halifax harbor. It was a glorious summer day, the sails were full, and many of my friends were on board to celebrate both my induction into, and retirement from, the practice of law. My entire legal career had spanned three working days. I loved Canada, and I had made many good friends in my adopted hometown of Halifax, but already Africa was in my blood, and I wanted to move on.

The next day I was on a flight to Heathrow, where I connected with a British Airways flight bound for Khartoum, where I would meet with UN officials and begin my assignment. I had signed a contract for three months; no work was guaranteed after it expired.

Years later, I had the opportunity to meet the man who had inspired our Christmas airlift to Ethiopia and thereby changed my life. While on leave from Khartoum, I arranged to have a Tusker beer with Mohammed Amin at the Thorntree Cafe in Nairobi. I told him my story, knowing full well that he had probably heard the same words many times over from people like myself who had been shaken by his images of hungry children from Korem. He was characteristically modest about his accomplishments, and gave more credit to the relief workers who followed him than the media that had broken the story. "We just take the pictures," he said to me. "You guys are the ones who feed the kids." The words he used to describe the human disaster at Korem, comparing the scene to an air crash, proved prophetic. Mohammed Amin was among 125 people killed in the crash of a hijacked Ethiopia Airlines plane off the coast of the Comoros Islands in the Indian Ocean on November 24, 1996. He had been returning home to Nairobi from Addis Ababa.

If today you walk the streets of the bleak shantytowns that have sprung up all around Addis Ababa, you can find the survivors of the Ethiopian famine of 1984. They live on top of each other in rusting tin shacks within a stone's throw of the Hilton Hotel, the favorite playground for the city's diplomats and UN employees, with its clay tennis courts and natural hot-spring-fed swimming pool. These people from the ancient Oromo, Issa, and Affar tribes have become refugees in their own country and have the look of a defeated race. As children, they roamed the open rangeland; their line of sight reached unbroken to the horizon and they could see storms approaching from kilometres away. Now they stare into their neighbor's laundry line. The shantytown has no running water, but most shacks sport television antennas. Programming is in English and includes episodes of *Bay Watch* and *America's Funniest Home Videos*. The displaced are sullen and listless, and have few possessions to their name. For good reason, they are bitter about their present circumstances. I suspect that today, somewhere among their ranks, are the very same nomadic children whom I met in the Ogaden camps over 10 years ago. For me, the idea of these once-proud youth living in squalor among the rubbish of Addis Ababa is the enduring legacy of the 1984 African famine.

A NORTHWEST PASSAGE

In the age of ocean liners, travellers between continents had the opportunity to adjust to the culture, climate, and pace of life of their destination. Crossing the ocean at 15 knots allowed ample time to adapt, and inevitably there were veteran passengers on board who, for the price of a drink in the captain's lounge, were willing to share useful information about the port of disembarkation—where to get a cheap room, places to avoid, colorful local characters, and good prospects for employment.

A trip by sea and rail from London to Khartoum was at a minimum a two-week enterprise. A district commissioner newly posted to the Sudan would travel by ship from Portsmouth through the Strait of Gibraltar to Alexandria, where he would present his papers at the Egyptian Customs House. The journey would usually be broken for a few days at Cairo, allowing the DC to take in some of the city's sights—the pyramids, the Sultan Hassan Teaching Mosque, the city's renowned souks, the National Museum with its exquisite artifacts from the tomb of Tutankhamon, and perhaps the beautiful Azbakiya Gardens, created by the French landscape gardener Barillet in 1870 on the site of a tranquil pond. The travel allowance for DCs was generous, and his accommodation would likely have been at Cairo's famed Shepheard's Hotel, where a string quartet performed every night for diners in the chandeliered ballroom.

From Cairo, there were daily trains with first-class sleeper compartments to Luxor and on to Shellal, where passengers would transfer to luxurious Nile steamers for the lazy, five-day trip to the Sudanese port of Wadi Halfa. Nothing about travel on the Nile was rushed. While on board the steamer, the DC would be served his meals on fine china; after dining, he could retire to the first-class lounge for liqueurs and card games. Wadi Halfa was a bustling frontier town that catered to well-heeled travellers on the Grand Tour, and its better hotel rooms were often booked weeks in advance.

Trains left punctually for Khartoum on a narrow-gauge railway line built by the British Army that represented one of the greatest engineering triumphs of the age. Its construction had been interrupted by frequent sand storms in the Nubian Desert between the Red Sea and the Nile that were of such severity that 50-tonne locomotives pulling cars carrying materials and laborers were derailed. Sections of track as long as 30 kilometres would be submerged in the desert for weeks at a time and had to be dug out by coolies imported from India. After the desert crossing, the DC would arrive at Khartoum well rested, having had at least a fortnight to prepare for his new responsibilities.

The problem with modern airliners is that they are too convenient. The flight from Heathrow to Khartoum on board my British Airways Boeing 767 took seven hours and 10 minutes. My in-flight meal was soggy lasagna served on a plastic plate with plastic utensils, and we watched three films, including *Mad Max III: Beyond Thunderdome*, starring Mel Gibson and Tina Turner. The flight attendant volunteered her opinion that the Sudan should never have been granted its independence, that the entire country had fallen apart at the seams. She liked Khartoum least of all the British Airways destinations; she was doing the trip as a favor to a colleague who had come down with malaria after her last trip to the Sudan. She told me all the air crews stayed at the Hilton Hotel and they rarely left the hotel grounds. "There's nothing in the city to see anyway." It was only the British flight-safety regulations limiting the number of hours that air crew can work without a break that necessitated the layover in Khartoum. If they had their choice, the flight attendant and her colleagues would return to London aboard the same aircraft that had brought them to the Sudan.

We lost the sun over Baiyuda Desert near the ancient city of Merowe, and the captain lowered the plane's flaps in preparation for landing. I had just dismissed the flight attendant's remarks as the idle ramblings of a cynic when the co-pilot came on the intercom to inform us that Khartoum Airport, and the entire city, had just disappeared from sight. I later learned that during the wet season, silt and debris plug up the massive turbines at the Roseires Dam on the Blue Nile that provides most of Khartoum's hydro power, causing blackouts that can last for days at a time. We circled the city for more than an hour waiting for the airport authorities to fire up their diesel generators and flip the right switches to illuminate the runway. Underneath us, the lights of the city reappeared bit by bit until I could discern the point where the Blue and White

Niles converged. There was sand in the air, and everything was washed in brown. No one knows for sure how Khartoum got its name; one theory is that when seen from the proper angle, the land at the confluence of the two Niles takes on the shape of an elephant's trunk, which in Arabic is similar to the name of the city. That night, I saw no sign of the elephant's trunk, nor have I in any of my subsequent approaches by air to the city.

Khartoum was a city of ghosts. I was surprised there were so few cars in the streets. White-robed figures drifted across my taxi's headlight beams and then were lost from sight. It was not late, but all the shops that lined Jamhurria Avenue were already shut tight. A few men were gathered outside a newspaper kiosk, oblivious to the racket of the portable Honda generator at their feet. None of the street lights were operating. I saw a group of children foraging through a rubbish tip in the alley leading up to my hotel.

Carolyn Head, the administrator for the World University Service of Canada's project in the Sudan, was waiting for me in the lounge of the well-worn Sahara Hotel, just off Jamhurria Avenue. She had gone to the airport to greet me, but the arrival hall had been evacuated when the power failed. None of the airport officials could provide any information about the status of arriving planes, and nobody had updated the low-tech chalkboard on which the arrival times of incoming flights were irregularly posted. Carolyn handed me a six-centimetre-thick briefing package about the Sudan and a copy of WUSC's draft transportation plan for emergency relief commodities. "A little bedtime reading," she said with a smile.

Bill McNeill and John Watson, the duo who ran WUSC back in Ottawa, had earned a reputation for identifying and hiring motivated and professional staff who, at first glance, might seem to be unlikely candidates for overseas postings with an international development agency. They came from all walks of life. The WUSC country director in the Sudan, Rudy Rodrigues, was a former mall manager from suburban Edmonton. Carolyn Head was no Africa hand, but already she had developed an impressive network of Sudanese contacts. Although it was our first meeting, she treated me like a confidante. "This place is tough," she told me. "But you're going to love it."

"Tough" was the most flattering adjective anyone other than a loyal employee of the Sudan Tourist Corporation could use to describe the condition of the country in 1985. A quick reading of the briefing documents Carolyn had provided revealed that the British Airways flight attendant had not been so far off the mark. The Sudan, Africa's largest country, was indeed falling apart at the seams. The office of Winston Prattley, the newly appointed special representative of the

Secretary-General for United Nations Emergency Operations in Sudan (UNEOS), had produced a quarterly review for the period between April 15 and July 15 that painted a very pessimistic picture of relief operations across the country. More than 8.4 million people, over one-third of the country's total population, were affected by the drought. An authoritative nutritional survey conducted by Oxfam in the Kordofan region estimated that approximately 530 children were dying of malnutrition every day. In the words of the review, "The sudden and catastrophic acceleration of the nutritional curve is inevitable if food does not arrive soon." In plain English, millions of people in the Sudan were on the brink of starvation.

The problem in the Sudan was not that the famine had gone unnoticed or that relief supplies had not been dispatched. The situation was entirely different from that of Ethiopia a year earlier. Aid agencies in the Sudan had provided plenty of warning that the famine was imminent, and donor countries had responded generously. By June 30, 1985, the United States had delivered 372,000 MT of grain to Port Sudan and another 560,000 MT had been pledged. But the country's only port was seriously congested, and there was simply no place to off-load the grain. Despite years of effort and millions of dollars invested by the European Economic Community to upgrade the port facilities, it had never functioned at its advertised capacity. Massive hydraulic cranes required to off-load containers had fallen into disrepair; there were no spare parts, and no preventative maintenance had ever been attempted. Labor strife was common. Trains required to transport supplies to inland destinations were infrequent and subject to breakdowns. Before independence, during the time of the Anglo-Egyptian Condominium, several trains a day would depart from Port Sudan on schedule with supplies for Khartoum and other Sudanese destinations; by the 1980s, it was a rare occurrence when more than three Sudan Railways Corporation trains would depart from Port Sudan during any given week.

Representatives of donor countries and aid agencies looked on with growing anxiety as the sacks of grain were piled on every available flat surface in and around the port. As of July 14, 1985, there were 392,000 MT of grain stacked up in Port Sudan, a quantity sufficient to feed the entire population of Darfur Region for 10 months. Five food-aid ships were anchored off shore waiting to berth. The mountain of grain represented one of the largest stockpiles of food anywhere in the world. Much of the bulk grain shipped in great haste by donor nations to feed hungry children was packed in 45-kilogram bags that were poorly hand-stitched. Through rough handling by careless forklift drivers, many of the bags had ripped open and were spilling onto the off-loading area adjacent to the railway terminal. The port was overrun by rats the size of dachshunds. The intense 45-degree summer heat and suffocating humidity of the Red Sea had taken their toll, and much grain had already been rendered unfit for human consumption. The port authorities stated categorically that storage space for the sorghum was not available at any cost. However, they could not explain to exasperated relief workers why, at that very moment, 40 warehouses in Port Sudan were filled to the rafters with baled cotton, the Sudan's most important cash crop, awaiting ships for export.

Nothing epitomized the sorry state of relief operations in the Sudan as dramatically as the saga of the Sudan Railways Corporation. In early 1984, in response to growing evidence of an impending famine in the Sudan, the U.S. Agency for International Development designed and funded an ambitious plan for the transport and distribution of relief commodities. USAID's scheme relied heavily on highly optimistic promises of performance put out by Sudan Railways Corporation officials, despite the SRC's long history of broken contracts and numerous warnings received by USAID from relief agencies. USAID contracted with the Sudan Railways Corporation to deliver 1,300 MT of sorghum, approximately the capacity of one freight train, on a daily basis to the town of Nyala in South Darfur. The goal was to pre-position food stocks in Darfur before the arrival of the July and August rains. In turn, USAID contracted with Save the Children U.K., giving them the exclusive right to distribute and monitor USAID sorghum at the village level throughout Darfur. Arkel Talab, a private company based in Baton Rouge, Louisiana, was brought in by USAID to manage the entire operation.

Ironically, after more than two years of drought, it was the very rains that the Sudanese farmers had prayed for that crippled the American relief operation. Heavy precipitation in May and June of 1985 washed out the railway track in nine locations, resulting in the loss of two locomotives and seven rail wagons. The lifeline linking Port Sudan with Darfur was cut; in the three weeks leading up to the publication of the *Sudan Quarterly Review* by the United Nations in July, 1985, not a single grain of food had been delivered to western Sudan. By June, 1985, the $100-million transport plan lay in ruins, and hopes of averting widespread famine in western Sudan were dashed. The authors of the review did not mince words: the over-reliance by USAID on the railway to deliver vital relief food "must now be viewed as a serious misjudgment of calamitous proportions." In a section entitled "Prognosis," the authors wrote: "It is not possible to be optimistic about the next quarter. Despite all efforts, the same problem areas will persist. A properly planned, sufficiently supported, and well-implemented program can do little more at this point than minimize the losses. People are suffering; people have died. This situation will not be corrected as long as international and national policy and decision-makers in Khartoum continue to have a high threshold for other people's pain. Immediate and decisive action is required before any degree of salvation can be expected."

It was too convenient to blame the complete and total failure of the Sudan Railways Corporation on the sudden and cataclysmic arrival of the seasonal rains. Washouts and bridge-collapses had been perennial problems in the Sudan since the railway was constructed in the 19th century, and should have been factored into any emergency transport plan funded by foreign donors. The truth was that Sudan Railways was a notoriously inefficient, government-owned corporation rife with corruption that over the years had proved immune to outside pressures. Images on Sudan's national television-news programs of starving villagers in Darfur breaking open anthills in search of grain made no impact on the SRC officials; bribery was the only incentive that moved them. The *Sudan Quarterly Review* noted that although the SRC had difficulty finding space on its rolling stock for relief commodities destined for the isolated western region of the country, for several weeks freight trains rolled into Khartoum filled with pastries and sugar especially prized by the middle-class Sudanese during Ramadan celebrations. More than one relief worker had remarked that USAID would have been much better off to hand over its $100-million transport contract to some of Khartoum's hard-nosed merchants: as long as they could make a healthy profit, the grain would eventually reach its destination.

Relief workers, once they accept employment, have little control over where they will be posted. I knew only that I would be working in Darfur, a region larger than the entire United Kingdom. I was told in advance to prepare for the worst. According to the July, 1985, *Sudan Quarterly Review*, "Individual amounts of grain distributed in Darfur have been little more than token, and wholly inadequate to guarantee immediate survival of the population." In a telex to the WUSC headquarters in Ottawa that was appended to my briefing documents, Rudy Rodrigues wrote that during the month of June, 1985, 34,000 MT of grain were required to supply three million people. Actual deliveries were less than 5,000 MT. Rodrigues questioned whether privately owned trucks were of any use whatsoever, noting the rainy season was traditionally a time when many truck owners put their vehicles on blocks to avoid possible damage on flooded roads. Spare parts and fuel were in short supply. Even if trucks could be found, they would barely make a dent in Darfur's immediate food requirements. A return trip from Khartoum to Nyala at the best of times required 10 days; simple arithmetic proved that moving 30,000 MT of grain by trucks that had a maximum capacity of five MT each would require more trucks than were available in the entire country.

A report by Oxfam U.K. dated June 10, 1985, provided the most comprehensive and authoritative analysis of the nutritional status of the population of Darfur. Oxfam had been keeping a close watch on Darfur since mid-1984, when heavy livestock losses, a collapse of livestock prices, high grain prices, and large population movements indicated the region was already gripped by famine. In the hardest-hit area north of El Geneina on the Chadian border, 77 per cent of all children between the ages of one and five were suffering from some form of malnutrition. Large numbers of people in rural areas were moving to towns where they believed food would be available. Much of Darfur's population was now almost entirely dependent on external food relief. With the failure of USAID sorghum to reach many villages in significant quantities, people had been surviving largely on traditional famine foods, particularly the fruit of the mukheit plant. Families migrated to forested areas known to contain wild foods such as koreb (grain gathered by ants in their nests) and lalob (wild dates), but even famine foods had now been exhausted.

The June 10 Oxfam report got into the hands of European and American journalists who had been keeping tabs on the progress of the famine across the Sahel. On July 8, 1985, the *Washington Post* published a piece by Jonathan Randal entitled "AID Learns How Not to Run a Famine Relief Project—Sudanese Will Die Because the Trains Never Came." Randal told the story of USAID putting all its eggs in the Sudan Railways Corporation's basket. The whole scheme had been doomed from the start. Randal quoted Andrew Timpson, the Sudan country director for Save the Children U.K.: "After six months, you'd think we'd done no work at all. You go out to Darfur and you'd think we'd only started. And the rains are coming."

Still smarting from its dismal performance in Ethiopia only a few months earlier, the international community was determined that the scenes of starvation in Bati and Korem would not be repeated across Darfur. Ethiopia was a client state of the Soviet Union, and the Western media had largely attributed the high toll from famine in Ethiopia to the alleged but totally unproved corruption and inefficiency of its government agencies. The Sudan had a different pedigree that was supposed to offer a measure of protection. Since 1969, when

Colonel Jafaar Nimeiri seized power, the Sudan had enjoyed close political and economic ties with the United States. In 1985, Sudan received over $1-billion in foreign aid, including $350-million dollars from the United States. The U.S.-based oil giant Chevron had invested tens of millions of dollars in oil exploration in the southern region of the country. The Sudan was strategically important to the U.S. and the West, and was viewed as a counterweight to the neighboring countries aligned with Moscow that the U.S. State Department dubbed members of the "Aden Pact"—South Yemen, Libya, and Ethiopia.

Immediate action was required. The UNEOS's Winston Prattley hastily convened a meeting at his office. In attendance were representatives of all major donor nations with embassies in Khartoum, as well as CARE, Save the Children U.K., and the various UN agencies. A sombre Andrew Timpson reported to the assembled group that only 19 per cent of the 95,000 MT of grain the SRC had undertaken to deliver to Darfur had actually arrived by June 30. Local warehouses were empty, and relief centres were being flooded with new arrivals. His words should not have surprised anyone reading reports on market prices from Kordofan and Darfur, but they hit hard. Ethiopia was happening all over again, and this time there would be no place for any of the big Western donors to hide.

In the weeks just before I arrived in the Sudan—while I was writing my bar-admission examinations—Prattley and UNEOS officials drafted a blueprint for the transport of grain and supplementary-feeding supplies to North and South Darfur using a fleet of heavy-duty four-wheel-drive trucks that would fly the UN flag. The government of Italy donated 110 Fiat military transport trucks that would form the backbone of the land-bridge fleet, which would be co-managed by Sudan's fledgling Relief and Rehabilitation Commission and the United Nations World Food Program (WFP). A Dutch company with expertise in the transport and storage of food commodities had been contracted to provide logistics expertise for the trucking enterprise, which had been given the cumbersome name of the Relief and Rehabilitation Commission/United Nations World Food Program Road Transport Operation, or RTO for short. The trucks would operate between Port Sudan and the most isolated regions of Darfur, and would have their own mobile recovery and maintenance units. It would be a massive undertaking, requiring the pre-positioning of fuel, the grading of sections of road, the repair of bridges, and the setting up of remote field stations with high-frequency radio-communications capability.

Prattley requested the World University Service of Canada position a team in the Sudan that would have the responsibility of scouting a northern route from Khartoum across open desert to El Fasher, Nyala, and El Geneina in Darfur. In addition, WUSC was requested to place three monitors in the field who would provide information on the transport and distribution of relief commodities and the nutritional status of the local population. I was to be one of those monitors.

According to a report prepared by WUSC, much of the route to Darfur was not really a road at all "but simply an ever-shifting series of tracks across the desert. It is isolated, difficult to follow, and has few facilities and communities en route." The same rains that had washed out the rail line in nine locations had flooded the seasonal rivers, known as wadis, throughout Kordofan and Darfur, making the route impassable in several sections. It was not marked on any map, and was more commonly transited by camel caravans than trucks. The paved portion of the road ended approximately five kilometres west of Khartoum. The RTO trucks would transit some of the most hostile terrain in all of Africa. There were several formidable wadis that would have to be forded; with the heavy rains, we could count on their flowing fast and deep. There were few towns along the 1,500-kilometre route, and only the most primitive truck-repair facilities. The northern route was avoided by commercial truckers because of long sections of soft, deep sand in which large transport trucks were known to disappear.

Carolyn Head had hinted at what my specific role in Road Transport Operation would be: Rudy Rodrigues had selected me to be the advance scout for the entire convoy. I was to report to Rodrigues the next morning, collect the keys for my vehicle, locate and purchase provisions for the expedition, and then head out across the Kordofan Desert. Just days after being inducted into the practice of law, and while my fellow graduates were settling in to their resplendent, oak-panelled offices, I was about to drive a Toyota Landcruiser loaded to the roof with jerrycans of diesel fuel to the outpost of El Geneina on the border of Chad. Somehow I was expected to find and chart the Sudan's version of the Northwest Passage—a route through to the west that six- and 10-MT trucks could navigate. I was thrilled at the prospect.

The RRC World Food Program Relief Transport Operation had established its headquarters within the walled compound of the Sudan base belonging to Total, the French oil company. It was located at the east end of Khartoum's airport. Total had grown impatient with the continuing hostilities in South Sudan and had radically scaled down its oil-exploration activities throughout the entire country. There was only a skeleton staff left at its Khartoum offices to protect the significant investment Total had already made in the country. As in the case of every other multinational company doing business in the Sudan, the Total compound was a world unto itself. Everything had been brought in from France, from the Duralex drinking glasses to the lighting fixtures. A noisy diesel generator provided the power for the air conditioner, which maintained the premises at an ambient temperature that approximated Arctic conditions.

I located Rudy Rodrigues in the RTO logistics room, working on a wall-sized map of the country, sketching in planned locations for fuel depots and maintenance sheds. Rudy is a Kenyan-born Canadian of Goan origin and the father of three children. WUSC had given him one week from the time he was hired to report to Khartoum; his family was packing up in Edmonton and was not far behind him. As a young man, Rudy had enlisted with the Kenyan army, and had been educated at Sandhurst, England's renowned officer-training academy. Although his most recent employment had been as a mall manager, Rudy was in his element in the Sudan, heading up what was essentially a military-style operation. He had already earned his salary many times over. While on a reconnaissance trip to Port Sudan, he had spotted 25 shiny-blue Mercedes trucks sitting idle. They had been donated by the OPEC countries but no provision had been made for their operating costs or insurance. Rudy swung into action; in less than one week, he had completed negotiations with the Saudi and Sudanese authorities to incorporate the trucks into the RTO fleet. Scooping up the Mercedes trucks was a major coup, and the UN brass were impressed.

I liked Rudy's assertive and decisive nature, and he immediately commanded my respect. After a few short words of welcome he briefed me on my assignment. Carolyn had been right: Rudy didn't want me in Khartoum long enough to warrant unpacking my bags. The spanking-new red Toyota Landcruiser I had spied on entering the building had my name on it. It came equipped with a special heavy-duty desert-option package, but in Rodrigues's opinion, it still required some modifications to make it suitable for a desert crossing.

Emergency-relief operations attract a disproportionate number of veterans of assorted foreign wars and the Sudan was no exception. On my first full day in the country, I was introduced to Neil Winship, the operations chief at RTO, who was a former British tank commander. Rudy's closest advisors at RTO were Ernest Vienna, with whom Rudy had served in the Kenyan army, and Sigmund Fossland, a veteran of the Danish army. Fossland was a walrus-like character in his late fifties who had spent the last 20 years of his life in Africa. He travelled everywhere in Africa with a Bic lighter and an ink pad. When required to provide any kind of official documentation, he forged the papers himself and used the end of the Bic lighter as a generic stamp.

Instantly recognizing me as a novice in need of assistance, Sig Fossland took me under his wing and put me through his crash course on crossing the desert without being lost or killed. Sig walked me around the Toyota Landcruiser, informed me that the fancy radial tires were useless in soft sand conditions, scribbled down the name of the metal-workers' souk where I could have a set of sand tracks made, and warned me of the danger of overloading the roof rack and thereby raising the vehicle's centre of gravity. An English relief worker had a few weeks earlier been crushed to death when his Land Rover flipped on the highway between Port Sudan and Khartoum. He had made the mistake of loading two 44-gallon drums of diesel fuel onto its roof.

In the RTO logistics room, Sig employed an umbrella—completely useless in the Sudan, and left behind by a confused volunteer who had lasted only a few days—to show me on the wall maps the route he intended me to follow. From my canoe-tripping days, I knew enough about the scale of maps and contour intervals to understand my assignment was formidable. I began to worry I had over-sold my skills as a rugged adventurer, that perhaps my résumé was too well written, but it was too late to change the script.

I went searching for my sand tracks. There are no hardware stores or shopping malls in the Sudan, but before there was Sears, there were souks. What you can't find, the tradespeople will make for you, usually on the spot—but come prepared for hard bargaining. Souks are usually organized thematically, with the leather-workers exiled to distant quarters because of the foul odors associated with tanning. Cairo's Khan el-Khalili souk, founded in 1400 by Sharkas el-Khalili, is known for spices and perfume. The souks at Aleppo in Syria, for centuries recognized as the finest anywhere in the Middle East, feature gold, silver, copper, and textiles. Reflecting Afghanistan's troubled recent history, the souks at Kabul are a mercenary's paradise: virtually every kind of weapon, from hand guns to shoulder-launched missiles, is available for a price. In recent years, American officials have been alarmed by rumors of heat-seeking Stinger anti-aircraft missiles, provided by the CIA to the Mujahadin during their campaign against the Soviet army, turning up in Peshawar alongside sabres and grenade-launchers.

Khartoum's souks are more functional than exotic, with large sections devoted to the repair of sewing machines and air-coolers. With its constant din of banging and filing, the metal-workers' souk was as distinctive as Cannery Row. I found it by rolling down the Toyota's window; it sounded as if 10

Caribbean steel bands were performing different tunes at the same time. There were more than 20 workshops spread about the souk, the majority featuring household furniture destined for Khartoum living rooms made from wrought iron painted in clementine and lime green. Security was becoming an issue in Khartoum, and break-ins were common, so a number of workshops manufactured metal grates for doors and windows.

After a bit of searching I found a workshop that specialized in automotive items, including jerrycans and roof racks. The proprietor was a bearded gentleman in a jellabiyah who looked like a prophet from the Old Testament. His name was Ishmael, and he spoke impeccable English. Ishmael immediately understood what sand tracks were, but he had no examples to show me. He had crafted his last set during World War II for an SAS officer who was en route to Libya. He explained that sand tracks had to be strong enough to withstand being driven over by a fully loaded vehicle, but light enough for one person to carry easily and slide under the wheels. Ishmael assured me that with a good set of sand tracks, I would be unstoppable; I could travel the width of the continent if I cared to. A custom-made set of sand tracks could be made for me in 24 hours. After a bit of haggling over the price, he served me excellent coffee seasoned with cardamom and introduced me to his great-grandsons, who had been hired as his newest apprentices. The youngest was only 12 or 13 but manipulated his welding torch with dexterity. The old man assured me that although the kid had never seen sand tracks in the course of his short life, he would have no difficulty designing a suitable pair. The success of the $10-million dollar RRC World Food Program Road Transport Operation was now in the hands of this pint-sized Hephaestus.

My search of other nearby souks was equally fruitful. I located jerrycans, cooking pots, a kettle, cutlery, plastic water jugs, vacuum bottles, heavy-duty rope strong enough for towing purposes, tire irons, mosquito netting, a bedroll, portable water filters, kerosene lamps, an axe, and storage boxes. After Sig Fossland's warning about keeping the centre of gravity of the vehicle low to the ground, I opted not to attach a roof-rack. Back at the RTO compound, a Total technician installed the HF radio and whip antenna.

I drove the Toyota to the grocery stores located in a residential area known as Khartoum II, just off Airport Road, with the intention of stocking up on all the food items I would need for the journey. From Carolyn's reports, I had gleaned that little food would be available in any of the villages I visited across northern Kordofan and Darfur. Even drinking water was at a premium. The stores at Khartoum II catered to the city's merchants and middle class, but the variety of items on the shelves was very limited. The Sudanese pound was not traded on the international currency markets, and most importers had to pay for foreign goods with U.S. dollars, which were hard to come by. Import restrictions imposed by the government on a variety of food items had also taken a toll. As electricity was sporadic at best, it made no sense for merchants to buy products that required refrigeration. The result was that all the stores I visited stocked only the kinds of items one would find holed away in bomb shelters. There was no milk, cheese, butter, rice, fresh meat, fish, sugar, choco- late, or flour. There were no eggs, potatoes, tomatoes, heads of lettuce, berries of any kind, beets, carrots, onions, or melons. The last canned vegetables had been sold three weeks earlier. People in the stores smiled when I asked about the availability of apples or pears. I found some excellent zucchini and fresh beans. The only fruit I could locate were grapefruit and oranges. Even salt was being rationed. After much scrounging, I came up with 36 cans of corned beef that had expired six months earlier, eight cans of Irish stew, five kilograms of macaroni, 22 cans of tomato paste, powdered milk, rock-hard biscuits, dates, canned beans, powdered lemonade, coffee, tea, toilet paper, and mosquito coils.

The Sudan had been embroiled in a civil war that had been percolating for the last 25 years between the mainly Arab north and the Nilotic and Bantu people of the south. The Sudan is 73 per cent Moslem and only 5 per cent Christian, but the war is about much more than religion. The south is rich in oil, gold, and other minerals. Vast resources had been wasted by both sides in ferocious battles waged in the remote southern regions of the country populated by the indigenous Dinka, Nuer, and Shilluk tribes, who made up approximately 20 percent of the country's total population of 21.5 million. There was no sign that either side was gaining the upper hand or that the war would ever be won.

Countries at war with themselves are hypersensitive about security issues; as a result, good-quality maps of the Sudan were almost impossible to find any- where in the country. The most detailed maps had been produced by the British during and just after World War II, but they were hoarded by the Sudanese military and treated as contraband. Sig had shown me a map of Khar- toum in his office only after I promised not to tell anyone it was in his posses- sion. It was a standard, military-issue topographic map on a scale of 1:10,000 with a contour interval of 50 feet. Although it was 40 years out of date, Sig insisted that in 10 months of searching, it was the best map of the city he had ever laid his hands on. "Look, it shows everything," he said with the zeal of an adolescent boy showing off the latest *Playboy* centrefold.

Indeed, the map was explicit: the British cartographers had gone to great lengths to chart out the railway that snaked across the city, the British military barracks, the officers' club, the airport, water towers, and radio huts. It was a perfect snapshot of Khartoum circa 1942, even noting the location of the swish Sudan Club on the banks of the Blue Nile.

Khartoum is a city that has always attracted eccentrics. After the city was razed by the Dervishes in 1885, Lord Kitchener rebuilt Khartoum according to his own hand-drawn street plan that incorporated a series of interlocking Union Jacks. He constructed a gun battery at the centre of the city for defence purposes. Peering over Sig Fossland's shoulder, I could make out the flags' faint outlines. The legacy of Kitchener's idiosyncrasy lives on today in the form of snarled traffic at six-way intersections and automobiles attempting to negotiate 120-degree turns. On the island of Elba, residents sing the praises of Napoleon, who, during his abbreviated period of exile, built aqueducts, bridges, and roads that are still in use today. In Khartoum, on the other hand, people curse the memory of Lord Kitchener.

Sig's map could get me over the Blue Nile Bridge and pointed west, but I needed something that would get me across a good portion of the Sahara Desert. Sig shrugged his shoulders. Kordofan and Darfur had last been mapped by the British in the late 1940s, but all known copies of the charts had since been confiscated by the military. Southern Kordofan, the home of the Nuba people and the site of continuing civil unrest, had been designated a security zone. The Sudanese government was nervous about anyone travelling in the vicinity of the Nuba Mountains. The explanation proffered was that attacks by bandits were common, but it's more probable that authorities in Khartoum feared the presence of rabble-rousers from the outside. The Nuba, an island of black African people surrounded by Arabs, were fiercely independent and not easily governed by outsiders. Ever since George Rodger and Leni Riefenstahl had published their stark photographs documenting the Nuba, the area had held a mystic fascination for foreigners and European-based human rights organizations.

Sig Fossland gave me the name and address of a trader on Jamhurria Avenue who kept a collection of old books and manuscripts from the days of the Anglo-Egyptian Condominium; Omar would be my best bet for maps of western Sudan that bore any resemblance to what I would actually encounter in the desert.

I didn't drive directly from RTO to Jamhurria Avenue. I had been in

Khartoum for almost 18 hours and I hadn't yet walked along the Nile to see the few remaining buildings from the era of General Gordon. The Khartoum I knew as a child from my *Boys' Own Annuals* ran the length of Nile Avenue and encompassed the governor general's palace where Gordon was killed, the graceful Anglican cathedral, the elegant Grand Hotel, and the Secretariat. From Airport Road, I turned left at the football grounds adjoining the University of Khartoum. While most of Khartoum was dusty and barren of trees, here along the river there were traces of what the city must have been like at the height of its glory. The old buildings from my storybooks were still there, covered with thick layers of grime, dilapidated, some looking abandoned. Many of them were partially overgrown by shrubs and plants; evidently no one had attempted any heavy gardening in the last 30 years. Overhead was a thick canopy of palm trees that almost blocked out the sun. It was late afternoon, and the trees were filled with finches and warblers. I parked the Toyota outside the U.S. embassy and walked along the river's edge, past the Khartoum Yacht Club. The river was in full flood and no sailboats were moored, but bobbing gently in the waters of the Blue Nile moored to the bank with heavy cable was the *Melik*, a boat whose name immediately brought to mind an episode from British colonial history that I had read and reread as a child.

The boat that now served ignobly as a clubhouse for expatriates who sailed the Nile on their days off deserved a place of honor in a naval museum. The *Melik* was an 1898 Class armored Screw gunboat and had played a critical role as part of the British expeditionary force that retook Khartoum in 1898. When the *Melik* was built, it had been fitted with two Nordenfeldt guns, one quick-firing 12-pounder gun, one Howitzer, and four Maxims. At the time, it was one of the most heavily armed vessels afloat anywhere. The *Melik* and its two sister gunboats, the *Sultan* and the *Sheikh*, had been carried in sections across the desert by rail and floated on the Nile just south of Atbara. The British expeditionary force that advanced on Khartoum included 8,200 British and 17,600 Egyptian soldiers, along with 2,469 horses, 896 mules, and 3,524 camels. Forty-four years later, after the fall of Tobruk, when it looked as if the Germans might sweep as far south as the Upper Nile, the British had installed an anti-aircraft gun on the deck of the *Melik*, and it was still in place. I expected there would at least be a historical marker telling of the gunboat's exploits, but I could not find anything.

Just before the palace, I turned away from the river in the direction of Jamhurria Avenue. All shops in Khartoum close from midday until early evening, so I was surprised to find that Omar, the trader whom Sig Fossland had recommended, was open for business. With fuel shortages plaguing Khartoum, Omar was unable to return home every day to his family for his lunch, and instead brought a simple meal to his shop each morning. He had a few tamiya left over, which he offered to share with me. He poured me a cup of tea from a vacuum bottle he kept behind the counter. When I told him what I was after, he motioned for me to be silent, peered outside the shop to see if anyone was in the vicinity, and then bolted the door shut.

"Ya salaam!" he exclaimed, his eyes bulging out of their sockets. "How long have you been with the agency?" he inquired sotto voce. It took a minute for me to comprehend that the agency he was referring to was the CIA. I explained I was nothing other than a mild-mannered relief worker, but Omar would have nothing of it. I had only dug myself deeper into a hole; Omar was on to the ruse. The CIA had a history of burying spies within the ranks of humanitarian organizations. I relented. What had tipped him off? The only customers he had for military-specification topographic maps were the many spooks who were based in Khartoum. World War II vintage maps of Darfur were prized by the Americans because the region shared a border with Libya, the homeland of Colonel Gadhafi, President Reagan's nemesis, and because in the desert, little had changed during the ensuing 40 years. Even in an age of satellite photographs, such maps were still very useful. It was well known that Libyan desert patrols camped at the same oases as the WW II British convoys. Someone with an American accent had purchased his last two maps of Darfur just a few months earlier. I was out of luck.

However, Omar had a set of what he called SPS maps from 1928 for me to examine. In the age when three-quarters of the world's land mass was colored pink, the Sudan Political Service was the division of the British Foreign Service reserved for diplomats and functionaries who were responsible for all aspects of day-to-day government throughout the colony. Members of the SPS were considered an elite, and were recruited exclusively from the ranks of upper-class English males. A disproportionate number were graduates of schools such as Harrow, Rugby, Marlborough, Winchester, and Eton. What Omar referred to as SPS maps were maps printed by the colonial authorities in London for the purposes of good governance. The map he showed me was of excellent quality. I noticed several stark warnings: the words "Beware—bandit activity" were printed in the vicinity of the Kawra Mountains west of El Fasher. Someone had carefully added markings of their own, penciling in at one desolate spot, "Good water here." The map was a real find; I sensed I had discovered my own version of the Dead Sea

Scrolls. With my trusty Silva compass for which I had traded in my law books, I now had a fighting chance of crossing the desert intact. I purchased Omar's map with a crisp new $20 bill and bid him a cheery "Ma'salaama."

There was no time for any kind of formal send-off. Carolyn Head helped me load my supplies into the back of the Landcruiser; Sig Fossland reminded me to pack the sand tracks last as I would soon be making use of them. I topped off my fuel tank and found room on board for an additional 11 jerrycans of diesel. Estimates of how long the trip to El Geneina would take ranged from 10 days to a month. There was a considerable body of opinion among seasoned relief workers recuperating at the Acropole Hotel that the northern route I was attempting was impassable. They doubted I would even reach Sodiri, halfway to El Fasher. Souk lorry drivers who gathered every evening at the Omdurman market reported the wadi at Bir Abu Zaima was flooded and no vehicles could get across. I could be marooned in the desert for weeks.

On Rudy's recommendation, I hired a driver who could double as a mechanic. If my vehicle broke down, it would be up to Abdullah and me to fix it. The mobile service units that RTO had been promised were languishing in Port Sudan awaiting customs clearance. Apparently, somebody needed to be paid a bribe. I programmed the HF radio to our assigned frequency of 7768 and had my first conversation with Mike Kilo, the RTO base-camp radio operator. I had been assigned the handle "Ruff Road Seven." Sig warned me that radio transmissions from Kordofan and Darfur would be of poor quality during the middle of the day because we had inadvertently been assigned a low-range short-wave frequency that was highly susceptible to electronic interference. He suggested I check in by radio every night at nine o'clock, when the desert had cooled and when radio waves could travel greater distances.

Sig had devised his own short form for me to use when sending messages, utilizing a system of colors and numbers. He expected daily reports on the status of the section of the northern route I had travelled, and he wanted whatever information I transmitted to be unambiguous. He reminded me that within two weeks, the big Fiat four-by-four trucks would be loaded with relief supplies and sent west according to the road instructions I had provided. Nothing would prevent their departure. "Find my route to the west—and find it quick," Sig pleaded. He pounded the roof of the Toyota, then signalled me off.

I was glad to be finally on my way. We crossed over the White Nile bridge to the old town of Omdurman, and Abdullah guided me through the souks and onto the paved road that pointed west. Within minutes we were off the asphalt and following the deep ruts left in the soft sand by the souk lorries. They went off in all directions and there was no one main path to follow. I shifted the Landcruiser into four-wheel-drive, and with my 1928 SPS map as my guide, plowed through the golden sand toward the setting sun. It was Thursday, August 29, I was 13,000 kilometres from home, and the dunes and ridges of the Sahara Desert stretched as far as the eye could see.

Since the time of the ancients, the desert has been a place to retreat to, a place for contemplation and reconciliation, a place for mystics. Its power mirrors the forces of the divine. The desert compels and confounds us. Our best efforts to contain it have failed; the desert frustrates our most resourceful engineers who spend hundreds of millions of dollars from development agencies in efforts to halt its advance. Nothing seems to work. The desert has its own rhythm. It moves forward, gathering momentum along its course, threatening cities in its path, then with no warning it shifts direction. At times, defying the scientists who plot its every move, it retreats into itself. The Bedouin look on with amusement at the busy foreigners who arrive with their noisy machines to drill, dredge, and irrigate along the banks of the Nile. The Sahara cannot be tamed, and it hits back hard at those who try to build kingdoms among the sand dunes.

For centuries, great armies have marched into the desert with imperial designs, never to be seen again. The poet Shelley, coming across bare ruins amidst the "lone and level sands" of Egypt, tells us of the fate of a desert king named Ozymandias whose statue was reduced to "Two vast and trunkless legs of stone" and a nearby "shattered visage." The desert humbles us and reminds us of our own mortality. Alexander the Great, after conquering most of the civilized world, knew, when he gazed out over the Sahara, that he had reached the southern limit of his empire. We are told he gathered his generals in his tent, announced his decision to retreat to the north, and quoted the ancient poet Lao Tzu: "The wise general, daring to march, dares also to halt."

Arabic, Amharic, and Aramaic are desert tongues. They lend themselves to the stories and songs about the land that are traded by the fires of Bedouin camps. When confronted by the desert, our own clumsy language fares no better than our soldiers. We are forced to resort to allusion, simile, and metaphor. We employ tired adjectives. How many writers have portrayed the desert as unforgiving, empty, barren, or hostile? At moments, it can be all or none of these things. In desperation, we search for elements of the romantic in the topography of the land and in the rituals of the people who inhabit it. But the only writers who find sentimental elements in the harsh lifestyle of desert peoples are those who have never lived through a dry season, with crying children, withering crops, and dehydrated livestock to care for. We speak of "waves of sand," but in truth, the desert has nothing in common with the sea. In truth, the desert is like nothing else on the face of the earth.

I was no T. E. Lawrence, Erwin Rommel, or Saint-Exupéry. I passed my childhood in the suburbs of a middle-class Canadian university town. My desert experience consisted of a few weekends in the 1960s I had spent with my paternal grandfather exploring the badlands between Tucson, Arizona, and the Mexican border, and my 14 days in Ethiopia eight months earlier with John Godfrey. With the help of the concierge at the Sahara Hotel, I had taught myself a dozen useful Arabic phrases, such as "Is this good water?" and "I don't have a gun." I now knew the words for spice (shatta), salt (millih), orange (portoocan), and truck (arabia). We were only 20 kilometres west of Khartoum when my driver Abdullah, who in our first meeting had described himself as an experienced desert guide, confessed he was really a city kid at heart and was terrified of open spaces. I had expected him to come equipped with the paraphernalia one associates with a desert crossing: a sharp knife, a sturdy water container, fire-making implements, and a good set of tools. Instead, Abdullah chose to bring Vuarnet sunglasses and the latest-model Sony Walkman. I suspected he was in big trouble back in Khartoum and needed to get out of town.

We made camp just after midnight under a starlit sky. I laid out my bedroll and rigged up my mosquito netting, tying the support strings to the roof of the Landcruiser. Abdullah was petrified of what he called "jackal packs," ferocious wild dogs that would rip apart anyone sleeping out in the open. According to Abdullah, they were known to walk off with small children between their jaws. He chose to make camp amidst the jerrycans, spare tires, and storage boxes in the back of the Landcruiser. He would breathe diesel fumes all night, but he would be safe.

The Sudan is more than 2.5 million square kilometres in size and borders on seven countries and the Red Sea. South Sudan alone is a region the size of France. In his definitive biography of the greatest traveller of our age, Wilfred Thesiger, Michael Asher writes of the diversity of the country:

> Perhaps the most fascinating country in Africa, the Sudan's vastness and diversity of cultures qualify it almost for the status of a miniature continent. It encompasses a complete cross-section of Africa's landscapes, from the ultimate sterile desert in the north, grading down through desert scrub and savannah of every

describable degree, to tropical forest on its southern borders. There are the fertile lands of the Nile valley, the placid beaches and arid mountains of the Red Sea Coast, the volcanic Marra range in the west, and isolated fastnesses like the enclave of the Nuba Mountains in the middle. It is home for hundreds of different tribes, speaking more than 100 different languages: in the north there are Arab Bedouin herding camels, goats, and sheep as far as the Libyan borders: in the southern grasslands and forests stalk naked cattle-herding Nilotic tribesmen like the Dinka and Nuer, standing tall and thin as thorn-trees. In the east roam the wild Beja nomads of the Red Sea Hills, who rear the best camels in Africa and wear their hair in uncut plumes as a sign of manhood, and in the west, the shym, hill-farming Fur and Tunjur, the black Saharan camel-men known as Zaghawa and Bedayat, and the Africanized Arab tribes that have been called 'the frontier tribes of Arabdom'—the ferocious cattle- and horse-riding Baggara nomads who formed the backbone of the Dervish army. In the 1930s, the country teemed with every kind of game: elephant, lion, buffalo, leopard, and any number of gazelles, antelopes, small mammals, and birds.

Apart from the destruction of the wildlife, the Sudan of 1985 had changed little from the land encountered by the young Thesiger, assigned as an assistant district commissioner to Darfur in 1934. The area where I would be based, in the region of El Geneina, was a day's drive across the desert from the town of Kutum where Thesiger had been posted. If anything, the conditions I would experience were likely to be even more primitive than those of colonial times. In the 1930s, there was regular passenger- and freight-train service between Khartoum and El Obeid, the capital of Kordofan. New roads had been cut through the desert and telex lines linked even smaller towns with Khartoum and the outside world. The British had built schools in all major towns. Gordon College in Khartoum provided a standard of university education for Sudanese students on par with anything available in the British Empire. Hospitals were constructed and outfitted with equipment brought in fresh from England, and wells were drilled. In 1940, the British built airfields in El Obeid, Nyala, and El Geneina. Weather stations were established, and a crop-monitoring program put in place. Commerce flourished. Merchants in El Obeid could receive orders for gum arabic or hibiscus leaves from dealers in London and, making use of the excellent rail and sea connections, could guarantee delivery within three weeks.

By 1985, the infrastructure left behind by the British had totally rotted away. Nothing had been adequately maintained over the years. In the words of Bob Geldof, "The Sudan was in a state of permanent chaos." Most bridges across the wadis had long before collapsed. Hospitals had been drained of everything that wasn't fastened to the floor, walls, or ceiling, and had no running water or sewage systems; local residents had made off with the copper pipes. People in El Geneina spoke nostalgically of the old days when electricity had been available and potable water would flow merely with a turn of the tap. The EEC air-bridge between Khartoum, Nyala, and El Geneina was encountering problems because the air strips had not been resurfaced since the 1950s and huge potholes were emerging. Schools in rural Kordofan and Darfur had no supplies, and teachers went for months without being paid. The British had run the country without interruption from 1899, when the Anglo-Egyptian Condominium was formed, through 1956, the year the Sudan was granted its independence. Along the dusty trail west of Khartoum, I encountered not a single trace of the Sudan's colonial legacy. Fifty-seven years of investment, planning, and management by the Colonial Office had been, for all intents and purposes, erased. No hint of the Empire remained. Once again, the desert had triumphed.

On Friday, August 30, I woke up at 5:15 a.m., having escaped attacks by roving bands of jackals. It had rained overnight and the air was cool. Abdullah and I breakfasted on oranges and coffee, loaded up the Landcruiser, then pressed on in the direction of El Fasher. It was hard going in the soft sand, and we had to stop at regular intervals to let the engine cool. As boats have an optimum speed at which the hull rises out of the water and begins to plane, so I learned that in the desert, the idea was to drive at a sufficient speed to allow the Toyota to ride the crest of the sand and not bog down. Some sections of terrain we travelled were wide open, with no sign of a path or track of any kind. If the sand was hard enough, I would accelerate to 80 kilometres an hour, kicking up clouds of dust behind me. The sense of speed was exhilarating; like a skier, I would negotiate slalom turns around clumps of scrub brush. Our nemeses were the prickly thorn bushes. They were camouflaged against the desert sand and popped up out of nowhere. Driving over them was not advisable; their razor-sharp needles could easily pierce our sand tires. On our first two days we had four punctures.

I kept the 1928 SPS map folded to the appropriate quadrant, and mounted the Silva compass in the plastic well designed for coffee cups and loose change. It was essential to follow the map closely. There were few if any landmarks to go by, and the land was so flat that triangulation was not a possibility. At times, when we were crossing especially rough terrain, I would be tempted to follow in the tracks of a souk lorry. I assumed they would be a good marker; lorry drivers, paid by the trip rather than the hour, would be travelling the shortest distance across the desert. But Bedford trucks have huge balloon tires with a 1.5-metre diameter, and their bodies are jacked up to provide them with at least one metre of ground clearance. The danger following in their wake is that one can easily bottom out on the mound of sand that piles up between the two tracks, leaving the vehicle suspended on its transaxles. I soon became proficient at estimating which souk tracks were navigable and which would leave us teetering high and dry.

It was slow going. By 7:20 a.m., we had travelled only 77 kilometres since we had left Khartoum. We had already been forced to stop twice to dig the vehicle out. The military-surplus shovels Rudy had found for me at the last minute were proving more valuable than the sand tracks. The winch, powered by the Toyota's mighty eight-cylinder diesel engine, was useless, as there were no trees or other fixed objects for kilometres around to attach the winch cable to. We had been told in Khartoum to keep an eye out for the UN's Road Transport Operation road-maintenance team, which had been dispatched along the northern route to clear the way for the Fiat trucks, but since we had left Khartoum, I had seen no sign of their work. Their mission seemed futile. Transferring sand from one place to another would achieve nothing at all. There was simply no road to maintain.

At Jebra Es Sheikh we received bad news. Souk lorry drivers explained to Abdullah that the route west was impassable at Bir Abu Zaima. The rumors we had heard in Omdurman were true: the wadi was flooded and was running at its highest level in years. The drivers had attempted to get across, but their trucks had stalled and had to be winched back to the shore. Our only option was to turn south and pass via Umm Inderaba and Bara to El Obeid, joining up with the southern route. Our hope of finding a Northwest Passage to Darfur was dashed.

It was blisteringly hot—46 degrees Celsius—and there wasn't a single tree that could provide an iota of shade. The track to Umm Inderaba and Bara was impossible to discern, and the sand was thick and soft. We let air out of our tires for better traction and kept the transmission in the low range with our differentials locked. The sand tracks from the metal souk proved indispensable. At times our wheels would be completely buried, and merely digging them out without providing support served no purpose: the Toyota simply sank deeper into the sand.

At noon, 336 kilometres west of Khartoum and en route to Bara, I heard Sig Fossland's thickly accented English coming across the radio. He was on board the UN Cessna 210, November 125 Charlie Foxtrot, heading toward Bir Abu Zaima, and he had expected to find us on the road. Where the hell were we? Using our pre-arranged code, I reported that the road condition was red west of Jebra Es Sheikh on account of the water at Bir Abu Zaima. We had no alternative and had diverted to the south. Sig was furious, and ordered us to turn around and proceed directly to Bir Abu Zaima. In my diary I noted: "Sacrificed for the cause so back we go."

I loved the isolation. Despite the absence of water, there were aspects of desert travel that reminded me of my canoe-tripping days in Quetico Provincial Park and the Boundary Waters Wilderness Area on the Ontario-Manitoba border. In the desert, we camped shortly after sunset, and made a fire with wood and brush that we had scrounged along the route to cook our cans of Irish stew and to heat our tea. Abdullah was a good conversationalist and was proving to be an agreeable travel companion. I soon realized that when he described himself back in Khartoum as a camel man, he was referring not to his experience as a pastoralist but rather to the brand of cigarettes he smoked. He was also a born raconteur and a good singer. He would have preferred to camp in one of the little villages we passed, but I craved the peace of the desert.

The few minutes just before and just after sunset, when the smallest ridge would stand out against the evening sky, became my favorite time of day. At dusk, I could make out colors in the grass and in the earth and in the rocks that were invisible under the midday sun. Nightjars would appear, drawn to the insects that hovered around our camp. In less than a quarter of an hour, dusk would be replaced by darkness, and I would watch the Southern Cross rise out of the sand. My last act before crawling under my mosquito netting each night was to strip naked, pour water from the jerrycans over my body, and without the aid of a towel, allow it to evaporate from my skin. It was complete bliss. The sand absorbed huge amounts of heat during the day and continued to radiate warmth for hours after the sun had set, but once the earth had cooled, the desert became chilly, and with the clear skies overhead the heat was sucked far out into space.

On more than one occasion, the light from our fire attracted Bedouin. We would hear the sound of the camel bells before we could make out the forms of the travellers with our eyes. After exchanging greetings, we shared coffee, water, dates, and nuts, and then the storytelling would begin. I couldn't understand a word; Abdullah did his best to translate. One group of Bedouin had travelled the Forty Day Road into Egypt, and had seen the pyramids. Man had done such great things long before the arrival of machines, they acknowledged. At that moment, I pointed to the moon and commented on the herculean feat of the American astronauts who had walked on its surface. My remarks were met with more than one minute's silence. Finally the oldest Bedouin spoke: "We respect our hawaja friend because he is a fellow traveller, but please do not think that we are so stupid as to believe such a silly story." Then he chuckled, and we all joined in. I apologized for my deception, and all was soon forgiven.

Along the route to Darfur, my diary entries ranged from the trivial to reflections on the devastating impact of the famine around me:

> September 1, 1985. Had an excellent shower last night—the bowls of clear, warm water were heavenly. Good sleep under the stars—a full eight hours. Last night I heard the CBC French service on the short-wave, complete with the first four notes of "O Canada."

> 475 kilometres. Just bypassed much black mud. I became stuck and was pulled out by a huge D2 grader that's part of the UN road maintenance team. Then hard rally-driving around mud to the village of Abu Hadid. Radioed Sierra Nyala to have them pass along to Mike Kilo that the road maintenance team is out of fuel. Some good news—we came across a souk lorry heading along this route to El Fasher. We even found Abu Hadid on our map. We are bypassing stations 3 and 4, Jebel Haraza and Hamrat El Wuz, and proceeding west to Sodiri, station 6, then bypassing station 8, Hamrat esh Sheikh, and heading southwest.

> Hot hot hot day. It's 1:40 p.m. and it must be 45 degrees Celsius. We stopped for tea in some shade. We took on extra water and fuel at Jebra Es Sheikh. I now have 10 jerrycans of fuel plus an almost full main tank. There was a fine well in Jebra—clear, cool water. The question now is how is the track from Hamrat El Wuz to Sodiri. With this hot, dry weather, the roads to the west should be improving.

> 490 kilometres. 15 kilometres due west of Abu Hadid we encounter a large wadi. The sight of stuck souk lorries is very

discouraging. We make camp at 5:30 p.m. Good dinner of soup and stew. Fine location, with birds and mountains in the east. Problem with bugs—but Abdullah rigs up the mosquito netting.

556 kilometres. We meet two farmers and a child who are grateful we are helping to feed their people. Thought at first they might be upset that we were driving through their field. They assured us a lorry had made it through on the same route some days before. People here are desperate. We come across only the very young and the very old—everyone else has gone.

645 kilometres. EnRoute to Sodiri. Soft sand but it can support the Toyota since it rained yesterday. Trying to reach Sig on the radio but no luck.

666 kilometres. We reach Sodiri and find out that the road to the west is closed. Which way now?

In Sodiri, we came upon a small convoy of trucks. They were souk lorries en route to the west, loaded with commercial supplies sent by Khartoum merchants hoping to cash in on the famine. Even the most basic goods, such as candles and tire patches, could be sold at a handsome profit in the Darfur souks. Diesel fuel was particularly coveted. The merchants stayed away from food items because the foreign-aid agencies were distributing large shipments of free grain, vegetable oil, and salt. Food trucked in by the merchants would therefore be less valuable; it was safer to stick to items that were not on the agencies' shopping list. The truck drivers had travelled to the edge of the wadi at Bir Abu Zaima and then turned back. It wasn't passable. Abdullah told me if anyone could get through the wadi, they could. The drivers work as a team, dragging each other across the wadi. Sometimes it would take 50 men and five camels to free a truck stuck in the mud.

I sent another radio message to Khartoum: "Local intelligence is that best route is south to Bara and El Obeid, then west to En Nahud, Umm Keddada, and on to El Fasher. Request permission to detour south to En Nahud." I received a reply an hour later from Sig and Rudy: "Try to detour to the north of the wet area. Southern road not acceptable. Area survey two days ago by November 125 Charlie Foxtrot shows some dry area through northern route."

We obeyed our orders, and against the advice of the souk lorry drivers followed their old tracks west toward Bir Abu Zaima. Here, along the northern edge of Kordofan, the drought had hit hard. Entire villages had emptied out and wells had run dry. We stopped to pick up an old man en route from his village, now abandoned, to Sodiri. He said it had not rained in more than two years, and anyone with the strength to leave had packed their belongings and begged rides on souk lorries to the big towns of the east. It was the worst famine he had seen in over 50 years. He prayed constantly for rain. "Allah karim," he repeated to himself over and over again.

God will provide. I had first heard the words "Allah karim" uttered by residents of Khartoum when confronted by beggars asking for food or something to drink. It's an ancient equivalent of "Don't worry. Be happy." The beggar is assured, despite his pathetic condition, that in the end, his needs will be met. There is no need for the rich to intervene or to feel guilty. Too often, "Allah karim" was nothing more than an excuse for inaction, a justification for callousness on the part of well-fed middle-class Sudanese back in Khartoum, and the international community. If it is all in the hands of God, then we can ignore the pleas of the beggar and let nature take its course in Kordofan and Darfur.

In July, 1985, Malcolm McLean of Oxfam prepared a report that he titled *The deterioration of nutritional status in Kordofan region between February and June 1985, with special reference to Northern Kordofan*. I had a copy of the report stuffed in the glove compartment of the Landcruiser as I crossed through the very area that McLean had studied. Despite the awkward title, it was a readable and useful document. In January, 1985, Oxfam had set up a nutritional-surveillance and drought-monitoring project in Northern Kordofan. Children between the ages of one and five from 15 randomly selected villages and six nomadic settlements were assessed. The survey results showed their nutritional status over the four months had deteriorated rapidly. According to the study, the children who were severely malnourished had very little chance of survival. McLean was direct and almost clinical in his detachment: "They are likely to have all died by now." He estimated that 8,640 children had died in Kordofan since the survey had been carried out, but the mortality rate was increasing rapidly as supplies, including famine foods, in most communities were being exhausted. In McLean's opinion, "A severely malnourished child is likely to die within two weeks of being measured, depending on whether the child has complicating infections—nearly all do— the child's age, and parental care." In September alone, McLean estimated there could be 25,200 deaths among children. For the remainder of the famine, he estimated that 533 children would die each day—one every 2.7 minutes. He added, "It is worth noting again that the trends are more likely to be logarithmic in nature rather than linear. Hence these estimates may well be conservative."

As a foreigner driving an expensive Toyota packed with supplies in a region levelled by drought and famine, I was worried I might be subject to harassment, if not violence, but along the route we encountered few people begging, and no one ever threatened us. People were too hungry and weak to challenge us. We had been told by Rudy to report at each police station we passed, but our first check-in with local authorities had cost us almost half a day while our documents were examined and re-examined, so I decided to forego the formalities. We never again reported to a police station. No one ever pursued us or even asked if I had a driving permit for the Sudan. (I did not.) In the Middle East and North Africa, travellers are afforded a special status; the Koran actually makes provision for travellers, allowing them to forego fasting during Ramadan. They are only required to make up the days at a later date. In hamlets depopulated of everyone except the old and the infirm, we were treated with kindness and generosity, and were usually ushered into the home of the sheikh, if there were one, or someone who had some tea or coffee to offer us. My basic Arabic was improving and I could carry on a simple conversation. Greetings always invoked God's blessings: may God be with you, they would say: "Al Hamdu lillaa." The words "If God wills it," or "En Sh'Allah," were tagged on to almost every sentence indicating an intention to act. When asked where I was heading, I replied that I hoped to be in El Geneina within two weeks—En Sh'Allah.

In the end, we were able to cross the wadi at Bir Abu Zaima. We attached our tow rope to the front of the Toyota and more than 60 men and boys dragged us 150 metres across the wadi. They had first lightened our load, carrying all our provisions over their heads to safety on the far side, stacking them in a neat pile. It was an extraordinary sight. Sig had warned me that if it ever came to this, I should stuff plastic bags in the exhaust pipe of the Toyota—at all costs, keep the engine dry. Water and diesel fuel don't mix. Once we were across, I extracted the plastic bags from the exhaust pipe and the engine started easily; the whole crowd cheered. I had nothing to give them and nothing was requested from me. We loaded up the Landcruiser and continued our trek west.

The next day we were waved down by a shepherd family of three generations. With the wadi flooded, no vehicles were getting through, and we were the first truck they had seen in over two weeks. If we made it through, then hope could not be far off. They wanted to slaughter the whitest of their goats in celebration of our arrival, and I had to persuade them to spare the creature's life. I gave them some empty plastic jugs. I had squirrelled away some chocolate in the first-aid kit, which I handed to their child. He had no idea what it was and cautiously nibbled at it. I'm sure he would have preferred a piece of fresh fruit, but we had not seen a single orange or melon for over 300 kilometres.

We carried on in the direction of Umm Gozayn. After 10 days on the road, our supplies were depleted and my energy was flagging. I was plagued with doubts about whether we would be able to accomplish our mission. Every hungry girl or boy who tried to wave us down, to beg anything that would dull their hunger pangs, reminded me of our responsibilities. I had no faith in the ability of the souk lorries, or even our heavy-duty Fiat trucks, to ford the wadi at Bir Abu Zaima. I radioed Sig Fossland and suggested he fly in a portable Bailey Bridge that could be assembled on site. The only other option was to wait it out until the water level subsided, which could be a matter of weeks. Despite our best efforts, we could not find the track to Umm Gozayn; in the end, a 10-year-old shepherd boy appeared out of nowhere and offered to be our guide. I assumed he wanted a ride and had no idea where we were heading, but he confidently led us across a field and through a little valley bordering the village. We could never have found the route on our own.

In Umm Gozayn, the market stalls were shut tight and there was not one item for sale in the town's few shops. We searched without luck for diesel fuel. We had consumed our last macaroni and pasta sauce, all our Irish stew, and were down to a few cans of Argentinean corned beef. Our water was sufficient for at least another five days if we used it sparingly. People staggered directionless around the market. One mangy dog wandered about; I kept clear of him. By noon, the temperature had reached 42 degrees Celsius and nothing moved. We decided to push off.

Hunger is part of the life cycle of the people who inhabit Northern Kordofan and Darfur. They must expertly manage the few resources available or risk starvation. By the end of the dry season, most families will have exhausted their household food stores and sold off any livestock they cannot sustain. During the dry season, adults commonly lose 5 per cent of their body weight. In order to obtain the necessary seeds and tools for planting during the wet season, farmers are forced to take out "sheil" loans at interest rates between 50 and 75 per cent. Even with a good harvest, the farmer must hand over much of his crop to the merchant who provided him with the loan, leaving him and his family in a precarious position for the impending dry season. By 1985, after four consecutive years of insufficient rainfall, most boreholes had run dry or had not been properly maintained. Nearly a quarter of Kordofan's 730 water yards required repairs before they could function. Even in the regional capital of El Obeid, water had become a commercial commodity when the 1000-litre-per-day capacity of the town's 25 wells proved insufficient. In rural areas, much of the water was of dubious quality; health workers attributed a 60 per cent incidence of diarrhea in children below the age of five in the area around El Obeid to contaminated wells.

Across Kordofan in 1985, approximately 425,000 people had been internally displaced. Many nomadic families were forced to move to towns and cities as far east as Omdurman in search of food and water, where they often came into conflict with local farmers. Rising food prices reflected the scale of the crisis: over a six-month period, the price for sorghum, known as dura, in most towns had tripled from 45 to 130 Sudanese pounds per 90-kilogram sack—about $100 at the official exchange rate. An estimated 2.8 million people were affected by the drought and needed to be supplied with grain—the same stocks that were being held up 1,300 kilometres away in Port Sudan.

Resentment against the central government in Khartoum was growing day by day. For more than two years, village councils and regional officials, noting rising food prices and diminishing village grain stores, had alerted the appropriate authorities in Khartoum that famine was imminent. Even the arrival of tens of thousands of displaced residents of Kordofan and Darfur on the doorsteps of Khartoum failed to budge the Nimeiri regime, which displayed little sympathy for their plight. In large measure the overthrow of President Nimeiri in July, 1985, can be attributed to the callous indifference that he and his administration demonstrated to the people of Kordofan and Darfur at the time of their greatest need.

I was driving along a corridor of despair. Never before had I felt such anxiety that at times verged on terror. Nothing that I had learned at college had prepared me for catastrophe. I had no local knowledge to build on. For long periods, mine was the only vehicle on the road. In some villages there were a few trucks, but their fuel had run out weeks before and they were stranded. Before Bir Abu Zaima, I would see souk lorries every hour. Now families were forced to walk single file in the open sun, often with a single, skeletal donkey in tow. My daily radio reports to Mike Kilo at the RTO base camp became more despairing. All the local warehouses were empty; even the police and local officials couldn't find food. Schools had been closed for two years. Farms had been abandoned. Families had been ripped apart, with almost all young men heading to the cities in search of sustenance. People had lost all hope.

After nine days and 1,207 kilometres on the road, we arrived in El Fasher on September 7 at 1:00 p.m. All our jerrycans of diesel were empty and we were down to a quarter tank of fuel. I was physically and emotionally spent, and staggered into the UN office, my face streaked with sweat and grime from the journey. My arms were covered in grease up to the elbows from changing a broken fan belt on the road from Umm Kaddada to Abyad.

The UN office was neat, orderly, and cool. A generator outside provided electricity for the air conditioner and the ceiling fan that whirled overhead. There was a new IBM computer purring away on the desk. I spied a water cooler in the corner. I wanted to assault it, but held off. The men in the office were wearing clean white shirts and ironed khaki trousers with cuffs; their hair was neatly combed back. None of them were Sudanese. They were taken aback by our appearance, and they kept their distance from us. Over nine days, I had lost eight kilos. I hadn't shaved for a week. My desert boots were caked with mud. They nodded in our direction, acknowledging our presence. "Where are you coming in from?" they inquired nervously. They didn't believe we had reached El Fasher via the northern route, as few souk lorries were getting through. No traffic had arrived via Sodiri and Umm Gozayn in over three weeks. They had been expecting the big construction trucks of the road-maintenance crew and had assumed we would be a good distance behind the Americans. People had been dreaming of having a grader in town that could plow through wadis and build roads. I asked for a glass of water for Abdullah and me and collapsed into an office chair.

Now I understood the lure of an oasis. El Fasher is built around a seasonal lake known as the "fula" that lends the settlement the ambience of a sleepy Mississippi town. For hundreds of years, El Fasher has been known as the beginning and the end of the famed Forty Day Road, the 1,400-kilometre camel-caravan route across the eastern Sahara linking Darfur with Asyut in Middle Egypt. To this day, caravans still load up at El Fasher, for the trek to Egypt, and you can find the camels grazing under the big acacia trees at the water's edge. For me, after nine days of sand and grime and mud, the town had a dream-like quality. In El Fasher, you could hear birds singing just before sunset, and thick, green palms shaded the streets. Stores were open, and people had fuel for their trucks. On the way into El Fasher I noticed the fields of green tumbac, or tobacco, that marked the perimeter of the town. They were doing well with the recent rains. Clearly El Fasher was faring better than many of the villages we had seen.

Abdullah relished the idea of hanging out in the El Fasher souk for a few days, but I was anxious to complete our journey and arrive at my posting. We stayed just long enough to fill our jerrycans with diesel and water, and to stock up on cans of corned beef and Irish stew, apparently the only tinned-food items that the authorities allowed into the country.

Abdullah took the Landcruiser to a local workshop, where we replaced the oil and air filters; after 1,200 kilometres of punishing desert travel, no additional maintenance was required. I made a mental note to write a letter to the people at the Toyota Motor Corporation in Japan. They had designed and built a truly miraculous machine that out-performed every other vehicle in its class. The only place for a Jeep in the Sudan was on the tarmac roads of the nation's capital, where the most serious obstacles they would encounter were potholes and pedestrians. The Jeeps proved useless in the very conditions they were advertised to thrive in. The newest-version Land Rovers were finicky. In Africa, it's easy to recognize people accustomed to the idiosyncrasies of Land Rovers; knowing that doors rarely open from the inside, they will automatically reach through the open window and open the door using the outside handle. The Mercedes four-wheel-drives, custom-built in Austria, were plagued by weak engine mounts. With the Landcruiser, the Japanese had done their homework.

After six hours in El Fasher, we continued our trip. West of El Fasher the landscape changed dramatically. This was rugged mountain country that reminded me of the American southwest, with rocky promontories, dried-up river beds, and huge outcroppings of granite. We began to climb steeply as we approached the town of Tawila, heading for the pass at Kebkabiya. It was late in the afternoon, and the views in all directions were spectacular. Egyptian hawks circled overhead looking for prey. Just south of us loomed the extinct volcano at Jebal Marra. I had heard stories about the mysterious lake at the base of the volcano and the wild horses that lived within its confines, cut off from the rest of the world. For generations, the area of the Kawra Mountains has been famous for bandits, so we maintained a lookout, particularly when we stopped for a break. We kept our engine running in case we had to make a quick getaway. As we approached Kebkabiya, we were buzzed by a big Luftwaffe Transal transport plane heading in the direction of El Geneina; the pilot tipped his wings in greeting, then disappeared through the pass at an altitude of not more than 400 feet. He was making his last run of the day and had just enough light to land at El Geneina before heading back to Khartoum.

I had to brake hard as we descended the winding track that led from the Kawra Mountains to Birka Sayra. According to my map, Birka Sayra was 275 kilometres from El Fasher, almost two days' drive, allowing ample time to cross flooded wadis, but our progress was slow.

After having reached El Fasher in defiance of all predictions, I felt as if nothing could stop us. But my overconfidence proved costly. Just 10 kilometres west of Kebkabiya, I misjudged the conditions of a wadi I had presumed to be firm and dry. We had advanced about 10 metres across its surface when we hit wet sand; I watched in horror as we quickly submerged up to window level in the thick, black ooze. I thought at one point that the Landcruiser was lost. Should I send a mayday call to Sig more than 1,000 kilometres to the east in Khartoum? The shame of losing a $40,000 desert-equipped Landcruiser in a mud hole was too much to contemplate. I considered the option of reporting the vehicle stolen by bandits; it would be much less humiliating.

It was impossible to open the doors, so Abdullah and I clambered out onto the roof through the windows. Mercifully, the vehicle did not sink any farther. Like Murphy's Law, one of Sig Fossland's Rules of Off-road Driving in Africa is that whenever a winch is really required, there won't be a solid object within 100 metres suitable for attaching a winch cable. Sure enough, the nearest tree was 150 metres off in the distance. Our army shovels proved useless in the thick mud. Unless the road-maintenance crew dropped out of the sky, this miserable wadi was our new home for the duration. And I'd worried about bandit attacks.

I was beginning to learn the ways of the desert, though. Allah karim—God will indeed provide. We had not been in the wadi more than 30 minutes when 20 Bedouin mounted on magnificent Bishari camels appeared on the horizon. They were heading our way. At first I thought they were an apparition. The camels were loaded up for a long journey. A number of children were among the riders. Attached to their saddles with twine and leather strands were drinking gourds, plastic jugs, cooking pots, sacks of charcoal, firewood, sheathed knives, camel-hair blankets, and rolled-up beds fashioned from palm fibre. Abdullah and I must have looked very silly sitting on the roof of our sinking Landcruiser.

A chorus of "Wallahi" and "Ya salaam"—"By God" and "By heaven"—ensued. The travellers dismounted and cautiously approached the Landcruiser. We uttered the traditional greetings of travellers, praising Allah for His greatness and thanking Him for His mercy. I gave the Bedouin a tour of the vehicle.

They were particularly intrigued by the HF radio, which erupted every few minutes with bursts of static-laden radio babble in English, Dutch, and Arabic, and by Abdullah's yellow Walkman. Abdullah suggested he let them listen to "Just the Two of Us," a tune with which he had tormented me from the moment we had left Khartoum. I threatened to take Abdullah back to the Kawra Mountains and tie him to a tree. Between the bandits and packs of roving jackals, he would have little chance of surviving the night.

The Bedouin asked, of course, why I would ever have attempted to drive across the very kind of sand that is well known to envelop anything heavier than a camel, but they knew that hawaja, as foreigners are called, did stupid things. Then, with no further discussion, they used our tow ropes to attach their animals to the front of the Toyota. It was an ingenious arrangement, with two separate pods of camels harnessed to the tow hook. Experienced camel-herders can speak and sing to their animals, and from all indications, the camels understand everything they are told. The Bisharis waited until all the preparations had been completed and then rose in unison on command. The first efforts to free the Toyota failed, so two more camels were hitched up. After much grunting and kicking, the vehicle was pulled clear of the mud and dragged to the west side of the wadi. I caught the whole episode on film.

We drove through the night. At one point I started hallucinating, brought on by intense fatigue and hours at the steering wheel of the Toyota without a break. In the glare of the headlights the sand appeared to me as snow. We had been caught in a once in a lifetime Sahara blizzard—or so it seemed. Just after 3 a.m., we pulled into Birka Sayra, hungry and tired. We had made good time, covering the 200 kilometres from the wadi in less than six hours. We were on the main souk lorry route again, and despite the late hour, six trucks were in the market, refuelling and letting off passengers. Straw mats were spread out on the ground for travellers to rest, and the whole area was illuminated by oil lanterns. Under the light of a quarter moon, the souk took on a timeless quality. I lay back on the mat, sucked the sweet juice from the sections of five oranges and sipped coffee laced with cardamom and ginger heated over a charcoal fire. In the distance, two kids were singing to the accompaniment of a lyre played by their father. Apart from the presence of the trucks, the scene was one that had been played out in the desert since ancient times. I fell asleep on the mat and was awakened just before dawn by the cry "Allah akbar" that summoned people to the mosque for the day's first prayer.

We were closing in on El Geneina. We passed through the village of Saraf

Umra, and then followed a muddy road through Alamasrob and Naima. Our spirits were high. At Birka Sayra, we had taken on fresh water and five kilos of sweet oranges. We radioed Mike Kilo, the RTO radio base in Khartoum, that the road from El Fasher to El Geneina was passable, but that the Wadi Bago just east of Birka Sayra was troublesome. In my journal I noted: "Today was a real push day—just 140 kilometres until Geneina. Stuck four times, twice in soft sand and once crossing muddy tracks. The road was much better than I had expected. We stopped for lunch at Saraf Umra, a beautiful souk with lots of trees. As usual, we had at least 10 people ask us for rides to El Geneina. I'm getting good at saying no."

Friday, September 13. I got lost again. I knew we weren't far from El Geneina but we were going in circles, and both Abdullah and I were getting frustrated. We had pushed through fields of thick thorn bush and scrub, followed a dry river bed for several kilometres, then turned due west and taken what we hoped was the path of least resistance through a section of steep, sandy hills. I wasn't paying close attention to my compass, and at one point we doubled back at least eight kilometres. Sharp thistles punctured two of our tires. It was hot, and we weren't getting anywhere.

In the end, it was an airplane that showed us the way. A C-130 Hercules transport aircraft came out of the eastern sky and swooped low overhead. I recognized the distinct, bull's-eye pattern of the Royal Air Force markings on its lower wings. Suddenly the plane went into a banked turn. It was circling us. The RAF Hercules was only 100 metres above us; I could make out the pilot motioning us with his hand. He wanted us to follow him. The plane peeled off, heading at least 45 degrees south of the direction in which we had been travelling. We corrected our course accordingly and picked up speed.

Thanks to the RAF Hercules, we located a track we could follow. We crossed a long section of soft, deep sand, then, with the engine straining, made our way up to the edge of a steep, rocky shelf with the transmission in low-range four-wheel-drive for maximum torque. After 20 minutes of climbing, with the engine perilously close to overheating, we reached the summit.

I had grown accustomed to the isolation of the desert. For days we had travelled through sparsely populated areas, often our only company the musical voice of Simon Akol, the Southern Sudanese known as Mike Kilo who operated the RTO radio base more than 1,000 kilometres distant in Khartoum. Sig Fossland, following military protocol, strictly prohibited the use of real names over the open radio. My WUSC colleague Rod Sidloski in Nyala had to be addressed as Ruff

Road 8. Whenever I became discouraged, it was Simon who urged me on. He had access to *Newsweek* and *Time* magazines, and he would regularly feed me little snippets of information. At my request, he would radio his counterpart at the U.S. embassy and get the latest National League baseball scores as they came in on the secure embassy telex machine. Other than Simon, we usually had the desert to ourselves. I had the sense that Darfur had been tilted on its edge and emptied out, that the region had gone out of business, that the entire population had packed up and left.

The view from the summit shocked us. Spread before us was a makeshift city, hundreds of little huts constructed from twigs, rags, and plasticized grain bags. It was the largest concentration of people in one place that we had seen since Khartoum. Dozens of cooking fires were burning and the sky was filled with smoke. It was just after 6 p.m. We were there for the day's last light.

In my journal I wrote: "I arrived at Assirni and remember why I came to the Sudan in the first place. Green tents stretch as far as the eye can see. I am mobbed by hungry stick children—hundreds of them." Assirni was the largest refugee camp in western Sudan, with a population of 28,000 displaced Chadians and Sudanese sheltering on three barren hillsides. We made our way to the UN tent at the centre of the camp, with its blue-and-white flag turned orange in the setting sun, but we were too late; a guard informed us the UNHCR team had already departed for its quarters in El Geneina. If we wanted, we could look around the camp on our own.

A small child led me proudly around the camp, as if showing off his neighborhood. Then he took me down to the big wadi that formed the western border of Assirni. Some kids were playing in the water, tossing an empty, plastic vegetable-oil container around like a beach ball. Their hoots of delight reminded me that no matter how grim their circumstances, kids exploit every opportunity to amuse themselves. I brought the boy back to the Toyota, sat him behind the wheel, and presented him with three of our succulent Birka Sayra oranges. His face just beamed.

THE END OF THE EARTH

After 15 days, 21 flat tires, and 1,615 kilometres of desert travel, the last leg from Assirni to El Geneina was all downhill. Eight-wheeled UNHCR DAF trucks carried supplies to the camp along the same route every day, so the track was easy to follow. Abdullah dubbed it the Autobahn. Someone had thoughtfully installed a Bailey Bridge over the last wadi on the road into El Geneina. It was the first functioning bridge that we had seen since crossing the White Nile at Khartoum, and it reminded me of the drawbridges that guarded the entrances of medieval castles.

Rudy Rodrigues had instructed me to report immediately upon my arrival to the UNHCR office in El Geneina. It was situated on El Geneina's main street, the length of which was buried in sand. I was greeted at the door by an Irish woman named Frances Cavanaugh. "We've been expecting you," she told me, ushering me into the utilitarian residence that she shared with three other relief workers. Apparently Mike Kilo had told them to keep a lookout for me. We walked out onto the screened-in porch, the walls of which were painted lime green. Four armchairs were arranged around a dented coffee table that was covered with magazines and books. I noticed that someone subscribed to *The Economist.* One leg of the coffee table was broken and had been propped up with a stack of UNHCR manuals on policies and procedures. Frances caught me examining their handiwork. "That's the best use we ever made of all that claptrap," she commented. "Someone in Geneva writes them. Khartoum sends them on to us. We're too busy running refugee camps to ever get around to reading them."

Frances cracked open a fresh pack of Marlboros, offered me one, then slumped into one of the chairs. Without having been invited, I followed her

167

lead. The house doubled as the UNHCR headquarters for western Sudan, and I could hear the crackle of an HF radio in one of the back rooms. Frances was expecting a radio call from Khartoum at any moment and cocked her ear every time we heard a voice. There was no sign of any of her UNHCR colleagues, and I didn't inquire as to their whereabouts. Nightbirds clung to the porch screen looking for a handout. They played in the light from an oil lantern, casting artful shadows on the compound wall. Frances offered me a flask of Johnnie Walker Red Label that she pulled out from a filing cabinet off to the side of the room. "Nothing like a little mother's milk to revive your spirits." I hadn't seen any alcohol since Sig had served me a pre-mixed martini out of his canteen back at the RTO compound. I had a few sips and it went straight to my head. I hadn't had a proper shower since Khartoum and I smelled like a camel. But it could wait until the morning. I curled up in the chair and fell asleep, still clutching the plastic thermos cup of Frances's mother's milk in my hand.

"You're not a hippy, are you?" asked the moustached UNHCR worker as I made my way toward the latrine the following morning. "I hate hippies." His name was Ekber Menemencioglu, and he was in charge of the entire UNHCR emergency operation on the Sudanese-Chadian border. I had been warned about Menemencioglu. People at UNHCR in Khartoum said that he had the disposition of a drill sergeant, and had little tolerance for the procession of shabby sandal-wearing foreigners who turned up at his office claiming to be relief workers. He told them to their faces to return only after they had had a bath and cut their hair. Menemencioglu shared the house with Frances, a UNHCR field officer named John Singh, and a guard named Jebril. Now I regretted not having taken a shower the night before. My face was covered in stubble. Menemencioglu demanded to know my credentials. I gave him a précis of my curriculum vitae. He was impressed that I was a lawyer, that I had gone to good schools, and that I came equipped with my own set of Sudan Political Service topographic maps. I could stay. I would be allowed to bunk at the UNHCR house until I found a place of my own. But he was busy and he didn't want to be bothered. He was leaving that morning on an expedition to Beida, a village 110 kilometres south-west of El Geneina that was being overrun with refugees from Chad. The Sudanese residents of Beida, barely coping with the famine themselves, were insisting that the Chadians be loaded onto trucks and shipped across the border. Menemencioglu would play the role of negotiator and firefighter. He hoped to be back within three days.

In Arabic, El Geneina means the garden, but there was nothing pretty about my new home. I couldn't make out a shred of green to relieve the monotonous desert browns and grays of the surrounding hills. The town looked as if it had been assembled in some kid's sandbox. El Geneina was a rough frontier outpost and had seen better days; during the time of the Anglo-Egyptian Condominium, it had flourished as the gateway to Chad, and as a major trading post for the nomads and farmers east of the Wadi Kaja. El Geneina still had its own sultan, who lived in a resplendent palace built into the side of the jebel, complete with a spectacular outdoor dance floor that overlooked the valley below. In colonial times, musicians would perform at the Sultan's house by moonlight. If you had the energy to dig down through the metre of sand that filled El Geneina's streets, you would find cobblestones, neatly laid out more than 50 years earlier by skilled masons brought in from Egypt especially for the purpose. On certain street corners were spouts and troughs where, years before, fresh water had flowed for the convenience of residents and their animals. The pipes had rusted away in the 1960s and had never been replaced. Telex service had arrived in El Geneina in 1918 and telephones in 1922. Now the only links with the outside world were the radio sets owned by the commissioner of El Geneina, Abdul Affis, the local police, and the various relief agencies. The last time the electricity had been turned on was in 1982, when President Nimeiri came to town for a day.

Abdullah had driven the Toyota to the souk looking for a new spare tire. Walking the streets of El Geneina took me back to my days as a child exploring remote towns along the Arizona-Mexico border. El Geneina was a Wild West settlement. People rode through town on horseback and tumbleweeds bounced down the main street. I could imagine gun fights at high noon. The corrugated-steel storefronts would not have been out of place in the gold country of California's Sierra Nevada east of Sacramento. If you added covered wagons and a saloon with swing doors, El Geneina would make a perfect Hollywood set. I had heard stories that before the arrival of Sharia law, El Geneina was the Sudan's own sin city, complete with imported dancing girls and a casino run by the local police officers. Now all alcohol was consumed behind closed doors and people rarely played cards in public.

During its heyday, El Geneina flourished as a trading centre for the region. The horsemen of El Geneina are among the most accomplished in Africa, and their stallions are famed for their speed and strength. For years, buyers came to the town from all over Europe and the Middle East to attend its annual horse auctions. But the El Geneina I found in 1985 was the epicentre of drought and famine in all of Africa. Many of its trees had been cut down for firewood, and almost nothing was for sale in the market. The town had a new population of displaced Sudanese and Chadians who had wandered in from the surrounding area. The ones I saw in my initial tour around town were in horrible condition, completely emaciated. There were no stray dogs in El Geneina; they had long before been killed for meat.

Yet the famine that had devastated most of Kordofan and Darfur had also rescued this sleepy town from complete irrelevance. The relief agencies had become the town's biggest employers and had created an artificially overheated economy. A new restaurant had opened not far from the UNHCR office, and local residents complained that foreigners with thick wallets had forced up the cost of the few offices available for rent. You could see the agencies' signs as you drove into El Geneina from the airport. The town was the administrative centre for a huge region and the headquarters for emergency relief operations along the Chadian border. For such a little outpost, the foreign presence was almost overwhelming. They were all there: Save the Children U.K., the Islamic African Relief Agency, UNICEF, the UN World Food Program. Even the EEC had set up a base. With the EEC air-bridge now in place, El Geneina was serviced by more regular flights than anywhere else in the country other than the capital. If you could sweet-talk your way onto a plane, you could reach Khartoum in two hours and 45 minutes.

Rudy and Sig in Khartoum were holding back the entire RTO truck convoy until they received my report on the northern route. Frances cleared a space for me at the UNHCR office where I could work. I rolled out my topographic map on a desk in Frances's office, and traced onto a separate sheet of paper all the obstacles and important features that we had encountered. Abdullah's recall was almost photographic. He remembered specific road hazards, washouts and rock slides, and wells where we had found potable water. We marked down where we could purchase diesel fuel—at places such as Saraf Umra and Kebkabiya. We recommended that the fleet detour around Wadi Bago and Wadi Beri. With luck, all the wadis would soon be drying up under the hot sun, and within a few days the truck-eating wadi at Bir Abu Zaima could be attempted. I made a list of items needed for my office, including a generator and an antenna for the radio station. I folded the list into the map, scribbled Carolyn Head's name on the outside, and delivered it to the EEC air-bridge office for immediate transport to Khartoum.

Over the next few weeks, I made El Geneina my operating base. The commissioner, Abdul Affis, was an easy-going man who had given himself over to fighting the famine. I made a point of visiting his office every week, seeking his counsel and asking his permission before I undertook any major initiative. Bureaucrats in Khartoum cared little about El Geneina, and the commissioner had only a tiny budget to administer. His only transport was a battered 25-year-old gasoline-powered Land Rover that had to be jump-started any time he wanted to use it.

The commissioner's most treasured possession was a small short-wave radio; like many Africans, he was an avid fan of the BBC World Service. He didn't trust his own country's official voice, Radio Omdurman. Only if the news came across on the BBC could it be believed. Affis said sports enthusiasts didn't even rely on the Radio Omdurman football scores. Throughout Africa and Asia, BBC correspondents such as Mark Tully, Mike Woolridge, and Andrew Whitehead are household names, and are welcomed as celebrities wherever they travel. One day when I arrived for coffee, Affis informed me that there had been a coup attempt in Khartoum. I asked if he had received an emergency dispatch from the capital informing him of the developments. "No," he replied. "I just heard it on the BBC." Affis was extremely accommodating of the requests of the relief agencies, some of which verged on the absurd. One agency wanted a family business that had operated out of a particular building for more than 30 years to be evicted so that it could set up its office.

The EEC air-bridge was the big game in town. With the wadis between Khartoum and western Sudan flooded, only a trickle of grain was coming in on the souk lorries. Although the Oxfam report I had brought along for the desert crossing had derided the EEC air-bridge as playing only a token role in averting famine and starvation, in reality the transport aircraft were the lifeline for many villages in Darfur. El Geneina was the westernmost of the three towns reached by the air-bridge, and it was the central distribution point for an area more than 1,400 square kilometres in size. There were 120,000 refugees from Chad already resident in the region and more were on the way.

Nothing in Sudan worked as well as the EEC air-bridge. It was beautifully choreographed. With military precision, as many as five C-130 aircraft landed at El Geneina's chewed-up airstrip every day. The planes pulled up alongside the terminal building that had been built by the British in 1940 and that would not be out of place in Surrey or Essex. The inside of the transport planes resonated with African rhythms as the laborers sang and chanted. They worked in teams, without forklifts or any other technology. The sacks of sorghum and supplementary feeding supplies were passed hand over hand, out the huge ramp at the rear of the aircraft and onto the waiting Bedford lorries. The last man on board, using a hand whisk, would sweep up the individual grains from the aircraft floor. The operation would be completed in minutes, with one engine left running to provide electricity and cooling.

There was no time to waste. The trucks would deliver much of the sorghum directly to the souk in the centre of the town, where it would be transferred onto the backs of camels organized by Peter Verney of Save the Children U.K. for transport to communities throughout the district. The camels carried four 45-kilogram bags each, and caravans were made up of as many as 120 animals. Verney's camel caravans travelled in the cool of the night and slept during the day. Although they received little attention, Verney and his herders were responsible in large measure for sparing dozens of isolated villages southwest of El Geneina from total devastation.

Peter Verney and Ekber Menemencioglu were at opposite ends of the spectrum of personalities drawn to Darfur in 1985. Verney was the very hippy that Menemencioglu was most suspicious of. The first time I met him, he was wearing hand-made leather sandals and traditional nomadic dress. Verney was El Geneina's own T. E. Lawrence. He spoke passable Arabic, and was more comfortable smoking Sudanese Chesterfield cigarettes in the company of his camel drivers than mingling with the fast-talking Save the Children executives who flew in from Khartoum on the air-bridge. Often he accompanied the caravans, swathed from head to toe in desert garb for protection from the wind and blowing sand. From a distance, people often mistook him for an Arab. He went for days without a shower or other amenities, but that didn't bother him. His nightmare scenario was being posted to Khartoum and chained to a desk in the Kuwaiti Towers, home to his friends at UNHCR.

Verney spoke candidly with the media and other visitors, enjoyed whiskey, and was a connoisseur of araqi, an overproof brew concocted from fermented dates. I gave Save the Children credit for recognizing that in a sophisticated emergency-relief operation, Verney was the organization's eyes and ears on the ground and had a vital role to play. What he didn't know about the customs of local tribes wasn't worth knowing. He was familiar with Darfur agricultural practices and traditional grain-storage methods. He kept a close watch on the price of grain and other commodities in the markets of El Geneina and surrounding villages. He knew which local officials could be trusted and which were involved in the business of selling relief supplies. Verney showed me the mukheit bushes that grew in even the driest terrain, and demonstrated in his kitchen over a kerosene stove how the poisonous berries, after many hours of boiling, became edible. After we had swallowed a handful, Verney mumbled that he hoped he had cooked them sufficiently. "If you start vomiting in the middle of the night, you're in deep trouble," he said. "And those EEC pilots don't like taking people on board who might dirty up their aircraft."

Ekber's bark proved worse than his bite. He was the consummate field man and personified the best qualities of the United Nations. Looking after the refugees within his jurisdiction to the best of his abilities was the only thing that mattered. His primary responsibility was the camp at Assirni, which had doubled in size in only three months. He bent the rules for the sake of the men, women, and children in his care. Although all its residents claimed to be Chadians and therefore eligible for assistance from UNHCR, Ekber knew that many were destitute Sudanese from villages as far away as 200 kilometres who had assumed the guise of refugees in order to qualify for daily rations. But it made little difference to him where they were from, and he ensured that his official reports to Khartoum and Geneva contained only the most obscure references to country of origin.

Providing food, medical supplies, and protection for 28,000 people camping out in the open required equal measures of dedication and ingenuity. Ekber had both in spades. On a regular basis, he berated his superiors in Khartoum over the open radio. I heard him complain that no diesel fuel had been sent in weeks; his trucks were running dry. It was cold at night in the camp and he needed blankets for the refugees. And where were the medical kits he had been promised? One radio message consisted of only five words: "Send more food, fewer journalists."

The great majority of UN staff members are happiest when they are perched behind a metal desk in their air-conditioned offices; Ekber insisted on being close to the action. He had faced his biggest challenge in May, 1985, when the wadi adjoining Assirni flooded, transforming the camp into an island. No food was delivered for more than three weeks, and dozens of children had starved to death. Prospects for the camp were bleak. Local authorities and representatives of the aid agencies told Ekber that the people of Assirni had to wait it out. It was a tragedy, but nothing could be done for them. Ekber refused to sit idle. Instead, he swung into action, commandeering dozens of inflatable rubber boats that had languished in government stores in Khartoum since the days of the Condominium. He fastened the boats together with rope and organized a system to ferry tonnes of relief commodities across the wadi. Ekber's navy was launched, and hundreds of lives were saved.

My lawyer friends back in Canada often asked me who (apart from me) would be mad enough to take up employment in the middle of the Sahara Desert. As with many relief workers, Ekber came to the Sudan via a circuitous route. He was a Turk married to a ballerina from Ankara. His father was a diplomat, and as a child he had been educated at Ottawa's elite Ashbury College for boys. He had attended the American University in Washington, D.C., and for several years worked as a producer for Turkish television, which partly explained his flair for the media. He was equally at ease at both ends of the camera, and the television crews who schlepped their crates of cameras and equipment all the way to the Chadian border loved him. He was an easy shoot; they could do their entire interview in one take. He looked the part of the rough-and-ready field worker, complete with the blue-and-white United Nations armband. On cue, Ekber would recount dramatic episodes, such as the flooding of the wadi at Assirni camp, and he had the latest statistics regarding refugee movements in Darfur at his fingertips. Although the media asked him to tell the same stories over and over again, his accounts always sounded fresh and unrehearsed. On many occasions, he exasperated his bosses at the UNHCR in Khartoum, but he was their rising star and they were smart enough to leave him alone. UNICEF and UNHCR were the only UN agencies in the Sudan that invested any significant resources in public relations, and that attempted to have at least one person on their payrolls who was articulate and confident in front of a camera. Most UN employees I knew became instantly tongue-tied the minute a microphone was shoved in front of their face.

I rented a house on the edge of town. It was bigger than I needed, but it had a yard large enough to accommodate the communications equipment that I hoped would be flown in from Khartoum. In addition, the landlord was willing to accept a short-term lease. Within days of my sending a request for a generator and radio tower to Khartoum, the EEC office in El Geneina radioed me that supplies with my name on them were arriving on an incoming aircraft. I went to the airport expecting to be able to hand-carry a five-horsepower gasoline generator, strong enough to run one or two electric lights and to charge my radio batteries. But Carolyn Head of WUSC had outdone herself: from the belly of the Hercules emerged a humongous 180-horsepower Volvo diesel generator that could meet the electricity requirements of a small town. In addition, she had managed to scrounge two 15-metre-high French-made antenna poles from her mates at Total. I needed three Bedford trucks just to bring the equipment back to my house, and had to engineer a system of pulleys to hoist the antenna poles into position. Abdul Affis commented that my radio station was better equipped and more powerful than that of the local military commander.

Over coffee one morning, my neighbor, Mr. Hassan, asked if I would be so kind as to allow him to run an electric cable to the generator, as his eldest son was about to be married and there was going to be a party. Electricity would allow celebrations to continue well into the night. Of course, I would be invited. I acceded to the request, thinking that at least he had been polite enough to ask. It would have been easy for him to attach a cable to the generator without my ever noticing. Over the ensuing weeks, Mr. Hassan established the El Geneina Power Company, charging people to hitch up a line to his fuse box. It didn't cost me any more diesel, and it was doing no harm. I became very popular in El Geneina. From that day on, anyone with a special event that was expected to run late would do everything to convince me to run the generator long past sunset. My circle of Sudanese friends expanded; I shared araqi with the families who for generations had made El Geneina their home, and heard all about the history of the town and the region. Part of my evening ritual was to make the trip up the hill where I kept the generator; with the flick of a switch, I would extinguish lights across half the town.

It was mid-October before the first RTO trucks arrived at El Geneina. I held a small reception for the first six drivers at my house. They had been hand-picked for their jobs in Khartoum and put through a rigorous obstacle course by representatives of Fiat. The drivers had lived their lives in and around Khartoum, and were startled by the scenes of drought and famine that they had witnessed along the northern route through Kordofan and Darfur. People had waved them down, begging for food. Khartoum was effectively insulated from the famine and many of its residents were unaware of the extent of the crisis. None of the RTO drivers had ever seen a severely malnourished person before. They had children of their own and were shaken up by the young kids who gathered around the trucks whenever they came to a halt, who begged a bit of grain, or milk powder, or whatever they were carrying in exchange for washing the trucks. But the trucks had only diesel and spare parts on board, nothing that could satisfy a hungry child.

I may not have been paid a lawyer's salary, but I loved my job and I was captivated by Darfur. As a field worker for the Road Transport Operation, my responsibilities were varied. No two days were the same. I had to supervise the drivers, arrange for warehouse space, maintain an inventory of spare parts, monitor market prices for sorghum and other commodities, write and transmit regular field reports to Khartoum, liaise with Commissioner Affis and other officials, report on unusual population movements, and run our field office. There was little time for paperwork, and all the UN bureaucrats were a safe distance away in Khartoum.

UN authorities in Khartoum allocated Ekber and me our own jet helicopter, an Aerospatiale Ecureil. The helicopter was a finicky craft and it didn't take well to the desert heat. Eventually, it flew home to Switzerland. Ekber and I weren't disappointed; it had proved to be more of a nuisance than anything else. Camels were slower, but they were more reliable, they used less fuel, and they never required spare parts. When we landed the helicopter in villages, I was always worried that some kid might walk into the tail rotor, which cut through the air at exactly neck height. The Australian pilot had packed up and left without much warning, leaving behind six 44-gallon drums of perfectly good Jet A-1 fuel, a highly refined kerosene—a commodity in very short supply in Darfur. With this fortified fuel source, my kerosene-powered refrigerator ran colder than ever before and produced the first ice cubes of its career. Kids coming to the office were fascinated by them, staring at them, biting them, playing catch with them, and were ultimately disappointed when the cubes melted in their hands.

The Fiat-made RTO trucks proved to be worth their weight in gold. The drivers had never seen anything like them. They were unstoppable. With their snorkel exhausts extending high over the top of the cabs, they could cross flooded wadis two metres deep. The Fiats had a hatch on the roof that the driver could pop open, originally designed for a gun mount. Drivers would climb onto the roof and smoke, read, or pray. The trucks were on the road seven days a week transporting sorghum and supplementary feeding supplies to communities on the verge of starvation. Their arrival in the villages was always a cause for celebration. The drivers were greeted like triumphant warriors, and showered with thanks and praise. "Al Hamdu lillaa! Al Hamdu lillaa!"

We pushed on with the trucks to Umm Tajok, Kongo Haraza, Kerenik, and Misterei. Everywhere it was the same story. It was the worst drought of the century. Food prices were ten times their normal levels—if any food were available at all. Grazing areas had been wiped out. Farmers first were forced to sell their sheep and goats, then calves, mules, and cows. People traded all their possessions, including farming implements, for minuscule amounts of grain, beans, or oil. Many of the smallest children were already dead. All the young men had departed for points east. On several occasions, we went to villages where we found nobody—they were ghost towns. I thought of the opening scene from my favourite Michael Crichton novel, *The Andromeda Strain*, where soldiers walk through a desert town in which all the inhabitants have been killed by a mysterious microbe carried aboard a downed satellite. My drivers would shake their heads and mutter prayers under their breath. This was the heartland of their country, and it was dying before their eyes.

In many cases we were too late. Many of the children between the ages of one and five at our destinations had already perished. In El Geneina and the surrounding district, an estimated 400,000 people were subsisting on the most meagre of diets. There was simply nothing left to eat. People had been reduced to eating the leaves of plants and digging up insects. In one village, I looked on as three young girls picked through the maggot-infested remains of a donkey. In El Geneina, when I ate in the little restaurant at the centre of town, a group of children would stand in the distance watching my every move. As soon as I rose from the table they descended on my plate, grabbed the little scraps I had left, known as carta, and disappeared into the night.

Famines are as much a medical as a nutritional crisis. Growing up in Canada, I was accustomed to receiving the world's best health care free of charge. The El Geneina hospital was the only medical facility for a district with a population of more than 400,000 people. Anywhere else in the world, the building would have been condemned. The hospital had no running water and no electricity. Patients were expected to arrive with their own bed sheets, and depended on relatives to bring them their daily meals and to change their dressings. The hospital's only doctor was from Khartoum, and I became good friends with him and his family. Dr. Douza was well trained and among the town's most esteemed citizens. He was a devout Muslim, and considered it his religious duty to care for the sick. His salary was the equivalent of $30 per month, but it wasn't an issue for him. He was happy to be there for people who were in need. "God has given me a gift, and it is my duty to use it," he would say to me.

Dr. Douza had intended to stay in El Geneina for a number of years, and had moved his family to the doctor's house located on the hill behind the hospital, built forty years earlier by the British. But then his own 11-year-old daughter died from a stomach disorder. The doctor and his wife believed that if they had been in Khartoum, she would never have been sick. They quickly packed up their belongings. When I last saw Dr. and Mrs. Douza, they were consumed by guilt; we said "Ma' salaama" without even making eye contact. I never heard from them again.

El Geneina never recovered from the departure of Dr. Douza. Khartoum assigned a replacement, but for unknown reasons he never arrived. Most recent Sudanese university graduates wanted to stay in the city where there were basic amenities and where they could earn a respectable income. I could hardly blame them. On one trip to the El Geneina hospital, I found a boy who had been badly burned by a lamp that had exploded. He was lying on a plastic sheet covered in his own urine and faeces. The second- and third-degree burns were infected and oozed yellow pus. Nobody had bothered to care for him, not even to clean his wounds. The kid was in excruciating pain, but there were no sedatives in the hospital. With help from a teacher at the elementary school, I cleaned him the best I could and wrapped him in fresh dressings. I brought him a toy helicopter that one of the boys in the souk had made from Kanny milk-powder tins. It was a working model, complete with a rotor and wheels that could spin. I returned to the hospital to visit the child after a three-day expedition to Nyala, but he was already dead. I found his body on the bed, covered with a sheet. Someone had already taken away the little helicopter.

No town was worse off than Beida, located just 300 metres from the Chadian border. In November, Ekber and I made the 110-kilometre trek to Beida in my red Landcruiser to assess the needs of the refugee population. Civil war and famine had driven thousands of Chadians, most of them women and children, across the border into the Sudan. All the communities in the area had experienced an influx of refugees. Umm Balla had a population of 24,500 Chadians and Anji Koti, 22,500. The camp at Beida was the home for 4,500 new arrivals from Chad. Almost all were women and children. The residents of the camp had walked as far as they could manage and then collapsed from hunger and exhaustion. According to United Nations official regulations, refugees who were within five kilometres of a national border were not entitled to assistance. The camp at Beida was therefore illegal. But poor women and children do not travel with copies of the UN regulations in their pockets. They had journeyed for hundreds of kilometres across the open desert, and they had no arable land to return to. The UNHCR had investigated the possibility of transporting them in the DAF trucks to the camp at Assirni, but most were in such poor health that they would never have survived the journey.

If Beida was not the end of the earth, then you could see the end of the earth from Beida. The town's Sudanese residents had evicted the Chadian refugees, forcing them to walk to an area three kilometres south from the town, with no protection from the sun and no access to water. It was the most illogical and impractical location for a refugee camp and was totally unsuitable for human habitation. The Chadians had only the most basic materials with which to make their shelters. Their only possessions were a few plastic jerrycans, some rags, and a few empty tin cans. The women wore bits of cloth, most of the children nothing at all. Their skin was covered with scabies. Some had open wounds that were festering. I saw a kid with mucus running down from his eye; he had to shoo the flies away constantly. Many people were severely dehydrated. I saw the telltale sign of kwashiorkor—a severe form of malnutrition—in the red hair of the skinniest children who gathered around me. The local police chief reported that 15 people were dying every day out of a population of 20,000 Sudanese and displaced Chadians.

Relief workers are the 20th-century's angels of mercy, and I was awed by their selflessness. Many had put their careers on hold to work alongside the poor. Few Save the Children, Médecins Sans Frontières, or Red Cross volunteers saw themselves as humanitarians, or as doing anything worthy of recognition by the international community. They joked about their meagre salaries, their rumpled appearance, and their fondness for tobacco and alcohol. They rarely took the vacation and hardship leave they were entitled to. Instead of taking credit for saving lives, they felt profoundly guilty that they were not able to do more. "If only we had proper medical supplies. If only we had electricity and hot water. If only we had arrived sooner," they told me. Inevitably, the toughest postings attracted the most committed and idealistic personnel. Bernard Kouchner, the co-founder of MSF, has written about them:

> Living your life to help others is a contract: You agree to engage in full-time confrontation with the most perverse and brutal side of human nature. It is troubling; you begin to doubt man's superiority in the natural order and our ability to master our less-honorable instincts. Yet at the same time, humanitarian work has shown me that people are the same the world over; their distress is similar from one situation to the next. Mothers everywhere experience the same sense of despair whether they see their child dying of starvation, their husband being arrested by the police, or their son going off to war.

The League of Red Cross and Red Crescent Societies had set up a clinic and feeding station in the heart of the refugee camp at Beida. The staff of four included two volunteer nurses, Wendy Woodward from New Zealand and Inger Nissen from Denmark. People in El Geneina said that they were fearless, that they were personally waging a war against sickness and death. Against all odds, they had managed to maintain the population at something just above the subsistence level. Inger and Wendy had shamed the local Sudanese relief committee into allocating the Chadians token rations of food, and sent excruciatingly detailed radio reports to UNHCR in Khartoum chronicling the camp's death spiral. "In case anyone out there is listening, there are people dying here," the nurses would announce into the microphone. The UNHCR authorities may have decided that the camp was illegal, that it broke all the rules, and that it was not worthy of assistance, but Inger and Wendy were not going to let them off easily. For once, the guys wearing the suits had to take responsibility and feel some pain.

A company called Columbia Helicopters, financed by USAID, had begun to deliver sling loads of emergency relief supplies to Beida, Kongo Haraza, and other hard-hit towns. As a result, a supplementary feeding program for the moderately and severely malnourished kids of Beida had been launched. But it was not enough: Inger and Wendy were losing as many as eight children a day. They were too far gone to be saved, and many of them were already brain damaged as a result of severe malnutrition and vitamin deficiency.

For both Ekber and me, Beida represented the front lines of humanitarian catastrophe. It couldn't get any worse than this. In the Red Crescent feeding station, we walked between the rows of the dead and the dying. I imagined what it was like for the first American soldiers at Hiroshima and Nagasaki just after the Japanese surrender in August, 1945. I felt guilty just being there—healthy, well fed, white, from a rich country with fields of wheat as large as the land mass of France and Germany combined. In Canada, we fed sorghum to cattle; here, it meant life. Despite our trucks of food and our good intentions, our role as relief workers was more as chroniclers than saviors. Our job was to report back to powerful donor countries, to document our benevolence, to act as tour guides for the blond journalists armed with make-up kits and battery-powered blow-dryers. As Ekber put it, "Don't think for one moment that the UN put you here so these kids could feel better. Your job is to make the rest of the world feel better."

It was the season of the haboobs, the violent desert sandstorms. Just hours after our arrival, a haboob moved in from the north, darkening the sky in the middle of the day. In the course of 30 minutes, the temperature dropped 15 degrees and heavy rains began to fall. A ferocious wind threw dust and dirt everywhere. Visibility was reduced to a few metres. People ran to their tukuls or the Red Crescent feeding tent for cover. But there wasn't enough room for everyone. A young girl, perhaps 10 or 11 years of age, stood out in the open, wrapping herself in plastic in an attempt to stay dry. She cried hysterically. I tried to comfort her, but it was no use. She was hungry, cold, frightened, and on her own in a foreign country. Even if her family were alive, there was little chance she could ever find them again.

In such moments, I was shaken to the core. Why do children suffer? How can governments turn their backs on the death of a multitude? I had been taught in all my years at Upper Canada College and Stanford University that the system worked, that capitalism could provide for all, that there were safety nets for those who could not care for themselves. I believed in the idea of progress. I had celebrated the great accomplishments of science and technology, such as the Apollo space project and the development of the personal computer. I had aspired to be a part of the same system, to earn a handsome income, to own two houses, to enjoy long vacations. I had never called myself a radical and I shunned extremism of any form.

But seeing this young girl wrapped in plastic, abandoned and miserable, enraged me and filled me with doubt about everything my society had taught me and everything I had believed in. At that moment, I lost my faith in Western civilization and in the capacity for institutions to do good. At that moment, my years of education at some of North America's finest schools seemed all for nought. I asked myself why I had spent so many hours studying the poems of Ben Jonson and learning the English of Chaucer. My education had been totally self-indulgent. I had squandered seven years in college. What good was my legal training to the people of Beida?

The girl died two days later, and Ekber and I watched as she was buried without ceremony in Beida's children's cemetery just minutes before sunset. The Red Crescent workers had no burial cloths, so her body was wrapped in a discarded sorghum bag marked with the words "a gift from the people of the United States of America." There was no family present to pray for her or to say a few words on her behalf. We did not know her name or where she was from. The anonymity did not make her death any easier. We knew that she had lived, felt the warmth of the sun on her skin, and enjoyed the companionship of her friends and family. Her life had never been easy, and somehow she had learned how to cope. Most North American children her age, given the same set of circumstances, would live a few days at most. This kid had been a survivor, but in the end we had lost her. I felt angry, alone, and betrayed.

That night, Ekber and I sat around the metal table in the Red Crescent staff tent with Inger and Wendy. We played cribbage and drank Johnnie Walker Red Label. One of the Columbia Helicopter pilots had delivered a case of Belgian Stella Artois beer, which sat off to the side unopened. I didn't feel like getting drunk. We cooked a pot of pasta over a Bunsen burner and served it with warmed tomato paste mixed with one fried onion. Ekber smoked through the entire meal. Nobody talked about the day's events.

Inger and Wendy told us of the difficulties they had faced in the camp. Before the arrival of Columbia Helicopters, the deliveries of food and medical supplies had been irregular at best. Many kids had died. During the interim period, eye infections, malaria, parasites, skin ailments, and diarrhea were constant problems. The nurses badly needed vitamin A and D tablets. The Red Crescent had been hard-pressed to find an expatriate physician willing to work in the camp. Inger and Wendy had been losing weight themselves. It was very difficult to eat when so many children living only a few metres away were going hungry. On the back of a health chart, Wendy scribbled a shopping list for my next trip to Khartoum—cheese in tins, biscuits, tea bags, tissues, beans in tomato sauce, canned fruit juice, and Irish stew.

When Ekber and I woke the following morning, Inger and Wendy had already left for the clinic. We stopped in on them on our way back to El Geneina. Wendy was holding a baby gazelle in her arms that had wandered into the camp a few days before. It had been abandoned by its mother and they were nursing it back to health. Amidst the scraps of plastic, the flies, the mud, and the misery, they had found a thing of beauty. They named him Skippy; I thought of the kangaroo from the Australian kids' television series. Three weeks later when I was back in El Geneina, Peter Verney passed me a hand-written message that had come up from the camp via one of his camel caravans. It was from Wendy, thanking me for the few food items I had managed to send on one of Ekber's trucks. But the last line saddened me. Despite their best efforts, the gazelle had died.

After Beida, whatever patience I had evaporated. I sent missives to my bosses in Khartoum demanding that I be allocated more trucks. Visitors from the capital had told me that many Fiat four-by-fours were being used on the highway between Port Sudan and Khartoum, the entire distance of which was paved and could be travelled easily by 20-year-old Bedford souk lorries. It was a total waste of resources. "Send me trucks or send me burial cloths," I radioed Khartoum.

Evidently I got through to someone. On October 13, John Jack of RTO in Khartoum allocated me 12 additional Fiats and three of his top drivers: Ahmad Babekir Haroun, Abakar Oushan Imam, and Abdal Haman Siwyr. Ahmad Babekir arrived with a short note from John. "These drivers have done a terrific job for me. All they ask is a fair deal and honesty. Ahmad Babekir speaks reasonably good English. Abakar Oushan led the convoy from Khartoum across the desert. Seems to be a walking road map."

I needed someone to lead these men. I appointed Garret Adam, a Northern Sudanese and devout Muslim, as the foreman of the combined fleet. He was the father of six, and had served as an officer in the Sudanese army. During my long absences, he had assumed control of the RTO operation in El Geneina and had earned the respect of the other drivers. They called him the General. With a hawaja in command, fuel-pilfering and the theft of relief commodities would be everyday occurrences. There was nothing I could do about it. Diesel in the desert was gold. There were other problems: truck drivers would take on dozens of passengers for their return trips, which was dangerous and illegal. Near Nyala, an RTO truck carrying passengers had flipped over, crushing 12 people to death. Policing the carrying of passengers was impossible. With Garret Adam as the drivers' leader, the situation was at least manageable. He set the rules, and enforced the discipline among his men.

The relief operation in western Sudan was front-page news in Europe. As a result, a healthy contingent of celebrities visited Kordofan and Darfur. Princess Anne, the patron of Save the Children U.K., arrived in the desert on board a Royal Air Force Hercules. I am no monarchist, but during her short stay Princess Anne impressed all the relief workers with her extensive knowledge of the mechanics of emergency operations, and with her sincerity. She had been well briefed, and she was tough. Local officials, at the urging of the British embassy, had invested a considerable sum in constructing a special toilet for her to use. Princess Anne preferred the same pit latrine the relief workers frequented.

In October, Bob Geldof, the moving force behind Band Aid and Live Aid, toured Assirni camp with Ekber and his colleagues from UNHCR. Geldof, well over two metres in height, was immediately at ease among the dust-covered Chadian girls and boys who flocked around him. I have always believed that many kids come with a built-in radar that tells them which adults they can trust and which they should fear. Their affection for Geldof was intense and spontaneous. Few people in the camp knew who Geldof was—that he had single-handedly galvanized the Western world to take action to fight famine in

Ethiopia and the Sudan, and that he had organized spectacular concerts in London and Philadelphia, featuring the likes of Bruce Springsteen, Bob Dylan, Bono, and Sting, broadcast around the world, which raised more money for a single cause than any other event in history. But Geldof preferred the anonymity. He didn't want anyone to fuss over him. A few days earlier, when he had checked into the Khartoum Hilton, the receptionist had insisted that he settle the bill each morning of his stay, not believing that the ragged, unshaven foreigner could afford such posh accommodation. In fact, all of Geldof's travel costs were being covered by a London newspaper, the *Daily Telegraph*.

In the feeding centre, Geldof was overcome by the sight of a severely mal-nourished boy. He held the boy's tiny hand and whispered to Ekber, "Is this kid going to die?" He fired question after question at the camp staff. What supplies did they need? Was food getting through? When would the refugees be able to return to their own country? If time had permitted, he would have stayed overnight at the camp. His only worry was that his visit had distracted the relief workers from looking after the children, and that he was getting in their way.

Geldof was deeply principled: members of the British press were with him, but he refused to be photographed at the side of a hungry child. He set the rules with the media. "Respect and honor these children," he requested the paparazzi from Fleet Street who accompanied him. Geldof, a former slaughterhouse worker and bulldozer operator, has the forearms of a man who knows how to look after himself. The photographers backed off, and for one brief moment the Irishman was left alone with dozens of girls and boys who called the camp at Assirni their home. Many of the kids were orphans and all were stateless. These weren't the children of Chad or the Sudan or the United Nations. These were Geldof's kids.

Relief work is waged in the manner of war, and large humanitarian organizations are invariably hierarchical structures built along the lines of the British military, with elaborate chains of command and centralized top-down decision-making. Even the language of emergency-relief organizations mimics military-speak: in the Sudan I learned about target populations, MREs (meals ready to eat), and drop zones. As in times of intense combat, people who demonstrate any talent at all—and who survive—are quickly promoted. After three months in the field, I received an obliquely worded memo from WUSC headquarters (another term borrowed from the army) in Ottawa informing me that my initial three-month contract had been extended, and that I would be asked to take on new responsibilities. I should assume that I would be in the Sudan "for the duration of the emergency." No one had asked me whether I wanted to stay on.

After months in the desert, I was becoming an old Africa hand. My persistent cravings for Dairy Queen milkshakes, McDonald's French fries, and Harvey's cheeseburgers disappeared. I was leaner and in the best shape I'd been since I ran cross-country races at Upper Canada College 15 years earlier. I had read the maintenance manual for the Toyota Landcruiser cover to cover, and knew exactly how hard I could drive the vehicle without inflicting serious damage. The sight of one metre of water in a wadi no longer terrified me. I knew the tracks linking El Geneina with villages 200 kilometres distant. At the age of 28, I was running a large-scale humanitarian operation—fighting hard to keep thousands of children alive. Back home in Canada, many of my colleagues from law school were doing grunt work for uninspiring senior partners.

But there was another side to all this. Too often in the Sudan I saw representatives of international-development organizations, equipped with the latest models of computers, four-wheel-drive vehicles, and HF radios, running roughshod over local officials. We were the new colonial masters, and few of us took the time to include skilled and eager Sudanese in our programs. That we got away with so much attests to the patience and tolerance of our hosts. In El Geneina, I was allowed to set up a powerful radio station with no official authorization and no licence. I never thought of asking anyone's permission. In any other country, including the United States and Canada, I would have been arrested. Under the banner of humanitarianism, we could do anything that we wanted. UN special representative Winston Prattley complained that "the government was more or less pushed aside. It was an undignified experience." Government officials were viewed by most foreigners as bumbling fools. Prattley commented to Canadian reporter Jim Travers about the pimply-faced foreigners fresh out of schools in England and America who now were making policy decisions regarding the future of Kordofan and Darfur. I worried that he was talking about me.

Predicting famines and allocating relief commodities is a complex business, requiring reliable and consistent information from the field provided in a timely manner. On several occasions, Commissioner Abdul Affis remarked to me that the young employees of the relief agencies in El Geneina had access to better statistics about crop predictions and market prices than his own officials. In Khartoum, the director of the Relief and Rehabilitation Commission, Dr. Kamal Showgi, complained that the relief agencies—which, unlike the government, had vehicles, fuel, and sophisticated communications equipment—did not provide his office with even the most basic harvest information. Crop forecasts were circulated among representatives of various agencies, but no one thought of making them available to the RRC. Agencies rarely submitted copies of their studies on the incidence of disease to the Sudanese Ministry of Health. As a result, it was almost impossible for the government in Khartoum to play any kind of co-ordinating role among the numerous foreign organizations involved in the relief effort. When they did try to assert some authority, they were accused of meddling.

Among the most celebrated of the foreigners who descended on the Sudan during the drought and famine were the pilots who flew for the EEC air-bridge, and for the Columbia Helicopter operation in southern Darfur. Many of the Americans at the controls of the Columbia helicopters were Vietnam veterans. In Europe, flight regulations prohibit pilots from performing stunts or carry out low-level flying. In the Sudan, there were no such limitations. One relief worker on furlough at the Hilton Hotel in Khartoum received a radio message telling her to have a look outside her window; minutes later, she was shocked to see a C-130 Hercules fly within 200 metres of the hotel with her favorite pilot at the controls.

Relief planes returning empty from El Geneina to Khartoum occasionally conducted what they called "bombing practice." One C-130 Hercules would fly directly above another with its ramp lowered. The loadmaster would lie flat on the ramp, his legs held by another crew member. The goal of the exercise was to drop cans of Heineken beer onto the roof of the second aircraft. There were other antics. More than one souk lorry driver was surprised by the sight in his rearview mirror of a C-130 bearing down at a speed of 200 kilometres an hour at an altitude of less than 50 metres. Despite the horseplay, the EEC air-bridge never had a single fatality, but there were some close calls. While watching the off-loading of a C-130 Hercules that had just landed in El Geneina, I looked on in horror as two Oxfam employees drove their Land Rover under the massive four-bladed spinning propeller. It cleared their roof by less than five centimetres; they were oblivious to the danger they were in.

The air-bridge was our time machine. After spending weeks in the field, parched and hungry, unshaven and scraggly, I would ease myself into the jump seat for the flight from El Geneina to Khartoum. After I had fastened my seat-belt, the pilot would reach into the cooler at his side and pull out an ice-cold Heineken. The sight alone almost made me delirious. I would savour every sip, and vow that never again would I take the availability of cold beer for granted. I usually rode on Juicy Lucy, named after the company that owned and operated the plane, St. Lucia Airways. Within three hours, I would be at the RTO headquarters in Khartoum, with its neat offices, air conditioners, fluorescent lighting, and refrigerators stacked with bottles of Coca-Cola. All the RTO team members drove new white Renault automobiles that had been diverted from UNICEF by Rudy Rodrigues. In the evening, they would descend on WUSC House for partying, music, and dancing. Some of the WUSC employees had even formed their own band, called Sweet Charity. I preferred to make my way to the Sudan Club, where I would peel off my filthy clothes, linger under a hot shower, and plunge into the swimming pool. On the club's covered patio, I would sip Nous-Nous, a combination of lemon and hibiscus juice, with Carolyn and Rudy. El Geneina and the famine seemed a million kilometres away. On one occasion, I emerged tattered and torn from the field just in time to take my seat on the Sudan Club lawn for a production of Noel Coward's *Private Lives*. Tea was served at intermission, and the theatre-goers exchanged pleasantries about the weather and their most recent trip to England. On weekends, the same crowd packed picnic baskets and folding chairs into their cars and made their way to the Khartoum Cricket Club. Matches were played on a sun-burnt and dusty pitch by men wearing bleached-white ducks and shirts. "How's that?" they barked out at the umpire with every ball bowled anywhere near the wickets.

The best of the relief workers were the most engaging people I have met anywhere in the world. In El Geneina, the heroine of the EEC air-bridge was a red-headed Irish firebrand named Christine Brown. She was our Joan of Arc. Every morning, she stood on the edge of the runway, shivering in the pre-dawn cold, listening for the drone of aircraft engines. From the tone, Christine could tell whether it was a Hercules or a Transal. She knew all the pilots, the names of their wives and girlfriends, and what they smoked. They loved her spirit.

All the loaders fed off Christine's energy. "Yella! Yella!" she ordered. "Let's get moving!" She led the men into the belly of the aircraft, sometimes hefting a 45-kilogram bag over her own shoulder. Christine set the rhythm for her team. The goal was to get the plane emptied and back to Khartoum as quickly as possible so that it could return with a second load before sunset. The El Geneina airstrip lacked runway lights, so the last Hercules had to depart shortly before 6 p.m. It was always a race to get the plane unloaded and turned around before it was too dark to take off. A night stop in El Geneina was the air-bridge pilots' worst nightmare. "What's your hurry?" Christine would ask them. "This isn't such a bad place." The crews were bunking at the Khartoum Hilton, and although they had memorized the room service menu, they wouldn't eat anywhere else in the city. They even brought along Hilton-supplied box lunches on their flights to the west.

Every day, Christine negotiated with army and police officers who were hoping to hitch a ride to Khartoum. She received so many requests that she could have run an airline, but the EEC agreement with the Sudanese Ministry of Transport prohibited carrying anyone other than relief workers. The pilots urged Christine to abandon El Geneina—to hop on board for the flight to the capital—but the air-bridge was her passion. She would see the last plane off, congratulate her loaders on a job well done, and prepare the daily radio report for the EEC office in Khartoum. Christine was paid a fraction of the salary of the UN staff, but she was every bit as professional, and then some.

The long hours, oppressive heat, and constant pressure associated with emergency relief work eventually took their toll on me. I lost another four kilos, and had to cut a new notch in my belt with a knife to hold my pants up. I looked and felt haggard. When I needed to be bucked up, I retreated to the relative comfort of the UNHCR house, where Frances Cavanaugh smothered me with attention. On one occasion, after a particularly rough expedition to Beida, I got up at five in the morning, threw together some clothes and my toilet kit, and drove to the El Geneina airport. I waited for the first Hercules to land just after dawn, hitched a ride to Khartoum, then checked myself into the Hilton Hotel. The owners of the Khartoum Hilton had a special deal for relief workers with proper identification; rooms were available for 25 per cent of the rack rate. I soaked for hours in the hotel room bathtub, and wrapped myself in huge, soft towels. I considered smuggling them back to El Geneina. I set the room's thermostat to the lowest level and luxuriated in the comfort of freshly starched sheets.

The next morning, I was the first one in line at the Hilton breakfast buffet. I treated myself to hot oatmeal, waffles with syrup, scrambled eggs, sausages, fruit salad, and fresh milk. Where were they getting all this stuff from? In the afternoon, I relaxed by the pool, and ordered a triple-decker pork-free club sandwich for lunch. As in other Muslim countries, Hilton had cleverly designed the hotel so that no rooms overlooked the pool. In any case, the only women who swam in the pool were foreigners. During my entire stay in the Sudan, the only time I saw Sudanese women swimming, they were fully clothed. Even young girls had to cover themselves. The bill for my two-day Hilton splurge came to $200, about one-third of my monthly salary. I reasoned that it was cheaper than a psychiatrist.

The famine attracted all types—missionaries, entrepreneurs, cowboys, mercenaries, and crusaders. Many foreigners came to the Sudan as English teachers, but with no promise of employment in their own country, they stayed on long after their original contracts had expired. Back home, they were unemployable. In the Sudan, merely by virtue of being expatriates with access to hard currency, they had a special status. Many managed to land relatively well paid jobs with relief agencies, and were entrusted with responsibilities that far exceeded their professional training and personal qualifications—jobs that should have first been offered to skilled Sudanese.

Stories about some of the more eccentric volunteers were traded among relief workers like bottles of good araqi. Brian in Wad Medani, located 160 kilometres upstream from Khartoum on the Blue Nile, was often seen walking around the town souk dressed only in his underwear, banging on a drum. Neil was employed for two months in El Obeid as a teacher, but succumbed to unspecified job pressures. He was put in a straitjacket in El Obeid Hospital and sent home.

"Dongola John" was another English teacher assigned to the town of Dongola in the Northern Libyan Desert, a two-day drive from Khartoum. He never reached his posting. After a night of carousing, he boarded the bus in Khartoum, vomited on several passengers, and was thrown off by the driver. Officials at the Ministry of Education of the Sudan never took him off their official list of teachers sent to Dongola; he continued to collect his paycheque for his entire stay in the Sudan. He spent the remaining five years of his contract living in the Tourism Hotel in Khartoum.

An MSF doctor in Awiel in South Sudan cracked up under pressure and was discovered running naked through the souk. She had to be evacuated to France. Cordelia came to the Sudan to forget her broken marriage back in England. She signed up with a relief agency working in Kordofan, then attempted to become a Muslim Sister. They didn't want her. She refused to eat or speak to anyone. An infamous member of the British National Front, a far-right-wing organization, established an English-language school in the town of Kosti. He advertised his school, collected fees from hundreds of students, and then disappeared without a trace. Mark, an English teacher based in Zalingei, just west of Jebel Mara, was best known for a portable toilet that he built using a plastic chair he had purchased in Khartoum. He wouldn't let anybody else use it. In the end, he grew homesick and concocted a reason to be flown back to England.

A UNHCR officer on a two-year contract arrived on the semi-weekly Swiss Air flight to Khartoum and checked into the Acropole Hotel. Unfortunately, he made the mistake of leaving his hotel window open. While he was sleeping, a haboob descended on the city, filling his room with three centimetres of dust and sand. The officer reported to the UNHCR headquarters on Nile Avenue and announced that he was resigning his post. He returned to Geneva on the same Swiss Air plane that had brought him to Khartoum. An information officer for an American relief agency, intimidated by the prospect of setting foot outside of Khartoum, spent three months sequestered in the Acropole Hotel. He never appeared in public without his Indiana Jones–style hat. Instead of venturing into the field, he treated hungry relief workers to free meals at the hotel, and used the information he coaxed out of them to file detailed reports with his superiors in Los Angeles. They thought he was a genius.

Although many countries made mistakes in funding development projects in Darfur, Italy had more than its fair share of white elephants to account for. In 1986, the Italian minister of international development committed $76 million for an ambitious relief and rehabilitation program in Darfur, to be implemented in co-operation with the United Nations Development Program. Among the first projects to be funded through the Italian program was a European-standard highway linking El Fasher to Nyala, a distance of approximately 220 kilometres. The project had been sitting on the UNDP shelves for years, with no donor willing to touch it. According to experienced development organizations active in Darfur, improving the road from El Fasher to Nyala was very low on the list of priorities. The existing road was a dirt track that, although inelegant, was perfectly adequate for the souk lorries and other vehicles that travelled its length. Relief agencies had suggested that if donors were truly interested in road improvement, the construction of Irish bridges at critical wadi locations should be the first item addressed. Moreover, when the minister made the decision to fund the highway, he was under the mistaken impression that the Italians would be engineering the final link in a highway across the desert. He was unaware that there was no highway in place between Khartoum and El Fasher—it was 900 kilometres of open sand. The Italians were building an autostrada from nowhere to nowhere.

The Italian Relief and Rehabilitation Program included millions of dollars dedicated to the improvement of village-level grain storage in Darfur. Over the years, various relief agencies, such as Oxfam and German Agro Action, had emphasized the need to augment the capacity of local grain storage to guard against future famines. An Italian delegation visited Darfur in October, 1985, specifically to ascertain storage requirements at the community level.

Unfortunately, the 1,200 prefabricated Fiberglas silos that the Italians eventually delivered could only be filled by sophisticated mechanized hoppers. The only opening for the grain was located at the top of the five-metre silos. Throughout Darfur, grain had traditionally been stored underground or in special clay pots. Hoppers did not exist in Darfur, and villagers had no fuel available for their engines. In addition, the silos needed elaborate concrete bases.

When the silos arrived in Khartoum, the relief agencies took one look at them and declared them useless. The Italians couldn't give them away. UNHCR, CARE, and Save the Children refused to take them. An informal contest was held among the relief agencies to come up with alternative uses for the silos, which had been delivered to the Sudan cut in half lengthwise. Suggestions included cattle dips, duck ponds, Jacuzzi liners, and prefabricated housing. UN special representative Winston Prattley was the hands-down winner; at a meeting of relief agencies, he announced that the Sudan now had the hulls for 2,400 boats—potentially the largest navy in the world.

The luckiest refugees in all of the Sudan had to be the 200 permanent residents of the Saudi Arabian–funded camp just a few kilometres outside El Geneina. Dubbed Club Med by relief workers, the camp included spacious, air-conditioned accommodation with hot showers and refrigerators stocked with cold drinks. All food items were flown in on a weekly C-130 transport flight from Saudi Arabia. At one point, Saudi social workers employed at the camp noted that the children appeared to be bored with their new surroundings. The next week, six of the latest arcade video games were installed. Huge generators ran 24 hours a day to provide electricity for the camp.

Gaining admission to Club Med was akin to winning the lottery; it was suspected that most of the residents were not poor Chadian children at all, but rather the sons and daughters of affluent Sudanese looking for a summer camp for their kids. During all my time in the Sudan, Club Med was the only place where I encountered kids who were rude and disrespectful. I once was invited to the camp for a meal. It was a veritable feast. We were served platters of meats, including succulent roast lamb. I had never seen such an array of sweets anywhere in Africa, all Saudi specialties flown in from the motherland for the occasion. The Saudi medical doctor sitting next to me told me the sole reason he had accepted the assignment in the Sudan was the pay: he was receiving the equivalent of $100,000 for six months of work.

The selling of relief commodities was commonplace in the Sudan, and undermined the legitimacy of the entire emergency operation. District councils, police, and local relief committees were all involved. A consequence of the decision by USAID to sell its sorghum rather than give it away was that price gouging became common. In one village, I saw a woman walk into a market with a pathetic pile of onions she had collected to trade for USAID sorghum. In Kongo Haraza, I received reports about a family, who for years had been among the most powerful merchants in the area, confiscating and selling thousands of bags of sorghum and other relief supplies delivered in their district. I often found relief commodities donated by the EEC for sale in village markets. UNICEF pharmaceutical supplies could be purchased at pharmacies in major Sudanese towns.

A certain level of trade in relief commodities could be expected and, in any case, could not be prevented. A 45-kilogram bag of sorghum became a unit of currency at the village level, and would be traded by a family for other badly needed supplies, such as vegetable oil or sugar. But the quantities of relief supplies for sale in local Darfur markets were so significant that corruption on the part of local officials and representatives of relief agencies was clearly interfering with their free distribution.

The famine was providing extra income for many people, including merchants, truck drivers, soldiers, and representatives of relief agencies. It wasn't only food that was being misused. In Khartoum, Rudy Rodrigues looked on with astonishment as senior officials of the Relief and Rehabilitation Commission cracked open a container that had been shipped by Band Aid in London. The container was filled with toys and children's clothing, the best of which the RRC officials divided up among themselves. Rudy knew that only the remnants would ever make it to the village level. When he confronted the officials, they explained that since most of the toys required batteries, which were not available in the regions, the booty would be useless in poorer communities.

If I had my way, all relief workers would have to swear the Hippocratic Oath—to promise that, at the very least, they would do no harm. The 1985 emergency operation in Darfur provided a textbook example of the dangers associated with large-scale indiscriminate food distribution. The rains of 1985 meant that farmers who had access to seeds and tools could harvest their first crop in three or four seasons. Instead of relying on food aid from the outside world, the people of Darfur and Kordofan had a slim chance, once again, of feeding themselves. Even if the quantities grown were not sufficient to maintain the entire population, local purchase programs could be instituted, rewarding farmers for their efforts. It would be an important step toward self-sufficiency.

However, it took months for the relief operation to gear up. By the time it was in full swing, farmers were ready to harvest their crops, the proceeds of which would go against the massive debts they had incurred during the years of famine. Farmers expressed the very real concern that at the exact moment their sorghum went to market, foreigners would dump more free grain. In the grain distribution business, timing is everything. The international community's rescue efforts in Darfur were about one year too late. According to Kevin Browne of Save the Children U.K. "They're sending in the cavalry. Unfortunately, the battle is long over."

Because of the urgent nature of the humanitarian operation in Kordofan and Darfur, important recovery and rehabilitation projects went by the wayside. Most agencies with expertise in community-based development were distracted by the large dollars and potential profits associated with the transport of sorghum. The USAID contract was worth $20 million to Save the Children U.K.

Some smaller agencies, such as Oxfam and German Agro Action, insisted on proceeding with development projects that, although less spectacular in nature, were vital to the economic recovery of the entire region. GAA was working in remote locations of Darfur rehabilitating old government buildings to use for village-level grain storage. GAA provided all the materials, and the local community contributed the labour. In every village, the project was being enthusiastically embraced by residents. Oxfam was supporting a village seed-bank program, providing zinc roofing materials so that villagers could upgrade their local seed-storage capacity at relatively low cost. Oxfam's goal was to ensure that every farmer had enough seed on hand to cultivate their entire field. In addition, GAA and Oxfam were working to intensify vegetable production in wadi gardens.

When Save the Children U.K. agreed, after much pressure from USAID, to take on the food distribution responsibility in Darfur, a real problem was the paucity of information about the region's emergency food requirements. In the words of Andrew Timpson, "Darfur was virgin territory. There was no early warning system for famine, and there weren't people on the ground from the international agencies as there were in Ethiopia." Donors in late 1985 had difficulties coming to grips with the dimensions of the famine. Estimates of the number of people at risk across the country, and the amount of grain needed to fend off starvation, fluctuated wildly. Among the agencies themselves, there was little agreement as to the criteria to be used in assessing needs.

The delays and lack of planning proved almost as catastrophic as the famine itself. Under the terms of the USAID contract, truckers were allowed to

deliver their loads to the most accessible locations. Isolated villages, which usually were most in need, were bypassed. Most of the grain ended up being
dumped in towns across Darfur. Peter Verney reported that in November, 1985,
farmers in the El Geneina market begged him to stop the grain distribution.
They would soon be harvesting their first crop, but with free sorghum still
being handed out by the relief agencies, they would not even be able to recoup
their costs. Sorghum was so cheap that people were starting to build houses out
of it. None of the relief agencies had made funding available for the local purchase of grain. The free distribution of sorghum created a strong disincentive
for farmers to plant anything other than cash crops such as tobacco. In the face
of massive foreign handouts, it had become completely uneconomic for the
farmers of Darfur to grow food for their own people to eat.

Alex de Waal, of Save the Children U.K., had the answers, but no one
would listen. In 1985, de Waal carried out one of the most detailed studies
ever of traditional practices employed by people in rural areas to cope with
famine. Entitled *Survival in Darfur*, it suggested that the international community, when planning its humanitarian strategy for the Sudan, failed to take
into consideration the tried and true techniques used by farmers and pastoralists since time immemorial to wait out famine. The people of Darfur
were far more resilient than anyone had ever imagined. In my conversations
with de Waal, he criticized the tendency of relief agencies to distribute
sorghum without first carrying out comprehensive surveys. You had to know
first where the grain was needed. He stated that he couldn't sleep at night
thinking of the damage that relief agencies would do by distributing food
without effective targeting.

De Waal would have ceased all distribution of sorghum at the end of
October, 1985, except for localized distribution in the Millit and northern
Jebel Mara area. He recommended that relief agencies employ a monitoring
team made up of a social scientist, a nutritionist, and an enumerator to determine local needs and to draft a distribution plan. Proper targeting of food aid
was required to reach the estimated 40 per cent of the population who were
most in need—in particular, the one- to five-year-olds and lactating mothers.
De Waal claimed that Save the Children U.K. was distributing 60,000 tonnes
of sorghum in Darfur with no baseline data. De Waal's teams would have
examined five factors: the nutritional status of the population, the availability
of animal and wage labor, the size of the population, the mortality rate, and the
expected size of the local harvest.

Grain distribution in Darfur continued well into 1986, and many farmers suffered the consequences. Many went further into debt; some lost their land. Because of poor targeting, vulnerable people continued to suffer and die. The total cost of the famine in human lives is impossible to calculate. In Darfur alone between October, 1984, and October, 1985, an estimated 77,600 people, most of them children, died on account of the famine. Alex de Waal estimates the excess mortality in Darfur during the total famine period at 105,000. Between November, 1984, and November, 1985, the mean number of animals per house-hold in Darfur dropped from 18.8 to 3.6. By November, 1985, 49 per cent of Darfur families had no animals. The population had reached rock bottom.

In hindsight, Save the Children U.K. should never have taken on such an ambitious contract. The agency was stretched far beyond its limits. The trans-port and storage of large quantities of grain required a specialized set of skills and a highly developed infrastructure. Save the Children's expertise was in designing and funding small-scale relief and rehabilitation projects, not in man-aging a trucking empire. Andrew Timpson later admitted that the USAID con-tract was a departure for SCF; it had not undertaken such a large-scale transport operation since Biafra in 1968. But no other organization—including the UN World Food Program—was willing to accept responsibility for food distribution in Darfur, and somebody had to do the job. Because of delays by WFP, Save the Children was forced to work blind. No comprehensive survey of the region's needs had been carried out. Nor could Save the Children be held responsible for the total failure of the Sudan Railways Corporation to meet its obligations under the USAID contract. Under the circumstances, the SCF field workers, charged with an impossible task, did an admirable job. Thanks to the resourcefulness of field staff such as Peter Verney, thousands of lives were saved, but Save the Children received little credit for its efforts.

It was fortunate that donors had decided to find an alternative to the Sudan Railways Corporation for the transport of relief supplies. It took months for the railway wash-outs to be repaired. Despite constant pressure from the EEC, load factors never improved significantly. Apart from the poor condition of the track itself, the rolling stock had never been properly maintained. Of the 160 locomo-tives that the SRC owned in November, 1985, 101 were inoperative. All 17 state-of-the-art Hitachi locomotives bought by the SRC in 1976 had broken down due to problems with the engines and the tractor drives. Of the 101 inoperative locomotives, 50 were beyond saving. Many had already been cannibalized for spare parts. The EEC had just entered into a contract with General Electric to refurbish 10 derelict locomotives. The engines were being totally rebuilt. At least some lessons had been learned: the SRC officials insisted that the repair work be carried out by Sudanese mechanics as much as possible, so that they would be able to maintain the locomotives long after the foreign experts had departed.

I filed a complete report on the RTO operations through the end of 1985 in El Geneina district with my office in Khartoum. It turned out to be my final report. In December, 1985, Rudy Rodrigues informed me that I was being reassigned to Khartoum to assist with the management of the entire World Food Program Road Transport Operation. He called it a promotion, and said my work in the field had impressed UN officials in the capital. But I was deeply disappointed at the news. I had made many friends among the local residents of El Geneina, and I enjoyed life on the frontier. I had no interest in living in Khartoum, with its snarled traffic and its large population of foreigners. Despite the presence of the Nile and the few bits of history that remained, Khartoum held little appeal for me. My place was in Darfur, helping people at the village level, not behind a desk. I had made preliminary plans with one of the school teachers in El Geneina to raise money for the rehabilitation of the local elementary school. I had been working with a woman from the town who had recently graduated from the University of Khartoum to develop a primary schooling program for young girls, who were often excluded from formal education. After three months in El Geneina, I was just beginning to feel settled.

But I had no choice in the matter. The decision was final, and my replacement had already been recruited from Canada. He would be arriving in El Geneina within 10 days and taking over the keys to my beloved red Landcruiser. I haphazardly packed my belongings into two wooden crates. My friends at the UNHCR house held a small farewell party for me. Ekber was most gracious, allowing the sandal-clad, jellabiyah-wearing Peter Verney onto his premises, probably for the first time. Christine Brown arrived with a healthy donation of Stella Artois from the Belgian pilots. Commissioner Abdul Affis walked to the party from his house, his white Land Rover having finally given up the ghost. I had enjoyed my talks with Abdul about El Geneina in the years before the famine had moved in. He was always a gracious host and a superb storyteller. "The sad thing is that you will always associate the name of this place with misery and with suffering," he said. "Come back when the fields are green, and when the schools are open again, and it will seem like another world."

But I did not have to see the schools populated with smiling students to know that El Geneina was a special place. Most foreigners associate Africa with the palm-fringed coast of the Indian Ocean, the open savannah of the Masai Mara, or the teeming wildlife of the Serengeti. The Africa I came to know and love did not lend itself to postcards and will never be a victim of mass tourism. For me, the appeal of El Geneina was that it was rough around the edges and you had to work hard to like the place. It attracted people like Christine Brown and Peter Verney and Ekber Menemencioglu because of the challenges it presented, not in spite of them.

I have never been good at saying goodbye. My drivers had been ferociously loyal to me, going far beyond the responsibilities that they had been contracted to carry out. Their efforts had made me look good. They drove hundreds of kilometres at a time, stopping only to pray. They had not seen their families in Khartoum since September. We had been through a great deal together, and had seen things that no one should ever have had to see. But there had also been good times. On long trips when we camped for the night, the men would park their Fiat trucks in a big circle, like the wagon trains of the American West. We would build a fire at the centre and there would be stories long into the night.

I loved sleeping in the back of the trucks on top of the grain bags, with a warm breeze blowing off the desert and a cloudless sky overhead. To this day the smell of sweet sorghum takes me back to my Darfur days. I remember the faces of the people in the villages where we delivered the first food they had received in many weeks, and how the children on their hands and knees would pick out from the sand the individual grains that had escaped from the bags. I remember the nameless girl at Beida, wrapped in plastic, tears streaming down her cheeks, crying out in the wind and chaos of the haboob. I remember how the kids in Kongo Haraza and Beida showed off the toy helicopters that they had lovingly constructed from dried-out reeds and bits of twine. They were perfect copies of the Columbia helicopters, complete with sling loads they had deftly cut from the USAID sorghum bags.

I departed El Geneina on the morning of December 14, 1986. I loaded my two crates into the back of a C-130 Hercules, then walked to the edge of the runway. My eighteen drivers had made their way to the airport to see me off, and had arranged themselves into an informal receiving line. These men were the best employees I had ever worked with; I have never had a stronger team. They had loaded sorghum onto the Fiats the previous evening and were heading off to Beida that morning.

Garret Adam was standing last in line. He had been fascinated by my SPS map. Whenever I had taken it out on road trips, he had peered over my shoulder, pointing out important features to me, suggesting routes, sketching in changes and additions to the map. Between us, Garret and I had made substantial revisions, he in Arabic and I in English. We improvised our own key at the bottom of the map with different symbols for the various road hazards we had encountered. When I said farewell to Garret Adam, I presented him with the rolled-up map, and for a moment he was speechless. He had always insisted that I wouldn't make a very good military man—I lacked the discipline and I didn't take orders well. As we parted, he stood at attention and gave me a crisp farewell salute; the simple gesture was one of the greatest honors I had ever received.

I was happy my last flight out of El Geneina would be on board Juicy Lucy, my favourite Hercules, with Captain Norbett at the controls. A strong wind was blowing directly up the runway from the west, which made our take-off easy. When we were airborne, Captain Norbett made straight for the long line of RTO trucks, which was already winding its way south toward the wadi. In the day's first light, the clouds of dust kicked up by the big tires made the trucks easy to pick out.

We flew low over the Fiats, and Captain Norbett banked the plane so I could see them out the starboard window. They would be in Beida by nightfall, with barrels of vegetable oil and bags of sorghum for thousands of Chadian kids whom nobody wanted or cared for. Somewhere, buried amidst that valuable cargo on board Abakar Oushan Imam's Fiat number 127, were six soccer balls I had bought in a sports store on Jamhurria Avenue in Khartoum. I had promised them to a gang of kids in Beida I had met on my last visit. Abakar assured me he would see that the soccer balls got into the children's hands.

Captain Norbett tipped the C-130's big wings in farewell as we crossed over the trucks, and then we peeled off toward the east, the Hercules's turbine engines roaring. The sun was already well above the horizon. For the first time, I noticed that the hills around El Geneina had a faint tinge of green, the color most sacred to Muslims. With any luck, more rains would be on the way and the seeds the Darfur farmers had so frantically planted would take root. With any luck, for the first time in years there might be grain to store and people could return to their homes. With any luck, God would at last provide.

Sunday and Moj

I missed Darfur, and I was still hoping Rudy Rodrigues might reconsider his decision to post me to Khartoum. The city's climate was among the most hostile anywhere on the planet, with temperatures hovering between 35 and 45 degrees Celsius. After a haboob moved through Khartoum, the entire city was coated with a thick layer of sand. It stuck to everything, from windows to cars to the leaves of plants. Khartoum had no cultural life and no performing arts of any kind. Foreigners flocked to the few concerts staged by musicians imported by the British Council. Sharia law, imposed on Muslims and non-Muslims alike, prescribed the limits of any social gatherings. Alcohol was strictly prohibited. Other than elaborate engagement and wedding parties hosted by establishment families, I never witnessed any kind of celebration in the streets of the city.

Khartoum, the capital of Africa's largest country, isn't much to look at. You have to scrape off more than 40 years of accumulated grit to find any evidence of its resplendent past. The city exists solely because of its location at the conjunction of the White and Blue Nile rivers, but there is nothing marking the spot. Khartoum's architecture is nondescript, as is the surrounding area. In 1986, 77 per cent of Khartoum families still relied on charcoal as their main source of domestic fuel. The result was that the city was encircled by its own miniature desert totally denuded of trees; today, the situation is even worse. Even in the wealthy suburbs, trees are regularly felled by private citizens and city workers. Khartoum has no public parks or gardens. There are no sidewalks for pedestrians, and aggressive drivers make walking anywhere in the city a risky proposition.

As he had for novices attempting a desert crossing, Sig Fossland had his own rules of engagement for anyone encountering Khartoum, which he shared with me on my first full day back in the city. Elevators in office buildings were death traps and had to be avoided at all costs. The only buildings where elevators could be trusted were the Kuwaiti Towers, where the U.S. embassy was housed, and the Hilton Hotel. For unknown reasons, people had begun to make off with manhole covers and sewer grates, so walking at night in Khartoum was perilous. I wondered how blind people coped. Sig said it was best to assume all Khartoum dogs were rabid. They should never be approached or petted. Water and electricity were totally unreliable. Sig advised newcomers to the city to fill every spare container in their apartment, house, or hotel room with water for the days when none would be available. Whenever Sig flew to or from Europe, he gathered up as many of the packaged handy-wipe towels as he could find on the aircraft, even raiding the little storage cabinets in the lavatories, which are rarely locked. He preferred KLM over any of the other airlines because of the quality of their towelettes and other toiletries.

The Sudan had little to show for its 30 years of independence from the British Empire. According to all the internationally accepted criteria for evaluating the quality of life and standard of living in a country, the Sudan was a basket case. The infant-mortality rate was among the highest in the world, and 10 times the rate of any member of the EEC. Only 22 per cent of the population had access to safe drinking water. Life expectancy was 48 years, compared to 74 years for citizens of the United Kingdom. The literacy rate among males was 38 per cent and among females, only 14 per cent. There was one physician for every 8,800 citizens. Per-capita annual income was $360. The economy was in ruins. The Sudan had borrowed heavily in the 1970s and early 1980s, and had an accumulated debt of over $9-billion. Annual repayments on the debt—if they were made—would amount to three times the value of the Sudan's total annual exports. The Sudan was already $400-million overdue in repayments to the International Monetary Fund, so further loans were impossible to obtain. The Sudan had become a beggar among nations, forever holding out its hand looking for contributions. In 1985, foreign aid accounted for 79 per cent of the total national budget. Only generous support from the U.S., Saudi Arabia, and other Gulf states allowed the country to stagger from crisis to crisis.

The United Nations rated the Sudan as an extreme-hardship posting for its staff, rivalled only by Chad and Mongolia. UN salaries were topped up to compensate for the day-to-day inconveniences that people experienced. The nearest medical care for UN employees and their dependents was over 1,500 kilometres away in either Cairo or Nairobi. The Khartoum American School provided a reasonable standard of education up to Grade 8, but high-school-aged children of UN employees had to be shipped overseas. Other than the cheerless hotel dining rooms, Khartoum featured one Chinese, one Korean, and one Ethiopian restaurant, all located along Airport Road. Sports facilities were only available at the private clubs. Many of the animals at Khartoum's pathetic zoo were sick or injured; some of them had been poached for food. Their tiny cages had not been cleaned in months.

The Sudan's capital city did have one unusual diversion. Years earlier, the hapless crew of a Sudan Airways 707, just acquired from Ireland's Aer Lingus, executed a perfect landing on the Blue Nile, 15 kilometres upstream from Khartoum. Apparently they had mistaken moonlight reflected on the water's surface for the airport runway lights. A more probable explanation is that they were drunk on Irish whiskey. Luckily the plane was empty and there were no fatalities. The 707 settled into the mud and took on a new life as a giant jungle-gym for Sudanese and expatriate children alike. Air Lingus hastily dispatched a team from Dublin to Khartoum to paint over all the airline's markings. Word went around the community of international airlines that in future, all planes sold to Sudan Airways should have any distinguishing marks removed before being handed over.

Every day after work at RTO, I retreated to the Sudan Club for a swim. The American Club featured a larger swimming pool and a better restaurant, but it lacked the faded elegance of this little relic from colonial days. The display case in the sitting room was lined with tarnished trophies honoring past champions in lawn bowling and tennis, long since dead. On the wall was a letter to the club president from Winston Churchill. The Sudan Club library contained hundreds of dusty, leather-bound books that hadn't been opened in years. A gaggle of aging British expats stranded in the former colony made the Sudan Club their beachhead in a valiant struggle to fend off any encroachment by the late 20th century. Every year, a Christmas pantomime was performed, in addition to one play. At the rear of the club were two open-air squash courts. Khartoum squash rules were amended to compensate for the city's intense heat: matches comprised the best of three rather than five games.

A fixture at the Sudan Club was 78-year-old Nora Robinson, a 30-year resident of Khartoum. Her husband, long deceased, had served with the Sudan Political Service, and she recalled the days when foreigners in Khartoum would spend the weekends in Port Sudan on the Red Sea. The men wore dinner jackets on the train from Khartoum, and the meals were served with silverware. All the cars were air-conditioned. It was the height of luxury. Mrs. Robinson chaired the garden committee of the club, and spent most of the day on the premises. She was not happy in post-colonial Sudan, but as the British Empire had disintegrated, she had nowhere else to go. The club, with its watercolor on the dining-room wall of the Queen Mother with a youthful Princess Elizabeth, was the only place she felt comfortable and could afford on her modest government pension.

The unofficial headquarters for aid organizations working in the Sudan was the Acropole Hotel, located in the heart of Khartoum a few blocks from the Sudan Club. Owned by three Greek brothers, the Acropole was an island of efficiency. From street level, the hotel was unimposing, but the rooms were always clean and the service was excellent. More importantly for employees of international organizations, the Acropole Hotel telephone was one of the most reliable in the city. There often was a line-up of hotel guests and outsiders waiting to use the phone or the telex. A number of small aid organizations very effectively operated out of the Acropole, using the hotel lobby as their only office. The restaurant on the second floor served hearty, home-cooked meals, including roast beef with mashed potatoes and gravy, and Nile perch. Excellent Greek coffee was offered at the end of every meal. On Friday nights the Acropole roof-top patio was the place to be in Khartoum, as the hotel featured recent English-language films. Many of them were pirated videos that were still in the theatres in North America and Europe. Anyone could attend, but you had to come early to get a good seat.

The Acropole became my second home in the Sudan. Although nothing in Khartoum could approach the hospitality I received from the residents of El Geneina throughout my stay in Darfur, the welcome extended by the Pagolatos brothers and their families came close. When I arrived at the hotel I informed George Pagolatos I needed a room for one week; one month later, I had not yet checked out.

My job at the Road Transport Operation involved assisting Rudy with the overall management of the truck fleet. After Darfur, the assignment wasn't much of a challenge. Rudy had already assembled a formidable team, including Ernest Vienna, Al Ford, and John Jack; roles and responsibilities had been established, and there wasn't much left for me to do. I felt I was just putting in time. On Rudy's behalf, I met with representatives of the various aid agencies with the aim of co-ordinating the transport and distribution of relief supplies. The Technical Co-ordination Committee convened weekly on the top floor of the recently renovated Relief and Rehabilitation Commission building located just down the road from the Khartoum zoo. The cast of characters around the table included representatives of all the UN agencies, Oxfam, Save the Children, CARE, World Vision, and indigenous Sudanese organizations such as the Sudan Council of Churches and Sudan Aid. The meetings were chaired by Per Bergen, a Norwegian associated with Redd Barna, Norwegian Save the Children, who had been seconded to UNEOS. Per Bergen was fond of saying he had been drafted to the Sudan "for the duration," not unlike the soldiers of the Great War.

The TCC meeting was a valuable forum to get up to speed on all emergency activities across the country, and I tried not to miss a session. Anita Mackie, a senior official with USAID, was one of the most active and vocal members of the committee, and I learned much just from listening to her. On one occasion, officials from southern Kordofan had come to the meeting pleading for food aid. They informed us conditions were so bad in their part of the country that hungry lions were attacking and eating villagers. It was a horrible situation and the TCC had to take action. They required an immediate shipment of sorghum and supplementary feeding supplies. A prolonged silence descended on the room. Finally Anita Mackie cleared her throat and addressed the delegation. She had a modest proposal: perhaps, under the circumstances, it would make more sense for the technical co-ordination committee to allocate food aid to the lions than to the local population.

I missed El Geneina. I became good friends with Simon Akol, the radio operator at Ruff Road Base who was the voice behind Mike Kilo. RTO had recently installed a new digital transmitter, and I used it to contact Ekber and Frances on a regular basis. We developed our own code. Frances would ask me if "Mr. Walker was coming to town," which meant that her supply of Johnnie Walker Red Label was running low. Could I please smuggle some on board Juicy Lucy?

I longed to be back in the field. Although my work at RTO was useful to the overall relief effort, it lacked immediacy. In El Geneina, I was part of a community and I knew I was needed. In Khartoum, my work was coming dangerously close to resembling that of my lawyer friends back in Canada. I was sitting behind a desk, with an In tray at one end and an Out tray at the other. Rudy even had me examine the lease for the building that RTO occupied. It was sheer drudgery, and I considered returning to Canada.

In the end, my redemption came in the form of a boy named Adam. I had parked my white Land Rover, on loan from the Royal Ontario Museum's dig in Upper Nubia, in an alley adjacent to the Acropole Hotel for the night. After dinner, I realized I had forgotten some documents in the car and went to fetch them. As I turned down the alley, I saw a shadowy figure crouching low on the far side of the car. A thief! Evidently he hadn't seen me, so I stealthily approached the Land Rover. It was a child, and he was using a nail to jimmy the lock. I pounced on him and spun him around. "Harami! Harami!"I yelled, but the streets were empty and nobody came to my assistance. The boy tried to escape but I held him fast. He started whimpering, then crying hysterically. Suddenly I was worried I had hurt him. He was tiny and frail, and dressed only in a pair of blue shorts. I saw he had no shoes and one of his legs was cut. He obviously was from the south, perhaps a Dinka boy. The kid was terrified of me, and buried his head in his arms as if expecting me to strike him.

He was not the first street child I had seen in Khartoum. The raging civil war in South Sudan, in combination with drought and famine in the north, had resulted in more than 10,000 young boys migrating to the city. They lived rough in the streets, eating out of garbage dumpsters. They were everywhere. Some had even made the zoo their home. I had seen children sleeping in the long grass near the Coliseum Cinema and outside the central police station. They hung around hotel entrances, begging from relief workers and local businesspeople. Khartoum residents considered them a real nuisance. I had heard stories that they were incorrigible criminals and were responsible for many break-ins in the city. Some people said they were dangerous.

This boy looked harmless enough. I slowly released my grip on him, but did not let go completely. "Ismik minu?" I asked. He told me his name. "Kam sanaa?" He was 11 years old. "Inte min wein?" Adam was from Malakal, on the White Nile, the heart of Dinka country. He had been in the city for almost a year, and he lived in a cardboard box near the Meridien Hotel. He was surprised by my questions, and he started to relax. But he was still shaking, and it was obvious he was hungry. He told me he was looking for anything in my car he could eat.

I told Adam to wait by the car, that I would go up to the hotel restaurant and find him a snack. I had a hunch he might take off as soon as I was out of sight and I would likely never see him again, but there were no restaurants open in the city centre and no stores where I could buy any food for him. If I spoke to George, the hotel might be able to gather up some leftovers.

George had entertained many unusual requests from hotel guests during his 20 years in Khartoum, but I was the first to ask him for food for a street child. He probably considered me naive, and he may have worried that feeding street children by the entrance of his hotel would only encourage more kids to move into the area. Many of his guests had already complained about the street children. They were dirty and they smelled. The kids were amused by car mirrors, and were always wrenching them out of position to stare at their reflections. Just a few days earlier, a British woman had told George she was horrified when one of the street children had spoken to her 12-year-old son. She had wanted to call the police, but the boy had not been harmed in any way and George had persuaded her not to. The police would cause problems for everyone.

Adam was waiting for me by the side of the car when I returned with his dinner. We sat on the hood of the Land Rover and I unwrapped the items George's cook had collected. There were two pieces of chicken, some bread, and two oranges. Adam's almond-shaped eyes grew to the size of saucers. I don't think he had eaten a piece of meat in weeks. In seconds the meal disappeared down his throat, and he licked the chicken bones clean. He had a big smile on his face. "Inte kwais?" I asked—was he feeling better? He nodded his head enthusiastically. He found my Arabic amusing. I had been taught by my drivers in Darfur. Their language was rough, and they had recommended I not use it in polite company.

The kid hadn't attacked me, nor had I been swarmed by the members of any gang he might belong to. I had already checked my pocket and my wallet was still there. The chicken, bread, and oranges hadn't cost me or the Acropole anything. But for the first time in many days, this child would be going to sleep with a full stomach. At last I felt I had done something good for someone in Sudan's miserable capital city. Perhaps making a difference didn't necessitate leading truck convoys across wadis or delivering emergency food supplies to isolated refugee camps. In a dreary alleyway of Khartoum within a few metres of the Acropole Hotel, I had found my El Geneina.

The next morning, the Royal Ontario Museum Land Rover was in a different condition than I had left it the night before. It was cleaner than I had ever seen it. Adam had found a rag and a bucket, and in the early morning hours had scrubbed away every speck of mud and dirt from top to bottom. He had even washed the tires. He was putting the finishing touches on his *oeuvre* just as I arrived, and he was proud of his work. "Shokol katir," he said. It had been a great deal of work. I had guessed Adam might be waiting for me, and during breakfast I had squirrelled away a few items from my table. One of the waiters had spotted me and raised his eyebrows. He probably assumed I was hoarding some food for lunch. Adam chomped away on a piece of toast while I explained that I was off to work, but that I would be back in the early evening. He promised to meet me outside the hotel on my return.

Rudy and his colleagues at Ruff Road Base were incredulous when I described my encounter with Adam to them. They had been in Khartoum much longer than I had, and they knew the street children were up to no good. The ruffians were not to be trusted. The kid was probably a member of an organized gang of thieves. The RTO base had experienced some break-ins recently, and had been forced to step up security measures. In his native Kenya, Rudy had become familiar with the phenomenon of the "parking boys," the children who made the streets of Nairobi their home. Many of them came from the Mathare Valley, Nairobi's burgeoning shanty town. Half the population of Kenya was under the age of 13 and a growing proportion of them lived in urban areas. Nairobi's parking boys were not popular among the local citizenry and were largely blamed for the city's skyrocketing crime rate. Carjacking was a common occurrence, and what once had been a charming provincial town was becoming one of Africa's most violent cities. People didn't dare to go out at night any more.

I ignored the advice of Rudy and his colleagues. That evening when I returned to the Acropole Hotel, Adam, as he had promised, was waiting for me just outside the entrance. He stood ready with a bucket of fresh water and a clean sponge, and no sooner had I parked the Land Rover than he went to work. I knew at that point there was no turning back. Adam was unknowingly dragging me away from my desk at the RTO base, but I didn't put up much resistance.

People's motivations for taking action are often difficult to fathom and usually mixed. Why do we do the things we do? For me, guilt was not a factor. In Darfur, I had already met American helicopter pilots atoning for unspoken atrocities they had committed in Vietnam 20 years earlier. Some people were motivated purely by religion, but I had little Catholic angst left in me. I could respond in the words of a lawyer, and say I believed in the concept of inalienable rights applying to all citizens and not just to those of a certain social status or skin color. Kids have the right to be protected from abuse and exploitation, and to receive a basic education. But I think that's too easy. I suspect the real reasons I got involved with the cause of street children have more to do with my own childhood and adolescence, from my days working with inner-city kids in Toronto's poorest neighborhood to setting up after-school basketball programs in East Palo Alto. I have always admired underdogs, and few people could be worse off than the kids living in Khartoum's gutters. Perhaps my unresolved grief resulting from the drowning of a 12-year-old child had something to do with it.

I began to research the phenomenon of street children. On January 15, 1986, I wrote some notes in my workbook:

> Street kids are:
>   – profoundly poor
>   – illiterate/uneducated
>   – sick
>   – illegitimate/from single parent families
>   – rejected by society
>   – hungry/badly nourished
>   – wearing rags
>   – lacking organized support from the government or relief agencies
>   – on their own.

The list contained no great revelations or insights, but in my mind I was attempting to work out who these kids really were, where they came from, and what hardships they had endured and were now encountering. I tried to be as logical as possible. I was, after all, a lawyer, not a social worker.

Khartoum's street children came from all over the country. I had driven across the breadth of Kordofan and Darfur, and I had witnessed the human consequences of drought and famine. I had seen thousands of people on the move. With their crops destroyed, their tools sold, their wells dry, and their seeds exhausted, there was nothing to keep them on the land. Adam and his friends did not choose to be in the street. The street children of Khartoum were the vanguard of the Sudan's urban landless poor, and their numbers were bound to increase.

I learned that approximately half of Khartoum's street children were ecological refugees from western Sudan. In many cases, their own parents sent them off to fend for themselves after the family's grain supply had been exhausted on account of the drought. They rode on the tops of souk lorries, often negotiating with the driver to wash the vehicle in exchange for a free ride. The kids hid away on trains on the route between El Obeid and Khartoum. The children from South Sudan were fleeing years of intense civil war that had spilled over from the main towns to rural areas. Many of the children were from the Dinka tribe, the community most closely associated with the Sudan People's Liberation Army, the main rebel group. The government forces still held the three main towns in South Sudan—Juba, Wau, and Malakal—but the SPLA controlled most of the surrounding rural areas. The government was therefore forcing people from the bush into the larger towns. Their villages had been destroyed by government soldiers and their huts set afire. Some of the children had seen their own parents killed. They escaped the war by stowing away under bags of coal on old Nile steamers. The government could dig a moat around the capital, but it would have no impact. Desperate people will do anything to survive. One way or another, these children would find a way into Khartoum.

The children I saw living in Khartoum's streets were the lucky ones. Many of their friends had died en route. Most people saw street children as riffraff, as refuse, as vagabonds and thieves. For me, Adam and his friends were the pioneers and explorers of their generation. These children were survivors. Some of the country's bravest citizens were living in the streets of Khartoum.

I needed to do more research. If I really wanted to learn about street children, who better to teach me than one of the kids? When they arrived in Khartoum, the children gravitated to the garbage dumps, learned the ways of the streets, and soon fell in with other unaccompanied kids. I wanted to apprentice with them, to learn how they adapted to this completely foreign environment and how they coped. Adam agreed to give me a tour of the street-kids' Khartoum. He took me to places that few foreigners visit. Not all the spots were miserable. I went to the Coliseum Cinema and saw one of the Hindi films. The kids paid 25 piasteres, about 10 cents, to get in. Alternatively, kids could buy their way into the cinema with elastic bands they collected during the day. The cinema staff needed them to wrap tickets with and none were available in local stores. The Coliseum was an open-air cinema, which is common in the Sudan. It rarely rained, so a roof was more of a nuisance than anything else. The place was packed with street children. One kid introduced himself to me as The Vampire, and that's what all the other children called him. "What's your real name?" I inquired as he chewed on a piece of chat, a mild narcotic imported from the south. "I dunno. Go ask my mom. She knows," he responded. Some kids passed around sticks of marijuana. Most of them obviously had seen the film several times before. They acted out their favorite scenes in front of other kids, they sang and danced. It was wild. The Sudan has an ultra-conservative board of censors, and whenever there was a kissing scene, the projectionist intentionally blurred the image, at which point the kids screamed hysterically.

Adam took me under the bridges where many of the children lived. They had an informal support system set up among themselves. Older kids looked after younger kids. Tasks were assigned each morning to all the members of the group. Some boys had to go to the market to work as porters. Other kids would wash cars. I was introduced to a boy named Isaac who had no legs. He had been riding on the roof of the train from Nyala to Khartoum. Somehow he had fallen off and was run over by the wheels. Both of his legs were crushed. His friends immediately jumped off the train. They carried Isaac to the nearest hospital, where the doctor saved his life. At first, there had been no money for a wheelchair, so the boys carried Isaac around from place to place.

I wanted to learn more. I asked the kids who helped them and who hurt them. Their enemies were too numerous to name. The police regularly conducted round-ups of street children, called kasha. The children were taken to the central police station and interrogated. Some were badly beaten by the police officers. The kids spoke of a prison called Kober in Khartoum North, where street children were locked up for months at a time. A number of their friends had disappeared into Kober and had never come out. Then there was the notorious Dar Tarbiat al Ashbal reformatory for juvenile delinquents. It was packed full with children from South Sudan who had been scraped off the streets and accused of being thieves, even gun-runners for the rebels. Just the name of this place instilled fear in the kids. I was told boys were drugged, whipped, and given electric shocks. Some were as young as seven or eight years old.

The street children of Khartoum had made few friends among middle-class Sudanese society. The kids from South Sudan were accustomed to having racist slurs hurled at them. They were called monkeys and slaves. Public buses never stopped for street children. People hit them and spat on them. One child told me the rich foreign kids were among the nastiest, never missing an opportunity to taunt them or throw things at them. Shopkeepers would threaten them with clubs if they even came near their stores. The Christians were no better than the Muslims. Many of the kids from South Sudan were Catholics and had been baptized. A number of them had wanted to go to Sunday mass, but the priest had chased them out of the church. He said they smelled and there was no room for them, despite the rows of empty pews.

The street children knew all the relief agencies by name, and easily recognized their logos on the sides of their four-wheel-drives. I was disappointed to learn that not one relief organization based in Khartoum had done anything on behalf of the street children. Apparently they, too, were worried the kids would steal their cars and break into their houses. Isaac was particularly clever and spoke good English. "If they call themselves Save the Children, then why won't they save us?" he asked me. I had no answer. According to the kids, the men from the UN Development

Program were the meanest. A number of the kids had gone to the UNDP offices asking for help, only to be threatened with violence by the guard.

Their list of good guys was short. There was an official from the French embassy named Robert Richard who had opened a small house for street children. He called his project Enfants du Soleil. The house was run by a Sudanese social worker. Every day after the embassy closed, Mr. Richard organized a distribution of sandwiches outside its gate. Then there was a woman named Blanka who ran an ice-cream shop who had befriended many of the children over the years. The kids recommended I go meet with her. "Maybe you'll get some free ice cream," Isaac suggested. There were one or two doctors who were willing to treat the children, but otherwise medical care was a big problem for them. Khartoum's street children were regularly denied permission to enter the city's main hospital. They were told it wasn't for them, with their rags and open sores. In any case, the kids had no money for medication.

The boys hinted at other problems. There were men who sexually abused them. Sometimes the boys were paid a few piasteres, but often it was simply rape. Police officers were among the worst offenders. The kids would be arrested, taken to the holding cells, and then viciously raped. One of the kids had been interviewed by a Sudanese social worker and had described such an incident. The social worker abruptly brought the discussion to an end, told the child he should be ashamed of himself for making up such stories, and threw him out of her office.

Following Isaac's advice, I visited Casa Blanka, the ice-cream store owned by the patron saint of Khartoum's street children. Blanka el Khalifa served me a coffee and a big scoop of her famous mango ice cream, and sat me down at a table in the corner. She had been born and raised in Croatia, and had met her husband while they both were enrolled as students in London in the 1950s. After graduation, they settled in Khartoum, where her husband had been appointed as a professor in the Faculty of Science at the University of Khartoum. He came from one of the most distinguished families in the nation—his grandfather was the legendary el Khalifa who, alongside the Mahdi, had led a populist uprising against the British, razed Khartoum, and led his Dervishes into combat at the Battle of Omdurman.

As a foreign woman in a predominantly Muslim society, Blanka's professional options were limited. She decided to open an ice-cream store, the first in the city, in 1975. Almost from the beginning, a few beggar children, attracted by the sight of other children entering the shop with their parents, turned up at Casa Blanka. At that time there were no vagrant children. Khartoum sparkled; city workers swept the streets clean at sunrise. Blanka made a deal with the kids:

if they promised not to bother her customers during the day, she would give them some ice cream just before the store closed at night. Being the mother of three boys, Blanka was well aware that ice cream was not the basis for a balanced diet, and began to serve them hot milk with sugar and bread instead.

Blanka had no intention of providing accommodation for the children. She knew it would never work. Instead, she did her best to ensure they had access to basic services such as health care. She arranged for a relative of her husband, Dr. Ali Abdel Karim, a noted pediatrician, to open up his clinic after hours especially for the street children. During the 1980s, the number of vagrant children in Khartoum continued to grow. With the advent of the famine, thousands of children were living on their own in and around the capital. They ranged in age from six to 16; most were between the ages of 10 and 13. I asked why there were no girls among their numbers. Blanka had investigated the issue thoroughly to satisfy her own curiosity. In Muslim society, no matter how poor the family, it would be completely unacceptable to allow one's young daughter to leave home on her own. In addition, a dowry system that had been in place for thousands of years rewarded the family of the bride on the night of the consummation of the marriage. As a result, girls and young women were a source of income for poor families. A financial incentive existed for parents to do everything in their power to keep their daughters at home.

A different phenomenon was at work in South Sudan, which was overwhelmingly Christian and animist. Boys and young men were being aggressively recruited by both the national army and the rebel forces. With the development of lighter weapons, often referred to as junk guns, boys could now be trained to serve as effective soldiers. They were often sent on missions that were considered unsurvivable. Child soldiers were known to be fearless and reckless. They were little killing machines; all you had to do was point them in the right direction. The experience in Mozambique, where South African-backed Renamo rebels recruited children from areas held by the government for the specific purpose of burning down their own villages and killing their own parents, demonstrated the degree to which children can be coerced and brutalized by adults with a mission. When an army needed new recruits, they went village to village and rounded up young boys for training. In South Sudan, girls were not at risk of being recruited by either side. Boys, on the other hand, had to run for their lives.

The street children had spoken of the contempt of middle-class Sudanese society toward them. Blanka had another interpretation. She agreed some people were hateful to the children, beating and abusing them, but in her opinion, they were a distinct minority. Muslim society has as its cornerstone the integrity of the family unit, and the Koran requires people to provide for the poor. The phenomenon of young boys living rough in the city streets was completely foreign to most Sudanese. There was no precedent for it. Many Sudanese honestly believed the children were refugees from Chad or Ethiopia, or that they were criminals. Blanka suggested the indifference shown by the citizens of Khartoum was the result of their lack of experience with urban poverty. Khartoum was not São Paulo or Bangkok—although it was quickly heading in that direction. The ignorance of the Sudanese should not be interpreted as hatred or racism.

Blanka's conscience had been seared through one particular episode involving a poor child she had met. Jaksa was a boy from South Sudan who had turned up at Casa Blanka with a horribly infected leg. He was an aspiring athlete, and had named himself after one of the Sudan's most famous football players. Blanka could smell the rotting flesh. She took the boy to Dr. Ali, who suspected the leg might be cancerous. Jaksa was put on the operating table. In order to determine where the rotten flesh ended and the healthy tissue began, the doctor could not give Jaksa any anaesthetics, so the boy had to be held down by two assistants. Dr. Ali stripped away the rotten flesh and did his best to save the leg, but the infection had reached the bone. The leg needed to be amputated.

Blanka explained to Jaksa why the amputation was necessary, but the boy would not agree to have the operation. Blanka pleaded with him, making it clear that unless the leg was removed, he would die. She coaxed him with a comfortable bed, fresh sheets, a pillow, pyjamas, even eau de cologne. But nothing worked. Finally Jaksa told Blanka he wanted something else. He had never owned a pair of shoes. He agreed to the amputation on the condition that just once, he be allowed to walk with shoes on his feet.

Blanka went off to the Bata store on Jamhurria Avenue and bought him a pair of beautiful leather shoes. They came wrapped in their own box. Jaksa opened it like a treasure chest. In Blanka's words, when Jaksa put the shoes on, he shone like the sun. On the day of the operation, the surgeon examined his leg one more time and exclaimed that something miraculous had happened. Jaksa's leg had improved dramatically; the operation would not be necessary. The boy made a full recovery, attended school, learned to be a carpenter, and now played football during every spare minute of the day.

In 1985, with children flooding into the capital by the hundreds, Blanka realized there was a critical need for a safe place where they could go for help. Her idea
was to set up a day shelter where street children could receive a hot meal, wash
their clothes, learn basic social skills, and receive counselling from social workers.
She found a house in Khartoum II next to the cemetery and the UNICEF office
that was perfect: it had a courtyard, several good-sized rooms, and few neighbors.
As Blanka said to me, the UNICEF people wouldn't care and the people in the
cemetery wouldn't complain. The centre opened a few weeks later. Blanka named
it Sabah, which means "morning" in Arabic. It was Khartoum's first drop-in centre
for street children, and it was an instant success with the kids.

Blanka and I bonded the day we met. Almost every evening I visited her
shop. Blanka treated me to mountains of her best ice cream. She was determined to bring me back to my proper body weight. Blanka had her eye on me
from the start; she needed someone to champion the rights of the kids. Only a
non-Sudanese could speak out about the conditions the children faced in the
streets. If I was thrown out of the country—a common fate of advocates for
minority groups in the Sudan—it wouldn't really matter. I was not planning to
stay for long. I could make my mark and then move on. Weeks before, Bob
Geldof had told me that with Band Aid, he never wanted to establish an institution that would be around for 40 years. His goal was for Band Aid to be like
a shooting star—short and spectacular.

I had been hired to work in the Sudan on a three-month contract, and had
to make a decision about my immediate future. My family had always expected
me to return to Canada after one year in Africa. In my father's words, I needed
to get Africa out of my system. Even some of my friends questioned the
wisdom of throwing away a potentially lucrative law career. I had an ability to
persuade people, and as a lawyer, I would never go hungry. My friends saw one
year away from Canada as an adventure and an opportunity, but in their
minds, giving up my chosen profession to work with the "ragamuffins and
hooligans," as they called them, verged on folly.

I needed advice. From my participation at the TCC meetings, I had gained
respect for Per Bergen, one of the senior advisors to the Relief and Rehabilitation Commission. I did not know him well, but from the meetings, I realized
he was a person of integrity and vast experience. He had spent most of his adult
life working in the field of international development. I asked him to join me
for a working dinner at the South Korean–owned Friendship Hotel on the far
side of the Blue Nile. Over pasta, I described my experience with the street

children, how they had adopted me, and shown me where they lived and where they worked. I talked about my discussions with Blanka el Khalifa, and the centre for street children she had just opened. I told him about my training as a lawyer, and the expectations of my friends and family back home. After all this, I had one question for him: were street children worth a career?

I had done most of the talking and I had not taken a bite of my dinner. Per had almost finished his meal. He placed his knife and fork together and looked me in the eyes. "They're worth a thousand careers," he responded.

Thirteen months earlier, I had walked among the women and the children at Gode in the Ogaden Desert. I had been inspired by their tenacity and their ability to cope with overwhelming obstacles. In the eyes of the children in the camp at Gode, I had seen fear, longing, and despair, but I had also recognized courage. I knew at that moment there was another path for me, but I did not know where that path would lead.

An 11-year-old apprentice thief had shown me the way. Blanka and Per, without consulting each other, confirmed what I already knew: I had to follow my heart. There was a lifetime of work with destitute children ahead of me, if I truly wanted it. The choice was mine.

In his book *Civilization and Ethics*, Albert Schweitzer explores the subject of empathy and compassion for others:

> You are happy, they say; therefore you are called upon to give much. Whatever more than others you have received in health, natural gifts, working capacity, success, a beautiful childhood, harmonious family circumstances, you must not accept as being a matter of course. You must pay a price for them. You must show more than average devotion of life to life.
>
> Open your eyes and look for a human being, or some work devoted to human welfare, which needs from someone a little time or friendliness, a little sympathy, or sociability, or labor. There may be a solitary or embittered man, an invalid or an inefficient person to whom you can be something. Perhaps it is an old person or a child. Who can enumerate the many ways in which that costly piece of working capital, a human being, can be employed. Search, then, for some investment for your humanity, and do not be frightened away if you have to wait, or to be taken on trial. And be prepared for disappointments. But

in any case, do not be without some secondary work in which
you give yourself as a man to men. It is marked out for you, if
you only truly will to have it.

January and February are Khartoum's best months. The air, for once, is free of
sand and dust, and the temperature rarely rises above 25 degrees. The Nile is at
its lowest level for the year and is easily navigable. At the Khartoum Yacht
Club, people launch their sailboats on the river, gaff-rigged dinghies cut from
the same plate steel as the great Nile steamers. An eccentric Brit working at the
shipyards had designed and built a fleet of the boats in the 1930s. They were
too heavy to transport anywhere and their hulls were almost indestructible, so a
good number of them still survive to this day. A friend was a member of the
club and had offered me the use of his boat whenever I wanted it. I had to get
away to think over Per's advice. I sailed from the boat's mooring beside the
Melik under the Khartoum North Bridge and upstream on the Blue Nile. The
only other craft on the water were feluccas with triangular cotton sails, identical
to the boats employed on the river by the Egyptians and Nubians thousands of
years before. I sailed under the shade of the date palms that lined the shore.

Since the night I met Adam, I had been mulling over an idea. The street children had told me they dreamed of going to school—but not any school would
do. The Sudan's public-education system had totally failed them. The curriculum
was based on an antiquated colonial model that had little relevance to their day-
to-day needs. The street children did not have the luxury of time; they could not
afford to spend 12 years of their life sitting in a classroom studying grammar and
learning their multiplication tables. Merely fighting for their admission to Khartoum's regular primary and secondary schools would achieve nothing until the
curriculum had been radically changed. That could take years.

The street kids of Khartoum wanted their own school, and they wanted
me to be the principal. They dreamed of a place where they could learn their
choice of trades. As Adam explained, being thieves, they were naturally good
with their hands. "We could take Sudan apart and put it together." Imagine the
possibilities if they could put this talent to a productive use. I had always
assumed street children had dreams of becoming fighter pilots or travelling to
the moon. In reality, they were very reasonable in their aspirations, even traditional. These kids wanted a place at the table. They wanted to belong to the
community. Perhaps the school would be the door that would allow them into
mainstream Sudanese society.

215

Not far from the Blue Nile was an area of the city known as Geref. In my travels around Khartoum on behalf of RTO, I had discovered a magnificent school in Geref that always appeared to be empty. One day I parked my car at its gate and went for a walk within its compound. It was called the Belgian Sudanese Technical School, and it was light-years ahead of anything I had seen in the country. In the classrooms were all the tools students would need to learn their respective trades. There was a shop devoted specifically to car mechanics that had several engines and chassis on display. Another classroom had a blast furnace, forge, and anvil for students interested in metalwork. Everything was neat and organized. The only thing the school lacked was students.

The next day I arranged a meeting with the school director, a Belgian named Luc de Groote. He explained to me that the school was a development project of the Belgian government and was devoted exclusively to the training of middle-class Sudanese for technical professions, but the school was something of a white elephant: very few middle-class Sudanese were actually interested in learning a trade. They dreamed of sitting behind desks in white-collar positions. The students were on their annual school break, which explained the empty classrooms. I inquired about the possibility of using the school after hours for the street children. We could design a special curriculum for them that emphasized practical skills, which would allow them to get jobs soon after graduating. Luc was immediately intrigued by the idea. He and his colleagues had been concerned about the plight of the street children, and had wondered themselves if there were any schooling opportunities for them. He agreed to help me draft a proposal.

Luc and I were both working in the dark; neither of us had ever actually seen a school for street children, and we didn't know if a technical-training school for street children had ever been tried. I consulted with one of Khartoum's most influential businesspeople, Yosef Sid Zaki Ahmed, the head of a Sudanese manufacturing conglomerate. The opinion of a businessperson, and potential employer of the children, was more valuable than that of a university-educated government social worker. There was no point in training street children for jobs that didn't exist. After speaking with Yosef Sid Zaki Ahmed, I went to the tough Arab businesspeople who owned the concessions for Mercedes Benz and Toyota, and put a question to them: if we properly trained street children to become car and truck mechanics, would they be willing to offer them apprentice positions?

I had an ulterior motive for visiting Yosef Sid Zaki Ahmed and his colleagues: the street children needed allies who had some clout in Sudanese society. I guessed that successful entrepreneurs, some of whom had overcome poverty themselves, might identify with tenacious and resourceful street children. A number of my Sudanese friends were surprised Yosef Sid Zaki Ahmed and his colleagues would show any interest in vagrant children who were suspected of being criminals. However, the Khartoum business community had a very pragmatic approach to the phenomenon of street children: they recognized that unless something was done to address the problem, the kids would be a source of political and economic instability. It was in their best interests to support a program that would get the children off the streets and into meaningful jobs. In the end, it was cheaper to keep the kids in schools than in prisons.

Luc de Groote and I labored to put together a nine-month curriculum for the first group of boys who would attend the school, but funding was still an issue. We needed a guardian angel who would bankroll the project. I canvassed the larger international-development organizations such as CARE and World Vision, and there was little interest in the idea. Their employees—all foreign experts—believed the street children would attack their teachers, steal the tools, and burn down the school. Nobody was willing to give the kids a chance.

George Pagolatos had introduced me shortly after my arrival in Khartoum to Alastair Scott-Villiers, the Band Aid representative in the Sudan. Alastair's partner Patta Scott-Villiers was a social anthropologist who had worked for CARE in northern Kordofan. Between the two of them they had a good understanding of the forces at work behind the phenomenon of street children. They were intrigued by the proposal for the technical training school, and when they saw the facility sitting empty, they knew it was the perfect place to launch the project. No funds were needed for bricks and mortar, and all the tools were already in place. The proposal called for employing Sudanese teachers experienced in technical training. To open the doors, we required $50,000 for salaries and operating costs, as well as meals and simple accommodation for the kids. Alastair promised to put the proposal in front of Penny Jenden, the executive director of Band Aid in London.

We had a response within a month. Geldof had scribbled 12 words across the top of our proposal: "It probably won't work, but I can't think of a better idea." Band Aid cut us the cheque, and the Technical Training School for Khartoum Street Children was on its way to becoming something more than an idea.

There was much work to be done before the doors opened. Prospective students had to be interviewed and selected by the staff at Sabah. We needed to find accommodation for them. Street children craved stability in their lives. They could not be expected to perform in their classes unless they had a safe place to sleep and three square meals a day. I went house-hunting. Landlords were very excited to show a foreigner dozens of houses in the Geref area that were sitting empty. They dreamed of being paid in U.S. dollars, which, when traded on the Sudanese black market, were worth between five and 10 times the bank rate. However, when they learned the houses were intended for Sudanese vagrant children, "No Vacancy" signs suddenly sprang up everywhere we looked. The landlords were worried the children would damage the residence and the neighbors would protest.

The leaders at Sabah, Munir Ahmed and Sulieman el Amin, went to bat for us. They were both university graduates and highly motivated young men with promising futures. Instead of working for local businesses or emigrating to the Gulf states, they had decided to devote several years of their lives to assisting Khartoum's destitute children. Using all their persuasive skills, they found a landlord willing to rent two houses to us. We had cleared another hurdle.

My efforts on behalf of the street children were not universally appreciated by the people at the United Nations World Food Program Road Transport Operation. I still had not adequately dealt with the issue of the RTO lease with Total. Rudy was becoming increasingly uneasy about the many hours I was devoting to what was considered non-United Nations work. I decided it was time to look for another employer.

In 1986, UNICEF in the Sudan was under the leadership of an Egyptian named Samir Basta. He had been trained professionally as a nutritionist, and spoke fluent Arabic, English, and French. Basta had inherited a staff he described as lethargic, uninspired, and hopelessly bureaucratic. In the midst of the famine, UNICEF closed its doors on schedule at 2:30 every day. Basta had been astounded by his own employees' lack of mission. They had no fire in their bellies. There was little awareness of the crisis the Sudan faced in the west and in the south. Basta said if it weren't for the members of the international media who trooped through Khartoum recounting horror stories of the extent of the famine in Darfur and Kordofan, few UNICEF employees would have noticed that kids were dying.

I knew Basta only socially. I went to his office and explained my idea to set up a program especially for the street children. I described the facilities available at the Belgian Sudanese Technical School, and summarized my discussions with members of the Khartoum business community. I told him I was not seeking a career in the United Nations, but I required a home for my project. At the same time, I believed UNICEF needed to demonstrate it was aware of the growing phenomenon of street children and was developing a strategy to deal with them.

Basta had a position available on his staff as director of the UNICEF Emergency Unit. The employee who had held the position, a Norwegian named Egil Hagen, had resigned to take up new responsibilities with a relief organization working exclusively in South Sudan. As the director of the Emergency Unit, I would be responsible for a large discretionary budget and oversee the implementation in the Sudan of UNICEF's programming for war-affected children in the south. Basta thought the definition of emergency could be interpreted broadly enough to encompass street children, and I could include them within my mandate. Thirty minutes after I had knocked on his door, he offered me the job. I accepted.

I knew intervening factors over which we had no control could possibly delay the opening of the school for the street children. I tried to plan for every eventuality. Luc and I met with representatives of the Ministry of Education and the Ministry of Social Welfare. Munir and Sulieman smoothed the way, and convinced intransigent officials the project was in the best interests of the government of the day, as well as the children. The one contingency I had never included in our calculations was the threat of international terrorism.

On April 15, 1986, U.S. Air Force planes bombed Tripoli and Benghazi in an attempt to kill Colonel Gadhafi. Their plan almost worked, and one cruise missile killed members of Gadhafi's family, but the primary target survived. For several years, Khartoum had enjoyed a close relationship with Tripoli, and Libyan operatives moved freely in and around the capital. In addition, hundreds of Libyans were based in Darfur, plotting against President Hissène Habré of neighboring Chad. The day following the U.S. Air Force attack, an employee of the U.S. embassy in Khartoum named William Calkins was shot. The attack was widely believed to have been carried out by Libyan security-force members as a reprisal for the American raids. More incidents could be expected. An evacuation plan for all American citizens went into effect.

Holding a Canadian passport provided me with absolutely no measure of protection. I looked more American than most of the American citizens who were resident in the Sudan. On April 18, I met with the chargé d'affaires of the American embassy in Khartoum, who strongly recommended I leave the country. In his words, the situation in Khartoum was grave. He would hold a seat for me on the aircraft that the U.S. government was flying into Khartoum to evacuate American citizens.

The Technical Training School for Khartoum Street Children was due to open in less than a month. Sabah staff had just begun the process of interviewing prospective students. I was days into a new job at UNICEF. The timing couldn't have been worse. But I have never suffered from a martyr complex. I wouldn't be good to anybody dead. I decided to accept the offer of the chargé d'affaires, and reported to the U.S. ambassador's house in Khartoum at 6 p.m. on April 21.

The pre-evacuation party hosted by the ambassador was a relaxed affair. If it weren't for the dozens of U.S. Marine guards patrolling the complex, searching the surrounding area with their binoculars, one might have thought it was a garden party. Servants hovered around the ambassador and his wife, and offered us canapés. We had been told to bring two bags each, and to expect weather that was cooler and wetter than Khartoum's, but our final destination was being kept secret.

At 8 p.m. we were transported by a convoy of unmarked vans from the ambassador's residence directly to the tarmac at Khartoum Airport. The motorcade was flanked on all sides by U.S. Marine guards carrying machine guns in soft tennis-racket cases. The Americans had chartered a Swiss Air A-310 Airbus for the evacuation. Some concerns had been expressed that Libyan terrorists might put a bomb aboard the aircraft. We had been assured every precaution had been taken to guarantee the security of the flight.

After the shooting of the American embassy employee, there had been much anxiety among members of the international community in Khartoum, and just after we were in the air, the passengers burst into applause. I was ambivalent about leaving Khartoum, and could only think about all the work we had put into opening the technical-training school. After we had been in the air for 10 minutes, the captain announced our destination: we were off to Nairobi. I had been hoping to have an opportunity to travel to Kenya, but had never had the time or the funds. Thanks to Uncle Sam, my wish had come true. My accommodation, meals, and long-distance calls in Kenya were all paid for by the U.S. government. After two days in Nairobi, I got bored with the city and rode an overnight train pulled by a steam locomotive to Mombassa on the Indian Ocean. I travelled to the mysterious Muslim island of Lamu and by tramp ferry to Zanzibar. Of the more than 300 people evacuated to Kenya, fewer than 20 ever returned to the Sudan. I was back at my post with UNICEF in Khartoum within two weeks, tanned and rested.

I assumed my responsibilities with new-found vigor. Thanks to the super-human efforts of Munir Ahmed and Sulieman el Amin, the Technical Training School for Khartoum Street Children opened its doors on schedule on May 13, 1986. It was the happiest day of my life. The children were delivered to the school aboard one of the RTO DAF trucks that Rudy had loaned me for the project. Despite his voiced reservations about my new-found vocation, I think that underneath, he had been rooting for me all along. Rudy had a bit of the street-fighter in him and he recognized the kids had guts. When the children saw their classrooms, their jaws dropped—never in their wildest dreams had they imagined they would attend such a beautiful school. One kid was overcome with emotion and passed out.

I had grown accustomed to the kids' rough appearance, but others were shocked. The boys had no place to wash, and their clothes were only rags. Their skin was marked with sores and open wounds. Hours after their arrival at the school, their teachers requested a meeting with Sulieman el Amin, who had been appointed as our project director, and me. The teachers were worried the students might attack them, and asked that we hire two security guards. I suggested we wait and see. After the first day in the classrooms, the kids had completely won the teachers over to their side. Within a week, a strong bond had formed between the adults and the children, akin to the relationship between a father and son. The teachers told me the street children were natural artisans and learned at a much faster rate than their middle-class counterparts. After one week, we knew the project was bound to succeed.

Our experience at the Belgian Sudanese Technical School suggested Blanka had been right: the reaction of Sudanese people to the street children was due primarily to the fact that they did not understand them. But despite the progress we had made convincing the Sudanese of the innate talents of the children, the expatriate community demonstrated little support for our cause. They were petty and malicious. The street children had become accustomed to their random acts of cruelty, but I had not. I once accosted a Swiss national outside the Acropole Hotel who was in the process of beating up a 10-year-old street child whom he suspected of touching his Mercedes four-wheel-drive. I grabbed the guy by the neck and told him if I ever saw him hitting another street child, I would give him the same treatment. The rat went whimpering off to his car.

Many working people in North America and Europe are unaware of the lifestyle assumed by their fellow citizens when living and working in developing countries. Men and women who are quite accustomed to raising their own children and doing their own dishes suddenly assume the air and habits of royalty. Many employees of the UN agencies such as UNICEF, the World Health Organization, and the UN Development Program have nannies to look after their children, cooks, gardeners, maids, and cleaners. They live the life of Reilly, with memberships in private clubs, spacious homes, and endless receptions to attend. Although they are employed by international organizations dedicated to the alleviation of poverty, they acquire a studied indifference toward the poor. They spend years living high on the hog overseas as consultants and international civil servants.

Khartoum was considered anything but a plum posting, but it still attracted a disproportionate number of UN employees with aristocratic roots. During my time in the city I met one prince and two princesses, all of whom were employed by the United Nations, including Princess Maria Pia of Liechtenstein, who worked with the UNHCR, and Princess Helen of Romania. The WHO representative in Khartoum, a member of a noble European family, spent much of his time throughout the famine driving from reception to reception in a limousine that flew a UN flag on its bonnet. The WHO office was moribund. I visited it once and was astonished at the hundreds of dust-covered files stacked about on every available surface. I found two of the employees asleep on the floor. In Juba, the WFP representative, an obscure Hungarian prince, refused to be evacuated during a period of heavy shelling by the rebel troops until the government held an official farewell ceremony for him.

My nemesis at UNICEF was an administrator whom I will call Tristan. He did everything in his power to sabotage the projects we started for the street children. He once called me into his office and told me he had received complaints from fellow UNICEF staff members that street children had been seen sitting on the floor of my office drawing pictures with crayons. Was this true?

I held my breath and counted to 10. "My friend Tristan," I began, "sometimes it takes someone who has been with UNICEF for six weeks to remind someone who has been with UNICEF for 16 years that the letter C in the word UNICEF does not stand for car, or cash, or credit card. It stands for children. These dirty, foul-mouthed, snot-nosed street children who visit my office are the very reason you receive your big salary, your per diems, your fancy car, and the private-school education for your children—and don't you forget it."

Administrators are powerful people and not the type one should upset. Henceforth my pay cheques stopped being automatically deposited in my bank account in Canada. I went four months without a salary. Tristan smiled every time he walked by me in the office.

UNICEF has a beautiful mandate—protecting children around the world. Unfortunately, many of the UNICEF staff I came to know were not up to the challenge. One official with UNICEF in the Sudan was an Italian who, due to his total incompetence, had been bounced from post to post around the world. He was a living representation of the Peter Principle. In India, UNICEF's single largest country program, he had been placed in charge of the entire water department, with disastrous results. The program was soon in shambles, and the Indians were understandably outraged. He was shuffled off to Khartoum. Word of his ineptitude eventually reached UNICEF's New York headquarters. Jim Grant, the executive director of UNICEF, considered firing him, but instead decided it was easier to promote him. He became the first UNICEF representative assigned to Kampuchea. The last time I saw him he was worried sick about how he was going to transport his pet mynah bird to his new country.

After a magnanimous contribution by the government of Italy to UNICEF Sudan's expanded program of immunization, more Italian staff members began to appear on the payroll. A young health advisor arrived in the country with a Porsche 911. His goal was to sell it and make a huge profit. He wore the latest Italian suits and loafers with no socks, à la *Miami Vice*. When his purebred Irish setter had puppies, he pinned up advertisements at the American and Sudan clubs offering them for sale at $500 each, $140 more than the average per-capita annual income in the Sudan. He was eventually posted to Juba, a town under siege with a population of thousands of internally displaced Sudanese facing starvation. Roberto insisted on flying in ground meat for his pets from his Khartoum butcher on the UNICEF Twin Otter. His housekeeper in Juba was a very practical Dinka man, and when Roberto was away on leave for a week, he did what any sensible person would do: he took the ground beef and fed it to his own children, and gave the dogs a mixture of sorghum and wheat. When Roberto arrived back from his vacation, the animals' coats had lost their sheen and he was livid. The cook was sent packing the same afternoon.

Despite their generous pay and benefits, United Nations employees were notoriously cheap. Before heading back to New York, one senior UN official and his wife hosted a lawn sale. Among the items for sale were half-empty jars of jam, unmatched socks, and hotel samples of shampoo. The street kids who washed cars knew the foreigners with UN licence plates always demanded perfection but paid them little for their work. Only diplomats and UN employees had access to the treasured commissaries that sold items not available in Khartoum stores, such as canned and frozen goods. Members of charities with more modest resources who wished to buy commissary items could obtain them from entrepreneurial UN employees at a substantial mark-up. Several UN staff based in Khartoum were suspected of being involved in illegal activities for personal gain, including currency trading, the selling of relief commodities, and car smuggling.

Observers of the international humanitarian-assistance business have noted a curious phenomenon: often the higher a foreign worker's salary, the lower the level of motivation. The Irish nurses who worked for GOAL, a non-government organization providing health care in camps for displaced people living on the edges of Khartoum, were paid $100 a month. They lived communally in a simple house near UNICEF known as the GOAL Post. They never turned me down when I arrived, often late at night, with a street kid in my arms who needed treatment. They were fiercely dedicated to their cause and worked in the harshest possible conditions. I never heard them complain. In contrast, many UNICEF international staff working in Khartoum received a per diem of $100 over and above their healthy salaries.

The UNICEF office in Khartoum had 70 local employees, but the southerners were hired for only the most menial positions. Many of them had gone to mission schools in the south and were well educated, but found it impossible to advance beyond the rank of warehouse-keeper or radio operator. All the senior positions were reserved for Arabs from the north.

There was one shining star in the UNICEF office—Marie de la Soudière, a dynamic Parisian married to Pierce Gerety, the American-born deputy director of UNHCR in the Sudan. During the Cambodian crisis, Marie and Pierce had been employed in Thailand by the International Rescue Committee co-ordinating the repatriation of survivors from the Khmer Rouge killing fields. Marie and her colleagues at IRC had organized a highly innovative tracing and reunification program, whereby the pictures of unaccompanied children whom IRC had come across were posted on the sides of public buses that went from village to village. Whenever a bus pulled in to a new destination and honked its horn, mothers would surround the vehicle and search desperately for their lost children. If they recognized a child, they were directed to special children's centres set up by IRC. Marie witnessed many tearful reunions, and over 550 families were located for unaccompanied Cambodian children.

Samir Basta proved to be an excellent boss, running interference for me with obstructive UNICEF colleagues in Khartoum, letting me freewheel as director of the Emergency Unit. At the same time, Marie took me under her wing, and gave me a crash course on how to survive in the labyrinthine bureaucracy of the United Nations. Marie was tenacious and articulate, and worked closely with me to develop a strategy to deal with unaccompanied children in the Sudan. Conventional approaches to street children at the time emphasized institutionalization—taking the kids off the street and putting them into orphanages or even reformatories. Nobody understood the concept of young children existing independent from families. Marie had assembled a small library of materials about unaccompanied children, and most of the publications were hopelessly paternalistic in their approach to the children, describing them in pejorative terms and emphasizing their deviant nature. Governments saw street children as a policing problem and an issue of crime control. Marie's goal was to help UNICEF, and the governments it worked with, to develop more humanistic and progressive programming that recognized street children as unique individuals who, with proper guidance, could become contributing members of their societies.

It is a popular misconception that UNICEF works directly with children, that it is in the business of feeding hungry kids and providing them with medical care and schooling. UNICEF works bureaucrat to bureaucrat, not adult to child. Marie de la Soudière and I were among the very few of Samir Basta's staff in the Sudan who had any direct contact with children whatsoever. Most UNICEF employees spend their time writing reports and meeting with their counterparts in the Ministry of Social Welfare or the Ministry of Health. I was surprised to learn that in most countries, UNICEF has no mandate to intervene directly with children and youth. It's restricted to supplementing and buttressing the government's efforts by providing materials, training, and direct funding. Because of the emergency situation in the Sudan, UNICEF had been authorized on an exceptional basis to provide direct assistance, and in the Emergency Unit, I was determined UNICEF would help children who the government could not—or would not—reach.

One of the Sudan's ministers made disparaging remarks about the street children at every possible opportunity. She once told Blanka her plans for the street children: "We are going to get rid of the garbage. We are going to take the children far from the city and dump them. Then we are going to build impenetrable barriers around Khartoum to keep them out." Marie and I met with her several times, and remained silent as the minister lashed out at the kids, who she called vermin, perverts, and scum. This from the woman who had the responsibility to care for and protect them. Similarly, the government had no interest in doing anything for the large numbers of children who were in jails and reformatories. On paper, these children did not exist, and the government denied there were any juveniles in detention in adult prisons. But Adam and his friends had told me lurid stories about the detention centres; their descriptions were graphic, and they had the ring of truth. Under the auspices of the United Nations, and with Samir Basta's protection, I was determined to get inside the reformatories and jails, and see for myself.

One day, two small Dinka children named Sunday and Moj bounced into my office, looking for employment. They had heard I had jobs for street children and they knew about the Belgian Sudanese Technical School, which some of their friends were attending. In fact, I did have work for them. My secretary was totally overwhelmed by the number of papers sitting on her desk. Since returning from Nairobi, I had written extensive field reports updating the drought-relief programs in Kordofan and Darfur, and sketching out options for UNICEF in South Sudan, where as many as one million people were at risk of starvation. In the south, the problem wasn't famine; the war had prevented crops from being planted and harvested, and local commerce had ground to a halt. I had several hundred copies of research documents scattered about my office that needed to be collated and stapled, so on the day of their arrival, I put Sunday and Moj to work.

The two boys had gone to mission schools in their towns in the south and both spoke reasonably good English. Over the course of the day they became more comfortable with me, and they told me their stories. Moj's two older brothers had been recruited by the SPLA at the age of 16. They had been given a rifle and basic training, and then sent off to war. They both had been killed within three months of being inducted into the SPLA. Sunday was from a small town, 80 kilometres upstream from Malakal on the White Nile, that had been attacked by government troops. The town's residents were suspected of being sympathetic to the rebels, although Sunday said he had never met or even seen an SPLA soldier. One day, all males in the town over the age of 16 were rounded up by Sudanese government troops and summarily executed. Sunday's father and brother were among those killed. Then the soldiers used flamethrowers to set all the huts on fire. Women grabbed their small children and any possessions that they could carry. Everyone ran into the bush.

Over the next few days, there were further attacks by government soldiers and more young men were rounded up and executed. Like Sunday, they were all from the Dinka tribe, and accused of being SPLA members. Rumors started circulating that children—boys in particular—were next on the government's hit list. Sunday's mother urged him to flee. He was 10 years old, although he could have passed for an eight-year-old. He hugged his mother and, with tears in his eyes, told her he would be back to look after her as soon as it was safe enough for him to return.

Sunday made his way to the thickly overgrown banks of the White Nile. He walked north for three days to a village where barges were tied up. At night he made his move, stowing away on an old Nile steamer under the cover of darkness. Exhausted, Sunday fell asleep under some bags of coal. He was woken in the morning by the sound of the ship's big engine. He searched the cargo hold for something to eat. There were some cans containing oil, lubricants, and chemicals, but nothing he could eat or drink.

In desperation, he crawled out of the hold and surrendered to the ship's company. They laughed when they saw him. He was filthy and scrawny, and was wearing only an old pair of gray shorts. They were southerners like himself, and they proved to be sympathetic to his plight. They gave him a metal tub of hot water and soap to bathe in, and some clean clothes. That morning, Sunday ate the biggest meal of his life. The men on the steamer were traders working with a Juba merchant and they had many food items on board that Sunday had never seen before. They included canned beans, chocolate, even Tusker beer from Kenya. Sunday had to work for his keep. They gave him a bucket of water and a mop, and he had to scrub below deck, but he enjoyed his new responsibilities and the company of his new companions.

They were travelling on the edge of the Sudd, one of the world's largest swamps, 19,000 square kilometres in size. Long sections of the White Nile were choked by acres of water hyacinths. The current in the river was imperceptible, and at times, Sunday thought they were going to lose their way. But the traders had navigated the river many times and they steered the steamer with confidence. Sunday soon became accustomed to the vibrations of the engine. The rhythm was almost soothing to his ears. At night they would tie up along the edge of the river; it was hot long after the sun went down, and by the light of kerosene lanterns and candles, the men would trade yarns, smoke, and sing songs. The language was rough, and Sunday did not understand all the stories, but he always laughed when they laughed. He would sleep alongside the men on the ship's deck.

After three days on the river, they reached their destination, the town of Kosti. Sunday had to stay hidden below deck when the ship was boarded by the police and the military, who were checking for weapons and other contraband. The men working on the steamer said Sunday was welcome to stay with them while they were docked in Kosti, and if he wanted, he could make the return trip with them to the south. But with every bend of the river, with every kilometre they had put behind them, Sunday had felt he was that much closer to safety. His village had been destroyed, and his father and brother were dead. The men on the steamer had spoken about Khartoum, about buildings eight storeys high with electric elevators that moved from one floor to another. All you had to do was press a button, the doors closed automatically, and you were on your way. He had heard of streets filled with automobiles, and cinemas where they showed the latest films from America and India. There was a big airport in Khartoum, and every hour of the day, jetliners from around the world took off and landed. Many of the people in Khartoum were rich and lived in big houses surrounded by walls with gates. Already he had a plan: when they docked in Kosti, he would take the train to El Obeid and then change onto another train for Khartoum. With luck, he could be in the capital within 10 days. He would get a job, or maybe go to school. He would look for the tall buildings with the electric elevators.

The first night they were docked in Kosti, Sunday bade farewell to the men on the steamer who had become his friends and slipped away into the darkness of the town. The men had taken a liking to him, and among them they had collected 20 Sudanese pounds so he could buy a meal and a train ticket to El Obeid. When he found the train station, it was closed, and the sign with the trains' schedule was only in Arabic, which Sunday could not read. While he was standing outside the train station, two police officers pulled up in a four-wheel-drive vehicle. They focused a small spotlight on him. Sunday feared the worst and nervously explained to them that he was on his way to Khartoum. He showed them his 20-pound note. They asked for identification, but he had none. They told him to come with them, and Sunday obeyed, but he was fearful.

When they got to the police headquarters, the policemen gave him some tea, showed him where the washroom was, and pointed to a room where he could sleep. There was a mattress for him on the floor, and although it was dirty, it was better than sleeping on the ground. The same two officers were there when Sunday woke in the morning. They served him tea and hard biscuits for breakfast. The boy was in luck: the first train to leave Kosti in more than two weeks would be departing that afternoon. The officers drove Sunday to the station and purchased a ticket on his behalf. He didn't even have to use his 20-pound note.

The officers shook Sunday's hand in farewell and wished him luck.

So far, everything had gone well. He was beginning to forget the killing of his brother and his father, and the torching of his village, but he missed his mother intensely. Sunday went to the market in Kosti. There wasn't much available in the stalls, but with 10 pounds he bought some food for the trip— some groundnuts, bananas, and some dried-beef sticks. He didn't know how long he would be travelling, and he guessed there would be no food available on the train. Amidst a pile of garbage in the market, he found a plastic bottle and matching cap. He would use it for drinking water.

Sunday's account of his voyage was interrupted by the arrival of a young UNICEF employee in my office with a tray of hot milk, tea, and juice. Sunday and Moj each asked for all three items, then Sunday continued with his story. Periodically, I interrupted him. He remembered all the details. Sunday told me he had never told his story in full to anyone before, and no one had ever asked him about it. Some parts of the trek he glossed over. He didn't want to talk about his mother, nor could he tell me much about his brother or his father.

The train for El Obeid did not leave as promised that afternoon. It was more than 48 hours before it finally pulled out of the train station at Kosti. By that time, every available seat was taken and some people were even sitting on the roof. People brought parcels and boxes with them—anything they could carry. There were at least 10 goats on board. Sunday had to fight to keep his place on the train. Unlike many passengers, he actually had a ticket, which he proudly showed the man who was serving as the conductor.

Sunday was told the trip would take two days; he calculated that if he were very careful, his food might just last. When the train stopped, there would be the opportunity to collect fresh water. Three days later, they had not yet arrived at their destination and Sunday's supplies were exhausted. He grew hungry and faint. There was a man from Juba on the train who was better dressed than most people. At one point he had come through the train compartment asking if anyone wanted to sell their seat to him. Sunday found him at the back of the train sitting on his big red suitcase. He sold the man his seat for 10 pounds, then traded the money for food from other passengers.

Sunday was relieved to have the war far behind him, but as the scenery changed and as the trees became more sparse, he grew apprehensive. He had never seen the desert before. It was flat and featureless. He was far away from the Nile now, and everything was brown and gray. Most of the people on board the train were Dinka and Nuer, and during the trip, Sunday heard frightening stories about the Arabs. Women and children were being kidnapped and sold as slaves. Sunday had better be careful or he would be clubbed on the head and dragged off to work as someone's personal servant, or end up tied to a stake on a farm, like a big ox. People told him to watch his back and be on alert for anyone who was overly friendly to him.

They arrived in El Obeid five days after leaving Kosti. Every square metre of space in the train station was occupied by a person or piece of luggage. Travellers came from southern towns such as Malakal, Juba, Wau, Yambio, and Yei, but they were also from Darfur. As far as Sunday could tell, they were all attempting to get on the next train to Khartoum. Among the people waiting in the station were children who were on their own, like himself. Sunday befriended them, and learned their circumstances were not much different from his. None of them had any money. They told Sunday it didn't matter—they could sit on the train roof all the way to Khartoum. Besides, it would be too hot inside the train. It was much more comfortable sitting on the roof. No one could tell him when the train was leaving or how long the trip would take. There didn't appear to be any kind of organized line for the train. There was just one big mass of people facing in the direction of the door that led to the tracks.

Sunday had to pee. It took him 15 minutes just to make his way through the crowd and navigate around the piles of baggage. While he was outside the station, he heard a commotion and saw people running out of the station's main doors. He recognized one of the kids with whom he had made friends and stopped him to ask what was happening. Apparently the police had arrived at the station. They were examining the documents of all the passengers waiting to board the train to Khartoum. They were sealing off the doors of the station. People who didn't have the proper documentation would be sent to jail.

Sunday and the boy ran as fast as they could away from the station. They saw more police vehicles pulling up in front of the station, including a truck they guessed was used for transporting prisoners. That night, Sunday and his friend slept in the market, having crawled under the empty stalls searching for any discarded items they might be able to eat. But the rats had already been through the market and had picked it clean. Sunday wondered how he would ever get to Khartoum. He had no money and no identification. He was beginning to think he should have stayed with the men on board the steamer at Kosti.

The next morning, Sunday found a group of trucks gathered around a borehole not far from the market. The drivers were pumping the water to wash their vehicles. They were souk lorry drivers. They spoke in very loud voices and they wore nice clothes. Sunday noticed they all seemed to know each other. They had assistant drivers helping them wash the trucks, except for one man who was working on his own. He drove a blue Bedford truck with colorful yellow markings. Sunday approached him and asked him if he could help pump water for him. The driver readily agreed, and Sunday quickly filled three buckets with water. Without asking, he took the brush lying next to the truck and started scrubbing the tires. Sunday's stomach was empty, and he couldn't help but notice the man was munching away on a piece of bread filled with beans. Although he could not read Arabic, Sunday could speak it well, so he could converse with the driver with no difficulty. After finishing with the wheels, Sunday moved on to other parts of the truck, starting with the headlights, fender, and engine grill.

It was already very hot, and he was beginning to feel faint. Using the hand pump, he doused himself with cool water. When the driver saw this, he motioned for Sunday to climb into the cab with him, where he had a vacuum bottle of tea mixed with milk and sugar. It was warm and sweet, and Sunday quickly finished it off. The man poured him a second cup, then reached behind the seat and pulled out a small metal box containing tobacco, dried dates, chewing gum, some canned food that Sunday did not recognize, and pieces of dry bread. The driver offered the box to Sunday and told him to help himself. Sunday hesitated for a second, then grabbed a handful of dates and a piece of bread. "Fadul, fadul," the driver said. He insisted that Sunday help himself to more, so the boy took the remaining dates and a second piece of bread. Then he grabbed a package of chewing gum. He left the tobacco untouched.

The driver's name was Abdul, and he was from Omdurman. He had a wife and four children, one of whom was Sunday's age. He had just delivered a load of automotive supplies to a rich merchant from El Obeid and would be driving back empty to Khartoum. Usually he would be taking a load of agricultural goods from the nearby farms, but because of the drought, the items that were for sale were prohibitively expensive. He predicted that with the first crop, things would soon be back to normal.

Abdul wanted to know what Sunday was up to and what he was doing so far away from home. Sunday gave him an abbreviated account of his journey, omitting the parts about his village being burned and his father and brother being killed. He had been told to be suspicious of northerners, and was worried Abdul might think he was an SPLA sympathizer. Sunday's excuse for leaving the south was that there had been no food for him at home to eat and all the schools were closed on account of the war, which was completely true. Abdul seemed satisfied with the explanation.

After Sunday had finished carefully washing and shining the truck, he had a proposition. Could he accompany Abdul to Khartoum and wash the truck whenever he stopped for a rest? The idea had already occurred to Abdul, and they quickly made a deal. Abdul appointed Sunday as his spanner boy; Sunday loved the title. When Abdul fired up the truck's engine and the two of them rolled off in the direction of a gas station to fill up with diesel for the journey, Sunday was elated at his good fortune. As they drove past the train station, Sunday could see that the crowd waiting to board the train now spilled out of the departure hall onto the front steps. Sunday searched for the children he had met in the departure hall; maybe he could convince Abdul to give them a ride in the back of the lorry. But he couldn't find any of them. With the arrival of the police they had likely taken cover.

Sunday helped Abdul fill the truck's big tanks with diesel. Then Abdul checked the tires' air pressure. He showed Sunday how to use the gauge. One tire was low, so they used the compressor at the fuel station to pump some air into it. Abdul said they were lucky; the town's electricity was working. Otherwise they would have had to pump the diesel manually and use a foot pump for the tires. Their last stop before they left El Obeid was at the city's largest mosque. Sunday waited inside the truck while Abdul disappeared inside the mosque for noon prayers. Sunday used the time to carefully inspect the truck's cab. It was beautiful. Abdul took good care of the truck. Everything was clean and orderly. There were several gauges on the dashboard that Sunday did not recognize. Abdul had a photograph covered in plastic affixed to the dashboard just to the right of the steering wheel; Sunday recognized Abdul in the centre of the picture, and knew the other people must be his wife and children. There were three girls and one boy. There was a little flag hanging from the rear-view mirror. Printed on the flag were words in an elaborate Arabic script. Sunday guessed it was a prayer from the Koran.

I had not expected such a long and detailed account from Sunday of his journey. While Sunday talked, he and Moj kept arranging my photocopied reports into neat piles. I had long since abandoned any hope of getting my weekly report on emergency operations for New York written. Instead, I had taken out a pen and began writing notes in my workbook, summarizing Sunday's story. It was after 1 p.m., and I suggested the three of us head off to Khartoum II for something to eat. Sunday, who had not been quiet for more than a few seconds to drink his tea, milk, and juice, was immediately silenced by my offer. The three of us went off to the Land Rover. I took my workbook and pen with me.

Over a lunch of tamiya, bread, beans, and juice I heard the rest of Sunday's account of how he came to live more than 800 kilometres from his home. Moj didn't open his mouth except to eat. Sunday was very animated when he spoke, and the three of us attracted the attention of a number of restaurant patrons. The street children were never allowed into restaurants and were rarely seen in the company of foreigners. The people in the restaurant were predominantly Sudanese, but I saw two aid workers sitting off at a corner table. Sunday and Moj were not wearing any shoes, and their T-shirts and shorts were filthy, but it was obvious to me that these kids had not been raised by wolves. They both had washed their hands before they sat down at the table, and they ate their beans and bread carefully, a bite at a time. Their manners were better than many of my well-bred boarding-school chums' back in Canada.

In between bites and sips, Sunday picked up where he had left off. The drive from El Obeid to Khartoum took about 10 hours. Abdul was a good driver, and Sunday liked watching him change gears as they approached a hill and when they went through sections of soft sand. The truck was strong and they never got stuck. They stopped three times, twice so that Abdul could pray and once so they could eat at a roadside restaurant. Sunday fell asleep at one point, and when he woke, it was already dark, and Abdul announced they would be arriving in Khartoum in less than two hours. Where would he be staying for the night? Sunday was hoping Abdul might invite him to his house, at least for his first night in the city, but it didn't happen. He told Abdul he would sleep in the market or near the train station. Abdul could let him off wherever it was easiest for him.

It was completely dark now, and the orange lights from the instrument panel reflected off the truck windshield. Sunday thought it made a beautiful pattern on the glass. Both he and Abdul were silent; Sunday began to think about his mother, and wondered how she was going to be able to look after herself. His father had owned cattle, but they had been abandoned in the rush to escape the village. Maybe after a few weeks it would be safe for her to go back to the village, and she would be able to rebuild the hut where they had lived.

Sunday hated the war. It was dangerous to walk in many places in the south because of the land mines planted by government soldiers and the SPLA. He knew a child whose legs had been blown off; the people didn't find him until two days after the incident, and he had already bled to death. Because of the intense fighting around the village, the crops went unharvested; mangos fell from trees and rotted on the ground. The village school had been closed for more than a year and the nearest church was no longer functioning. The priest said it wasn't safe any more and had departed for Juba. He had always said he would stay with the community through thick and thin, but he was one of the first people to leave.

It was almost midnight, and Sunday was surprised there were so many trucks on the move across the desert. The sand was flat and hard, and the trucks seemed to take any route they wanted. At times it resembled a race. They darted in and out, passing one another, honking their horns, sometimes one truck cutting another truck off. Abdul pointed off into the distance; if you followed the lines of the red tail lights, they converged at a point where the horizon glowed. The trucks ahead of them were kicking up a lot of dust and the light was diffuse. Sunday thought it almost looked like a setting star. It was Khartoum.

Sunday had heard many stories about the city. Some kids in the train station at El Obeid had said the streets were paved with gold, but Sunday didn't believe them. He wasn't so excited about the prospect of riding in an electric elevator any more. Alone in the truck cab with Abdul, on the last leg of the journey, Sunday became fearful. He was riding into the heart of the enemy. The glow on the horizon grew brighter and Sunday began to make out distinct shapes. Khartoum was a desert settlement, and a predominantly Arab town. It was also the headquarters for the Sudanese army and the air force. Within that same city lived the men who planned the destruction of the south, who sent the trainloads of troops to burn all the villages and to kill all the men. Apart from the attack on his village, Sunday had never seen fighting, but back home at night, he had occasionally seen bursts of light on the horizon. He knew what they were. Big guns were being fired, and bombs were being dropped. The war was closing in on them. He remembered an old woman in his village screaming out that if they didn't move quickly, they would all be killed. Everyone said she was crazy. There were no SPLA soldiers in their village, so there was nothing for them to fear. The government troops would leave them alone.

When they finally arrived at Khartoum, Sunday was disappointed. The houses and stores were all pushed close together. There was garbage everywhere. El Obeid had seemed a much nicer town. Sunday saw a street light, but it wasn't working. He had thought there would be flashy electric signs on the storefronts, but there were none. They were dark and drab. Some looked as if they had been abandoned.

At a big intersection, Abdul stopped the truck. "There's your market," he said, pointing to an open area with a few covered stalls. Sunday thanked him for the ride and they shook hands. That was it. For the second half of the trip, Abdul had become more serious and less friendly. Sunday wondered if he had said something wrong, or done something to upset him. After they left El Obeid, Sunday had wanted to ask Abdul to write down his full name and address so Sunday could track him down if he ever needed help, but now it didn't seem appropriate to ask. Sunday slammed his door shut, and watched as the truck drove off into the distance, turned the corner, and was lost from sight. He was on his own again.

We had finished our lunch and it was late. All the other diners had already left and their tables had been cleared. I had many questions for Sunday, but I could tell he was fatigued. Moj was growing impatient. "We have to get back to the Meridien Hotel," he repeated several times to Sunday. They had made a deal to rendezvous with other street children. They were going to try to make some money in the market, and with their savings go to the Apollo Cinema that night. I told them I had more work in the office if they wanted to help out, but Moj insisted he and Sunday head off to the Meridien. Sunday wanted to come back to the office with me, but after a little more persuasion from Moj, both boys got up and went to the sink at the side of the restaurant to wash and dry their hands. I offered to drive them to the hotel, but they said they could make their own way there. Sunday gave me a big smile, and promised he would be back at my office the next morning to finish off organizing all my documents. Then he skipped off, kicking his heels in the air, and broke into a run so he could catch up to his friend.

A Reason to Live

Back at the UNICEF office I tracked down Marie de la Soudière and told her about Sunday's flight to safety. During her months at the Baenkang Holding Centre on the Thai-Cambodian border, Marie had interviewed dozens of unaccompanied children, and she cautioned me: you can't believe everything they tell you. Their intention is not to deceive you, but rather to please you. The children become very good at recognizing what kinds of stories the interviewer wants to hear. She had a good point. The Heisenberg Uncertainty Principle applies to the interviewing of street children as much as to everything else. Merely by observing the children, we were changing their behavior. Some elements of Sunday's story were obviously untrue: no barges or river boats were getting through between Malakal and points as far north as Kosti. And if Sunday had arrived in Kosti, then Khartoum was easily reachable by road and not by train via El Obeid. But street children often go with the prevailing wind rather than taking the most direct route, and few travel with road maps in their pockets. Perhaps Sunday and Moj had the idea that if they spoke long enough about their horrible circumstances, they would be rewarded with a snack. The meal they ate with me at Khartoum II was likely beyond their wildest expectations.

At the same time, Marie agreed there was nothing in the story that was patently outrageous. Sunday hadn't claimed to have hitched any rides with fighter pilots, nor had he bragged about killing a dozen government troops with his bare hands. Like any other child, he missed his family. Sunday and Moj had not asked for anything in payment for the work they had performed in my office. Marie emphasized that letting the kids tell their stories was therapeutic. They needed someone to debrief with, to unpack experiences that would easily traumatize adults twice their age. They were penniless, they were vulnerable, and they were living in a totally hostile environment.

When I arrived the next morning at my office, Sunday and Moj were already busy stapling and collating the stacks of documents. My secretary had let them into the office. "Your assistants will put you out of work," she remarked. Without any coaxing from me, Sunday began talking. The subject today was the Hindi film he and Moj had seen the night before. Sunday provided his own version of the plot. It was standard Hindi fare—unrequited love, mistaken identity, broken hearts all around, the usual stuff. Sunday acted out his favorite parts of the movie, providing voices for the various characters, at one point leaping onto my desk and doing his own version of an Indian dance. The kid certainly wasn't inhibited. Moj just watched, shaking his head.

Sunday and Moj became regular visitors to the UNICEF office. I officially deputized them as UNICEF volunteers, making plastic identity cards for them, complete with the blue-and-white UNICEF logo. Some of my colleagues were bewildered, others were outright hostile toward the kids. To them, UNICEF was an elite organization, an exclusive club, and they didn't like the idea of Sunday and Moj or any other street children darkening the hallways. Two employees tried to ban Sunday and Moj from the lunch room, but Samir Basta backed me up, and the kids were allowed to bring their own lunch and eat it quietly in the corner. The UNICEF office was dominated by northern Sudanese, and they were wary of southerners, even two 11-year-olds. Rashied, UNICEF's deputy director in the city, put out the word that the boys were likely spying on behalf of the SPLA. He instructed the UNICEF security guards to keep an eye on them, and for people to lock up their desks at night.

I visited the Technical Training School for Khartoum Street Children almost every day. Following Yosef Sid Zaki Ahmed's advice, Munir and Sulieman invited prospective employers to the school to meet the children. The idea was to match up each student with an employer so they would have a job to go to the day they graduated. The kids progressed faster than anyone had expected, completing two years of curriculum in less than nine months. Their technical training was supplemented with classes in Arabic and mathematics. We had very few discipline problems. UNICEF began to feature the project in their in-house publications. The *Washington Post*'s Cairo-based correspondent Blaine Harden wrote a piece about me and the kids, which went as a wire story around the world. As a result, I received letters from people in South Africa, Thailand, and Mexico who wanted to replicate our success.

It was far too early for us to be held out as an example for others. We were still learning lessons from the children, particularly from those who had problems adjusting to the routine and to a classroom environment. Some of the most promising kids dropped out of the school. When Sulieman el Amin interviewed them, he learned that although they liked the curriculum, the boys did not have the patience to wait nine months before earning any income. They needed money immediately. Some of the street children had been sent to Khartoum by their parents with the task of earning enough money to send a portion home every month to support them. Inevitably, this was a pipe dream. Jobs of any kind were hard to come by in Khartoum; street children earned a few piasteres carrying items in the market and cleaning offices, but never enough to live on. Many of the kids longed for their families and felt guilty that they had failed to honor their promise of contributing to the family income.

Within a few days, Sunday and Moj finished all the collating, stapling, and filing I could possibly rustle up for them in the UNICEF office. I circulated a memo among my colleagues, advertising their services and recommending them highly, but there were no takers. A senior-level administrator from North Sudan had got to the staff first and had effectively frozen Sunday and Moj out of any opportunity for employment at UNICEF.

Although they had done an admirable job, repetitive and mundane office work did not come naturally to Sunday and Moj. I needed to find employment for these young people that could build on their love of freedom and their knowledge of the streets. Sunday's story had inspired me. Under his own steam, the boy had negotiated his way along the Nile and across the desert, a perilous journey of more than 1,000 kilometres. North American kids his age weren't allowed to take a bus across town on their own. Sunday had moxie. He told me he wanted to make money and be a "big man" some day, owning his own business and driving a car. He had already figured out that a job at UNICEF was too boring. Sunday wanted to be where the action was.

For kids with an entrepreneurial bent, I knew that a small business could be their ticket out of the garbage dump and along the road to self-sufficiency. They needed something that required little or no infrastructure and that allowed them to be their own bosses. I thought of various kinds of enterprises, from setting up a printing shop to making simple crafts, but printing is highly competitive and requires a substantial up-front investment for equipment. I had already seen several craft projects for refugee and internally displaced women run by non-profit organizations, and very few actually turned a profit.

They depended on continuous injections of money and expertise by their non-profit sponsors, and sold most of their production to sympathetic members of the expatriate community. My idea was to design a project for Khartoum's street children that was modelled after a business rather than a charity. The challenge was to identify an enterprise the kids could run themselves, that met the needs of the local market economy, and that ultimately could be self-supporting.

In Khartoum, communicating with people, either at their home or at their office, was a constant source of frustration. The postal service in the Sudan was unreliable at best. When letters arrived at their proper destination, it was a cause for celebration. Telephones were purely ornamental and were put to use as paperweights on people's desks. During my first six months in Khartoum, I had successfully completed three phone calls, and eventually I abandoned trying to reach people by phone. Instead, I would climb into my Land Rover and burn precious fuel driving across town looking for the people I wanted to meet. Usually they were out in their cars looking for me. The UN agencies shared a number of state-of-the-art portable satellite telephones. Calls cost $15 per minute. They were intended to be used for priority communications with New York and Geneva, but were commonly employed by UN employees wanting to speak with someone at another office located a few kilometres across town.

I had an idea: why not set up a guaranteed, same-day courier service, with street children delivering mail and newspapers around the town? The kids knew the streets better than anybody else because they had broken into many of the buildings. Instead of putting them in jail, why not put them on bikes? We would call it SKI Courier, for Street Kids Incorporated. Most importantly, we would run it on a for-profit basis. Street kids everywhere have one thing in common: they love money. The more money we made, the more children could be involved in the project. The idea would be to provide a hand up, not a hand out. Through the vehicle of a small business, the children could learn basic social skills such as the importance of coming to work on time, personal appearance, dependability, and reliability.

I discussed my idea with my colleague at UNICEF, Saddiq Ibrahim, and with Abdul Mohammed, my counterpart at the Sudan Council of Churches. Saddiq was hesitant at first. He thought we would face major opposition from the Sudan's powerful postal union. Abdul suggested we start small, relying on the aid agencies and embassies for business. They would be more forgiving than Khartoum's hard-nosed merchants.

I drafted a four-page proposal for SKI Courier and shared it with Marie de la Soudière and Samir Basta. Both were enthusiastic. At the same time, they were concerned a high-profile bicycle-courier business could put the spotlight on the phenomenon of street children and the issue of displaced people living in and around Khartoum. The government was becoming increasingly nervous about the growing population of southerners living within the city limits. Politicians wondered out loud what would happen should the southerners decide to take up arms against the government or engage in acts of sabotage. Their concerns were absurd; anyone who visited the hastily constructed shanty towns could see the displaced people were living hand-to-mouth and had nothing in the way of tools or weapons with which to begin a rebellion. Visitors commented on their passivity, not their revolutionary fervor.

Samir and Marie emphasized that while it was perfectly appropriate for UNICEF to be advocating on behalf of street children, we should not do anything that would make them potential targets for politically motivated reprisals by the government. We should take seriously ministers' threats to deport and imprison the children. My challenge was to use the bicycle-courier business to engender support among the citizens of Khartoum for the cause of the street children, without giving the government an excuse to deal with the problem in an arbitrary and confrontational manner. I would be walking a tightrope.

I went door to door in Khartoum, searching for potential clients for the business, which only existed on paper. Some of the aid agencies and a few embassies were intrigued, but they doubted the scheme would work. The most common concern was that the children would steal their mail. Street kids couldn't be trusted with valuables or with their correspondence. After much discussion, seven agencies agreed to a trial period in which we would provide them with free service and during which they would be using the courier service to deliver bulk mailings that were of no particular importance.

I didn't like the idea of relying on the kindheartedness of Khartoum's expatriate community for our survival. The whims of foreigners working in the field of international development are notoriously fickle. Throughout the 1970s, enormous resources went into establishing co-operatives run by local women's organizations in South Asia for the production of batik, which at the time was all the rage in Europe and North America. But batik turned out to be another fashion fad, and after several good years, most of the projects were forced to shut down. I didn't want the bicycle-courier business to be the flavor of the month.

The reason the technical school for Khartoum's street children had succeeded was because of Yosef Sid Zaki Ahmed and his colleagues, and their promise that there would be jobs for the students when they finished their training. I needed to find a Sudanese business that relied on the efficient delivery of documents for its livelihood, with which we could form a working partnership.

Until fundamentalists seized power in 1989 the Sudan had always enjoyed a vigorous and independent press. The Sudanese have no tolerance for censorship and expect their newspapers to reflect a plurality of political opinions. Even during the dying days of Nimeiri's regime, when he allied himself with the Islamic fundamentalists and imposed sharia law, newspapers and magazines were allowed to print and publish whatever they wanted. In 1986, a prominent Sudanese, Bona Malwal, founded *The Sudan Times*, a six-page English-language newspaper, most of which he wrote and edited himself. The little newspaper quickly acquired a loyal following and was influential far out of proportion to its size and news-gathering resources. Information-hungry expatriates snapped up as many copies as Malwal could print. Malwal's writing was supplemented with articles brazenly copied from *Newsweek, Time, The Saudi Gazette*, and other publications. He knew his audience well; the newspaper regularly featured the Garfield and Wizard of Id cartoon strips, American baseball results, and county cricket scores from the U.K. Malwal wasn't about to be sued for copyright infringement; his business had no assets that would satisfy any judgment.

Within weeks of its first issue's hitting the streets, *The Sudan Times* became required reading for diplomats and senior-level employees of aid agencies. Articles were pithy and scathing in their evaluation of the government's performance in managing the economy, dealing with the displaced, and prosecuting the war in the south. Almost every week, *The Sudan Times* featured a new scandal involving government corruption or ineptitude. Malwal couldn't afford his own war correspondents and relied instead on his extensive network of friends and associates from South Sudan to provide up-to-date information on the latest government or SPLA offensive. The quality of information was so good that it was widely suspected Malwal had sources not only within the SPLA leadership, which was to be expected, but also among the government's own ministers. Malwal was equally critical of the foreign powers that for years had meddled in Sudanese affairs, and questioned the qualifications of many of the aid "experts" who had recently arrived in the Sudan. In a stinging editorial that perturbed representatives of the international aid agencies, Malwal asked, "Who are all these foreign youngsters racing four-wheel-drive vehicles around our country?"

Bona Malwal was a better editor than he was a businessperson. *The Sudan Times* delivery system was primitive. Copies were available for sale in hotel kiosks and at a smattering of stores around the city. But many of the shops kept irregular hours, and often they sold out of the newspaper before noon each day. I knocked on Malwal's door with a proposal that would help his newspaper and at the same time would provide needed employment for a few street children. I suggested he set up a subscription service and sign a contract with our proposed bicycle-courier business to deliver copies of the paper across the city each morning. Snarled traffic would present no problems for us; the bicycles could go where no one else could venture. Nor would persistent fuel shortages cause us difficulties. I assured Malwal that the children could be relied on—they had a vested interest in the business succeeding.

Malwal wasn't convinced, so in the end, I made him a deal he couldn't refuse: I guaranteed we would deliver copies of *The Sudan Times* to all his subscribers by 10 a.m. every day or we did not need to be paid. He had nothing to lose. We closed the deal with a cup of tea and a handshake.

On September 18, 1986, I launched SKI Courier out of a garage with half a dozen clients and three borrowed bicycles. Our first three employees were Sunday, Moj, and a 16-year-old named Pio, whom I had met at Sabah. I had the kids report to my house at five in the morning. They had slept the previous night in a park near the Meridien Hotel and looked scraggly. I made a mental note that we would soon need uniforms and access to a shower. Their first stop would be the warehouse space on Jamhurria Avenue where *The Sudan Times* was printed. Earlier that week, the four of us had huddled over a Khartoum street map I had purchased from the same man who had sold me my 1928 SPS map a year earlier. Using a ruler and pencil, we arbitrarily divided the city up into sections. Pio caught on immediately, but for Sunday and Moj, the idea of a map was very abstract and completely foreign to them. Eventually, all three became familiar with the map and were confident they could locate the addresses of the subscribers Malwal had provided. They included embassies, businesses, even government offices.

The boys did two trial runs and timed themselves. They knew to stay out of elevators and to always hand the newspapers over to the office manager. We had a rubber stamp made up that had four words on it: Delivered by SKI Courier. Every newspaper we successfully delivered would be an advertisement for Khartoum's first guaranteed, same-day bicycle-courier business.

When I sent the kids off on their bicycles that first morning, I didn't know if I would ever see them again. Even in their dilapidated state, the bicycles were worth more than I would pay the boys for a month of their hard labor. Surely they had already done the calculation themselves and knew they could abscond with the bikes and make a tidy profit. Rashied and others at UNICEF would have a field day at my expense. I was nervous. The sun wasn't up yet and I went back to bed, but I couldn't sleep. I felt like a base commander who had just sent his bomber pilots off on a sortie.

I worked out of my house that morning, pacing up and down, growing more and more anxious as time went by and the couriers had not yet returned. Ten o'clock passed and still there was no sign of them. They knew what the arrangement with Malwal was: if all the newspapers were not delivered by our deadline, they wouldn't be paid for any of them. Just after 11 a.m., I heard shouts at my gate. They were back! From their broad grins, I knew they had been successful. I anticipated they would be hungry and had prepared some breakfast for them. Between mouthfuls of beans and bread they gave me a run-down of their first day on the job. They all wanted to talk at the same time. Pio had seniority, being the oldest, so he went first.

The mission had been accomplished. There had been some obstacles, but nothing the founders of SKI Courier couldn't handle. When they arrived at the printing shop, the newspapers were not ready, and they had to wait 45 minutes for them to be bundled. Pio had a flat tire, but he fixed it within 10 minutes. Sunday had an encounter with a belligerent security guard who did not want to let him into the Kuwaiti Towers, but Sunday offered him a fresh copy of that day's newspaper as an incentive to let him into the building. It worked. They each had their own recommendations about how we could improve the service. First on their list was purchasing bicycles that were more durable. The three we were using were at least 10 years old and had never been properly maintained. One bicycle had faulty brakes and another had a chain that kept falling off. Moj had greasy fingers to prove it. But the fundamental concept behind SKI Courier was sound, and Pio already had plans to expand the business. "We'll build an empire," he proclaimed.

When I saw Malwal later that afternoon, he was ecstatic. When I had first approached him with the idea of SKI Courier, he hadn't thought the kids would be able to pull it off. In the past, he had tried using motor scooters to deliver newspapers, but they kept breaking down. Spare parts were difficult to find in the souk. He had never seriously considered using bicycles. In the Sudan, there was no culture of bicycles. Despite the fact that the city is completely flat, they are rarely used as a mode of transportation. Perhaps it's a question of Sudanese pride. People would rather be seen riding a bus than pedalling a bicycle to work. The result is that public transportation is stretched beyond its capacity. It's not unusual to see someone in Khartoum catching a bus by diving through its open window. Bicycles and street children were a perfect match. Bona Malwal predicted we were on to a good thing.

The first days in the life of SKI Courier were the hardest. So many people had said we would fail—that the kids would sell their bicycles, that they couldn't be relied on, that no one would trust them with their mail. Luckily, we didn't listen. *The Sudan Times* contract was manna from heaven for us. In a city where virtually nothing works, the thought of a morning newspaper arriving in time for one's breakfast tea made people delirious with joy. The kids would throw the newspaper over the walls of the compounds, then scoot off, spinning their tires and kicking up dirt. They rang their bells to shoo pedestrians out of their way. Nobody in the city had ever moved with such determination.

If we had been doing business in New York or London, we would have judged our success by the telephone ringing off the hook, but we had no telephone, and even if we did, we would never have expected it to ring. That's the reason we went into business in the first place! So instead, we waited for people to beat a path to our office, which is exactly what they did. Representatives of the aid agencies and the embassies came first, congratulating us on our success. I told them a handshake was nice, but we wanted their business. If they really believed in SKI Courier, they should sign up as clients.

The next wave consisted of businesspeople who wanted to know if we were for real, and if we could help them to increase their profits. They were the easiest to deal with. We had already developed special pricing for bulk mailings. A travel agency came to us wanting to advertise holidays on the Red Sea and the Kenyan coast for the Christmas and Eid vacations. They knew we were the most efficient way to reach Khartoum-based expatriates and the Sudanese middle class. Among the ranks of the businesspeople who visited us were potential competitors, hoping to develop a similar enterprise that would make them some money and put our street children back in the garbage dump. I didn't mind answering their questions. We had already done all the pricing. We were competitive because the children were willing to ride bicycles and because they did not demand fancy motor bikes or four-wheel-drive vehicles to do their jobs. Street children were the only ones gutsy enough, and hungry enough, to allow themselves to be seen sweating it out on a bicycle in the city. The work was below most northern Sudanese, and we knew they would never do it. Our kids had seen famine and war, and they understood what the alternative to SKI Courier was. Pio put it best when he said, "My bicycle has given me a reason to live."

I had never run a business before, so all I had to go on were my instincts. Keep It Simple Stupid, or KISS, became our watchword. After our first week, friends at the American embassy offered to supply us with 10-speed bicycles, but spare parts for these complex machines would be hard to come by, and without spare parts, we would be very vulnerable to breakdowns. We relied instead on the world's most popular bicycle, the Flying Pigeon, produced in Shanghai and built to endure China's bone-jarring roads and pathways. I'm convinced the Chinese stole the design for the Flying Pigeon from the classic Raleigh coaster bicycle. They're not fancy, but they get the job done, and throughout the developing world they're the standard in bicycles.

After 14 days of bicycling, the kids had already earned enough money for three new bicycles. They could either take the profits and divide them up among themselves or invest in new equipment. I let them make the decision. From the beginning, I wanted the boys to understand it was their business and not mine. I was, after all, a do-gooder from across the sea, and eventually I would pack my bags and leave for Canada. The decisions they made affected their future, not mine. It was a tough choice for them to make. They were still wearing rags and Sunday's toes were poking through the end of his smelly running shoes. But with little prompting from me, they put all their profits into three new Flying Pigeon bicycles that Pio had managed to purchase at a reduced rate from a local merchant to whom they promised to give all their business should SKI Courier become a going concern.

We quickly became the talk of the town. Officials at the French embassy, concerned that an urchin who resembled a dusty chimney sweep was gracing their chancellery twice a day, donated 200 Sudanese pounds so the three boys could buy proper uniforms. The boys took 20 pounds to a tailor they knew in a local market and had blue cotton shorts made. They used another 30 pounds to purchase six canary-yellow T-shirts. The remaining 150 pounds of the French contribution went back into the business. "We'll save it for a rainy day," announced Sunday with a smirk. He knew it hadn't rained in Khartoum in over 18 months and no rains were in the long-range forecast. Nick Cater, a London-based journalist for *The Guardian*, arranged to have sent out from the U.K. a dozen fluorescent orange newspaper bags printed with "SKI Courier, not tomorrow—today." Sunday, Moj, and Pio looked smart in their new kit, negotiating like Tour de France champions through traffic jams, dodging potholes, and venturing out even in the fiercest haboobs when the rest of the city had shut down. "The mail must get through," we declared to our incredulous and grateful clients.

With every letter and parcel successfully delivered, SKI Courier gained legitimacy. With the new clients we attracted, we could hire new couriers. Sunday, Moj, and Pio helped Sulieman and Munir of Sabah interview all the prospective candidates. They knew which kids could be trusted and which kids would abscond with our bicycles as soon as they were out of sight of the office. Despite their advice, additional couriers meant we had to come up with a system to prevent bicycles from being stolen. As with everything else at SKI Courier, the system had to be simple to be effective. We came up with something we called the "death penalty." It worked as follows: when children joined SKI Courier, we made them sign a contract. Article 1 of the contract stated that all the children shared the assets of the business, as well as its losses. Article 2 was the death penalty clause. It stated that if any child lost, sold, or gave away his bicycle, all the kids were penalized 10 days' wages to cover its cost. Sister Ann from my Grade 2 class in London had been the inspiration: whenever one kid acted up, we were all forced to stay behind after school. The death penalty was self-enforcing. The employees of SKI Courier understood they had a financial stake in anyone they hired being honest and hard-working. What more powerful motive could there be?

Sure enough, several weeks into our project, Sunday sold his bicycle. Of course, that's not what he told us: he had concocted an elaborate story about his bicycle's being stolen from the U.S. embassy while he was inside delivering a parcel. However, we knew from reliable sources—the other kids—he had sold his bicycle for approximately $40, more than one month's income for a SKI courier.

We knew what we had to do. We brought all the SKI couriers into one room and Munir and Sulieman explained the situation. We would impose the death penalty. All the kids would lose 10 days' wages to cover the cost of Sunday's stolen bike. Then the adults walked out of the room, letting the children sort out their dilemma. The children held a discussion with Sunday, during which the kid was roughed up. It was their own method for dispute resolution. The result of the discussion was that the bicycle was miraculously recovered within 24 hours. Apparently, Sunday stole the bicycle from the person he had sold it to. We never lost another bicycle.

SKI Courier prospered. With their distinctive blue shorts, yellow T-shirts, and fluorescent orange delivery bags, the kids stood out from the pack. We did

Yassir *(left)* and Moj *(right)* in Khartoum, May, 1987. Moj is wearing the t-shirt given to him by the BBC crew that made a documentary film about SKI Courier.

My last photo of Sunday and Moj, September, 1987.

Street kids
sniffing glue in
Garibaldi Square,
Mexico City.

DEREK LAMB

The Garden
Center developed
by Street Kids
International with
the Red Cross in
Lusaka, Zambia,
in January, 1992.

ANDREW BALL

A scene from Karate
Kids that some of
our critics found
objectionable.

ANIMATION BY DEREK LAMB AND KAJ PINDAL

PETER DALGLISH

These are the kids I bought out of jail for $20 each in the Philippines.

PETER DALGLISH

Children playing with a kite made from recycled plastic in Zanzabar, April, 1986.

Emma McCune in South Sudan. Emma had a natural sense of style and refused to dress down—even when visiting the remotest villages along the Nile River.

One of the Street Kids International schools set up by Emma McCune near Bor, South Sudan, in February, 1991. The children walked from villages ten kilometres distant to attend the classes.

With my friend Lual in Bor, South Sudan, February, 1991.

Nuer children playing soccer, South Sudan, February, 1991.

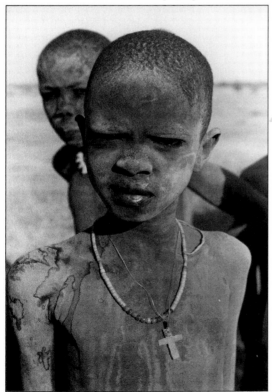

Dinka child, South Sudan, February, 1991. Children herding cattle cover themselves with a paste made from ash, dung, and cattle urine, which dries into a fine white powder that serves as an excellent natural insect repellent. Because the mixture stings, the children are careful to keep it away from their eyes.

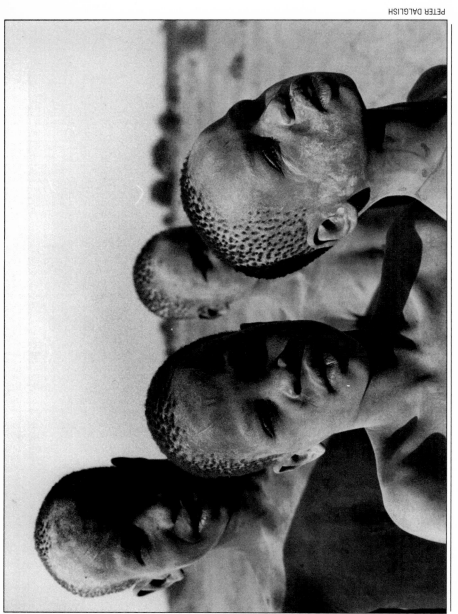

Dinka children, South Sudan, February, 1991. Although they had no material possessions, their life was rich: by the age of 11 they knew the land for 100 kilometres around, were familiar with the seasons of the Nile, could hunt animals and prepare the meat, and

Children I encountered along the edge of the White Nile trekking into Ethiopia in 1988. "Behind us is death," one of the boys said to me. Many of their sisters and brothers drowned attempting to cross the river. Others were attacked by wild animals or hunted down by Arab militia.

Students at a school for freed laborers near Lahore, Pakistan,
run by the Bonded Labor Liberation Front, May, 1992.
"We are free, we are free!" they shouted out in Urdu.

PETER DALGLISH

more than provide employment for a small group of destitute children. The SKI Courier kids were ambassadors for all their friends in the street. With every successful delivery, and with every new client, we challenged the prejudices stacked up against the children. Maybe the street kids weren't all criminals and deviants. Maybe they deserved to go to school and to sleep with a roof over their heads. Perhaps they could even be allowed into the state-funded hospitals.

Most kids who arrived at SKI Courier were illiterate. Pio, Moj, and Sunday—who could read—designed an elaborate color-coding system so the new couriers would know where the letters were being delivered. Many of our clients were embassies, all of which had flags flying outside their offices, and our color-coding system was therefore loosely based on their flags. But as the number of our clients increased, the system started to crumble under the strain. Things came to a head when one of the boys delivered a letter intended for the U.S. embassy to the delegation of the Palestinian Liberation Organization. I learned about it when a navy blue Chevrolet with diplomatic plates pulled up outside our office. A young officious-looking American emerged from the vehicle, delivered a letter with my name on it, and left without speaking. The letter invited me to a meeting with the chargé d'affaires of the U.S. embassy. It was a short but humiliating session for me. The incident was extremely embarrassing for everyone associated with SKI Courier, and it almost shut us down. The Americans were among our biggest clients and had been enthusiastic supporters of SKI Courier from the start. They did not like the idea of Yassir Arafat reading mail intended for their eyes only.

After my meeting with the American chargé d'affaires, Pio convened an emergency session of the informal SKI Courier management team. On their own, the kids proposed they should learn to read and write. It was the only way to ensure that letters would eventually be delivered to the correct addressees. Pio and I applauded the suggestion, but asked who would pay for the teachers? We had no extra funds available for salaries or for school materials.

I had already seen many literacy-training projects that failed for one reason: they were designed by well-meaning people who assumed there is an economic benefit that automatically flows from learning how to magically put letters into a combination to form words, and words to form sentences, and sentences to form paragraphs. Too often, however, literacy does not guarantee a job or even improved working conditions. Literacy may connote an improvement in one's class, but will not necessarily put better-quality rice on the table.

When the children of SKI Courier decided they wanted to learn to read and write, they were not trying to make me happy, or UNICEF happy, or even their clients happy. They were making themselves happy. We had already set up an incentive system that rewarded kids for their efforts. The kids earned points in five different categories: punctuality, appearance, bicycle maintenance, helping other kids, and performance. The last category was the most important and was counted like a triple-point square in a Scrabble game: kids were awarded bonus points based on their efficiency. At the end of each week, the points were translated into a cash bonus. The more letters the kids delivered, the more money they earned each day. Pio, Moj, and Sunday scored more points than the other children because they didn't have to consult the dispatcher or an adult in the street to determine where a letter was to be delivered. They could read, and they were getting rich as a result. That did the trick.

The boys of SKI Courier agreed they would collectively pay for a tutor to come to the office for an hour each day. They would learn to read and write in English and in Arabic. Their classes would be very practical, and would start with the names of the destinations they most commonly visited around the city on their bicycles. The boys learned their lessons quickly. The kids were attentive in their classes, since they had invested their own hard-earned Sudanese pounds in their education. At first we had a problem with teacher absenteeism. Then Pio took their tutor aside and informed her she would be docked wages for every day she came late. From that day on, Arabic class began punctually at 10 a.m.

Pio was the heart and soul of SKI Courier. After a few weeks I delegated all aspects of running the business to him. He was mature far beyond his years and had the qualities of a great leader. He rarely had to raise his voice with the kids. They respected his authority and his judgment. Pio was from Nasir in Eastern Equatoria, and he spoke enough English to be able to work with foreigners. He was the one who put out the fires, who negotiated disputes among the children. He was the one they turned to for advice. I once told him he would be a fine teacher or a youth worker. As with many young people from South Sudan, his dream was to return to his homeland, find his family, and help rebuild the communities that had been destroyed by the war. He had no interest in going overseas. His place was by the River Nile, and he dreamed of owning cows some day.

When I thought of Pio and all the kids from the south, I thought of a poem by Langston Hughes I had studied years earlier at Stanford:

I've known rivers:

I've known rivers ancient as the world and older than the flow of
  human blood in human veins.
My soul has grown deep like the rivers.

I bathed in the Euphrates when dawns were young.
I built my hut near the Congo and it lulled me to sleep.
I looked upon the Nile and raised the pyramids above it.
I heard the singing of the Mississippi when Abe Lincoln went
  down to New Orleans, and I've seen its muddy bosom turn all
  golden in the sunset.

I've known rivers:
Ancient, dusky rivers.

My soul has grown deep like the rivers.

Working for SKI Courier was a coping strategy for Pio, and for his friends from
the South. At the first hint of peace, they would pile onto the trains and steamers
and wind their way back to the villages where they were born, where they tended
goats and cattle, where they sang and danced by the light of the fire, where they
listened to the stories of their parents and grandparents, where the land was green
and the air was sweet, where you could smell rain in the wind days before it fell
from the sky. They had seen enough of Khartoum, and they had all, on more
than one occasion, been called "abid" or slave by one of the city's residents. They
were appalled and shamed by the living conditions of their brothers and sisters in
the shanty towns—Jebel Awlia, 40 kilometres south of Khartoum, and Dar es
Salaam, west of Omdurman. There were no services in the camps, and no shelter
from the sun or the wind. It was akin to taking up residence in a garbage dump.
All the street children from South Sudan realized there was no future for them in
the Arab north. They understood the war was more about race than it was about
religion. By virtue of being black, these children, battered, bruised, and tormented, had become the enemy the government feared.

Pio knew better than to recruit kids solely from South Sudan for SKI Courier.
Poverty was a great leveller, and racism was virtually unknown among the children.
They didn't care about a kid's skin color or religion as long as he could get the job
done. Only one thing mattered: could he deliver the mail on time?

One day when Pio was biking a letter to a distant part of Khartoum, he spotted a boy peering out from under a pile of rubbish. Pio brought the child to the office on the back of his bike. The 10-year-old from Northern Kordofan was named Yassir. He was small for his age, about the size of a child of seven or eight. Yassir was from a village just outside El Obeid. After the crops failed for the third successive year, and being the oldest male child, he was sent off by his family to fend for himself. He rode on the top of a train to Khartoum and lived in a dumpster for his first three months in the city. He gradually worked his way up the social ladder of the street, earning about 50 cents a day as a porter in the market. We put him on a bicycle to test him and his feet could barely reach the pedals. But Yassir could read and write in Arabic, and he was willing to learn English. Pio and his colleagues decided to hire him as the office dispatcher. Yassir was an instant success, and proved to be one of our best employees.

In one important aspect, we differed from most businesses: our goal was not to keep our employees but to lose them. We designed SKI Courier as a stepping-stone for street children along the road to self-sufficiency. We paid the kids a wage they could live on, but not so much that they would want to make a career out of riding a bicycle around town. We wanted them to learn some basic social skills and then move on.

The boys picked up mail twice a day from our clients and brought it to the SKI Courier office, where it was sorted. Through the course of their delivery activities, the boys came into daily contact with office managers, who were responsible for local hiring by their agency or company. The managers could see the boys were motivated and hard-working. One thing usually led to another: our best kids were constantly being lured away by offers of higher pay. The best compliment to SKI Courier was when a kid returned from his rounds with news he had accepted a job with another company. Every time a kid graduated, we held a small party. "Good luck and good riddance," we told them. They all knew that if they didn't accept the offer of employment, we would fire them.

SKI Courier had started to attract international media attention. Word about our courier business had reached London, specifically the headquarters of the BBC. With little warning, a television crew flew to Khartoum to record the story of these amazing children who were defying the obstacles and, like flowers in the desert, adapting to their harsh environment.

The BBC crew had arrived with a writer who was not sure what the angle of the story would be. Within a few minutes of meeting Sunday, she knew she had her star and would build their piece around him. Sunday had already emerged as our poster boy, with his good looks, his contagious enthusiasm, and his southern charm. He had a habit of walking up to foreign women, flashing a disarming smile, and asking outright if they would adopt him. Then he waited for their response. Some of them just melted.

Sunday was born to act and loved to perform for any audience. While in Nairobi, I had purchased a Sony Walkman, and friends in Canada had sent me a number of audio tapes. The one song that Sunday wanted to listen to over and over again was the 1960s Peter, Paul, and Mary tune, *Puff the Magic Dragon*. Aboard the Land Rover, we would be winding through the streets of Khartoum, looking for a lost courier or scouring the souks for bicycle parts, when Sunday would suddenly break into his own version of the song. He had little idea what many of the words meant, but he memorized them all just the same. I would join him for the chorus. We would have our windows down, the Land Rover being without the luxury of air conditioning, and pedestrians would often stare at us. There wasn't much singing in the streets of Khartoum, and what little there was, Sunday was likely responsible for. He was a one-child Vienna Boys Choir.

All the kids had different strategies for dealing with a city where they knew they were not welcome, where politicians spoke openly about having them rounded up and shot. Some kids engaged in their own personal vendetta with the enemy, fantasizing about blowing up the military barracks just off Airport Road. Pio survived life in the north by putting all his energy into SKI Courier, and into his plans to build an empire that would earn him a fortune. Sunday retreated into a world of music, song, and dance. In a city of darkness and repression, it was a source of light. It helped to keep him sane, and to keep all of us at SKI Courier happy. According to Yassir, the big advantage of Sunday over a Walkman was that he didn't require any batteries.

The BBC had arrived in Khartoum with the intention of filming a seven-minute item for the national news. It evolved into a 30-minute documentary, and it told a beautiful story. The cameraman attached a remote unit to Sunday's handlebars for some of the sequences. The "bikecam" shots showed Sunday finding the path of least resistance between the long lines of cars that crawled along Jamhurria Avenue and through Khartoum's central business district. Other media followed in the BBC's tracks. Jane Perlez, the *New York Times* correspondent for East Africa, penned a story about her first visit to the Sudanese capital. She described the corroded hulks of the more than 600 yellow Mercedes buses on the outskirts of Khartoum, "a sad metaphor of Khartoum's decay." She reported on her visit to the Foreign Registration Office, where "the lone worker was stretched out across two desktops sound asleep while a wood-bladed ceiling fan dispiritedly circulated the stifling afternoon air."

But Perlez discovered another side of Khartoum. Her piece concluded with a vivid description of SKI Courier:

> The flagship of the street boys is a messenger service. Decked out in canary yellow T-shirts and shorts, the boys ride on bicycles around the city, skittering around the standstill traffic to deliver messages, mail and newspapers.
>
> "The roads are very bad here," Munir Ahmed said. "No one would dare deliver mail by car, and all the telephones are dead." The booming service earns a profit and pays the boys a small monthly salary that they are forbidden to spend on drugs.
>
> Unlike the patterns in other cities of the world, there is little risk that a Khartoum messenger boy will become outmoded. It will be a long time, say the patient residents, before the phones work. The fax machine is but a dim dream in Khartoum.

But the kindest words about SKI Courier were written by a young English woman working with a U.K.-based youth leadership organization called Project Trust. In an unpublished essay entitled "A Vision in Motion: Dispatching Destitution," Kate Beckman wrote: "It is too early to say what the long-term effects of projects like SKI Courier will be. The cheerful atmosphere at SKI's office is clear evidence of its benefit to the first batch of free-wheeling dispatch riders. But hopefully, the example of SKI will stretch well beyond the immediate circle of its couriers. Firstly inwards, through the persistent tendrils of the grapevine, back to the streets themselves, to let the thousands of other boys there know that there are prospects beyond the begging hand and the shoeshine box. And secondly, to the wielders of power, to city councillors, to aid personnel and to ordinary citizens—to provide living evidence that destitution is not delinquency—that the children whom today we chase away from our cars and castles could tomorrow be walking side by side with us to work. 'There, but for the grace of God, go I.' Let us hope we will listen."

With two modest success stories under my belt, I wanted to do something about the many street children in detention in and around Khartoum. A boy turned up at Sabah with open wounds on his back, the result of a severe lashing inflicted on him while in police custody. Inevitably, the children who were treated most harshly by the police were from the south. Some were as young as seven and eight years of age, and they were often forced to share prison cells with adult detainees. Physical and sexual abuse by the guards, police, and other inmates were commonplace.

Using my status as a UNICEF employee more as a shield than a sword, I lobbied with officials at the Ministry of Social Welfare and with the Khartoum police to gain access to the prison in Khartoum North and to Dar Tarbiat Al Ashbal, where I suspected kids were being held. But time was on the side of the bureaucrats. I sat for hours in their steamy waiting rooms, sweating under the motionless ceiling fan, watching others being escorted into the offices to do their business. When I asked about the status of my meeting, I was always told that it was "ba'ad shwoya"—in a few minutes.

During my months in the Sudan, I had learned the value of patience, and I never turned up for a meeting with a government official without a good book to read or a copy of a report to work on, but the promised meetings at the Ministry of Social Welfare never materialized. The official I needed to speak with was always unavailable, or had been called away for a meeting with the minister, or was meeting with lawyers. At one point I camped out for three days at the ministry, hoping to meet the one person who could grant me permission to visit the prisons. In the end, I had a 15-minute session with an information officer, a government flack whose job it was to run interference for people like me asking prying questions that really were none of their business.

It didn't matter that UNICEF and the international community were underwriting the Ministry of Social Welfare's operating costs and programming. In the meeting I was handed a yellowed copy of a piece of legislation dating from colonial times that set out the terms for the care of minors in detention in the Sudan. The legislation provided for the construction of British-style Borstals for all juvenile delinquents. The official flatly denied there were any children or adolescents being detained in adult prisons. When I described the boy who had turned up at Sabah with lash marks inflicted by police officers, I was informed that as the child was from the south, he could not be trusted. Perhaps he had been punished by his own people and now they were blaming it on the government authorities. There were many explanations for the boy's wounds.

The official had some questions of his own. What exactly was my job at UNICEF? How long had I been in the country? Had I ever visited the south? He wanted to see my passport and a copy of my contract with UNICEF. I told him I could provide both documents, but it would take time. I could play the waiting game as well as the Sudanese.

The Sudanese bureaucracy was riddled with security agents, and although their methods were primitive and often brutal, they usually got their job done. I knew that merely by requesting to visit the prisons, my name would be put on a watch list and my movements around the city would begin to be noticed and probably recorded. For repressive regimes around the world, the most effective tool to intimidate and dispose of pesky diplomats and employees of human-rights organizations is to declare them personae non grata, and then to give them one day to pack their bags and leave the country. Most of the UN employees I met during my time in the Sudan were terrified by the prospect of being kicked out of the country. They might have to return to their home countries, face winters, pay taxes, and do their own laundry! But for me, to be PNGed by the government in Khartoum would be my own red badge of courage. I couldn't care less what they did to me, and I was determined to use my remaining time in the country to lobby as effectively as I could for the children who lived in the streets, and for the children who had been thrown into the country's dungeon-like prisons.

According to Lau Tzu, when one encounters resistance, one should choose another path. I decided to forego the formalities of official permission from the ministry and went directly to the prison in Khartoum North. I had the name of a child who was in detention, charged and convicted of murder. I had no idea how I would be received at the prison. The guard who answered the door was surprised to see a foreigner, but not alarmed. I showed him my official UNICEF identification card, but it did not seem to mean anything to him. I explained the purpose of my visit, that I wanted to interview a child who was in his care. His name was Salah Sharif, and he was 14 years old. The guard nodded his head. He knew Salah well and was familiar with his story. Had I been sent by his family? he asked. In fact, it was Robert Richard at the French embassy who had briefed me on Salah's case and who had asked me to see the boy, but the prison guard did not need to know the French embassy was involved, even informally, in the case. I explained the family had sent me to check on the boy's status and well-being, and all I needed was 10 minutes. To my surprise, the guard stood aside and welcomed me into his prison.

When you pass through the gates of prisons in a developing country, you leave behind the land of the living. I know street workers in cities such as Bogotá, Lima, and Nairobi who won't step into a prison without having a fresh plastic jar of Vicks VapoRub on hand to dab under their nose to ward off the stench. The smell hits you first because you can't see much until your eyes become accustomed to the darkness. In the prison in Khartoum North, I heard a shuffling sound, which I initially thought was an animal. But the prisoners didn't have many visitors, and the arrival of an unexpected person meant trouble—someone was about to be dragged away for questioning or transferred to solitary confinement. A prisoner was frightened, and he was taking cover.

The guard moved confidently in the darkness; he had to pause at one point so I could catch up with him. It would have been almost impossible for me to find my way back to the main gate on my own. I thought of the famous prison etchings of Piranesi, *Le Carceri*, that depicted the maze-like underground network of cells of medieval Rome. I know now that the Khartoum North prison wasn't a particularly bad place for children to be held against their will, as far as prisons go. But it was a far cry from the holding cell in which I had interviewed legal-aid clients in the Halifax police station while attending law school. No matter what kind of offence Salah had committed, no youth should have to live in such conditions.

Salah Sharif shared a cell with three other prisoners. There were only two bunks and one filthy blanket. In the corner was a single yellow bucket that was used by the prisoners to wash, bathe, urinate, and defecate. There was no window or source of outside light. The guard called out Salah's name. He rose apprehensively and made his way to the cell door. The guard asked the other prisoners to stand back before he unlocked and swung open a gate that reminded me of the sliding door of a hamster cage. Salah didn't say anything, and walked in step with the prison guard to the office that doubled as the visitors' room. In the centre was a wooden table, heavily marked and leaning to one side. The guard pointed to the table—there were two benches we could sit on. The guard asked both of us if we would like something to drink, then lit a cigarette for himself.

"Did Monsieur Richard send you?" Salah inquired. He knew as soon as he saw I was a foreigner that there must be some connection with Robert Richard, the only person who had ever shown any interest in his case. I explained the situation to him—that I was a lawyer, but that I was employed as the UNICEF emergency officer in Khartoum. I had begun some projects for street children, and I was aware there were many street children in prison. Salah glanced over to see if the guard was listening, but he was reading an old newspaper and enjoying his cigarette.

I thought it would be easier for Salah to talk about the situation of other children who were in prison rather than his own particular circumstances. I asked if he knew other youth in detention, and how they were faring. Salah nodded. "There are many of us," he replied. He quickly ran down the names of children who he believed were imprisoned in Khartoum North or other detention centres. He told me there were kids who had been in detention for more than two years, some of them for the most trivial of offences such as common vagrancy. The kids from Darfur were not treated any better than the children from the south. Some of the kids in prison were refugees from Chad and from Ethiopia. I asked Salah if officials from any other United Nations agency had ever visited the prisons to interview the refugee children. Salah shrugged his shoulders. "No one ever comes to see us," he sighed. "No one cares about us."

The guard continued to ignore us. We moved on to the subject of Salah's own situation in the Khartoum North prison, and the set of circumstances that had landed him in jail. He didn't want or need my pity. Salah insisted Khartoum North was one of the better facilities for children in the Sudan. The guards were decent people; some of them even treated the young prisoners as they would their own kids. No one had beaten him in prison. The guards ensured no young people were in a cell with any violent offenders or someone who might sexually assault them. But Salah alluded to "difficulties," and I suspected I wasn't getting the entire story.

I had seen some documentation about Salah's case, so I knew about the murder charge he faced. The prosecution's case relied on a confession the investigating police officers had obtained from Salah after hours of interrogation and beating. Salah had been forced to sign a statement that he had never read. Robert Richard had shown me a French translation of the original Arabic document. It was less than two pages in length, and described how Salah had followed a businessman to his house and used a club to bludgeon him to death. Neighbors had heard screaming in the house and had alerted the police, who had accosted Salah just as he was exiting the front door of the man's residence. There were no witnesses to the murder. Since Salah had signed a confession, his lawyer had insisted he plead guilty. Salah was told there was no way he could argue in court that the confession was obtained through coercion. "They've got you where they want you," his lawyer informed him. "The best you can do is get down on your knees in front of the judge and plead for mercy."

I was no crack criminal lawyer, but there were many holes in the prosecution's version of events. There was no sign of forced entry at the victim's residence.

Exactly how had Salah gained entrance to the house? The police report indicated the victim's body was covered with scratch marks evidently inflicted by Salah, but Salah had no similar marks on his body. There had been a struggle, but the official police report suggested it was Salah who had attempted to fend off the man, not the other way around. The weapon Salah used was not something he brought to the house in pursuit of the man, but rather an object he found among the man's possessions. The man was married and had a family, but on the day of the attack, he was the only person at home. How did Salah know he would be alone? Finally, the victim was a wealthy merchant, and the house was filled with valuable possessions, but the police report contained no mention of Salah's leaving the house with anything on his person other than his own possessions. Jewellery, the man's expensive watch, and cash in the victim's wallet were all left untouched. So what had been Salah's motive?

I explained to Salah I had done work as a legal-aid student representing inner-city children charged with various crimes, but I needed to know the truth if I was going to have any chance at all of having his case reviewed. But Salah was tight-lipped. In our first meeting, I didn't expect him to trust me, even if I were a friend of Monsieur Richard's. I asked him a few more questions about the conditions at the Khartoum North prison, and then the guard informed us my time was up.

It took three more visits to the prison for me to get the full story. On my subsequent visits, I made sure to bring along some Marlboro cigarettes to smooth things over with the prison guard. Salah liked to read, so I brought him copies of the latest editions of *Time* and *Newsweek*. On my third visit, the guard left Salah and me alone in the meeting room, and finally Salah was able to tell me exactly how he had ended up in the man's house and why he had clubbed him to death.

From my work with inner-city kids in Halifax and East Palo Alto, I should have guessed what had happened. It was so obvious from the evidence. Salah was living rough in the streets of Khartoum, destitute and defeated, when a man driving an expensive car pulled up beside him and offered him a meal. Salah was suspicious at first, but the man seemed friendly enough. He invoked the name of God, and said he felt sorry for the poor street children. Salah was surprised when they did not go to a restaurant as the man had promised, but instead drove across the Khartoum North bridge. The man said he had food in his house and he would cook something for the two of them.

Of course, when they arrived at the house, Salah found out what the rich man was really interested in. The man, who was tall and powerful, brutally raped Salah. Salah fought him every step of the way, but it was futile. The pain was intense, and Salah screamed for him to stop, but the man did not listen. Somehow Salah managed to break loose and ran to a corner of the room, where he found a wooden club that resembled a cricket bat. The man came at him again, and Salah took one big wind-up and slammed the man over the back of the head with the club. Salah told me he was attempting to knock him out, and was shocked to see blood drip out of his mouth and his ears. He cried hysterically, threw down the club, and ran from the apartment into the arms of the police officers, who were just arriving.

Salah had told the same story word for word to the police officers who interrogated him, but they refused to believe him. The man he killed was from an important family. Salah said he was willing to submit to a medical examination to prove he had been raped, but the police officer said no purpose would be served by having such a procedure carried out. Salah was a murderer, and he would likely be executed. The interrogation lasted for several hours, and Salah was severely beaten over his chest, face, and back with a whip. Someone had prepared a document for Salah to sign, but he refused to co-operate with the interrogators. It was only when they threatened to attach electrodes to his genitals that he caved in and signed his name to the document. He said his hand was shaking so uncontrollably that it had been almost impossible for him to write. His own sweat and tears had blurred the ink on the document.

No one at UNICEF was interested in Salah's case. I thought that since he was a northerner, there might be some sympathy among the staff, but they told me they all had important work to focus their attention on. Jim Grant, the executive director of UNICEF in New York, was soon visiting Khartoum, and many preparations had to be made. On account of the drought and famine, two film crews were coming to the Sudan, hosted by UNICEF. Most of the desk officers at UNICEF were tied up with regular business: negotiations with government ministries, ordering supplies, and routine office administration. There wasn't much room on the agency's agenda for discussion about young Salah, or the many other children from North and South Sudan who were wasting away in the country's adult prisons, all of which dated from colonial times and had not been renovated or upgraded in more than 30 years.

I found an eminent Sudanese lawyer who was willing to examine the details of the case. He met with Salah, with the victim's family, and with the police. After much discussion, it was determined the verdict could not be overturned. There was no evidence on which to challenge the veracity of Salah's own confession. But there was one reason to be optimistic: under Islamic law, the family of the victim is entitled to ask for dia, or blood money, to compensate for the loss of their loved one. If the individual who has been convicted of the crime is able to pay the dia, he is set free after a relatively short period of confinement. In this case, the victim's family initially stated they would not accept dia and wanted Salah put to death. Because of his youth, Salah was given a 15-year sentence with no opportunity for parole. Salah's lawyer had convinced them to reconsider their decision and they had agreed to negotiate. Eventually, a deal was struck. The dia was the equivalent of $5,000. If we could somehow raise the money, the boy would be set free.

A Swedish filmmaker was in the Sudan at the time, documenting the famine, and when I told him Salah's story, he expressed much interest in meeting with him and seeing if he could help the boy. I arranged for two meetings between Salah and the filmmaker, and an agreement was made that the filmmaker would raise the money among his friends back in Stockholm. He promised me we would have the cash within three weeks. Salah was ecstatic, and all his friends in the prison congratulated him. But that was the last we heard of the filmmaker. I sent him numerous letters and telexes, but heard nothing in response.

In the end, it was Robert Richard who was able to raise the money in France that allowed Salah to gain his freedom. It was the right thing to do, but both Robert and I knew Salah's situation differed from the hundreds of other children who were in prison in the Sudan only because he had made a friend at the French embassy and Monsieur Richard was willing to go to bat for him. What about all the other children locked behind bars? Robert Richard confronted me: weren't they my responsibility, as a lawyer and as an employee of UNICEF?

The process of getting to know Salah, and attempting to win support for his cause within the UNICEF office, had taught me the weakness of the UN system. Working exclusively through the auspices of the government meant that UNICEF inevitably practised its own variety of self-censorship. It was only willing to engage the government on issues that were not controversial and would not upset its counterparts at the Ministry of Social Welfare or the Ministry of Health. Human rights, even if the well-being of kids was at stake, were outside its jurisdiction.

UNICEF in the 1980s focused on a four-point program around the world that emphasized the importance of growth-monitoring, the promotion of oral rehydration salts, breast-feeding, and immunization. The items on the list were non-contentious, non-political, and relatively low-cost to implement.

Jim Grant and his country representatives pursued them with a level of intensity that verged on obsession. I argued that speaking up for children in jail, or beginning an advocacy program for street children, would not in any way compromise the Sudan's national-immunization program, which had been funded to the hilt by international donors. Immunization was such a sexy agenda item for the international community that two UN agencies—UNICEF and the World Health Organization—both claimed jurisdiction over it and took credit for progress that had been made in immunization campaigns in developing countries. Human rights, on the other hand, was a delicate issue that often got international development organizations into trouble. Amnesty International was frequently attacked by regimes around the world for meddling in their internal affairs, and governments did everything in their power to discredit the organization.

Médecins Sans Frontières was one of the few international development organizations that had successfully married the provision of emergency relief with humanitarianism. Unlike the United Nations and many of the larger agencies, they refused to kowtow to any regime, no matter how powerful. The credo of Médecins Sans Frontières is that people in need, no matter what their religion or race, have the right to a basic standard of medical care, and no government or politician has the right to prevent them from receiving such assistance.

The organization was co-founded by Bernard Kouchner, who, while working as a volunteer with the French Red Cross during the Biafran Civil War in 1968, was forced to wait several months for the Nigerian government to sign a piece of paper that allowed the Red Cross to provide food and medical care to children who were on the verge of starvation. By the time the documents were signed, the t's crossed and the i's dotted, most of the intended recipients of the Red Cross assistance were lying cold in their graves. During three years of hostilities, more than one million civilians died.

Kouchner vowed he would do whatever it took to challenge the power of states to use food and medical care as a weapon. Renouncing the oath of silence that the Red Cross required from its employees, Kouchner and another medical doctor, Max Recamier, spoke openly about the destruction of the Ibo people. Leftist French intellectuals, happy that Nigeria was flirting with the USSR, accused the two of messing with Nigeria's internal affairs. Kouchner and his circle of friends, including young chain-smoking journalists, Catholic social activists, and medical students from the Sorbonne, created an organization that challenged the legitimacy and questioned the competence of the Old

Boy networks that ran the traditional aid agencies. Audacity and chutzpah characterized all their actions. They paid no attention to the rules of diplomacy or national borders. MSF launched ambitious medical programs with the Mujahadin rebels in the mountains of Afghanistan, dodging the rockets of Soviet helicopter gunships. They exposed their volunteer staff to risks few UN employees would ever endure.

The men and women who make up Médecins Sans Frontières work in the most appalling circumstances, at times performing combat surgery in canvas tents only a few kilometres from the front lines of civil conflicts. They recruit fearless nurses, doctors, and logistics experts, invest heavily in their training before sending them overseas, then pay them $600 per month plus their expenses. Radio operators and truck drivers working for Médecins Sans Frontières receive the same wage as thoracic surgeons.

From its humble origins, MSF by 1986 had grown to include chapters in Holland and Belgium, and was beginning to flex its own diplomatic muscles. Kouchner had evolved the notion of the "right to intervene," which championed the authority of humanitarian organizations to challenge sovereignty—to cross state boundaries and provide medical care wherever it was required, no matter who might object. Policy-makers in Paris and Washington said the idea would never take root and was hopelessly naive, but Kouchner persisted, first in his capacity as the president of Médecins Sans Frontières, and later as the French Secretary for Humanitarian Action. Countries with bleak human-rights records cried foul and tabled the age-old excuse that criticizing their human-rights records infringed on their sovereignty. But that was the very presumption behind the right to intervene—the idea that sovereignty could no longer be used as a shield, and governments, whether democratically elected or self-appointed, had no right to starve their own citizens or selectively eliminate minority populations whom they considered a threat to national security.

The employees of MSF were activists, not bureaucrats. One of the reasons the UN employees I knew were so uniformly ineffective was that they were too comfortable and complacent. They were desk-hugging careerists, women and men overloaded with academic credentials who were motivated by the promise of a comfortable salary and a generous benefits package, rather than by any desire to make the world a better place. Most of the non-government organizations paid modest salaries, perhaps a few hundred dollars a month, but I did not notice any difference in the quality of their personnel. If anything, people such as Asma Dalallah and Inger Anderson of Sudan Aid had more highly refined technical skills than the UNICEF employees. At UNICEF, I often had members of local community-based organizations coming to my office asking me to loan them the services of a nutritionist, someone who could carry out a basic weight-for-height survey of their children, the first step in a monitoring program in times of famine. I was embarrassed to inform them that among the 60 or so personnel in the UNICEF office, I did not know a single one who had the ability to carry out such a survey. The statistics we gathered and sent to New York either came from government sources—which were suspect—or from organizations such as Oxfam, German Agro Action, Sudan Aid, or Save the Children. Nick Stockton, of Oxfam in Juba, had already accused UNICEF of taking credit for a feeding program that Oxfam managed.

Working for UNICEF in the Sudan was the first time in my life I had to accept compromises in the quality of the work I was engaged in, and it made me uncomfortable. People in the office spoke about "the art of the possible" and "focusing on the do-able," but too often it was a justification for mediocrity. It was too easy to use the war in the south, or the famine in the west, or the Sudan's lack of infrastructure, as an excuse for second-rate work. The children of the Sudan, who numbered among the poorest kids anywhere in the world, were exactly the group UNICEF had been designed to assist when it was founded in 1946 to care for the girls and boys living amidst the rubble of Tokyo, Dresden, Hamburg, and Berlin. If we couldn't effectively reach out to the kids in the south, whose villages had been burned to the ground, whose fathers had been led away at gun point, whose schools had been stripped bare of every piece of paper and bit of chalk, and whose cattle had been stolen by Arab raiders, then what good were we? Quiet diplomacy, the lingua franca of the UN system, had miserably failed these kids. There had to be another way.

IN SILENCE AND
IN DARKNESS

A few months after I had assumed my responsibilities as emergency officer for UNICEF in Khartoum, I had a new boss. In July, 1986, Jim Grant appointed an American, Cole Dodge, to succeed Samir Basta. Dodge had been the UNICEF representative in Uganda during the civil war in that country, and had front-line experience working with war-affected children. In UNICEF circles Dodge was known as an activist who was willing to take risks, and his appointment raised eyebrows among UN personnel based in Khartoum. Dodge was keenly interested in children living under especially difficult circumstances, including street children, working children, refugee children, and children in jails and institutions. I hoped that with Dodge at the helm, UNICEF might focus attention on the kids caught up in the war in South Sudan. Many Sudan observers believed that, while the government in Khartoum would tolerate a few soup kitchens for destitute kids living in the garbage dumps sprinkled around the capital, they would never accept the notion of a UN agency intervening directly in rebel-held areas.

Only days after his arrival in Khartoum, UNICEF staffers labelled Dodge a cowboy, more out of jealousy than anything else. During his time with UNICEF in Uganda, Dodge had emerged as a hero, brokering 48-hour cease-fires between government and rebel troops that allowed for the immunization of legions of girls and boys. He had cultivated a relationship with the charismatic rebel commander Yoweri Museveni, who went on to become president of Uganda. It was Cole Dodge who, only days after the war ended, walked into Museveni's office and requested permission for UNICEF to co-ordinate the decommissioning of the army of young boys that had played a key role in putting Museveni in power. Unless they received an education and had a chance to find employment, Dodge argued, the now idle youth would become a source of economic and political instability for the new government. It took some persuading on Dodge's part, but eventually UNICEF, working hand-in-hand with the new government, began an ambitious program whereby combat-hardened 13- and 14-year-olds who had never seen the inside of a classroom traded in their AK47s for grammar texts and pencils, sitting alongside girls and boys eight and nine years of age. As could be expected, there were transitional difficulties experienced in the classrooms, but on the whole the UNICEF initiative was successful in helping to ease Museveni's children's army back into Ugandan civilian society.

At our first meeting, Cole Dodge requested that I sketch out a plan of action for the UNICEF Emergency Unit and have it on his desk within two days. With a Toshiba laptop computer that I had just purchased with my first UN paycheque (the day I signed on with UNICEF, my salary quadrupled), I drafted a document with four priority areas—expanding projects for street children and children in jails and institutions, assisting the displaced population living on the edges of Khartoum, monitoring and evaluating populations in danger in the Sudan, and stepping up programming in South Sudan, including rebel-held areas.

The last point was by far the most contentious for Dodge and for UNICEF. As an agency of the United Nations, UNICEF was restricted to working only where permitted by the host government. Contact with rebel authorities was strictly prohibited, and distributing food and medical supplies to children living in rebel areas was out of the question. UNICEF had no presence in most of South Sudan, including all the territory east of the White Nile, which was held in its entirety by the SPLA. From authoritative reports issued by the various aid agencies active in the south, we knew that in 1986 300,000 children were on the verge of starvation. In particular, the town of Wau in the province of Bahr el Ghazal faced a critical food shortage. The town hospital had no medical supplies and all the medical staff had withdrawn to Khartoum. Rebels were reported to be within a few kilometres of the town centre. Wau was all but cut off from the outside world.

Dodge needed more information before making a case with UNICEF headquarters staff in New York that we should begin food distribution for children in rebel-held areas. He authorized me to travel to Nairobi to meet covertly with representatives of the SPLA to investigate the possibility of a co-operative program providing humanitarian assistance to kids in isolated areas of South

Sudan to which only the rebels had access. I had to be careful: if the Sudanese security officials suspected me of making contact with the SPLA, I would immediately be expelled from the country, so every time I travelled, I pretended to be on holiday, packing my snorkelling equipment and suntan lotion on top of my carry-on bag. I started shuttling between the Sudan and Kenya, departing Khartoum at 2:30 in the morning on the Kenyan Airways Boeing 707 and arriving in Nairobi just after dawn. The daily British Airways 747 from London arrived in Nairobi at the same hour, so I had to dash from my plane through the terminal to reach the immigration desk before the onslaught of British tourists. The movie *Out of Africa* had been released a few months earlier, and inevitably among the British Airways passengers at least three or four women would be dressed identically to the Meryl Streep character, including jodhpurs and riding boots. The polite, always dignified Kenyan customs and immigration officials would look on with amusement. At the safari lodges that dot the game parks of the Masai Mara, Samburu, and Tsavo, the wannabes were dubbed "Streeps." Some of them had even acquired the accent and affected manner of speaking.

My meetings with SPLA officials were conducted by the poolside of the Ambassador Hotel in Nairobi. They chose the location; I would have much preferred somewhere more discreet. I was terrified of being spotted by Sudanese security agents, whom I imagined to be watching with binoculars from behind trees and overhead in their hotel rooms. One SPLA official always showed up drunk, and I had to ply him with generous quantities of French fries and roast chicken from the room-service menu before he would be sober enough to carry on an intelligent conversation. The SPLA were sincere in their desire to feed and immunize their children, but they had no infrastucture, and UNICEF would not consider providing anything that could be used in a military capacity: vehicles, fuel, radios, tents, and even canned food were on the prohibited list. What we had to offer were emergency supplementary feeding materials, cooking utensils, basic school materials, vitamin supplements, and immunization supplies. Faces around the table would sag when I ran down my list. I was very blunt with the SPLA officials: were they interested in caring for their children or in equipping their soldiers?

If we wanted to save lives, we needed to act quickly. The conflict in South Sudan was gaining momentum, and displacing larger and larger numbers of civilians. An increasing percentage of Khartoum's street children were boys from the Dinka and Nuer tribes who, like Sunday and Moj, had made the long trek north from the war zones on both sides of the White Nile. Every day, I saw new faces in the streets—kids covered from head to toe in dust who drifted aimlessly about the city centre, frightened, underfed, and barefoot. Some of them were only seven or eight years of age. The new arrivals weren't accustomed to traffic; drivers would curse them as they darted between the cars at intersections. I gathered up the smallest children and transported them in my Land Rover to the reception centre at Sabah, where the social workers would register them, scrub them until their bodies glistened, feed them a nutritious meal, and tend to their wounds.

The war was forcing people throughout the south to take refuge in the government-held towns. As of July, 1986, Juba, Wau, and Malakal were the homes for approximately 50,000, 40,000, and 35,000 displaced people respectively, the majority of whom were women and children. Prolonged seasonal rains and the absence of any kind of shelter made their condition particularly desperate. Insecurity had prevented farmers from planting sorghum and maize. Cattle-raiding by Arab militia groups armed by the government had resulted in huge herd losses. Already much of the south was inaccessible to even the most resourceful of relief agencies. Roads were being washed out, and because of rebel or militia activity, many tracks were too dangerous to travel. The railway linking Wau with Awiel and the outside world had not functioned since 1981. Malakal, usually supplied by river, had not been reached by barges in almost a year. We knew that as the situation deteriorated, an unacceptable amount of any food we transported would be lost to rebels, militia, and the military. Monitoring the supplies we provided would be impossible.

When I updated the map on my office wall at UNICEF, I inserted green flags on the towns and villages held by the SPLA and red flags on the government positions. Apart from the largest towns, my map was a sea of green. Using the map, I began to envision how UNICEF might carry out an emergency program. Once we made the decision to push ahead with food shipments to towns and villages in the south, we would need to proceed with extreme caution: land mines had been planted indiscriminately by both sides throughout the south. Boreholes, walking paths between villages, and fields were all prime locations. No records or maps were kept of where they had been buried. Plastic land mines are virtually undetectable and can last for decades. A Khmer Rouge general once compared the land mine to a perfect soldier, "ever courageous, never sleeps, never misses." In January, 1987, I met with a Thames Television crew at the Hilton Hotel in Khartoum to brief them on their planned trip into the south from Kenya to interview SPLA leader John Garang. I advised against the trip because several truck convoys carrying relief supplies north from the Kenyan border had recently been attacked. In the end, they got their interview with Garang but paid a heavy price: on the return trip, one vehicle hit a land mine and rolled. The Thames Television director, an experienced and respected journalist named Alan Stewart, was thrown from the vehicle and crashed head-first into a tree. "I can't go yet. I've got to survive," Stewart whispered as he was cradled in a colleague's arms. He died minutes later.

I needed to learn more about the south first-hand. In January, 1987, the UNICEF representative in Juba, Noel Astillero, took an extended leave to visit his family in the Philippines. Dodge required someone to fill in for him and asked me to take the assignment. I jumped at the opportunity. My 10 weeks in Juba allowed me to work closely with the coalition of aid agencies that had already set up a food-distribution system for the displaced people from the Mundari tribe, traditional rivals of the Dinka, who were camped on the outskirts of the town. Oxfam in Juba had spearheaded the formation of the Combined Agencies Relief Team, or CART, through which the agencies pooled their resources, including food and vehicles, and directed them where they were most needed. The EEC was CART's major donor. Local truckers were hired to become part of the CART fleet at a fraction of the operating cost of RTO in Khartoum. The drivers knew all the roads and tracks between Juba and the Ugandan border, and extracted every ounce of horsepower out of the creaking Bedford lorries. CART received little press compared to the EEC air-bridge, but the team's can-do attitude won it supporters in every quarter of the south—except in the government of the Sudan, which accused it of gun-running.

Juba was the government's staging point for the war in the south. I watched with clenched teeth, barely able to contain my rage, as Boeing 707 cargo aircraft arrived at Juba airport filled with weapons, including American-manufactured cluster bombs, then returned the same day to Khartoum with badly injured soldiers—five young men strapped down on each cargo pallet. Many cried out in agony, their bandages dripping blood. Aging F-6 fighter aircraft belonging to the Sudanese air force flew sorties on a daily basis from Juba. Dinka cattle camps, packed with children and easily identifiable from the air because of the large concentration of animals, were regular targets for their bombs. With no danger of being shot down by anti-aircraft fire, the planes could swoop in so low over the camps that the pilots could make out the faces of the children. After an attack, the camps looked like a scene from *The Inferno*: kids' smooth bodies ripped apart, limbs flailing about, pools of cattle and Dinka blood intermingling on the ground.

Who was profiting most from the war? My time in the Sudan taught me that the powerful multinational arms manufacturers are the ones who must be made accountable for their actions. But I am not completely naive; I know that with their profits flowing into the Swiss bank accounts of politicians and policy-makers, there is little chance the carnage will end. Warriors may have a code of honor that governs the manner in which they kill, but businesspeople who control this dirty business have no conscience and feel no sense of responsibility.

Juba, a tiny town compared to Khartoum, had only a few resident foreigners, and without delay I was inducted into the community of aid workers, teachers, and volunteers. I became friends with a gregarious priest from Quebec named Father Claude, a member of the Pères Blanches order, who zipped about the region on his Ducati motorbike, dispensing food and prayer to the faithful and non-believers alike. Nick Stockton of Oxfam proved to be an indispensable ally. I scribbled his recommendations in my black notebooks as he talked and sipped coffee. Stockton insisted that the south had to be supplied by truck from Kenya or Uganda, and not by way of costly aircraft from Khartoum. While media tend to focus on dramatic air-bridges, planes flying relief supplies are always a sign that things have gone terribly wrong. UNICEF shouldn't wait until the only way to Juba was by chartered 707s. Feeding-stations for displaced children were urgently required. Stockton advised me to use trucks to pre-position supplies in the south as quickly as possible while some areas were still accessible by road.

Oxfam had earned its spurs in South Sudan through many years of effort with local tribespeople developing an innovative cattle-vaccination program. The premise behind the scheme was simple: by improving the health of the Dinka's, Nuer's and Mundari's cattle, you improve the health of their children. Cattle are the unit of currency throughout South Sudan, and by helping a tribesperson to increase his herd and augment his wealth, you can earn his respect and his loyalty. UNICEF had been surprised by the low numbers of children turning out for its immunization program in and around Juba and other government-held towns, but the problem wasn't difficult to identify. The vaccinators were officials from the government's Ministry of Health, of whom all southerners were naturally suspicious. Oxfam offered a solution: set up a vaccination cold chain and immunize only cattle for the first year. When the chiefs see how well their animals fare thanks to your efforts, you will soon have thousands of children lining up to be immunized. In the words of one Mundari chief, "When word gets out about our healthy cattle, people will carry their children across the Nile to be immunized." The same cold-chain equipment used for the cattle vaccines—including kerosene refrigerators and insulated cold boxes—could be used to transport and store vaccination materials for children.

Before Juba, my experience relating to emergency operations during wartime was purely theoretical. My office in Khartoum was littered with publications from Médecins Sans Frontières, the Red Cross, and various UN agencies that provided step-by-step instructions for constructing ventilated improved pit latrines (VIPs), helicopter landing pads, and primitive but effective water-filtration systems. I knew where to source the world's best kerosene refrigerators (Sweden), and could imitate the sound of both incoming and outgoing mortar fire. But I was completely unfamiliar with the limits imposed by combat. The war made the implementation of UNICEF's rigid national-immunization plan impractical. Oxfam focused instead on modest-scale local initiatives, taking advantage of any break in hostilities. Its vaccination and feeding programs were flexible and highly decentralized. Maintaining close relations with the local chiefs was essential. Nothing should be done without their blessing. Vaccinators were all members of the local displaced population, not officials with the Ministry of Health.

I radioed my recommendations to Cole Dodge in Nairobi, using a prearranged code employing the names of Canadian cities and hockey players to avoid tipping anyone off that we might begin operating in rebel-held areas. Dodge radioed back that he required irrefutable evidence that the road from the Kenyan border to Juba was open and that trucks carrying UNICEF supplies could make it through. After three days of searching for a courier, I persuaded a pilot from the Nile Safaris air charter company to hand-carry a small parcel to Khartoum, and arranged for Dodge's driver to collect it from the hangar. When Dodge unwrapped the parcel in his office, he had all the proof he needed about road conditions: inside was an unopened bottle of Kenyan beer. Unlike Khartoum where prohibition was in effect, beer was available in Juba at various bars around town, including the favorite watering hole of the aid workers, the Greek Club, and the old Juba Hotel, which once accommodated passengers of the Imperial Airways flying boats en route from England to South Africa. The beer was Tusker and White Cap bottled in Nairobi, coming in on huge transport trucks. Despite the presence of Tiposa guerrillas just north of the Kenyan border waiting in ambush, the drivers did manage to deliver their valuable cargo. I noted that during the first week of February, 1987, alone, 40 MT of beer arrived in Juba from Nairobi—one week's supply for a thirsty and battle-weary town. I suspected that the drivers dropped a few cases off the end of their trucks as payment to the Tiposa to ensure safe passage. The civil servants, aid workers, and merchants of Juba could enjoy cold beer and a daily game of darts, while the children of South Sudan, diseased and malnourished, subsisted on famine foods. "What's wrong with this picture?" I asked Cole Dodge.

Juba had a burgeoning population of street children, all of whom were kids who had lost one or both parents to the war. I met with a group of them every day after work under the shade of the jacaranda trees outside the Juba Hotel, bringing along a briefcase stuffed with tasty meat and vegetarian samosas from the Greek Club. The kids had witnessed acts of savagery by both government and rebel soldiers. War had robbed them of their childhood, and they had little hope for the future. Gido Ernesto, age 11, had lost both parents in hostilities near Terekeka. He dreamed of going to school and becoming a mechanic, but Juba's classrooms had no places open for displaced children. The principal had told him that he needed to produce a birth certificate and other papers before he could be admitted—documents that had been burned when his family's hut was torched by SPLA soldiers. Gido supported himself by washing dishes in popular local restaurants, and slept in the Juba market alongside dozens of other orphaned children. "Nobody wants us," he told me with the solemn voice of a man five times his age. "We fight with the stray dogs for food scraps." Among the kids who slept in the market was a nine-year-old Acholi girl named Beatrice, but she was shy and would not speak with foreigners. Her big brother, Anton Taba, looked after her, and washed army trucks for food money. Anton told me that the army soldiers sometimes offered him cigarettes, but he kept his distance. Men wearing the same uniforms had murdered his parents and older brother.

Throughout South Sudan, there were communities far worse off than Juba. The town of Wau, held by government troops but surrounded by rebels, had been isolated for weeks from the rest of the country. Small chartered aircraft provided the only link with the outside world. I was in possession of a letter from Bishop Joseph Nyekindi of Wau imploring the relief agencies to come to the aid of his people. The letter reported that armed conflict, combined with attacks by Murahaleen militia, had displaced tens of thousands of people in the Bahr el Ghazal region. Due to low food stocks, only the hungriest children were receiving any assistance. The bishop was desperate:

All pieces of land in the town are turned up for cultivation, but there is no rain. Hunger is at the highest peak in the town of Wau. Seeds planted are scratched out at night by other people for food. Life is at the verge of extinction!

We do not see a way how food can now be brought to Wau. Raga-Dein road is no more possible. Wau–Juba road is no more passable. The railway is dead. People feel doomed! ... This is our situation now in Bahr el Ghazal. We are doomed to die, but we do not want to die in silence!

Part of the draft plan I had submitted to Cole Dodge called for UNICEF to position a medical team in Wau to provide basic medical care for local women and children. I argued that UNICEF had to be proactive; we could not wait for the entire health-care system to collapse before we intervened. Wau was under government control, so we would not require any special permission to operate within the town limits. Dodge liked my proposal and sent it by courier to Jim Grant and his colleagues at the UNICEF headquarters in New York. Within a week, we had a response: food distribution in areas under SPLA control was out of the question, but we were encouraged to step up our operations in those few towns held by the government. In particular, New York approved the idea of UNICEF dispatching a medical team to work in the main hospital in Wau.

A problem of United Nations agencies is that when they are most needed— in times of war when people's lives are on the line—their personnel are often evacuated. Although we had received the authorization from New York to send doctors to Wau, UNICEF had no international personnel willing or able to work in the town. The assignment was considered too dangerous for the United Nations.

I knew where we could find the right people for the job. I had become friends with Jacques de Milliano, the founder of Médecins Sans Frontières in Holland. His organization was only two years old, but it had already operated in several conflict zones, including northern Uganda during the civil war. Over the years, employees of MSF have become inured to the sight of UN employees and their families standing in long lines in airports around the world with their suitcases at their side, awaiting the first plane out of the country, at the very moment MSF personnel are arriving to begin their emergency work. On my return to Khartoum from Juba, I proposed to Cole Dodge that UNICEF link up with Médecins Sans Frontières Holland and provide all the resources it required to set up an emergency medical program based out of the hospital in

Wau. Dodge quickly okayed the plan, and MSF in Amsterdam combed its files for physicians who could function in conditions that rivalled what it had experienced in Afghanistan or Ethiopia.

In March, 1987, I flew with Dodge and the MSF delegation to Wau. Jacques de Milliano had selected two young medical staff for the assignment, Marijke and Harry. Both had substantial experience in war zones and were known to keep their cool when under fire. They would be posted to Wau for an initial six-week period, and would work with local personnel to rehabilitate the hospital and restore basic medical services.

We were aware that risks were associated with the operation. SPLA rebels were camped only a few kilometres from the town and could begin an offensive at any moment. Furthermore, the security situation in Wau was precarious at best. Just like Beirut, Wau was divided in two by its own green line. One half of the town was controlled by the Dinka, the other half by the Fertit militia, with whom the army was closely aligned. Residents could not easily move from one sector to the other.

As soon as we arrived in Wau, Harry, Marijke, Cole, and I knew the town was doomed. As the SPLA soldiers had drawn near, Wau had been abandoned. Anyone who had the physical strength had escaped to the bush. The only people left were the very old, the very young, and the very sick. At midday, nobody walked the streets except a naked madman. The markets were closed, and all the shops on the town's ramshackle main street were shut tight. Arab merchants had become my own version of the canary in the coal mine: with their highly developed knack for both making money and staying safe they knew when to cut their losses and pack up for Khartoum. The hospital itself was in a horrific state. There had been no electricity or running water in over six months. Most of the beds were occupied by people in the last stages of life. Some were blind. Many had open wounds that were infected. The patients—if they could be called that, with no medical personnel within 100 kilometres— had not received any medical treatment for 10 weeks, and the hospital's medical supplies had been exhausted long before we arrived.

Cole and I were spooked by the place, and had serious reservations about leaving Marijke and Harry in Wau. They had no capacity to defend themselves should it become necessary. There was only one pilot in Khartoum who was willing to bring supplies to the team on a regular basis—the courageous Dutchman Eddie Folman. He flew a Cessna 404 for Sasco Airways, a Khartoum-based charter company owned by a businessman named Nur, and he was familiar with every landing strip in the south. But if the airport became unserviceable for any reason, such as heavy rain or shelling, then the team would be on its own.

Cole and I suggested that Marijke and Harry return with us on the UNICEF plane to Khartoum until the situation in Wau had stabilized, but they were determined to stay behind and begin their work. They had a new Motorola radio with which they could transmit and receive messages, and they promised to stay in regular contact with us. All four of us remained overnight in Wau with our pilot, camping out on the floor of the abandoned doctors' compound that adjoined the hospital. We didn't get much sleep; throughout the night, we listened to the moans of sick and dying patients for whom the MSF team had arrived too late.

In the morning, Cole and I took a final tour of the cursed town, then headed off to the airport. I was feeling uneasy about my optimistic plans for UNICEF programming in the south. Sitting behind a desk, they had seemed so easy; up close, Wau was lethal. Cole didn't say anything, but I knew he was revisiting the entire notion of UNICEF, with its limited expertise, becoming bogged down in a costly and potentially dangerous operation that had the potential to save very few lives. Nothing we did could pull Wau out of its death spiral. Cole was an expert at risk management and allocating UNICEF's material and human resources where they could do the most good. Wau was a sinkhole for the compassion of the international community.

The Wau police chief, an older Dinka gentleman, escorted us to the Wau airport, his weapon drawn and his forehead covered with beads of sweat. Once we arrived we saw that the UNICEF Twin Otter was being guarded by four military personnel who brandished automatic weapons. I wasn't sure whether they were there to protect or intimidate us. No civilian scheduled flights had been in or out of Wau in weeks, and there was a good-sized crowd at the airport who would do almost anything to get on board our aircraft. We had room for at least 12 people, but offering anyone a seat would have resulted in a full-scale riot. Eddie Folman had encountered exactly that situation when taking off from Malakal a few weeks earlier: a government soldier had shot dead an unarmed civilian who had scampered over the retaining fence and was running toward the aircraft loading area. I was relieved when we were finally in the air.

Many weeks later, we learned that our fears for the safety of the MSF team were justified. Just hours after our departure, Harry was approached by the police chief—the same man who had accompanied us to the airport. He explained to Harry that he and Marijke were in grave danger and had to be extremely vigilant.

The garrison military commander in Wau, Major General Abu Gurun, was conducting a search-and-kill operation designed to root out rebel supporters. His enemy were the Dinka, and he was determined to exterminate—that was the word he used—any Dinka who defied him. Abu Gurun was also highly suspicious of foreigners, all of whom he believed to be supporters of the SPLA. Many people had already been killed in town by Abu Gurun and his accomplices. The police chief warned Harry and Marijke that their only chance of survival was to fight fire with fire. They should never show their fear, and be prepared to resist. They had to be armed at all times and always on the lookout for the major general's henchmen.

The police chief suggested to Harry that the two of them ride in his Land Rover to the police station, where the police had a makeshift shooting range. Harry agreed. At the range, the police chief produced a revolver and gave Harry a crash course on firearms operations and safety. He then asked Harry to aim in the direction of the target, located about 25 metres distant. Harry calmly levelled the gun and pumped the trigger five times. All the shots scored at the centre of the target. The police chief looked on in amazement. Who was this Dutch doctor who could shoot like a sniper?

Harry possessed unique professional skills of which we at UNICEF and our friends at MSF were unaware. In order to maintain its reputation as a civilian humanitarian organization, MSF prefers not to hire women or men with military experience. During his interview with MSF in Amsterdam, Harry had neglected to mention that he had been a member of the Dutch army's elite anti-terrorist squad. He was a highly skilled marksman and an expert in demolition. He knew how to incapacitate and kill attackers with his bare hands. When he was recruited by MSF to work in South Sudan, he had just finished an Alpine training exercise with the Swiss military involving a simulated hostage-taking.

Harry reasoned that as long as Eddie Folman could fly to Wau with his Cessna 404 loaded with supplies, he and Marijke were safe; if necessary, they could use the plane to evacuate to Khartoum. I had flown with Eddie on several trips in South Sudan and I admired his expertise at the controls. Eddie was cautious, and for good reason. Aviators around the world have a maxim: "There are old pilots, and there are bold pilots, but there are no old, bold pilots." It paid to be careful and not to push the envelope. In the south, thunderstorms were common, and it was rumored that they had the force to rip the wings off healthy airplanes. Many of the local air strips were marginal at the best of times and were flooded five months of the year. Although charter planes were clearly marked as civilian aircraft, there was always the worry that the SPLA—or the government—might shoot them down in error.

There was strong evidence to suggest that the SPLA possessed shoulder-launched anti-aircraft missiles that were effective up to an altitude of 3000 metres. In August, 1986, a Sudan Airways F-27 was shot down minutes after taking off from Malakal. Everyone on board was killed. A relief worker based in Malakal had boarded the flight, but had been thrown off the plane minutes before take-off by a government official who demanded her seat. Although it was the first civilian flight out of Malakal in several weeks, and although the relief worker had a valid boarding pass, she lacked the stamina to do battle with the hefty bureaucrat. Her courtesy to the government official saved her life.

Eddie Folman loved the south. Whenever he had to stay overnight in a town, he was always offered a bed in the house of the chief, and he never went to sleep hungry. He had tales about places along the course of the Nile that I had never heard of. He was on a first-name basis with all the chiefs in both SPLA- and government-controlled towns, and he was wise enough to stay above politics. Although he did not consider himself invulnerable, his distinctive yellow-and-white twin-engine plane was well known to both sides. It would serve no one's interests to bring him down.

Less than two weeks after we had left Marijke and Harry in Wau, Alastair Scott-Villiers of Band Aid arrived unannounced in my office. Usually upbeat and talkative, he was ashen-faced. He told me that Eddie had flown to Wau that morning with supplies for an aid agency. The plane was long overdue, and it was suspected that he had been shot down.

Cole Dodge wasn't in the office, so I tracked him down by walkie-talkie and told him there were problems with the Sasco plane. Dodge is a pilot himself and he understood the gist of my message. I told him I was driving with Alastair to the Sasco hangar. When Alastair and I arrived, a grim vigil was already under way. The plane had left Wau for Khartoum shortly before noon, with enough fuel in its tanks for three hours. It was now well after four o'clock. Unless Eddie had landed on some unknown strip, he had gone down without sending a radio message. We had to assume the worst.

UNICEF had a talented pilot of its own based in Khartoum named Daniel. He and Marie de la Soudière were my favorite people on the entire UNICEF team. Daniel and I had been on dozens of trips together with the UNICEF Twin Otter, a Canadian-built plane with a respectable cargo-carrying capacity and a phenomenally short take-off and landing performance. With its balloon tires, the UNICEF Twin Otter could land in the roughest terrain. I had seen Daniel bring the plane down on a cattle track and within the confines of a football field.

Daniel was at the Sasco hangar, crouching with his ear only a few inches away from the HF radio, but there was nothing but static on the Sasco frequency. When it grew dark, the ground crew pulled the refuelling and unloading equipment back from the position where Eddie would normally park the 404. They had been standing outside the hangar, searching the sky with their eyes, hoping against all odds that Eddie's radio had failed, that somehow he had managed to land, and that now he was homeward bound. Pilots develop a special relationship with their ground crew, particularly during wartime. Eddie depended on them to maintain the aircraft and properly fuel it. They had never disappointed him. After they closed the hangar doors, the crew joined us around the radio, but they didn't look up from their feet.

We never did find out who shot down Eddie's 404. The wreckage was eventually located 100 kilometres northeast from Wau. The army blamed the SPLA, and the SPLA blamed the army. The plane was hit approximately 15 minutes after take-off by a projectile—presumably a shoulder-launched anti-aircraft missile. Eddie had his own method for evading missiles—hugging the ground. I had flown with him for as long as one hour at an altitude of less than 100 metres, just trimming the tops of the date palms along the shores of the Nile. Eddie's theory was that with the aircraft flying so low, troops on the ground could not hear its approach and would not have enough time to arm, level, and fire their weapons. Despite his talent for evasive action, Eddie had been shot at in the past, and his plane had more than one bullet hole in the fuselage. He called them his war wounds.

There was a memorial service for Eddie and his co-pilot at Khartoum's cathedral on Nile Avenue. The church was filled with their friends and with representatives of the various aid agencies and embassies. Eddie's brother arrived from Holland for the occasion. Eddie wasn't a religious man, and the service would not have meant much to him, but he would have appreciated the wake that was held a few hours later in the Sasco hangar. In defiance of the Sudanese government, beer and other alcoholic beverages were served on the wings of a Sasco aircraft. A sound system had been rigged up and the speakers blared jazz music, Eddie's favorite diversion. We all drank heavily, but as soon as we finished one cooler of Heineken, another was hefted onto the counter, packed with ice, courtesy of Eddie's loyal friend Wally Boon, the co-ordinator of the EEC air-bridge.

The shooting down of Eddie's 404 had practical consequences for all the aid agencies working in South Sudan. If Eddie could be brought down, then everyone was vulnerable. Nobody was willing to fly to Wau anymore. It was too risky. Now Harry and Marijke were completely cut off.

The two MSF doctors sent us daily radio reports on the condition of the local population, and on supplies they urgently wanted flown in when conditions permitted. They were invariably chipper and optimistic about their own circumstances, no matter what hardships they had to endure. But suddenly the radio messages ceased, and they didn't respond to our calls. Cole and I stayed in close contact with the MSF office in Amsterdam and their colleagues in Paris. Two weeks passed before an exhausted Dinka arrived by bicycle at the Sudanese–Central African Republic border with a single envelope that he asked to be posted by the customs official. He had ridden his bike over 200 kilometres, hunting small animals for his subsistence.

The letter was addressed to Jacques de Milliano at MSF in Amsterdam and was from Marijke and Harry. Their radio had been confiscated by Major General Abu Gurun, and their situation was very serious. Although he did not go into specifics, Harry hinted that their lives were at risk. Abu Gurun was out of control and was hunting down members of the local Dinka population. No one was safe.

Occasionally, MSF in Khartoum received short radio messages transmitted by Harry, who we presumed was using the police chief's radio. One communication explained: "Every week more patients here in Wau. Malnutrition is increasing. We need more money for the rehabilitation of the pediatric ward. Send also food for personal use. We are OK. Harry and Marijke."

Marijke and Harry survived in Wau for nine months before Cole Dodge, with Daniel at the controls, flew into the besieged town on the Twin Otter to rescue them. They had timed their flight to arrive shortly after dawn, when neither the SPLA nor the government troops would be expecting an in-bound aircraft. Cole and Daniel commandeered a vehicle at the airport and drove to the hospital compound, where they found Harry in a dazed and disoriented state. Marijke had fared much better. She was anxious to board the plane and return to Khartoum, but Harry had to be persuaded to leave. He insisted that he still had work to do.

What happened in Wau over those nine months has never been fully written or reported. In his debriefings with me in Khartoum, Harry was restless and fearful. He insisted that my office door be closed throughout our discussions.

The episodes he described stayed with me for several years in the form of recurring nightmares—evil stories about the gassing of citizens and the execution of young children.

The truth is that the garrison commander, Abu Gurun, was a psychopathic killer. Over the years, he had earned the distinction of being labelled "the devil of the Sudanese armed forces," and army officers in Khartoum referred to him as "our Hitler." Soon after his arrival in Wau, Major General Gurun began to supply the Fertit militia with all the weapons they required to wage war against the Dinka, who for the most part were unarmed. Kidnapping and torture of civilians, including women and children, became commonplace. On June 20, 1987, 18 dead Dinka were found in a heap just outside Wau. The bodies had been mutilated; genitals had been severed, and several victims had been decapitated. One pregnant woman's abdomen had been sliced open from end to end.

As the SPLA moved closer to the town, executions of civilians were stepped up. On August 11, 1987, Major General Gurun, responding to an alleged SPLA missile attack on a military transport aircraft, personally supervised the round-up of Dinkas in Hillet Dinka, a settlement in the northeast quadrant of Wau. Anyone without proper identification was arrested. Hundreds of people were taken by truck to the river's edge and machine-gunned. Dinka children between the ages of six and 10 were forced to kill their parents with spears. Sixty-two community leaders were jammed inside an ammunition storeroom at the Grinti army barracks, then a rubber hose connected to the exhaust of an armored personnel carrier was used to gas them to death. Harry examined their bodies, and knew from the crimson color of their lips that they had died of carbon monoxide poisoning. During August and September, more than 1,000 Dinka were killed in and around Wau by the army and members of the Fertit militia. I had to stop Harry during his recounting of the incidents so I could move away from my desk, take a deep breath, and recompose myself.

What would I have done under the same circumstances, given the same pressures? Harry and Marijke first tried to lie low, avoiding trouble. Then Harry started going on patrols near the perimeter of the town, always armed. During one patrol, he came across the bodies of eight naked girls and boys who had been impaled on spears. He recognized one of the kids as the girl who delivered tea to his house every morning. On other occasions, he found mangled body parts and severed heads.

Harry and Marijke began to fear for their own lives. Harry responded in the manner of a soldier, forming his own militia made up exclusively of Dinka men living in Wau, many of whom had served in the Sudanese army. Dinka soldiers are much feared by Arabs on account of their size, raw courage, and brute strength. Whether armed with spears or rifles, they are fierce combatants. Harry's militia were disciplined and ready to kill at the slightest provocation. Most of them had already lost family members at the hands of the major general. They secured the area surrounding the hospital and acted as bodyguards for Harry and Marijke whenever they travelled in town. They had regular contact with their SPLA brothers, who moved freely within the bush just a few hundred metres from the hospital. The militia members cached weapons in secret locations in Wau, including the hospital itself.

After months of isolation and with no reason to believe that they would be rescued, Harry set in motion a plan to kill the major general. The turning point was an unexpected invitation to dinner at Abu Gurun's house. He was immediately suspicious, and packed a revolver in a shoulder holster for the occasion. He was startled when the major general's manservant uncovered a steaming plate of meat served with gravy. No meat had been available in Wau for several months; a few chickens had been kept alive for eggs, but all the goats and cattle were long dead. Harry was finishing the last morsels on his plate when he recognized a human joint. He excused himself from the dining room, stepped outside the house, leaned against a tree, and vomited. Then he returned to his host's table for dessert and coffee.

When he climbed into the UNICEF Landcruiser following the dinner, Harry's hands were shaking so violently that he found it difficult to start the engine. He drove to the hospital compound that night with only one goal in mind. Several weeks earlier, he had cared for a patient who was sick with cholera, a disease that results in profuse and unrelenting diarrhea. Unless treated with aggressive rehydration therapy, people usually die within a few days of being infected. For reasons he would not specify, Harry had kept some of the cholera culture alive in an incubator that he had set up in a makeshift laboratory. His scheme was devious but fail-safe: he would reciprocate Abu Gurun's hospitality by inviting him to dinner at the doctors' residence. The meal would require some careful preparation: the MSF doctor planned to inject the live cholera culture into the food just minutes before it was served. Harry had the pharmaceuticals necessary to treat cholera and would take a dose to protect himself against the effects of the disease. He expected that Abu Gurun, after having consumed the pasta dinner, would be writhing in pain before breakfast the next day. His death would be suitably miserable. But Cole Dodge's unexpected arrival changed everything.

Despite all that he had experienced, Harry was determined to return to Wau as soon as physically possible. Less than 12 hours after arriving in Khartoum, he tracked down Cole Dodge at his residence, and inquired when the Twin Otter could be readied to fly him to Wau with fresh supplies. He was concerned about all the people he had left behind. Many children in the hospital were sick and needed treatment or they would soon die. But Dodge's flight into Wau to extract Marijke and Harry was a one-off operation and a highly risky mission. Returning to the town was not an option. After Harry and Marijke spent three days debriefing in Khartoum, Médecins Sans Frontières in Amsterdam instructed them to board the next available plane to Holland.

Months later, after I had resettled in Canada, I received anxious phone calls from Harry, often in the middle of the night. He never introduced himself. "I have to go back," he would blurt out. Harry told me he was wasting precious time in Holland tending the runny noses of rosy-cheeked school children. He had dreamed up a scheme to use ultralight aircraft to deliver relief supplies to isolated communities throughout the south. Through his contacts in the Dutch military, he kept himself apprised of the latest developments in the region, including troop deployments by the government and the introduction of sophisticated weapons, donated by Iraq. The Sudanese government portrayed the war as a kind of jihad—the front lines of Islam—thereby winning support from countries such as Libya and Iraq in the form of vehicles, aircraft, bombs, tanks, flame-throwers, air-to-ground missiles, mortars, land mines, satellite imagery, and cash. The Dinka and the Nuer had only rifles, knives, and their hands to defend themselves.

Harry was incensed that little pressure had been put on the government in Khartoum to cease and desist from exterminating civilians in the south. Western nations talked tough about human-rights violations against unarmed southerners, but continued to provide Khartoum with the latest weaponry. Harry documented the return of slavery in the Sudan, whereby Fertit militia would capture women and children in southern villages, transport them to the north, and sell them as domestic servants and farm workers. Rumors had been circulating in Khartoum among the churches and relief agencies about the abduction of civilians in the south, but the incidents were dismissed as isolated cases. We now know that Harry's information was correct, that the Fertit, Tiposa, and Mundari tribes, backed by Khartoum, raided many villages under SPLA control and kidnapped thousands of women and children to work as slaves in the north.

During my 10 weeks in Juba, I missed my many friends among the street children of Khartoum—and apparently they missed me. Within hours of my return to the capital, a contingent of them gathered outside the Acropole Hotel. Sunday and Moj were there on their bikes ringing their bells; I could hear the commotion from my window. When I appeared at the hotel entrance, showered and freshly shaved, they let loose a football-style cheer. The kids had many questions for me: Why was I gone so long? Was there any food in Juba? Was it true I had met John Garang, the rebel commander? Sitting on the pavement outside the hotel, they briefed me on life in Khartoum as seen from their perspective. The police were stepping up the roundups of street children; a number of the most popular kids had been dragged away. There were rumors of police torturing kids in special detention centres located in the middle of the desert. Two 12-year-old boys had just returned from a six-day journey to Port Sudan on the Red Sea. They had heard that a new Hindi film was showing at a theatre there, and hitched rides with truck drivers for the 1,500 kilometre return trip. Now they could boast about a film no one else had seen. The most dramatic news concerned a 10-year-old Dinka child who appeared one day at Sabah. He was a tough kid—a real scrapper—and had gone to Sabah after a street fight to have some deep cuts disinfected. The nurses had insisted he have a shower first, and low and behold the Dinka boy turned out to be a Dinka girl in disguise. She was the first girl among their numbers. "She's cute!" Sunday exclaimed.

The war had come to Khartoum's back door in the form of 700,000 displaced southerners, who now were facing almost daily threats of eviction by the government authorities. Their situation defied all the rules and conventions governing the treatment of a civilian population by state authorities. The southerners had fled to Khartoum as a last resort, abandoning their huts and their cattle. Many of them had been chased off their own lands by raiding parties made up of Baggara militia, a traditional enemy of the Dinka and the Nuer whose support the government had strategically enlisted, along with that of the Mundari and the Tiposa. The militia members were given weapons and ammunition, and carte blanche to do the government's dirty work

I heard from the women and children who lived in the camps how the Arab militia terrorized them, burning their crops, stealing their remaining livestock, even ripping the few clothes they had off their bodies. Many of their husbands and oldest male children had been shot by the Baggara. They fled into the jungle, trekking for as long as 14 days to get to the railhead, then packing themselves onto the trains that took them north to the edge of the desert. The camps for the displaced were built on land nobody else wanted.

281

Hilla Shok, for example, had been constructed on top of a garbage dump. The southerners hoped to minimize their chances of being evicted, but weren't always successful. On December 9, 1987, the commissioner of Khartoum Province, Karam Mohammed Karam, announced that anyone without full identification papers would be expelled from the city.

Most residents of Khartoum were hostile toward the presence of so many southerners near their city. Angry mobs regularly burned down huts in squatter areas. The Sudanese press—largely owned or controlled by Islamic fundamentalists—fanned the flames of hysteria with headlines warning, "Squatters Intrude into Capital and Cause Danger" and "Increase of Displaced People Is Part of Plan to Promote Insecurity." Even educated northern Sudanese began to stockpile food, fuel, and weapons in anticipation of a showdown between the army and the displaced.

My assistant warehouse keeper, Martin Hakim, was a southerner who lived in one of Khartoum's largest shantytowns. One day while traveling to work he was accosted by police and dragged off a public bus, the only apparent reason being the color of his skin. He left a note on my desk dated September 20, 1987:

Dear Sir,

Very sorry that any misconvenience has been caused. I had a fight with a police officer in a plain cloth in a bus while coming on duty on Thursday and has been locked in and got bailed this morning by Mr. Albino from the League of Red Cross. I am going home to change my filthy clothes and hope to come in the office tomorrow because I need to comfort my family who might be very worried by now since they never knew of my whereabouts. If you have an urgent need of cash pls find the sum of 200,000 Sudanese pounds enclosed in envelope. I will bring you the other cash balance tomorrow.

Thanks and sorry for all this bad moment.

Yours sincerely,
Martin Hakim

Martin's encounter was typical of the daily harrassment experienced by southerners living in and around Khartoum. I was astonished by their self-restraint and dignity in the face of naked aggression. I know that in the same circumstances I would be unable to contain my rage.

The camps I visited were completely exposed to the elements, and all water had to be brought in by donkey carts. A nutritional survey by Sudan Aid had shown that 30 per cent of children in the shantytowns were malnourished. The huts the families lived in were constructed of refuse they had salvaged from the garbage dumps, including cardboard, pieces of wooden crates, sections of corrugated metal sheeting, bailing wire, and plastic bags. When a haboob moved through the area, many of the huts would be swept away with the storm. The displaced children had no opportunity for schooling, and only the most basic medical programs were under way. The Irish nurses of GOAL had established three medical clinics and an ambitious supplementary-feeding program, but they were being overwhelmed by the number of women and children who requested assistance.

I directed our warehouse staff to turn over whatever materials we had to the relief agencies working hands-on with the displaced. They were to be provided with everything they needed. We had enough stock to make an army quartermaster jealous: bails of used clothing donated by people in the United States and Canada, 44-gallon drums of vegetable oil from the EEC, over 30 MT of medical supplies, thousands of sachets of oral rehydration salts, cholera-buffer stock, Ringer's lactate solution, intravenous administration sets, bicycles, bicycle tires and inner tubes, motor bikes, diesel fuel and gasoline, enough spare parts for a fleet of 25 vehicles, radio receivers and antennae, compressors and related water-drilling equipment, MASH-style portable hospital tents, water pumps, and assorted airplane parts. At one point, Tristan confronted me with the accusation that "at this rate the warehouse will be empty within three weeks." I told him that was the whole idea.

At the same time, Cole Dodge began to lobby members of the diplomatic community based in Khartoum, requesting that they support UNICEF's position that the displaced were entitled to food and medical care, and had to be protected from harassment by the police and the military. Already the issue of the displaced southerners was a highly sensitive one, and some ambassadors wanted to steer clear of the subject. Canada was ably represented in the Sudan by Marc Perron, a career diplomat and Middle East specialist who had no interest in playing diplomatic games with government officials, who he suspected were corrupt and incompetent. Canada has no embassy in the Sudan, and Perron worked out of a single room at the Hilton Hotel during his visits to the country.

Most diplomats love the perks that come with their jobs. Even in developing nations, most ambassadors travel around the city in limousines or the latest model Mercedes-Benz with tinted windows. My own rule of thumb is, the poorer their country of origin, the larger the limousine they drive. Ambassador Perron broke all the rules. He didn't consider it appropriate for Canada's representative to be chauffeured around the streets of Khartoum in a $60,000 vehicle. Instead, he began each morning on the steps of the Hilton Hotel, bargaining with taxi-cab drivers for the best rate for the day, saving Canadian taxpayers a sizable amount of money. When he arrived at embassies and government offices for meetings, he had to produce his credentials before his yellow taxi was allowed on their premises.

I went with Perron to Hilla Shok and looked on while he moved through the camp, drinking tea with the displaced and meeting with the nurses from GOAL. He asked all the right questions and made no idle promises that could never be kept. Perron shared Dodge's outrage that the Sudanese government officials had prohibited UNICEF and the other agencies from drilling boreholes to provide safe drinking water for the displaced. He heard how the commissioner of Khartoum was threatening to send bulldozers into the camps to level them, and how the police were arbitrarily arresting young men, dragging them off to the police station for questioning.

After visiting the camps, Perron would return to the Hilton, have a quick shower, and then attend meetings with Sudanese government officials. With crocodile tears, they would tell him how concerned they were about the plight of the Nuer and Dinka people newly arrived in the city, and the generous provisions they were making to ensure the displaced's well-being. Perron would keep silent, letting them talk themselves into a corner, and then he would clobber them. He had witnessed the appalling living conditions of the displaced southerners. Why was the government of Sudan doing everything in its power to make their lives so miserable? Who had ordered in the bulldozers to destroy their dwellings? If countries such as the United Kingdom, France, and Germany had had women and men of Marc Perron's calibre as their designated representatives in the Sudan, the government would never have been allowed to run roughshod over the rights of its own citizens. Perron did his best, but Canada could achieve very little acting alone.

The phenomenon of children living rough in the dust and dirt of Khartoum attracted the interest of academics. Munir Ahmed, the director of Sabah, received numerous requests from researchers, both Sudanese and foreign, who wanted to interview the street children. As an enticement, the researchers often dangled the carrot that a good research paper about the street children might lead to funding from their university for programming that would benefit the kids. Munir usually acquiesced to the requests because he wanted to be co-operative and was legitimately interested in finding out more about the children who were in his care. The researchers poked and prodded the kids, interviewing them at length, even collecting blood and urine samples. After they had gathered all the information they needed, they disappeared. Few even had the courtesy to send Munir a copy of their final paper. In no case did their research ever lead to funds being provided by their institution for Sabah's programming.

I once sat in on an interview by a British sociologist who wanted the life story of a particular child. The kid she selected at random happened to be a good raconteur and was known by the street workers as having a vivid imagination. The researcher placed a bowl overflowing with chocolate-covered biscuits on the table only a few centimetres from the boy's face. The more he talked, the more biscuits he was fed. The boy was from Darfur, and described in great detail his journey across the desert. He had been captured at one point by the police and locked up in a jail cell. He needed to go to the bathroom, and he convinced the guard to let him out of the cell. On the way back from the bathroom, he bonked the guard over the head with a board, stole the keys, and escaped from the jail.

The researcher was writing furiously. This was excellent material for her paper. The story became more and more outrageous. The child had hitched a ride with Bedouin from El Fasher along the Forty Day Road into Egypt and had seen the pyramids. He described them vividly to the researcher. She should have been tipped off by his casual reference to the swimming pool he dove into at the base of the pyramids, and his climb to the top of the biggest pyramid to get a good view. It was so nice, he stayed there for the night.

The boy then befriended some rich French tourists in Cairo and flew with them back to Khartoum. The man was a millionaire, and offered to adopt the boy. All the boy had to do was be their tour guide in South Sudan. They hired a truck and a driver, and took the big highway down to Juba. Along the way, they stayed in luxurious hotels.

The story went on and on, and the bowl of cookies was almost empty now. The boy was doing fine until he described how a fire-breathing dragon came out of the jungle and attacked the truck that he was traveling in with the French family. The researcher took her first break from writing on her scribble pad. "Fire-breathing dragon?" she inquired. The boy hesitated, then nodded. South Sudan was full of fire-breathing dragons. The kid looked at me anxiously, trying to elicit my assistance. But with his wild story, he was venturing into no-man's land and was on his own. The researcher turned to me. She was irate. The boy was a little liar. He had wasted all her time. She suggested that he should be punished. I suggested that she should pack up her things and go back to her comfortable hotel. Maybe she should invite the kid along for a swim.

The interest shown by foreign academics in the plight of Khartoum's street children did little to protect the kids from the racism and violence they encountered. The story of Paul, a 10-year-old from the Upper Nile town of Ayod, is illustrative. He turned up at my office one morning in May, 1987, clutching his left arm. I could see blood streaming down between his fingers and onto my floor. He showed me a wound that was about eight centimetres long, and told me how it had happened.

Paul had been walking outside a shop looking at the goods on display. He may indeed have been thinking of stealing something, but he hadn't yet laid his hands on anything. Suddenly the shopkeeper lunged at him with a piece of glass and gouged his arm. The wound was deep and bled profusely. Usually the street children would tend to each other's wounds as best they could, but this injury was too serious, so Paul was forced to go to the Khartoum Teaching Hospital.

Paul was a destitute street child with only a pair of shorts to his name. The man behind the reception counter at the emergency room of the hospital told him to have a seat. Paul waited patiently in the hospital, noticing that nicely dressed middle-class children, usually accompanied by their mothers, were being led in and out of the treatment rooms although they had arrived long after he had. He was being overlooked or forgotten. He went back and asked the man at the reception desk when he would be able to see a doctor. The man barked at Paul to take his seat and be quiet, then complained that he was dripping blood onto the hospital waiting-room floor.

After more than three hours, Paul was escorted into a treatment room where a doctor cleaned and stitched the wound. Throughout the entire procedure, the man never talked to Paul. He used a large needle and drew the thread quickly through the wound. The whole procedure was accomplished in less than 10 minutes. After the doctor had finished, he demanded that Paul pay for the treatment. The boy was flabbergasted. The man could tell by his appearance that he was a Dinka child and obviously did not have a penny to his name. Paul explained that he was from the street and had no possessions. "That's too bad," the doctor said with a smile. He then proceeded to remove the stitches.

If I were Paul I would have kicked and yelled, attacked the doctor, and broken every remaining window in the hospital. But Paul obediently sat at the table while the doctor took out each stitch one by one, and then the boy ran off to the souk, where he was consoled by his friends in the street. The incident reinforced their well-founded fears of anyone wearing a uniform. It didn't matter whether the person was a policeman or a soldier or a surgeon. Intoxicated by power, these people often abused those over whom they exercised control. Street children, existing at the lowest level of the social strata, were easy victims, and hurting these kids heightened the officials' sense of invulnerability and omnipotence.

I loaded Paul into the Land Rover and we drove to the office of Dr. Nadia Toubia, one of the country's leading physicians and someone who, from the beginning, had been very concerned about the street children. We had an arrangement with Dr. Toubia that we could bring kids to her office after her regular visiting hours, so the children did not upset any of her middle-class patients. She treated dozens of street children and never requested any form of payment. Many of the Sudan's health professionals were women, but after the Islamists seized power in June, 1989, those who were not party members were fired from their jobs. The regime instructed them to return to their homes and tend to the needs of their husbands and children.

The reluctance of members of the diplomatic community to speak out against injustices they knew were taking place within their jurisdiction, and on their watch, reminded me of the saddest chapters in the history of the International Committee of the Red Cross, when the leaders of that worthy organization sat on their hands while the Nazis led prisoners in their care to their deaths. Humanitarian organizations will rarely go on the record criticizing the actions of another organization, but once again MSF is exceptional. In its first *Populations in Danger* report, MSF levelled criticism at the United Nations for its tacit support of repressive government activities in the Sudan: "Some UN agencies such as UNICEF practise a policy of tactful understanding toward the government, which raises many questions about their real aims." In a special report entitled "Life, Death and Aid," MSF accused the UN agencies in the Sudan of kow-towing to the government: "In the face of massive human rights violations and official determination to hamper relief efforts for the most

threatened populations, the UN simply stuck to its ordinary operating procedures in an extraordinary situation. It was consistently pusillanimous, and as
such became party to a huge and needless tragedy."

Alex de Waal, now of Africa Watch, is more specific in his criticism, citing
the ineptitude of the heads of UN agencies posted to Khartoum: "Sudan has
been unfortunate in having a succession of senior UN staff members who
appear to have lacked the insight, integrity, or courage required to use their
resources and leverage to maximum effect." De Waal refers to the parade of
UN representatives who refused to confront the Sudanese government, even
when demolition of the shantytowns around Khartoum began in earnest and
500,000 people were forced to take refuge at special locations, set aside for
them in the middle of the desert, that were completely unfit for human habitation. The regime interpreted the acquiescence of the donor community as tacit
approval for its practices, which then were ratcheted up.

Spurred on by National Islamic Front zealots, in 1991 the government of the
Sudan launched a clean-up operation in and around the capital. Members of the
National Islamic Front attacked the shantytowns, then sent in bulldozers to
destroy the huts that had been carefully built from scrap materials to offer some
protection from the sun and the wind. The government official in charge of the
relocation operation, Sharaf Eldin Ibrahim Bannaga, explained to members of the
diplomatic community that the clean-up was necessary for environmental reasons: "These were environmental hazards, and we are bound by international
treaties that call on us to enhance our environment." Even the Sudanese Red
Crescent, an organization with a distinguished track record of providing humanitarian assistance throughout the country—including those areas populated primarily by Christians—was hijacked by the Islamists. With the Red Crescent
under their control, the Islamists now exercised a virtual stranglehold over the
distribution of all emergency resources available to the Christian and animist residents of the shantytowns. Again, UN agencies for the most part remained silent.

One person who had no qualms about speaking out was Mother Teresa. In
her address to a prayer meeting in Khartoum, the capital of a country being
ripped apart by war and famine, the nun from Calcutta lectured the congregation about the suffering of displaced southerners. People in the audience began
to squirm, but she didn't let up. "Will you, today, accept a poor person into your
house, and into your life? That is what Jesus is asking of you." I liked this lady.
The church was crammed with the town's glitterati: ambassadors, UN agency
representatives, members of the chattering class. Mother Teresa clobbered them.

During her five-day stay in Khartoum, I showed Mother Teresa the projects for the street children, and explained how the kids were acquiring practical skills that would allow them to get a job. "But are you teaching them the Bible?" I responded that if we taught the street children anything from the New Testament, the authorities would shut down our projects. She was a tiny person, but she was forceful and strategic. Bob Geldof described her to me as an operator. She had the subtlety of a steamroller. She knew exactly what she wanted and how she was going to get it. Geldof told me that when they were in Addis Ababa together in December, 1984, they met with the head of the Relief and Rehabilitation Commission. On her way into town from the airport, the nun had spied two government buildings, apparently vacant. She waited until the cameras were rolling before she ambushed the commissioner. "If you really want to help your people then you'll give me the two buildings to use as orphanages." What could the poor guy do? Representatives of the world's media waited for his response.

Mother Teresa knew never to waste time with middle-level managers. While driving with Steffan de Mistura of the World Food Program, she suddenly announced that she had to speak to the president. "The president of what?" de Mistura asked. She meant the president of the United States. Steffan made a U-turn and headed for the American embassy on Nile Avenue. Within one hour, Mother Teresa was on the phone with her friend Ronald Reagan in Washington.

Mother Teresa was travelling to Nairobi, and her sisters asked me to travel with her. It was my regular Kenyan Airways flight departing Khartoum at 2:30 a.m. Despite the late hour, she stayed up the entire flight, praying most of the time. She said a special prayer as we watched the sun rise over Mount Kenya. Before we landed, the flight attendants passed out arrival cards for immigration and customs purposes, which required passengers to declare all funds they were bringing into the country. Mother Teresa gave me her passport and asked me to fill out all the forms for her. I asked her how much hard currency she had in her possession. She said she had none. I asked again. Surely she had some money in her purse, the only item she was travelling with. "My son," she replied, "I have not had a cent on my person in 30 years."

When we arrived in Nairobi, Mother Teresa waited until I had collected my bag at the arrivals area, and then we proceeded together through customs. Just before we parted, she took my hand. "The challenge for you, Peter," she said, "is to recognize in the face of the poorest child in the street the image of God." "Mother," I responded, "it is easier for me to recognize the image of

God in the face of the poorest child in the street than in the face of a rich corporate lawyer back in Toronto." She smiled, then replied, "But there's God there too." I knew that she was right. We walked through the sliding glass doors into the airport concourse. More than 80 nuns from her order, the Sisters of Charity, carried her off to their bus. Three days later, Mother Teresa was on board a twin-engine plane that crashed while attempting to take off from Dar es Salaam. Two passengers were killed. Mother Teresa walked away unscathed.

In May, 1987, Richard Reid, the regional director of UNICEF in Amman, requested that I prepare a report for the agency on children in difficult circumstances throughout the Middle East and North Africa. I welcomed the opportunity to escape Khartoum, and to learn about working and war-affected children in other countries. I travelled to Turkey, Morocco, Israel, and the occupied West Bank and Gaza. In Turkey, I examined the situation of working children in Istanbul. In Morocco, my research focused on the "petites bonnes," the girls and young women who worked as domestic servants for middle-class and wealthy Moroccan families. It was an accepted tradition in Morocco that families would take in a very young girl to carry out domestic chores, but research by two professors in Tunis and Rabat had demonstrated that a high proportion of these young people were subjected to prolonged and systemic physical and sexual abuse by the families they were working for.

I referred in my paper to reports of girls as young as 10 and 11 working 14 hours a day for a slave wage and never being allowed to go to school. They were punished for the most minor infractions, such as dirtying their clothes or not completing their tasks in a timely manner. Prepubescent girls were being sexually assaulted by 14-, 15-, and 16-year-old adolescent males, who were often encouraged by their father to "take" these girls as their first sexual partner. Although few Moroccans were willing to admit it, initiating a young male sexually with a petite bonne living in his own household had become an accepted practice within many wealthy Moroccan families.

In the Occupied West Bank and Gaza, I investigated the reports of violence inflicted on children and youth in detention. Palestinian youths—some of them as young as eight and nine years of age—were systematically rounded up by the Israeli occupying forces, searched, detained, interrogated, and imprisoned. They could be held for as long as four weeks without charge, after which many of them would be released for a few hours and then re-arrested. Palestinian kids were tough, and they had learned to fight at an early age. They certainly were not angels, but they were entitled to a measure of protection from arbitrary violence, particularly by the soldiers who were occupying their land.

My report was completely apolitical, and included rough estimates of the number of children in detention in the Occupied West Bank and Gaza. I noted high levels of anxiety among Palestinian girls and boys who had endured years of war and the extreme hardships imposed by the occupying authorities. Schools had been closed for months at a time. Some children had seen their fathers dragged away in the middle of the night by Israeli soldiers. Children were terrified by the roar of the Israeli fighter aircraft, which often flew so low over their towns that their houses would shake. They never knew whether the planes were going to drop a bomb. Some kids wet their pants every time they heard a fighter overhead.

The one thing the Israelis had been very successful at was engendering hatred in a new generation of Palestinians. The kids with whom I spoke despised Israel and everything it stood for. It was Israel that was denying their families the ability to work and preventing them from attending school. They all laid the blame for their scrambled childhoods at the feet of the Israeli leaders and the young soldiers who seemed to go out of their way to hurt them. Less than six months after I wrote my report, the Intifada was under way, and the same Palestinian youths I had interviewed were taking matters into their own hands. The Israelis countered with brute force; CNN's footage of heavily armed soldiers clubbing children who wielded only rocks and slings disturbed almost everyone who saw it. Even the U.S. Congress was moved to criticize Israel for its use of excessive force.

Back in Khartoum, my friends congratulated me on the success of SKI Courier and the technical training school, but in reality these initiatives helped to keep me balanced and focused. Every visit to the camps for the displaced southerners fatigued and depressed me. The demolition of squatter housing continued unabated. Dodge's attempt to win support among major donor countries for the cause of the displaced came up empty. Some UNICEF staff started to make life difficult for Dodge and his family in the Sudan. They wanted a representative who was more diplomatic—someone who was good at cocktail parties and less passionate about kids. People suspected that since Dodge was a practising Christian, he was overly sympathetic to southerners. They wanted UNICEF New York to recall him. I was closely linked to Dodge, and I knew that a number of my colleagues wanted me out too.

My emotional nadir came in July, 1987, when evidence surfaced of a mass execution of civilians in the town of Al Daein in South Darfur. Two respected Sudanese academics, Dr. Suleyman Ali Baldo and Dr. Ushari Ahmed Mahmud, released a comprehensive report on the events of March 27 and 28, 1987, during which more than 900 Dinka residents were hunted down and executed by members of the town's majority Arab Rizeigat population. At least 200 Dinkas were burned to death in railway boxcars while police officers looked on. People who escaped the boxcars, their clothing in flames, were shot or clubbed to death. Eye witnesses testified that some police officers joined in the attacks on the Dinka. Drs. Baldo and Mahmud also documented that slavery was flourishing in South Darfur. Hundreds of Dinka women and children had been captured by Rizeigat militia and sold as household servants, common laborers, and sex slaves to Arab families. The authors concluded that "the kidnapping of Dinka children, young girls, and women, their subsequent enslavement, their use in the Rizeigat's economy and other spheres of life, and their exchange for money—all these are facts."

The report created a sensation in Khartoum, but for the wrong reasons. Drs. Baldo and Mahmud were accused of being liars, traitors, and rumor-mongers. The Sudanese government refused to accept any responsibility for the massacre, dismissing it as a revenge killing. I knew Dr. Baldo from his involvement as an advisor to Sabah and our technical training school for street children. He was thoughtful and level-headed, and always willing to speak out on behalf of the kids. To see him pilloried by Islamic fundamentalists was a chilling experience. Extremists were on the march, and I feared that the Sudan's days as a fledgling democracy were numbered.

I visited SKI Courier every day I was in Khartoum and was proud to see that the business was growing. By May, 1987, we had signed up 28 clients and had 10 boys working full-time. Pio developed a proof-of-delivery system, books of receipts that addressees would sign and the boys would subsequently deliver to our clients to demonstrate that their mail was getting through. Unfortunately, all 50 receipt books were printed and distributed with a small typographical error in our slogan that appeared on the front cover: instead of "SKI Courier—Guaranteed Same Day Delivery," they read, "SKI Courier—Guaranteed Some Day Delivery."

Most kids at SKI Courier lasted three or four months before moving on to other employment. Some kids dropped out of the program, unable to turn up on time for work or unwilling to pedal a one-speed bicycle around town in 40-degree heat. But the experience gave every kid who joined an injection of self-confidence, and the idea that perhaps there was an alternative to living on the margins of society, begging for a few scraps of bread and living in constant fear of the state authorities. Anyone who looks at photographs of Sunday and Moj with their uniforms and bicycles can see the pride in their faces.

I was the guest of honor at the graduation of the first group of boys from our Technical Training School for Khartoum Street Children. It was not an elaborate ceremony, but for all the kids it marked a turning point in their lives. They had sewn new clothes themselves for the occasion, and their hair was neatly combed. The director of the school, Sulieman el Amin, made a short speech, congratulating the boys for their enterprise and their willingness to persevere with their studies. Yosef Sid Zaki Ahmed and his colleagues from the Khartoum business community were present on the podium to symbolically receive the boys one by one after they were handed their certificates. Adam, the kid who one year earlier had broken into my Land Rover with a bent nail, was standing in the front row. He had a job waiting for him at Iveco in Khartoum, the Fiat truck division. The ceremony ended with a singing of the national anthem, and with hugs and cheers. Tears welled in my eyes. If only we had been able to open dozens of such schools! How many kids could have benefited from such fine teachers and from a curriculum tailored to their particular circumstances?

As proud as I was at that moment, I worried about the kids. The certificate meant a lot to them, but how would potential employers react to this piece of paper? Nothing could disguise the fact that these children were dirt poor. The technical skills they had learned at the school would not protect them from racism, violence, or the war in the south. The government was making noises about launching an all-out offensive to capture the SPLA strongholds in Eastern Equatoria. New recruits would be required, most of whom would be young people from families who were poor and had no other options. Some of the kids from South Sudan who were attending the school had spoken to me openly about using their skills as blacksmiths and mechanics to aid the efforts of John Garang and the SPLA, and to wage war on the government in the north. It crossed my mind that these same children from towns and villages all over the Sudan who had become such close friends could easily end up on opposing sides of the conflict. What would they do if they met each other in battle?

After two years at the centre of a humanitarian catastrophe, my spirits were flagging. Most of my colleagues from my Darfur days had long since departed for jobs in Europe and North America. I rationalized that there were other cities in the world where my energies could be put to better use. Reluctantly, I began to plan my orderly withdrawal from the Sudan and my retreat to Canada. It wasn't easy. I could hand over my professional responsibilities at UNICEF, but not my friendships with the kids in the streets. I knew that for Khartoum's bravest children, no explanation for my departure would suffice.

I had another incentive for returning to Canada. I had grown impatient waiting for any of the non-government organizations based in Khartoum to take up the cause of street children, and to develop programming specifically for unaccompanied minors. Their agendas were already crowded, and it was obvious that street children were never going to get the attention and the resources they deserved. Street kids were a new phenomenon and they required new expertise. After our successes in Khartoum, why not set up a charity based in Canada that would put a priority on creative programming rather than on warehousing children in institutions? If SKI Courier worked in Khartoum, why wouldn't it work in Kingston, Jamaica, or Bogotá, Colombia?

Working with street children in Khartoum, we had learned to cope with every conceivable menace. From the little I had gleaned from kids' lives, however, it was apparent that the biggest threat to their well-being in the 1990s would not be war, famine, or police violence. A disease called AIDS was moving relentlessly through the barrios and the shantytowns of Africa, Asia, and Latin America, fuelled by poverty and ignorance. Members of the international development agencies, not known for their prescience, were slow to pick up on the fact that AIDS was becoming a disease of the urban, landless poor. Street children are sexually active at a very early age, as young as eight or nine. The nurses at the clinic housed within Sabah reported to me that sexually transmitted diseases were among the most common ailments they were treating. We did not have to be Louis Pasteur to understand that unless we took preventive action, millions of girls and boys living on the edges of mainstream society would be laid low by a disease they knew nothing about.

One day in Khartoum, I went to the U.S. embassy in search of a film I could show the kids at Sabah. The Americans had a dozen copies of an old black-and-white documentary film about the construction of the Hoover Dam and one ancient Tom and Jerry print. I signed out the cartoon, borrowed a 16-millimetre projector and a screen, and arranged for a late-afternoon showing—the only time of day when we might reasonably expect to have electricity. That day, there were about three dozen kids at Sabah, as unruly as ever. We were all packed into a back room of the compound. As soon as the cartoon began to roll, we had their rapt attention: the children were mesmerized by the images of cats chasing mice, and they rushed back to the streets that evening to tell their friends what they had seen. The next day, we had over 100 street children at the Sabah gates demanding to be shown Tom and Jerry.

An idea was born: why not produce an animated film designed to teach street children around the world about AIDS? Unlike most health promotion materials, the cartoon would be entertaining as well as informative—something the children would want to see over and over again. One of Canada's quiet success stories is the National Film Board of Canada, which is internationally acknowledged as a leader in animation. Their films win awards at festivals from Venice to Vancouver. Could the NFB animators be persuaded to create a film for the world's poorest kids?

I did not relish the prospect of saying good-bye to any of the street children of Khartoum. Over the previous 18 months, they had become my life. Street children divide the world in two: those who help them, and those who hurt them. I could leave my white Land Rover unlocked anywhere in the city, knowing the kids would watch over it. At the Technical Training School, we didn't have money to pay for a doctor, so I had assumed that role, cleaning wounds, dispensing Biltricide pills to treat bilharzia and chloroquine for malaria, and shampoo for kids with lice. I had bailed more than a few of the street children out of jail and had recruited lawyers to represent them. I had no idea how I was going to break the news that I was leaving and would not be coming back.

Pio was the kid I had the most hope for. He was highly intelligent, principled, and hard-working. The other street children craved the natural leadership skills he brought to the business. He set the tenor for the office, picked the kids up when they were down, searched for new clients, and solved disputes. More than anything else, the success of SKI Courier was due to his energy and commitment. As long as Pio remained involved, I had faith that SKI Courier would grow and prosper.

I was worried about Yassir. We had become very close, and he needed a great deal of emotional support. He was smaller than the other kids and often very introspective. Yassir had taken me to the movies, and I had once tried to teach him how to windsurf on the Blue Nile. The sail was much too big for him, and he had spent most of his time swimming in the river, but at such moments he was happiest. At times, my mind played games with me. I imagined that Yassir could go to school in Canada and attend the same kind of summer camp I had gone to for many years. But, of course, the whole idea was unworkable. His future lay here in the Sudan, alongside his own people.

I had a set routine when I encountered street children fighting. Like a hockey coach, I would break up the fight, have the kids dust themselves off, and then ask them to shake hands and make up. We would finish off with two words in Arabic: "Nehna achwan"—we are brothers. I would hold onto the two combatants and not let them go until I heard those words cross their lips.

My flight for Europe was departing Khartoum at three in the morning. About 30 of the street children had trekked to the airport to see me off. They stood outside the departure terminal in their rags, waiting to shake hands with me one by one. I had to fight to keep control of my emotions. Yassir was the last kid I had to say good-bye to. He already had big tears in his eyes. I was about to extend my hand to Yassir's when he reached out his hand to mine and asked me his favorite question: "Nehna achwan?" Are we brothers?

Yassir wanted me to promise that I would be back soon and that I would never forget him. I had to be straight with him: I told him that because of the war, my life had become impossible in the north and I could not afford to put other people at risk. I would not be returning to Khartoum for a long, long time. But I assured him that I would never forget him. I told Yassir that he and his friends in the street had made the word courage real for me, and that they were as noble as the sultan of Brunei. "Who's he?" asked Yassir. I explained that he was the richest man in the world and controlled a Pacific island kingdom. There was no poverty in Brunei; all the kids went to school and had good jobs when they graduated. "Do you think he needs a bike courier?" asked Yassir with a wink.

When I reached the door to the airport terminal, I turned and saw that the children had not moved. They looked at me through the gaps of the chain-link fence. We were about 10 metres apart. Sunday, Moj, Paul, his little brother Mango, Issam, Isaac—they were all there. Yassir was sobbing uncontrollably now, and Pio had his arm around his shoulders. I hesitated for a second, then moved quickly from the shadows into the harsh light of the old terminal building.

BRAVE IDEAS FOR
BRAVE CHILDREN

My experience in the Sudan haunted me years after I had resettled in Canada. I felt profoundly guilty for leaving the projects I had started and for abandoning the children who had become my friends. Adjusting to life in Toronto was painful, and I searched for outlets for my restlessness and frustration. I walked empty streets at all hours of the night with no particular destination in mind, and played billiards till dawn with strangers in the smoke-filled pool halls of Chinatown and Kensington Market. I felt closer to the homeless than to the privileged, and learned the names of the panhandlers who, fortified by cheap wine, camped out on the coldest winter days at the entrances of subway stations in the city's downtown core. There were no shantytowns in Toronto, but there were poverty and despair aplenty. I found aboriginal youth high on gasoline fumes drifting along trendy Queen Street West, clinging to lampposts for support. Only three blocks away, a $400-million stadium with a retractable roof was under construction. According to local sports writers, the members of Toronto's professional baseball team—all of them millionaires—needed a home befitting a world class city. It was a matter of personal dignity.

As hard as I tried, I couldn't get the Sudan off my mind. In city parks, I stared at African-Canadian children who, despite their winter clothes and hockey sticks, reminded me of the kids I had played soccer with in the refugee camps of Beida and Um Balla. Having lived through a famine, I was embarrassed by the abundance of riches in my own country. In grocery stores, I panicked when confronted with five brands of toothpaste to choose from. Advertisements for the latest fast-food crazes from Pizza Hut and Burger King turned my stomach. The Canadian economy in 1987 was booming, and many of my friends from Upper Canada College were caught up in the business of making quick money. They bought and sold condominiums two at a time; their children wore running shoes that the SKI Courier kids could only dream of. Four-wheel-drive Range Rovers with leather upholstery costing $60,000 were all the rage, although their owners had no intention of ever using them in off-road conditions. I kept thinking of all the charities in the Sudan that lacked even a one-speed bicycle for their work. I cheered on Mother Teresa when, during a rare visit to New York City, she confounded the VIPs and luminaries who had turned out to greet her with the blunt admonition that while India was poor, the spiritual poverty that characterized middle America was far worse. They hoped that she would end her sermon with a smile, but she was glum during her entire stay in New York and announced that she longed to return to Calcutta.

I was suffering from culture shock and I didn't even know it. I refused to accept the idea that Toronto was my new home and I would not be returning to the desert. I held off opening a Canadian bank account for 18 months and never got around to ordering a telephone for my first apartment. I was moody and irascible, and my friends handled me with kid gloves as if I were a scarred veteran of the Vietnam War. Lawyer Rosemary McCarney and businessperson Don Simpson, both of whom had extensive experience working in Africa, recognized the symptoms of someone in pain. They offered me a desk in a renovated warehouse on Front Street East, along with the use of a photocopier and a coffee machine. With their guidance, I drafted a business plan for Street Kids International and shopped it around Ottawa. But few people were interested in the concept of a new charity focusing on street children, and I received little encouragement. An expert at the Canadian International Development Agency, Alberto Palacios Hardy, told me I was wasting my time, and reminded me that the failure rate among new Canadian charities was higher than the equivalent statistic for small enterprises. Representatives of three major banks turned down my application for a business loan. My only physical assets were my Toshiba laptop computer, an American Express card I had acquired during my days with UNICEF, and a battered diesel Volkswagen Rabbit that refused to start when the temperature dropped below zero. Bewildered bankers stared at me when I told them that the purpose of the loan was to help hungry kids living overseas. "Where did you say you went to law school?" they asked with more than a hint of disbelief in their voices.

But ideas are powerful, and the premise behind Street Kids International—that poor kids needed something besides traditional charity—was compelling.

On board an Air Canada flight to Florida, the well-dressed businessman sitting next to me made the mistake of asking me what I did for a living. More than one hour later, he had signed on as the first member of the Street Kids International board of directors. His name was Frank O'Dea, and he was the co-founder of the Second Cup, a chain of 188 coffee shops across Canada. He was going to Florida to visit his friend Sean O'Sullivan, once the youngest person ever to sit in the Canadian Parliament and subsequently a respected and influential priest. It was Father Sean who had conceived a controversial billboard campaign to draw Canadian men to the priesthood that featured a larger-than-life image of Christ on the cross with the slogan "Dare to Be a Priest Like Me." Now Sean O'Sullivan was dying of cancer, and had only a few weeks to live. O'Sullivan was staying with his friends the Bassetts at the Players Club, a condominium on Longboat Key along the Gulf of Mexico, a few hundred metres from my parents' building. I arranged to meet O'Dea at The Colony, a local tennis resort; we sketched out a strategic plan for our organization on a paper tablecloth. With Frank O'Dea on side, I had an experienced entrepreneur who knew everything about franchising. He also had money. Upon our return to Toronto, he walked me into the main branch of the Royal Bank of Canada and co-signed a loan for $30,000.

Frank O'Dea's life parallelled that of a street child more than I could ever have imagined. Many street kids resort to substances such as glue and gasoline to ward off pain. Frank's drug of choice was alcohol, something he discovered at age 13. It almost killed him. During his adolescence, he destroyed 17 cars, and once drove through a tollbooth on a Quebec highway at 195 kilometres an hour with a cold beer sandwiched between his legs. O'Dea worked as a milkman and stole the money left by his customers. While employed as a machinist for the Canadian Pacific Railway, he pocketed copper wire, which he traded for booze. Eventually, he ended up homeless, begging for his next meal. He slept in flophouses and on park benches. With the help of supportive and forgiving friends, he turned his life around. Now, through Street Kids International, he hoped to extend a hand to kids in places as distant as Bombay and Rio de Janeiro.

Having access to Frank's line of credit made everything easier. I was able to buy a table and eight used chairs for $200 at Goodwill Industries—now I could host meetings. Knowing that appearances are important for both charities and businesses, I invested $2,500 in the design of a logo for Street Kids International. Too many humanitarian organizations had logos that were real clunkers (the most commonly employed images are hands, globes, and doves, or ghastly combinations thereof). I wanted something original that conveyed the strength and determination of the children I had befriended in the Sudan. Our artist, Paul Gilbert, seeking inspiration, asked me for one word that exemplified the goals of our new organization. What was the most important thing we were doing for the street children? I responded with six meandering paragraphs of prose. Gilbert pushed me for one word, and after much thought I faxed my choice to him in letters five centimetres high: FREEDOM. Three weeks later, a package arrived by courier with Gilbert's bill attached. Inside, I found a drawing of a child in flight, arms reaching for the sky. As a boy I had felt like Icarus, always dreaming that I could soar toward the sun. I had stationery and business cards printed on donated stock featuring Gilbert's artwork. People found the image arresting. We ordered baseball caps and T-shirts emblazoned with the flying child, which high school students snapped up. I took a bus to Ottawa and left one of my new business cards on the desk of the civil servant who had dared me to launch my own charity for street children.

I assembled a staff that emphasized youth and zeal over paper qualifications. All I could promise them was that life at Street Kids International would never be boring. "Fasten your seat belts," I advised. "It's going to be a wild ride." A 23-year-old named Brian Grant put his plans for law school on hold so he could sign on as a full-time volunteer. On his first day, I told him that I hoped we weren't the *Titanic*. Roisin Burke, a native of County Cork, Ireland, whom I knew from her days as a street worker in Khartoum, became our project officer; for six months, she went without a paycheque. Peter Budreo, the former business manager at the Taylor Statten camps, agreed to manage all the financial aspects of the charity. Before his arrival, I had relied on a shoebox accounting system. Christopher Lowry, my hardest-working board member, came on staff when it became clear that the animation project I envisioned to teach street children about AIDS was a complex and lengthy undertaking, requiring someone familiar with all aspects of filmmaking. Anyone who walked into the office off the street would be handed an assignment for the day. We soon had a regular cadre of high school students hanging around the office, helping with whatever needed to be done. When the United Nations invited me to attend a human rights conference in Vienna, we sent James Khamsi, a 14-year-old volunteer, in my place. He was the youngest delegate by 10 years. To appease his parents' concerns about safety, we arranged for James to be billeted at a convent.

We used our small size to our advantage, exploiting new opportunities and relying heavily on computer technology. My Toshiba laptop was my constant companion. It never caused me any problems, despite being dropped down a flight of stairs, exposed to sand storms, and left to bake in the desert sun on the edge of the El Geneina runway, causing the plastic casing to melt and change color. I bought a primitive modem and signed up as a customer with America On-Line during its first year of operation in Canada. We were lean but focused, and willing to compete with organizations 10 times our size. Conditions of employment at Street Kids International violated all union regulations. I had a sign posted above my desk that warned, "If you are not fired with enthusiasm, you will be fired with enthusiasm." When we were working against a deadline and expecting a late night, we brought sleeping bags and thermoses of coffee to the office. Attitude was important: we saw ourselves as a start-up business with a promising future rather than a cash-starved charity. Visitors to our shared warehouse space were more likely to find copies of the *Wall Street Journal* strewn about our desks than back issues of *Refugee* magazine.

From the beginning we took risks, investing heavily in research and project development. As my knowledge of street children was limited to the Sudan, it was essential that we identify the most experienced organizations working with unaccompanied minors in other parts of the world and learn lessons from them. We knew that the Brazilians were on the cutting edge of projects for street children, including girls and young women. The National Movement of Street Girls and Street Boys, based in São Paulo, had organized a high-profile international media blitz, putting pressure on the government of Brazil to take steps to stop the murder of street children by police and hit squads. In Colombo, Sri Lanka, Dale Chandler and Andreas Fuglesang had written a training manual for street workers that was better than anything else I had come across. In Thailand, a health activist named Mechai was combating sex tourism and using unconventional methods to promote the use of condoms to prevent the transmission of STDs. I had seen a photograph of Mechai standing between two elephants, one of which had the words "Think Big" painted on its side, and the other the words "Think Condom." I wanted the youthful staff of Street Kids International to apprentice with these visionaries rather than with functionaries in Geneva and New York.

We went on the road. In April, 1988, Roisin Burke, Brian Grant, and two colleagues carried out a three-month survey of 17 potential sites for SKI Courier around the world, including Kingston, Jamaica, and Asuncíon, Paraguay. We were looking for cities that combined a growing economy with a poor commu-nications infrastructure. Everywhere the research teams went, people were intrigued by the concept of a bicycle courier service run by kids whom society had condemned to the rubbish heap. Belo Horizonte in Brazil was ruled out because of its hilly topography and dangerous traffic. In Harare, Zimbabwe, our research team determined that the phones worked too well; fax machines would soon arrive on the scene, threatening any courier operation. My board of directors questioned the wisdom of investing $17,000—more than half our available funds—in a reconnaissance exercise, but the intelligence we accumulated and the contacts we made with local community-based organizations proved indispensable over the years. In some cities, the arrival of the Street Kids International personnel was featured in the local newspapers. On June 12, 1988, the *Times of Zambia* carried a story entitled "Experts ready to help street kids," which reported that "two field workers of Street Kids International, Mr. David Brown and Mr. Brian Grant, have said that children roaming in various parts of Africa could be organized into useful citizens." The next day, both of my employees were arrested on suspicion of being South African agents; only after lobbying by friends at the African National Congress headquarters in Lusaka were they sprung from their cells.

Among Canadian non-government organizations, Street Kids International was the new kid on the block, and we refused to play by the rules. Most Canadian charities working overseas lined up at the government trough, relying on the Canadian International Development Agency for up to 90 per cent of their funding. The conventional wisdom in 1987 was that without core funding from CIDA, Street Kids International had no chance of surviving. We'd go belly-up before we could afford our own photocopier. But CIDA had introduced a regulation requiring organizations to be operational for at least two years before they could apply for financial assistance. CIDA's intent was to encourage new agencies to broaden their base of support, and in our case the strategy worked. Instead of going to government, we forged alliances with unlikely partners.

The people at the Bank of Nova Scotia, impressed by our chutzpah and can-do attitude, introduced us to a number of their private banking clients known for having deep pockets. The Swiss-based Oak Foundation became a perennial donor to Street Kids International, funding several projects in their entirety. Placer Dome, a giant among international gold mining companies, sponsored a study we carried out for the government of Papua New Guinea on the phenomenon of violent youth gangs in that country. New York Fries organized a kite festival for us, with primary school children buying Street Kids International kites at stores in shopping malls across the country. Butterfield and Robinson, a Canadian company that had popularized exclusive bicycle trips in France and Italy for North American travellers, adopted us as their favorite charity. Philip Greey, a Toronto real estate mogul, provided us with free office space. We sponsored the premiere of the film *Salaam Bombay!* by Mira Nair, with all the proceeds going to a bicycle courier project we were setting up in Bangalore, India. Two students at the Toronto French School, Kathryn Khamsi and Justine MacIntosh, founded a youth group that organized fund-raising events on our behalf, including the construction of a 100-metre-long banana split.

Street Kids International didn't have the cash on hand to pay me anything more than a token salary, and I was forced to live hand-to-mouth. My life became a riches-to-rags story. I lost weight and blamed it on malaria. I sold the collection of coins I had started when I was eight years old to pay my heating bill. I frequented the cheapest Vietnamese restaurants on Spadina Avenue, where the food was more nutritious and half the cost of a McDonald's meal. Our office was in the heart of Toronto's theatre district, but over the course of seven years I never had the money available to see a single show. When Stanford University held a swish reception for Canadian alumni featuring Secretary of State George Shultz and Prime Minister Brian Mulroney at the King Edward Hotel, only two blocks from our premises, friends from college days who had expected me to attend were surprised when I didn't appear. Too proud to let them know that I couldn't afford the $80 cost for the evening, I instead concocted the excuse that I was sick.

As Street Kids International became better known, I started speaking at fund-raising dinners and had to be properly dressed. I got by with one multi-purpose blue sports jacket, two Save the Children ties, and one pair of Rockport leather shoes. I was forced to turn down invitations to dinners and weddings that required a suit; at funerals, I always kept my topcoat on. When I turned up at the offices of the lawyers who served on our board of directors, receptionists often mistook me for a courier. Eleanor Johnson was the only Street Kids International board member who consistently voted to increase my salary, but with little success. The board assumed that since my parents were well off, I would be looked after; in reality, they had stopped supporting me the day I graduated from law school.

Out of desperation, I had financed Street Kids International during its first year of life with my American Express card, and my debts had piled up. I approached American Express officials with the novel idea that they consider my outstanding balance of $19,500 as a contribution to the cause of helping poor children, but they weren't interested. I informed them that I had every intention of settling my bill—when my financial situation permitted. American Express countered with a salvo of angry letters from lawyers threatening to prosecute me. They wanted to put Street Kids International out of business. Their counsel in Toronto showed no mercy and reinforced my decision not to take up the practice of law. In addition, I owed back taxes to Revenue Canada, whose employees, in comparison, were flexible and understanding about my predicament, proposing a long-term repayment plan. Two loyal friends came to my aid: Jim Hayhurst, an advertising executive and founder of the Hayhurst Career Centre, and Bill Graham, a professor of law at the University of Toronto. Both became accustomed to my arriving unannounced at their offices looking for a cheque to pay for my apartment and groceries. Over the ensuing years, they contributed many thousands of dollars to keep me solvent and keep Street Kids International on its feet.

Studies published by the World Health Organization in Geneva in 1987 showed that AIDS was gaining a foothold in some of the largest cities of the developing world, including in Asia. I felt enormous pressure to begin research in earnest for our proposed cartoon to teach poor urban girls and boys about the disease. Too many health promotion films featured white-smocked doctors wearing stethoscopes around their necks; we wanted a character who street children from Argentina to Zimbabwe would want to emulate. In late 1987, I carried out an informal consultation with groups working with street children in five cities around the world to determine who were the most popular heroes among the kids they worked with. The results surprised me: number one on their list was Rambo, as portrayed by Sylvester Stallone. Number two was President Ronald Reagan. Their third choice was Bruce Lee, whose karate movies are imitated with equal passion by kids on the streets of Bangkok, Lagos, and Rio de Janeiro. Children growing up in the shantytowns saw their family members and friends cheated, lied to, and beaten by local authorities. They learned the value of weapons, and the need to fight back when no one else will provide protection. Through television and movies, they saw crime and violence as urban adventure, and thugs and murderers as the new heroes.

We chose Bruce Lee as the model for our hero, and with the help of Peter Herndorff, a Canadian publisher and media executive, joined forces with the National Film Board of Canada, home to some of the world's most acclaimed animators. Two of the NFB's brightest stars, Academy Award–winner Derek Lamb and Danish-born animator Kaj Pindal, the creators of *I Know an Old*

Woman Who Swallowed a Fly, agreed to devote two years of their lives to the project. They were a big catch for a little organization like Street Kids International. Derek had worked as a producer, writer, and music composer for the Children's Television Workshop in New York City (the home of *Sesame Street*), designed title sequences for PBS's *Mystery! Theatre,* and served as visiting lecturer in animated film at Harvard University. In 1979, in response to a challenge issued by UNICEF to produce a cartoon in honor of the International Year of the Child, Derek and animator Eugene Fedorenko scripted a parable about an abandoned baby who is bounced from house to house by unsympathetic adults. The cartoon, entitled *Every Child,* was both clever and disturbing. To get around the problem of language, Derek commissioned Quebec mime artists Les Mimes Electriques to invent their own for the adult characters. *Every Child* earned its creators 12 awards, including an Oscar.

Kaj Pindal had been head-hunted by the National Film Board in the 1950s to work on a technical film depicting the workings of jet engines. In 1966, Kaj and NFB colleague Les Drew gained recognition for an animated film entitled *What on Earth!* that examined our love affair with the automobile. Many years ahead of its time, *What on Earth!* asked the question, "If Martians landed on earth tomorrow, wouldn't they think that cars and not humans controlled the world?" Kaj had been inspired by a visit to smoggy Los Angeles and the threat of a highway being built down the centre of his hometown. "You can do whatever you want with other cities, but leave my Copenhagen alone!" Kaj declared. When *What on Earth!* was shown on Danish television, it sparked a national debate, and the proposed highway was never built. The experience convinced Kaj that the best animation did more than make people laugh: it made people think.

With *Karate Kids,* our first cartoon for poor children, the National Film Board of Canada had come full circle. In the 1940s one of the NFB's legendary filmmakers, Norman McLaren, taught simple animation techniques to healthcare workers in China; now two of McLaren's protégés were taking their sketch pads to the streets of the developing world. I travelled with Derek and Kaj to Mexico City and Guatemala City in January, 1988, so that both artists could spend two weeks living and drawing among the street children, learning from the kids which characters and story line would be the most appealing. Neither Kaj nor Derek had any experience with street children, and they were apprehensive about their first encounter in Mexico City's Garibaldi Square. I told them to leave their wallets and watches in the hotel safe. Within minutes, the kids had won them over. We saw girls and boys painted up as clowns juggling amidst the traffic at a busy intersection; before the light turned green, they had collected handfuls of coins for their next meal.

A new world opened up to Derek and Kaj. We visited the shantytowns and the grimy police holding cells, and sought shelter from the rain under the highway overpasses where the kids lived and slept. In a Dickensian reformatory, we watched as children laughed along with the characters of a Laurel and Hardy–style slapstick comedy, their scarred faces illuminated by the blue glow from the television screen. "How can there be any joy in such a sad place?" Derek asked. At a simple restaurant in the city's historic quarter, we met Pablo, a remarkable 11-year-old boy with the maturity and composure of a man twice his age. He held down two part-time jobs to feed and clothe his younger sister, so he had no time to go to school. Despite his poverty, he was optimistic about his future. The boy strongly resembled the child star of François Truffaut's *Four Hundred Blows*. Derek commented that if the great French director had been with us, he would have dusted Pablo off to star in a new feature film.

In Guatemala City, we encountered the children who lived and worked in the region's largest garbage dump, competing with vultures for scraps of food. We watched scruffy kids emerge from cardboard boxes that doubled as their homes, and met young girls who for a few coins performed sexual favors for Guatemalan businessmen and military officers. Our guide was the 26-year-old American street worker Mark Connolly, who, with a bulging first-aid kit slung over his left shoulder, ministered to the kids' basic medical needs, from stomach ailments to STDs. In a country where human-rights workers were routinely tortured and executed by military and civilian police, Mark put his life on the line every time he appeared in public. He smiled in the face of danger, as if to say to the authorities, "Come and get me." The kids would perk up as soon as they saw Mark coming, then embrace him passionately. Dirty tears ran down their cheeks as they recounted their latest run-in with the police. When their friends disappeared, they always assumed the worst. Derek and Kaj provided a rare opportunity for the kids to laugh. The children were fascinated by Kaj's sketches, and wherever he went he attracted a crowd. On command, Kaj produced dozens of drawings of Mickey Mouse and Daffy Duck, then caricatures of the street kids. They were astonished to see themselves come alive on his sketch pad.

In the hill town of Antigua, Mark introduced us to his friend Everelda, a beautiful 12-year-old Indian girl who sewed the colorful friendship bracelets so popular among school children in Europe and North America. Her customers were the foreigners enrolled at Antigua's famous Spanish language schools.

Everelda was an astute businessperson, and could carry out currency transactions in four languages without resorting to a dictionary or a pocket calculator. We drove away with the sweet voices of a choir of Indian children in our ears, calling us deeper into the forest. It sounded like angel music. We didn't want to leave Guatemala, despite all its problems. When we returned to North America and I dropped Derek off in Boston, he told me that during our 14 days on the road, he had lived more intensely than he had throughout his years on faculty at Harvard University. Amidst the squalor of the barrios, we had witnessed acts of kindness and valor that often left us speechless. Without a word, hungry kids we handed oranges to would carefully break the fruit into pieces to share with their friends. Children set aside a portion of their meagre daily earnings to buy milk for stray cats they had adopted. The kids—most of them Indians—were barred from school because of their absolute poverty, but their minds were sharp. In their ability to tell stories and elicit emotion, the street children of Mexico and Guatemala were light years ahead of Derek's Harvard undergraduates. "If only my film students had half the creative energy," he lamented.

Based on this research, Derek and Kaj created a 12-minute prototype film at the National Film Board studios in Toronto under the leadership of our producer, Michael Scott. The idea was to package a take-back-to-the-streets AIDS health message within a dramatic adventure story that the kids would find irresistible. The test film was made up of 350 hand-drawn images transferred to video—a storyboard in electronic form. The picture sequence was accompanied by a simple script in five languages. At this point, the prototype had no sound effects, music, or moving pictures. Derek Lamb, Michael Scott, and I pre-tested *Karate Kids* in Nairobi, Colombo, Manila, Rio de Janeiro, New York City, and Toronto. We showed the test film in vegetable markets, out of the backs of trucks, and even in a Manila prison where I found three boys under the age of 12 incarcerated. After one week of frustrating negotiations with lawyers and government officials, I met behind closed doors with the prison warden and asked what it would take to set the children free. He asked for $60; with three US$20 bills I bought them out of jail. In Rio de Janeiro we spoke to pre-teen street girls who were regularly molested by the police. "We don't need condoms—we need knives," one girl remarked.

In the Philippines we met with mothers attempting to pry their 10-year-old girls and boys from the talons of pimps and procurers. In the 1980s a virtual industry based on the sexual exploitation of children sprang up in the Philippine town of Pagsanjan, located at the site of an often-photographed waterfall. It was just another sleepy Filipino community until an American film crew arrived in 1978 to film combat scenes for the Francis Ford Coppola film *Apocalypse Now*. Pagsanjan never recovered from the influx of wealthy foreigners, some of whom took advantage of the naiveté and natural affection of the local children. Over the ensuing years Pagsanjan was transformed into a mecca for pedophiles. Local children became fluent in French and German, and arrived at school with their pockets stuffed with foreign currency. They sported fancy clothes from Manila, and Nike running shoes costing one hundred and fifty dollars, equivalent to four months' wages for their parents. Some of their "foreign friends" built houses for the children and their parents. When mothers in Pagsanjan, outraged by the wholesale abuse of their young children, began to campaign against the pedophiles, they were shouted down by owners of local businesses hungry for foreign currency.

In Hell's Kitchen, the back door to New York City's Times Square, Trudee Able-Peterson showed our test cartoon at the centre for street children that she had founded. Many of her kids were involved in the sex trade, including girls and boys just on the edge of puberty who were picked up by their clients in the video arcades and movie theatres only two blocks distant. Trudee wanted her kids to have the best. The centre was equipped with comfortable furniture. There was a room where the children could watch television, and a washer and dryer for their clothes. We learned from Trudee and her young friends about poverty and abuse in America, about violence, drugs, and racism. In New York City in 1988, 55 per cent of black youths were unemployed. Young children were left unsupervised for extended periods of time. Approximately 85 per cent of black inner-city children grew up in single-parent homes. Today, the statistics are worse. Women are over-burdened with the combined responsibilities of providing for the family, managing the household, and caring for the children. Adam Walinsky, a lawyer writing in the *New York Times*, has described their predicament: "As they are the mothers of the child victims, they are also the mothers of the gang predators. They have given birth to and raised the violent ones, but they do not know them."

The 850 street children in six countries who watched our test cartoon were our toughest critics: although they enjoyed the story and identified with the characters, they had many practical suggestions for us. They wanted the female characters to be stronger, and the kids in the film to be barefoot, because many street children don't own shoes. They were frustrated that the villain in our test film, who infected a child with AIDS, did not die. They wanted more information about condoms. Derek and Kaj returned to the National Film Board studios in Toronto almost overwhelmed by the feedback they had received. Some officials had been very pessimistic about the prospects of the cartoon ever being seen by street children. In the Philippines, we were told that any depiction of condoms would result in the film's being blacklisted.

Animation is expensive. *Karate Kids,* including distribution costs, was budgeted at $1.5 million. Christopher Lowry knew the project was too big to be funded entirely in Canada. Why not approach European donors? Like two travelling salesmen, Christopher and I visited Stockholm, Copenhagen, London, Brussels, Geneva, and Oslo armed with our menagerie of cartoon characters so ingeniously designed by Kaj Pindal. The European development agencies, such as the Swedish International Development Agency and NORAD in Oslo, have always been at the forefront of the children's rights movement, and they fell in love with the karate kids: Pedro, Maria, and Karate Hero. Subsequently, SIDA, NORAD, and the Foreign Ministry of the Netherlands became our most reliable funding partners. They were not concerned that we worked out of a temporary office and that most of our staff were volunteers. When I asked the people at NORAD in Oslo why they were willing to contribute hundreds of thousands of dollars to the *Karate Kids* project, their answer was unequivocal: "Because your work is the best."

The advent of the VCR guaranteed that *Karate Kids* would reach a massive audience. Whereas film projectors are awkward and tend to be confined to institutions, VCRs are portable and easy to use. Although many community-based projects in the developing world do not own VCRs, they can usually borrow or rent one when necessary. While visiting Rio de Janeiro, I asked Anna Filgueiras, the director of one of that city's best-known projects for street children, if she would have trouble locating a videocassette recorder. She smiled before answering. "I have over a thousand street children in this project. If I tell them that we need a VCR to watch a cartoon, don't worry. The kids will find one somewhere."

After more than two years and 23,000 hand-drawn and colored images, *Karate Kids* was premiered in Yaoundé, Cameroon, in October, 1989, to resounding applause. Our project funders included the Canadian International Development Agency and the World Health Organization Global Program on AIDS. Thanks to the tireless efforts of Christopher Lowry, the cartoon, accompanied by a handbook and pocket-sized comic book, achieved an international profile we never dreamed of in 1987. Today, over 10,000 copies of the film are in distribution in 25 languages and over 100 countries, making *Karate Kids* the single most ambitious intervention on behalf of street children anywhere in the world. In the Copperbelt province of Zambia, Dr. Chandra Mouli used the *Karate Kids* cartoon as part of a week-long life-skills course for out-of-school youth. During a four-month period in 1990, he estimated that he showed the cartoon at least 60 times to children and teenagers. Hussein Ahmed, a paramedic in Dar es Salaam, Tanzania, wrote us to report, "Really it works well with our program. So far we have not missed a day without showing *Karate Kids* to the school, clubs, and private meetings." Dr. Jay Wortman used the *Karate Kids* materials extensively with aboriginal communities in northern British Columbia. In health workshops with these communities Dr. Wortman found that "the adults and elders are as fascinated by the video as the kids."

The worldwide success of *Karate Kids* resulted in Street Kids International being awarded the Peter F. Drucker Award for Non-Profit Innovation. As part of the award I had the honor of meeting Peter Drucker at the Mayflower Hotel in Washington, D.C. Drucker, well into his seventies, was still vital and energetic. He told me that, in the 1970s, he had correctly predicted the year in which the number of employees at the U.S. Department of Agriculture would exceed the total number of farmers in America. He described it as "the triumph of the bean counters over the bean planters." He reminded me that business people in North America and around the world had much to learn from my friends the street children. It was the great industrial designer Nicholas Hayek who once noted that the most successful chief executive officer never loses the awe of a seven-year-old child.

We parlayed the success of our *Karate Kids* cartoon into new opportunities for the organization. In September, 1990, I recruited Roisin Burke, who had apprenticed with Robert Richard in Khartoum, to work alongside the staff of the Red Cross in Lusaka, Zambia, to launch that country's first ever program for street girls and boys. I issued her a one-way plane ticket to Lusaka and a cheque for $25,000. With our technical assistance and financial support, the Zambian Red Cross built a non-residential emergency centre for street children where the kids would not be harassed by police—a place they could call their own. The program focused on providing basic health care and recreation facilities for both girls and boys, and included an innovative legal-aid component that supported the basic rights of poor children. The Garden Centre, as it was christened, was soon overrun with children from Lusaka's burgeoning shantytowns. Roisin brokered our modest investment into a $250,000 program, squeezing donations of cash and goods in kind out of local embassies and various international development organizations. Roisin is a strict no-nonsense type. For her own transport needs, with $300 she purchased a car constructed primarily of plastic fastened to a Volkswagen chassis. Her crowd in Lusaka included colleagues at the Zambian Red Cross, members of the local Wild Geese Society, a gang of badly behaved Frenchmen who worked for Médecins Sans Frontières, and a Catholic priest named Father Jude who was a former Irish national judo champion.

Street children like to make money, and many are natural entrepreneurs. A common problem of street children the world over is that they lack capital and a place to store the tools of their trade. David Wilson, who had served as the load master for Ethiopia Airlift, signed up with Street Kids International immediately upon graduating from King's College in Halifax. We shipped him off with Brian Grant to help set up our second SKI Courier project in Bangalore, India. Wilson's next posting was in the Dominican Republic, where he worked with the YMCA in Santo Domingo to help them begin a small business co-operative for the hundreds of street children who made a living through shining shoes. Traditionally, the kids worked through a middleman, renting a shoeshine box with brushes and polish at a cost of up to half their daily wages. The kids complained that while they slept, their money was often stolen from their pockets. They had no incentive to save money, so they often spent what they earned on glue for sniffing. We set up a savings program for the children, and a credit scheme whereby they could pay for their own shoeshine kit over a period of weeks. The kids attended classes in basic literacy and small business skills.

Our energy and staying power were our biggest assets. "Brave ideas for brave children" became our motto. I saved up my earnings for a suit, and used all my rhetorical skills to win over gray-haired accountants who controlled the purse strings of the big agencies. We were the Trojan horse of humanitarian organizations. Often our targets were blue chip institutions such as the Pan-American Health Organization and the Robert Wood Johnson Foundation. We went to Rotary International and asked it to bankroll the First Bank for Bombay Street Children, so kids could go into business for themselves. My board member Dr. Rebecca Cooke introduced Christopher Lowry and me to Dr. Malcolm Potts, the president of Family Health International, a giant in reproductive health services around the world. Dr. Potts helped us deal with the delicate issue of promoting condoms without offending local authorities.

In all our projects, a key factor for success was choosing an experienced and flexible local community-based partner. We wanted organizations that had a real presence in the streets, worked with girls as well as boys, were run by nationals rather than foreigners, and were willing to embrace a progressive agenda that included advocacy, reproductive health issues, and the promotion of entrepreneurial skills. For too many years, organizations with a heavy adult-centred approach have dominated the field of street children and working children. People are uncomfortable with the notion of kids living totally independent of families. It's all about power: adults like to control children. The entire issue of adolescent sexuality bothered adults primarily because kids were making decisions about their bodies by themselves. Many of the larger children's charities were run by people who hadn't had a new idea in 20 years—burned-out cynics who long ago should have been put out to pasture. Poor children deserve adults in their lives who are at least as brave as they are. Why do they so often end up with these losers?

Nobody in the child-serving field had seen anything like the *Karate Kids* cartoon before. Most health education films were dull 1950s-style presentations featuring a white doctor standing in front of a chalkboard lecturing his audience on the do's and don'ts of good health. After five minutes, most kids fell asleep. Our 22-minute cartoon opens with a chase scene that leads to a policeman being tossed into a chicken coop. From their experiences in Mexico and Guatemala, Derek and Kaj knew that making fun of a policeman would get the kids' attention. Children watching the test film began to seethe when the image of the policeman flashed on the screen, and they cheered when he ended up in the chicken coop. But this bit of harmless fun got us into hot water with local authorities in several countries when the completed cartoon was distributed.

AIDS is an issue of social justice, not just health and science. At Street Kids International, we believed that poor children had the right to information about AIDS that was specific, detailed, consistent, reliable, and practical. They needed to know how the disease was transmitted and how they could protect themselves. We argued that no institution, government, or church had the right to keep such information from destitute girls and boys. Our biggest problem was the ultra-conservative gate-keepers at ministries of health and within the ranks of the international development organizations. By their reactions to the cartoon, we could gauge whether they had any direct contact with street children. If they found the language or imagery too explicit, we knew they were desk-bound bureaucrats. Some officials objected to almost every aspect of the cartoon, from its comical portrayal of the policeman to the depiction of sexual relations taking place outside of marriage. The star of the cartoon, a martial arts expert named Karate Hero, cohabits with his girlfriend; some Catholic organizations in the Philippines and Kenya found this highly objectionable. A street child in the film steals a necklace and a wallet, and is able to escape punishment. Some agencies thought that he should have to pay for his crime. We listened to all our critics, but we did not diverge from our path. *Karate Kids* was a cartoon for the front lines, and it had to reflect the reality of the streets. Those adults who knew what the kids were up against understood the need for frankness and clarity.

The UN Centre for Criminal Justice in Vienna commissioned Street Kids International to investigate the involvement of street children in criminal activity. When I began my research, I was aware that in many countries poor girls and boys are recruited by adults to steal, run drugs, and participate in prostitution. Who was behind the kids? I corresponded with organizations in seven countries working directly with street children and put the question to them. My report for the UN, entitled *The Myth of Fagin*, identified the same group of adults in each country who played a key role in the shaping, training, and corruption of vulnerable youth: the police. From Buenos Aires, Argentina, to Saint Petersburg, Russia, police officers were the ones who conscripted hungry kids to transport and sell narcotics, pose naked for pornographers, and extort money from tourists. If kids refused to participate they were often beaten or arrested. In Bombay I heard about a boy at the Dom Bosco home for street children who had spent three months building a wooden cart with which to sell fruit in the market. During his second day on the job a policeman asked for a bribe, which the boy refused to pay. The cop smashed the fruit cart into tiny pieces in front of the boy's eyes. The street child was inconsolable, abandoned the Dom Bosco project, and was lost to Bombay's underworld.

Tim Bond, a child rights activist with Terre des Hommes, exposed the involvement of police in Thailand's child sex trade. In return for kickbacks, police routinely turned a blind eye to brothel owners featuring prepubescent girls and boys. In some cases, the brothels were owned outright by senior police officials. Sex tourism had become one of Thailand's major sources of foreign currency. The airlines, travel agencies, and hotels all benefited. The government was only upset because it was unable to tax the windfall revenues. When an American television network produced a hard-hitting documentary about child prostitution in Thailand, local child-welfare authorities expected that the resulting hullabaloo would force the police to close the biggest brothels. But the documentary had the opposite effect, acting as a public service announcement for the local sex trade. Over the ensuing months, the number of Americans arriving in Thailand looking for 12-year-old sex partners tripled.

In 1991, at the conclusion of the Gulf War, I visited Iraq as a member of a Canadian delegation assessing the impact of the war on the civilian population. As Baghdad airport had been heavily damaged in air attacks, we traveled into Iraq overland from Jordan, an 11-hour journey across the desert on a European-standard highway. Our hotel in Baghdad, the Al Rasheid, had a hole the size of a truck on its side from an American cruise missile, yet the telephones and television still functioned. The in-house entertainment system advertised John Wayne westerns and Bugs Bunny cartoons. The Iraqi dinar had been in a free-fall since the commencement of hostilities, and my room—one of the best in the city—cost $20 per night.

I went to Iraq with an open mind, but after many meetings and conversations with health workers, teachers, students, and the elderly I became convinced that the UN sanctions were not achieving their purported goal of forcing Saddam Hussein to comply with the cease-fire conditions that he had entered into, including handing over weapons of mass destruction. If anything the everyday hardships experienced by Iraqis on account of the UN sanctions only hardened their resolve to defy the United States. Their hatred of George Bush was palpable; we saw children carrying banners that read in English "President Bush—Murderer of Children." In hospitals I witnessed mothers begging for aspirin for their sick children. I spoke with an 11-year-old diabetic; her mother had only one disposable syringe which she had been reusing for three months. To sterilize her daughter's arm she splashed on men's cologne. While the poor and the middle class were hardest hit by the sanctions, the rich and well-connected—including business people, politicians and military officers—were profiting from the prohibition-style economy brought on by the UN sanctions. Artificial shortages of everyday commodities such as sugar, vegetable oil and flour meant that anyone with access to hard currency and truck transport could make a killing. Smuggling had already become Iraq's biggest business. Kuwaiti merchants were more than willing to trade with their Iraqi counterparts along their common border—commerce that for centuries had gone on between these desert peoples.

There was no shortage of ironies in post-war Iraq. The very countries that went to war against Iraq had provided Iraq with $90 billion of sophisticated weaponry during its eight-year war with Iran. Many rooms at the Al Rasheid hotel were occupied by American, French and German arms dealers eager to help Iraq to re-equip its armed forces. In the elevators I overheard two South Africans bragging about the deals they were cutting. While the Western media vilified Iraqis as blood-thirsty barbarians, in reality Iraq was among the most progressive countries in the Middle East, with women participating fully at all levels of society. Seventy per cent of Iraqi doctors were women. I spoke to a rabbi in Baghdad who told me that Iraqi Jews enjoyed complete freedom to practice their religion—a rarity in the Middle East. Iraqi universities offered a high standard of education free of charge to all students. The same European and American reporters who decried the looting of Kuwait by Iraqi soldiers could be found every morning exploring Baghdad's Souk Harami—Thieves' Market—trading U.S. dollars for Kuwaiti war booty, including Rolex watches and Sony HandyCams packed in their original boxes. After their stint in Iraq, they would return to Jordan with their GMC Suburbans loaded down with oriental carpets, silver and other Desert Storm souvenirs.

Although we developed projects with local partners in many countries, the Sudan continued to be my obsession. In 1988, due to a combination of drought, floods, locusts, and war, more than 250,000 residents of South Sudan starved to death. The silence of the international community—including the UN agencies—was deafening. Thousands of young boys undertook a trek of epic proportions from South Sudan to the refugee camps of western Ethiopia; more than one-third of them died en route. Many drowned while attempting to cross the Nile, some were hunted down and killed by Arab militia men, while others succumbed to hunger and disease.

In August, 1988, I managed to convince an American pilot I had known from my Khartoum days to fly me to the town of Ler on the White Nile so I could see for myself the condition of the Dinka and Nuer children in the region. Jim Gaunt landed me on a tiny metal airstrip left behind by the Chevron Corporation, which had been carrying out oil exploration in the area before hostilities recommenced in 1983. For several days, I lived on an abandoned barge with six unaccompanied Nuer children and a family of hippos. I used the barge as my base, venturing out as far as I could on foot during the daylight hours. On my second day, I was overwhelmed by the sight of over 800 children, almost all of them young boys, who had gathered on the west bank of the White Nile. "Behind us is death," one of the kids told me. Their villages had been torched, and they had been pursued for many kilometres by Baggara militiamen. The boys had crossed some of the roughest wilderness in all of Africa, fighting off wild animals, foraging for food, lying low to keep out of the sight of soldiers.

Along the way, some kids had been blown apart by land mines, while others were eaten by crocodiles. Many of the youngest boys, weakened by hunger and disease, lonely and tired, simply gave up hope. Ignoring the pleas of their older brothers and friends, they refused to walk any farther. They sat down and waited for the enemy to come to them.

The children I met that day on the bank of the White Nile had nothing to go home to. In particular, they longed to attend school like normal children. They wanted to learn to count, and to read and write in their own language. But their classrooms were in ruins. There were no school books, chalkboards, or pencils, and not a scrap of paper. My time in Khartoum had shown me that there was no future for Dinka, Shilluck, or Nuer children in the predominantly Arab north. We had to create the conditions in the south that would allow young children to remain in their own communities. I knew that Street Kids International could play an important role in helping to rehabilitate and equip local schools, creating an island of stability amidst the chaos of war. According to the conventional wisdom, only when peace broke out could schools re-open and classes begin. But the civil war showed no signs of abating and the kids of South Sudan could not afford to wait any longer. I needed to find someone who could spearhead an ambitious—and potentially dangerous—primary schooling program in the most remote locations of South Sudan.

It was Patta Scott-Villiers who introduced me to Emma McCune. We met over a lunch of chicken curry at the Fairview Hotel in Nairobi, where many relief agencies working in South Sudan were based. Emma had just emerged from her beat-up Land Rover, nicknamed Brutus. She was tall, elegant, and strikingly beautiful. In some ways, she was an unlikely choice to take up the responsibilities as the co-ordinator of our proposed schooling program in South Sudan. Emma was the eldest of five children born to a tea planter in India, and had been educated at the Convent of the Assumption in Richmond, North Yorkshire. She had lived a comfortable life, loved beautiful clothes, and enjoyed spending afternoons in London's art galleries. While working for the Refugee Study Group at Oxford, she was moved by the plight of the South Sudanese and went to Khartoum for six months to assist with the local displaced population. The appalling conditions she encountered in the camps bordering the capital city caused her to exchange Oxford and London for Dinka and Nuer villages along the White Nile.

Over the course of our lunch, I realized that Emma was exactly the right person for the assignment. She had already travelled extensively in South Sudan and had taught herself passable Arabic. She was resourceful, committed, and proudly independent. Years earlier, she had helped pilot a small aircraft from the United Kingdom to Australia and back, and was familiar with maps. She knew everything about two-way radios. Our proposed schooling program would require the endorsement of UNICEF, and I knew that with her natural charm, Emma would do a fine job of extracting whatever supplies we needed from the most recalcitrant UN official.

On May 1, 1990, Street Kids International launched a pioneering primary education program in South Sudan for 20,000 war-displaced children from the Dinka and Nuer tribes, with Emma McCune at the helm. Our partner was the African Relief Committee in Canada, an association of African-Canadians headed by Akwatu Khenti. I was proud that, thanks to Emma's intensive lobbying, UNICEF had agreed to provide support for the initiative through Operation Lifeline Sudan. Chalk, chalkboards, paper, pencils, and textbooks were purchased in Kenya, then transported by road and air to remote communities throughout Eastern Equatoria. Classes were held in the most basic surroundings, even under trees, if necessary. All the teachers were Sudanese volunteers. After the Sudanese air force bombed three of our schools, killing over 20 students, Emma arranged for the construction of underground shelters for the kids. I travelled throughout the region with her visiting the schools, and took consolation in the thought that sitting among the girls and boys so diligently learning their lessons were the younger siblings of the same street children with whom I had worked in the north.

Emma was the most extraordinary relief worker I had ever met. Although she came from a family of means, she was immune to the crass material needs that have paralysed so many of her generation. She wore whatever she could get her hands on, slept on the dirt floors of huts, and ate whatever food was being served in the village. Emma was bitten by scorpions and rats, and survived bouts of malaria and amoebic dysentery. She never complained about the lack of the most basic amenities, such as electricity or running water. Her only luxury was her solar-powered laptop computer, which she used to write detailed reports from the field.

Emma loved everything about the south. She craved the isolation from the Western world and the richness of living so close to the land. When I saw her in Nairobi, she was inevitably hurrying from one meeting to another, always running late. In the south, she was in her element. Emma was comfortable with the seasons of the Nile, and was a favorite visitor of village women. She learned how

317

to speak their language and how to dance for the celebrations that marked special occasions. She became their biggest backer, establishing self-help organizations for women, organizing the production of mats that the women could trade for other commodities. She founded her own charity called WomenAid. Emma was best friends with the Operation Lifeline Sudan pilots, and cajoled them into flying in items that she needed for her network of women's enterprises. Seeds, fishing hooks, yarn, needles, and thread were all items on her shopping list.

Emma believed in the power of primary schooling to transform lives. She wanted the children to learn to read and write in their own languages rather than in English, so she searched high and low in Nairobi for the old readers published by the missionary organizations in the 1950s and 60s. Eventually, she found the original plates for a Dinka book for children entitled *Marial and the Cow*, and arranged to have hundreds of copies printed for the first time in more than 20 years. She scrounged reading books in Nuer, Bari, and Lotuka. Emma gathered up the old wooden crates used for the transport of ammunition by the Sudanese army and the SPLA rebels alike, and established workshops so that they could be transformed into furniture and desks for the schools.

When Brutus, her Land Rover, was getting on in years and was not up to the punishing off-road conditions in Eastern Equatoria, Emma went to see her friends at UNICEF, and within a few days collected the keys for a Toyota Landcruiser, complete with winch and tape deck. With her new wheels, she would disappear into the field for months at a time. I would hear nothing from her, and then an eloquently written report would emerge from the fax machine at our Street Kids International headquarters in Toronto. Her reports combined personal anecdotes about the children she had come to know and love with statistics about the number of pencils and notebooks we had distributed. She wrote about the importance of kids learning to read in their own language.

The Street Kids International Primary Schooling Program for South Sudan was the most ambitious field-based project that we ever attempted, and also the most dangerous. Some of the schools were only a few kilometres from the front lines. Emma, working closely with her colleagues at the Sudan Relief and Rehabilitation Association, opened 110 schools in areas where there had been no formal education for the past seven years. Teacher-training courses were conducted in the town of Torit. Street Kids International was responsible for bringing in all the materials for the training courses, including mattresses, kerosene lamps, cooking pots, books, and writing materials. The teachers learned how to use the new mathematics, science, and language textbooks, as well as how to write lesson plans. Discussions were held concerning health education, agriculture, and immunization programs. Each person who attended the training course was responsible for returning to his or her own community, and in turn recruiting and training other teachers for the local school.

It was more than her responsibilities with Street Kids International that drew Emma into the heart of the jungle of South Sudan. In 1990, she met Riek Machar, the SPLA commander of the Upper Nile Region, at a hotel in Nairobi. It was love at first sight. On June 17, 1991, they were married in Nasir in a Presbyterian church built by American missionaries; the ceremony was conducted by the pastor wearing a pink bathrobe.

Street Kids International had gone to extreme lengths to maintain its neutrality and avoid any allegiance with the various factions at war in South Sudan. Emma's very public relationship with Riek put us in a bind. Shortly after the marriage, a rift developed between Riek and SPLA commander John Garang that followed tribal lines: the Dinka remained loyal to Garang and the Nuer sided with Riek. Khartoum exploited this fracture in the alliance between the two dominant tribes of South Sudan: a major government offensive succeeded in recapturing much of Eastern Equatoria, and many of our schools were forced to close as thousands of civilians took cover in the swamps and jungles. Emma was labelled the Yoko Ono of South Sudan, and was even accused by some of being paid off by Khartoum to marry Riek and engineer a split with John Garang. Questions were being asked about the role of Street Kids International. In the end, I had to fire Emma. I had asked her to step aside and serve as an informal advisor to the education program, but I knew she would refuse my request. She was never one for compromise. When she received my termination letter by fax, she called me from our office at Wilson Airport in Nairobi. The conversation was short and painful. "You're punishing me because I fell in love," she accused me. I told her that Street Kids International could not get caught up in the internal politics of the SPLA, that I was firing her for the sake of 20,000 children involved in our school program. But she wouldn't listen to me and hung up the phone. It was the last time we spoke.

On Friday, November 26, 1993, I received a phone call from the editorial desk of the *Times of London* asking for my help with an obituary they were running in the following day's newspaper. Of course I was willing to help them, but who had died? There was a silence at the other end. The journalist assumed that I had already been informed. Late on Wednesday night, Emma McCune, age 29 and five months pregnant, had been killed in a car accident in downtown Nairobi. After surviving disease, bombings, and ambushes, she had been killed in a mundane head-on collision with a minibus.

No foreigner in modern times had been so completely accepted into the world of the South Sudanese. When we arrived in the village in her new Land-cruiser, the local women would surround Emma and poke her, ask her many questions, and laugh and smile. They trusted her and loved her as a Sudanese. They were impressed that an English woman could be as tall as they were. They accepted her in a way they rarely accepted an outsider. In the end, when Emma decided to marry Riek and live among them rather than in England, people in the south understood, and few questions were asked. She had protected their children, built schools for them, and found books for them to read. She had earned their trust and their respect.

My favorite memory of Emma involves a young deaf-mute orphan named Kachinga, who served as Emma's unofficial guide in the town of Kapoeta in South Sudan. Emma thought that with the proper medical care, some of his hearing might be restored, and to test her idea she brought her Walkman along. She placed the headphones on the boy's ears and then played a tape at full volume. Emma and I watched Kachinga's face as he discovered that he could indeed hear; his eyes lit up, he leapt into the air, and then tears streamed down his cheeks.

Few people thought Street Kids International would survive more than a few months; this year the organization will celebrate its 10th anniversary. I left Street Kids International in June, 1994, to become the director of Canada's national youth service corps, and I now live on the shore of a pristine lake 25 kilometres northwest of Ottawa with my wife, Nienke Schaap, who works as a training advisor for Médecins Sans Frontières, and our daughter Annelie. Under Christopher Lowry's stewardship, Street Kids International produced a second animated film for poor children on the subject of substance abuse. Instead of punishing kids for drug use and marginalizing them even further, the cartoon explores the reasons why kids are drawn to glue, gasoline, and narcotics. *Goldtooth*, directed by Derek Lamb, premiered in January, 1995, and is already in use in over 80 countries around the world.

Hardly a week goes by when I don't receive a phone call or an e-mail from a young person who, inspired by the example of Street Kids International, wants to volunteer overseas. I keep an active file of community-based projects for street children that are willing to host a foreigner. The first student volunteer I sent overseas was Eden Godsoe, the 16-year-old daughter of a Canadian bank president, who volunteered for Kukula, a home for street children in Limón, Costa Rica. There was no bed for Eden in the home, so she slept on the floor. The first night of her stay, the sewer backed up and she awoke covered in putrid green sludge. Eden toughed it out, never complained, and returned to Canada confident that she could overcome any obstacle in her path.

Over the past five years, I have introduced several young people to a remarkable American Redemptorist priest from Longview, Washington, named Father Joe Maier, who has spent the last 26 years ministering to the Christian families employed in Bangkok's largest slaughterhouse in a neighborhood called Klong Toey. Buddhists aren't allowed to kill animals, so for generations the work has been the exclusive responsibility of Thailand's tiny Christian community. Before one enters the slaughterhouse, Father Joe provides a pair of gumboots. It seems a bit strange because there is no rain in sight and no mud on the ground. Visitors learn why as soon as they walk onto the slaughterhouse floor: the warm blood is six centimetres deep. Overhead in the rafters, they can see children sleeping in hammocks suspended only a few metres above the killing pens.

Father Joe runs an ambitious outreach program for the Klong Toey kids and their families. Sports and recreation programs are designed to foster leadership skills. In 1991, Father Joe opened a shelter for homeless kids, many of whom are refugees from Bangkok's notorious Pat Pong sex bazaar, where child prostitution is big business. The children arrive battered and bruised, their spirits broken. Reaching the youngest children before they get caught up in Bangkok's underworld of sex and drugs is a priority, so Father Joe operates a pre-school that features arts, crafts, music, and physical fitness. He has initiated a micro-credit program so that the women in the community can start small businesses for themselves. On account of the AIDS pandemic, Father Joe has been forced to establish the city's first hospice for children infected with HIV. All the patients have been involved in Bangkok's sex trade; when I last visited the clinic, the youngest was an eight-year-old girl. The volunteers I referred to Father Joe have set up a soccer league for the street children, drafted funding proposals, visited kids in prison, and become the best friends of children who have only a few months to live. All have been deeply affected by the experience.

Father Joe lives only a few metres from the entrance to the slaughterhouse. The butchering of the pigs is conducted at night, and their cries sound like the voices of children in distress. His wooden shack has no running water, and electricity is unreliable at best. He has few material possessions. On my last trip to Bangkok, I presented Father Joe with a copy of a favorite classical CD by the

Tallis Scholars. He had never seen a CD before and didn't own a CD player. "Don't worry," he said. "I can tie a string through the hole and use it as a shaving mirror."

The children of Klong Toey are lucky to have Father Joe, and Father Joe is lucky to have the children of Klong Toey.

I went to Africa to rescue destitute children, but they ended up rescuing me. The world's poorest kids taught me that my life is worth far more than the clothes on my back or the car in my garage. In sprawling shantytowns devoid of running water and electricity I had expected to find darkness and despair. Instead I discovered light and life. I learned never to place my faith in institutions, but instead to believe in people—no matter how young or poor. Politicians in Ottawa, Washington, and London call themselves leaders, but among the gangs of "throwaway children" I knew young people who could run circles around most elected officials. In the streets, leadership meant having food in your stomach at the end of the day and a warm place to sleep. Leadership meant looking after your friends, and keeping them out of harm's way. Leadership meant successfully negotiating with the police officer who needed a bribe, or the jailer who threatened violence. Leadership had nothing to do with press conferences, VIP receptions, photo opportunities or the Davos World Economic Forum. Leadership was about compassion and caring.

When I returned to Canada I was showered with compliments and awards for my work. But I felt undeserving, and being fêted for our modest successes at Street Kids International made me uncomfortable. The real heroes were the children I had left behind.

Epilogue

I never did return to Khartoum, but I kept my promise to Yassir. Although it has been 10 years since I last saw them, the street children of Khartoum have never been far from my thoughts. For months after my return to Canada, I dreamed about the Sudan. I never told anyone, but I held out hope that one day, sitting at my desk in Toronto, I would suddenly hear Sunday's distinctive sing-song voice and discover that the whole gang of them had managed to survive the war and escape the country. Using Canada as our base, and Pio as our captain, we would launch a SKI Courier empire around the world. Street children everywhere would have jobs and could learn to read and write. We would fight poverty through literacy. In the words of Bob Geldof, we would change the world.

Through contacts in the Sudan I tried to stay in touch with Pio and wrote him several letters. I received one response in 1991:

> Hello Peter. How you? How you to come Sudan? I'm fine but I need the tools to be carpenter. How is you family? When you coming to Khartoum? This is my letter to you. I am Pio Lokno.

In 1994, I learned what had happened to my friend Pio. He never got his tools, and he never had the opportunity to become a carpenter. For unknown reasons, he ended up back on the streets. Eventually, he lost everything. In desperation, he joined the ranks of the Sudanese army and was sent to South Sudan to take up arms against his own people. He never returned from combat.

The Islamists who seized power in 1989 stepped up their efforts to clean up the streets of the nation's capital. In September, 1992, and November, 1994, major round-ups of street children were conducted, with over 3,000 boys detained. The kids were sent to "rehabilitation camps" in isolated desert locations, where, no matter what their religion, they were taught the Koran, were given Islamic names, and had their heads shaved. Seven camps for street children were established between 1992 and 1994, each with a population of 80 to 1,250 between the ages of five and 15. Children "graduated" from the camps to the Sudanese military. It was a one-way trip: many of the street children of Khartoum have suffered the same fate as Pio, being sent by the regime in the north to fight against their own people on their own land. Sunday and Moj disappeared, and are presumed to have died in the war. I have a picture of them in front of me as I write; Sunday has his arm around Moj's neck. Both kids have big smiles. Sunday is wearing his yellow-and-blue SKI Courier uniform, while Moj sports the green T-shirt given to him by the BBC crew that made the documentary film about our little project.

After the fundamentalists took over, most projects for vagrant children in Khartoum were shut down. I had always worried that SKI Courier, because of its high profile, would be an easy target for the regime. In fact, SKI Courier is alive and well today in Khartoum, and has served as a model for courier projects in India and Ethiopia. Inspired by the success of SKI Courier and similar self-help projects, Street Kids International is developing a third animated film that will help poor girls and boys to set up their own businesses, manage money, and learn how to support themselves and their families. In many ways, Pio's dream has come true.

There have been sporadic sightings of Yassir in and around Khartoum. At one point, there were reports that he had saved up enough money for a plane ticket to the Gulf states. Friends told me that he had been offered a job in Saudi Arabia and planned to start a business of his own. Although there may be some truth to these stories, I know from my last conversation with Yassir that my best chance of tracking him down would be to travel to the Sultanate of Brunei and check out the local courier businesses. If Yassir did manage to escape the Sudan, and if indeed he is still alive today, he would have a courier operation of his own by now. It might be called SKI Courier, but it would more likely be named after his friend Pio, who plucked him out of a garbage dumpster in the world's most forlorn city, who breathed life into his soul, and who gave him a reason to dream.

GLOSSARY OF TERMS

AICF	Action internationale contre la faim
Al Hamdu lillaa	Praise be to God
Allah karim	God will provide
Anglo-Egyptian Condominium	the political and administrative structure put in place by the British following the defeat of the Mahdi at the Battle of Omdurman
Band Aid	the famine relief agency founded in 1984 by the Irish rock star Bob Geldof
bir	well
bore hole	machine-drilled well
arabia	truck
ba'ad shwoya	in a few minutes, soon
Bailey bridge	World War II-vintage modular bridge that can be transported by truck and assembled on site
Bedouin	desert-dwelling nomads of North Africa and the Arabian peninsula
bilharzia	water-borne disease transmitted by microscopic snails
C-130 Hercules	American built four-engine transport aircraft famous for large cargo capacity and ability to operate from rugged air strips
carta	left-over food scraps
CRS	Catholic Relief Services

Dar es Salaam	Place of Peace
Eastern Equatoria	region of South Sudan immediately east of the Nile
EEC	European Economic Community, now known as the European Community
ECHO	The international development agency of the European Community
En Sh'Allah	If God wills it
FAO	The UN Food and Agriculture Organization
felucca	traditional Nile sailboat
harami	thief
hawaja	foreigner
ICRC	International Committee of the Red Cross
Irish bridge	not really a bridge at all, but a reinforced concrete base constructed at wadi locations
Inte min wein?	Where are you from?
Ismik minu?	What is your name?
jebel	hill
jellabiyah	traditional dress worn by Arab men
Kam sanaa?	How old are you?
LWF	Lutheran World Federation
malish	too bad; I'm sorry
millih	salt
MSF	Médecins Sans Frontières
MT	metric tonne, or 1000 kilograms, approximately 2200 pounds
mukheit plant	drought-resistant plant producing berries that are a traditional famine food
Muslim Sisters	ultra-conservative lay association of Muslim women
Nuba	black African mountain-dwelling tribe of Southern Kordofan
ORS	oral rehydration salts, mixed with water and used to treat dehydration
portoocan	orange
Redd Barna	Norwegian Save the Children
Red Crescent Society	equivalent to the Red Cross

RRC	Relief and Rehabilitation Commission — the government agencies in Ethiopia and the Sudan responsible for co-ordinating famine relief within the country
RTO	the road transport organization managed by the UN World Food Program in the Sudan
SCF	Save the Children Fund
Sharia law	strict Islamic code of law
shokol katir	much work
souk	market
SRC	Sudan Railways Corporation
Sudan Aid	domestic humanitarian agency supported by the Catholic church in the Sudan
Sudan Council of Churches	umbrella group for the Sudan's Protestant churches
tamiya	Arab version of felafel—seasoned mixture of ground chickpeas cooked in hot oil
TCC	Technical Co-ordination Committee comprised of aid agencies active in the Sudan
tukul	traditional African hut made from sticks and animal hides
Twin Otter	Canadian built twin-engine transport aircraft
UNDP	United Nations Development Program
UNHCR	The United Nations High Commission for Refugees
UNICEF	The United Nations International Children's Emergency Fund
Upper Nubia	region of the Upper Nile along the Sudan-Egypt border
USAID	The US Agency for International Development
wadi	seasonal river
weight for height	The standard measurement used by nutritionists to determine levels of malnutrition. Any child below 80 percent weight for height is considered to be moderately to severely malnourished.
WFP	United Nations World Food Program
WUSC	World University Service of Canada
yella yella	let's get going!

BIBLIOGRAPHY

African Rights. *Food and Power in Sudan: A Critique of Humanitarianism.* London: African Rights, 1997.

Allan, Ted and Sydney Gordon. *The Scalpel, the Sword: The Story of Dr. Norman Bethune.* Toronto: McClelland and Stewart, 1952.

Amnesty International. *Sudan: Human Rights Violations in the Context of Civil War.* London: Amnesty International, 1989.

Amnesty International. *Sudan: The Ravages of War: Political Killings and Humanitarian Disaster.* London: Amnesty International, 1993.

Amnesty International. *Sudan: What Future for Human Rights? An Amnesty International Briefing.* New York: Amnesty International USA, 1995.

Amnesty International. *The Tears of Orphans: No Future Without Human Rights.* New York: Amnesty International, 1995.

Asher, Michael. *Thesiger.* London: Viking, 1994.

Berger, Thomas R. *The Report of the Mackenzie Valley Pipeline Inquiry: Volume One.* Ottawa: Supply and Services Canada, 1977.

Churchill, Winston. *The River War.* London: New English Library, 1985.

Conarroe, Joel, ed. *Six American Poets.* New York: Vintage Books, 1991.

FitzGerald, James. *Old Boys.* Toronto: Macfarlane, Walter & Ross, 1994.

Frank, Anne. *The Diary of a Young Girl.* Otto H. Frank and Mirjam Pressler, eds. New York: Anchor Books, 1995.

Government of the Republic of the Sudan. *The Emergency Situation in Sudan: Urgent Humanitarian Requirements November 1988.* New York: United Nations, 1988.

Hancock, Graham. *Lords of Poverty.* London: Mandarin, 1991.

Harrison, Paul. *The Greening of Africa: Breaking through in the Battle for Land and Food.* London: Paladin Grafton Books, 1987.

Hughes, Langston. "I've Known Rivers," in Elizabeth Roberts and Elias Amidon, eds., *Earth Prayers from Around the World.* San Francisco: HarperSanFrancisco, 1991.

Irving, David. *The Trail of the Fox.* New York: Avon Books, 1977.

Lee, Harper. *To Kill a Mockingbird.* New York: Popular Library, 1962.

Lewis, Richard S. *Appointment on the Moon.* New York: Ballantine Books, 1969.

LICROSS-VOLAGS Steering Committee for Disasters. *When Disaster Strikes: Emergency Logistics Handbook,* Geneva 1982.

Lifton, Betty Jean. *The King of Children: A Biography of Janusz Korczak.* New York: Schocken Books, 1988.

Lifton, Robert Jay. *The Nazi Doctors: Medical Killing and the Psychology of Genocide.* New York: Basic Books, 1986.

Médecins Sans Frontières, François Jean, Ed. *Populations in Danger.* London: John Libbey & Company, 1992.

McLean, Malcolm. *A Preliminary Report on the Deterioration of Nutritional Status in Kordofan Region Between February/March and May/June 1985, with Special Reference to North Kordofan.* London: Oxfam, 1985.

Oxfam, UNICEF & Darfur Regional Government. *Nutritional Surveillance and Drought Monitoring Project.* London: Oxfam, 1985.

Pratt, Brian and Joe Boyden. *The Field Director's Handbook.* London: Oxfam, 1985.

Randal, Jonathan C. "AID Learns How Not to Run a Famine Relief Project," in *The Washington Post,* July 8, 1985.

Relief and Rehabilitation Commission. *Review of the Current Drought Situation in Ethiopia.* Addis Ababa: Relief and Rehabilitation Commission, 1984.

Schweitzer, Albert. "Civilization and Ethics," in *The Light Within Us.* Westport, CT: Greenwood Press, 1971.

Thesiger, Wilfred. *The Life of My Choice.* Glasgow: Fontana/Collins, 1987.

UNICEF. *The State of the World's Children 1997.* Oxford: Oxford University Press, 1997.

Zutt, Johannes. *Children of War: Wandering Alone in Southern Sudan.* New York: United Nations Children's Fund, 1994.

INDEX